SUITE 3505

DEDICATION

This book is dedicated to my wife and our two children, Kip and Carole, in gratitude for their patience and understanding, especially during the years 1961 through 1964, and to the thousands of dedicated citizens throughout America who supported and who continue to support the cause of better government in our Nation and a just and lasting peace with freedom for all the peoples of our turbulent world.

SUITE 3505

**The Story of the Draft
Goldwater Movement**

F. Clifton White

with

William J. Gill

ARLINGTON HOUSE
New Rochelle, New York

Copyright © 1967 by Arlington House, New Rochelle, New York.

Library of Congress Catalog Card Number 67-12950

MANUFACTURED IN THE UNITED STATES OF AMERICA

BOOK ONE

GENESIS

THE COW PALACE

IT WAS THURSDAY NIGHT, July 16, 1964. In the huge trailer parked outside the walls of the Cow Palace near San Francisco I sat behind the big communications console from which the nomination of Barry Goldwater had been directed less than twenty-four hours before. Above my position was a television set on which I could scan the events unfolding on the floor of the 28th Republican national convention. Below me sat our six regional directors, each of whom had guided the voting of scores of delegates in a great bloc of states.

From this inconspicuous command post we had deployed the forces which had wrought an unprecedented revolution in the Republican Party and in American politics. For the first time in nearly thirty years the delegates to a national nominating convention of the Grand Old Party had been permitted to vote their convictions. The seemingly impregnable bastion of the powerful group that had controlled the party's conventions for decades had been breached. The first great victory was behind us. Now we were readying ourselves for the beginning of the second battle, a battle in which the odds against us would be much greater and the stakes far higher.

Those of us who had come to this time and place over a long and tortuous road knew that adverse odds could be mastered. But we knew too that they could only be whittled down by a concerted and organized effort. The vehicle for this effort would now be the Republican Party. Forged by Lincoln in the crucible of the Civil War, the party had undergone many changes since its first Presidential nominating convention in 1856. It had been corrupted by Reconstruction, remolded by the impact of the industrial revolution, rescued by the progressivism of Theodore Roosevelt, decimated by the Great Depression, revived again by Dwight D. Eisenhower. And now it was groping for a way to restate, for present and future generations, the importance of individual liberty in an era when the rising tide of totalitarianism is threatening to engulf the world.

Admittedly, the vehicle was flawed. Our party was divided, torn by dissension, wracked by acrimonious debate, counted out by all but a few of the great oracles. Yet we had been divided before and had managed to unite, winning through to victory in other elections when there had been far less at stake. Tonight the moment was at hand for drawing together all the conflicting forces within the party and welding them into a unified instrument that could inspire the latent values of the American people and rally the voters to our banner during the coming campaign. Within a few minutes Barry Goldwater would attempt this task in his acceptance address to the convention.

In the trailer, meanwhile, our duties were rather limited this evening, confined to keeping an electronic eye on the demonstrators massing outside the Cow Palace gates in an attempt to embarrass the Republican Party and its candidate. A fleet of automobiles equipped with two-way radios and a small battalion of volunteers with walkie-talkies were deployed on all approaches to the building and the galleries within. Their job was to report all "incidents" to us so we would have a running record of what actually transpired in the event an attempt was made to inflate these disturbances into *causes célèbres*. After the tension of the last four days this was a relatively relaxing hour. Insulated from the hubbub in the convention hall we were able to sit back and watch the proceedings on our television sets with a degree of detachment we could not have permitted ourselves before.

On the screen above my position, Richard Nixon appeared to introduce the candidate. Just four years earlier Nixon had himself been the nominee and until Goldwater's victory over Nelson Rockefeller in the California primary on June 2 there were many who had expected he would be again. But at this moment all of Nixon's efforts were bent on binding up the gaping wounds opened by the bitter attacks on Goldwater that his fellow Republicans had begun to make exactly one year before, and which had steadily mounted in ferocity until they had established what one columnist called "a new level of vituperation" with the famous Scranton letter of the previous weekend.[1]

This introductory address was perhaps the finest, and certainly the

[1] Robert D. Novak, *The Agony of the G.O.P. 1964*, The Macmillan Company, New York, 1965, p. 455.

fightingest, Dick Nixon had ever delivered, and the convention enthusiastically cheered him on. Like General Eisenhower, who on Tuesday night had urged Republicans to "scorn the divisive efforts" of "sensation-seeking columnists and commentators," the former Vice President struck out at the "faint hearts" who were afraid because the polls and columnists said that the party could not win in 1964. "The only poll that counts," he reminded the assemblage and millions watching on nationwide television, "is the one we *all* vote in."

"To the columnists who have closed their minds" and plan to make Senator Goldwater "the whipping boy of this campaign," Nixon said the Republican answer would be "the greatest army of volunteer workers in history going into the precincts and telling the truth." Then he gave the delegates, and the millions of party members they represented, their marching orders. "Let us," he declared, "think victory, talk victory, act victory—and we will win victory in November."

A moment later, as Nixon introduced the man we all hoped could give us that victory, pandemonium broke loose in the Cow Palace. The reverberations seemed to shake our trailer outside the walls. Amid a shower of hundreds of red, white, blue and gold balloons released from the rafters, Barry Morris Goldwater made his way to the rostrum. The ovation lasted for nearly ten minutes and its echoes must have carried all the way to the heart of San Francisco a half-dozen miles to the north. Behind the microphones on the platform, the Senator and his handsome family waved their gratitude, all but engulfed in the balloons hailing down upon them. But when Goldwater was finally permitted to speak there was no exhilaration in his voice. His tone was flat, a bit hoarse, almost harsh.[2]

He started routinely, accepting the nomination "with a deep sense of humility," calling for a "united and determined" campaign. In broad strokes, he outlined the issues on which he intended to do battle with the Democrats—foreign policy, morality in government, crime in the streets. Then he issued a solemn warning that for an instant must have stirred even the most Liberal Republicans as well as millions of thinking Democrats:

Those who seek to live your lives for you, to take your liberties in return for relieving you of your responsibilities—those who elevate the state and downgrade the citizen—must see ultimately a world in which earthly power can be substituted for Divine will. This nation was founded upon the rejection of that notion and upon the acceptance of God as the author of freedom.

Those who seek absolute power, even though they seek it to do what they regard as good, are simply demanding the right to enforce their

[2] See Appendix E for full text of the Goldwater acceptance address.

version of heaven on earth. They are the very ones who always create the most hellish tyrannies.

Absolute power does corrupt. And those who seek it must be suspect and must be opposed.

Turning again to foreign policy, he reminded America that "it was Republican leadership under Dwight David Eisenhower that kept the peace and passed along to this Administration the mightiest arsenal for defense the world has ever known." He reminded them too that men were dying in Vietnam, as they had in Korea, in a war in which their Commander in Chief "refuses to say whether or not the objective is victory." And finally he reminded them that "It has been during Democratic years that a billion persons were cast into Communist captivity and their fate cynically sealed."

Then, striking a more hopeful note, he said: "I believe that the Communism which boasts it will 'bury us' will instead give way to the forces of freedom." Almost fervently he attempted to reinstill a lost element in the nation's character when he promised to seek "an America proud of its past, proud of its ways, proud of its dreams and determined actively to proclaim them."

Though he paid tribute to the Republican Party throughout, only once did he really attempt to welcome the support of those elements of the GOP which had been warring against him:

Balance, diversity, creative differences—these are the elements of the Republican equation. Republicans agree, Republicans agree heartily to disagree on many, many of their applications. But we have never disagreed on the basic fundamental issues of why you and I are Republicans.

This is, this Republican Party, a party for free men—not for blind followers and not for conformists.

But scarcely twenty seconds later, as he drew toward the conclusion of his acceptance address, Goldwater cut loose with a salvo that seemed deliberately designed to blast apart whatever semblance of Republican unity might still exist and to ward off as well those myriad Democrat and independent votes the party needed to achieve victory:

Any who join us in all sincerity, we welcome. Those who do not care for our cause we do not expect to enter our ranks in any case.

And let our Republicanism, so focused and so dedicated, not be made fuzzy and futile by unthinking and stupid labels. *I would remind you that extremism in the defense of liberty is no vice. And let me remind you also that moderation in the pursuit of justice is no virtue.*

In the trailer I sat stunned as I listened to these words. I had not seen the speech beforehand, nor had any of the men working with me. But none of us had ever expected such a seemingly carefully calculated rebuff to the moderates and Liberals within our party and to the millions we had hoped to draw to our cause.

Inside the Cow Palace the crowd cheered insanely, and I wondered if they knew they were hailing disaster and defeat. This was the time for magnanimity, the time for building bridges across the gulfs that separated Republicans from one another and from countless thousands who were not Republicans and probably never would be. But now the magic moment had passed. There would be no recapturing it. Never again would Barry Goldwater have this opportunity. But far more tragically, I knew that perhaps never again would our nation have a chance to redeem itself from the mistakes of the recent past.

I do not mean to convey that I believe Goldwater could have defeated Lyndon Baines Johnson simply by opening his arms and his heart in this one speech. The cards were too carefully stacked against him to hope for an honest deal if he had delivered a thousand great and magnanimous speeches between July 16 and November 3, 1964. In retrospect, I see that no candidate who had been so indelibly branded as an "irresponsible warmonger" and "extremist" by leading members of his own party, as well as by large and respected elements of the press, could probably hope to be elected President of the United States. But with those fateful words, *extremism in the defense of liberty is no vice,* Senator Goldwater had seemed to identify himself with the very groups that the public had been led to believe would drive us into nuclear war with world Communism.

It was not the words alone, however. They were merely symptomatic of far deeper difficulties that had beset the Goldwater camp since the assassination of President Kennedy eight long months before. These difficulties were compounded of many things, all of which I intend to explore in this book. But not the least was the fact that Barry Goldwater, from the day he announced his candidacy onward, never had anyone around him who could advise him on the subtle nuances of American politics.

This observation is not made out of pique (though there are some who will undoubtedly claim that it is) that on the very day Senator Goldwater made his acceptance address I had failed to receive the appointment as National Chairman of the Republican Party. This was a post that I had sought, that scores of my friends in the Goldwater camp and even some prominent Liberals had hoped I would get, and that many newsmen had confidently predicted I would obtain. However, I accepted the Senator's decision then, and I would defend it now. The candidate has every right to pick his own National Chairman and his own campaign team. Indeed, it is incumbent upon him to do so.

But this observation is not mine alone. It has been made in one way or another by every leading Republican I know, including many who were intimately connected with the Goldwater campaign in 1964. Not all of these people had had the opportunity to observe for so long a period as I the events that led up to the nomination—and the ultimate defeat—of Senator Goldwater. But few who were within the Senator's camp, except for the tight little coterie that insulated him from all other Republicans, will disagree with the premise of my argument.

When the Senator ended his speech the crowd broke into an exultant roar. I reached up and turned off the television set. Abruptly the noise subsided to a muffled echo heard but faintly through the walls of the Cow Palace and the soundproof shell of the trailer. I pushed the master switch on my console for the last time and issued my final message to our leaders in the state delegations and our volunteers. "All call," I said, "all call. I want to remind you to turn in your communications gear at the trailer just as soon as possible. Again, my congratulations to all of you. No candidate ever had a finer team behind him. Keep up the good work and you will surprise them all in November. Good luck. Goodbye. Out."

I closed the switch and leaned back in my chair. The regional directors and their assistants rose and all but one of them was shaking his head in sorrow. With that single exception, they had been around in politics for a long time and they could smell defeat. One by one they came over to say goodbye. Three of them were former state Republican chairmen—Wayne Hood of Wisconsin, Stephen Shadegg of Arizona, Lloyd Waring of Massachusetts. Each grasped my hand in silence. There was nothing any of us could say. Edward Failor of Iowa, who had handled the Middle Atlantic region, waited at the door to collect the portable telephones and the walkie-talkies. State Senator Tom Van Sickle of Kansas, my administrative assistant since the National Draft Goldwater Committee days, left the stand-by console next to mine and went down to help Ed Failor. He flicked off the lights at the back of the trailer before he left and I sat alone in the semi-darkness, thinking back over the past four years.

I'm not sure why, but my mind kept returning to a family in Topeka, Kansas, whom I had never met. I had received a letter from them at our Draft Goldwater headquarters in Washington over a year before. The father, a machinist in a small factory, had written to tell me that he and his wife and their three children, who ranged in age from ten to sixteen, had held a conference and decided to cut corners on the family budget so they could send us $10 a month "until the time Barry Goldwater is elected President."

I thought of the sacrifices made by this family and thousands of others like them; of the unswerving dedication of the Goldwater volunteers in

California and all the other states; of the courage displayed by professional politicians and businessmen who had put their careers on the line for the Senator. And I thought of the unstinting devotion shown by the small group of men and women who had started meeting with me as far back as 1961 to plan for Barry Goldwater's nomination and election. Within an hour I would have to attend a party for the members of this original group. For one swift instant I wondered whether I could face them. The thought vanished as quickly as it had come. They were expecting me, and I knew that I would be there.

Ed Failor and Tom Van Sickle had gathered up all the communications gear. The telephone company men came in to finish dismantling the equipment and cart it off in their truck. I went outside and got in the car that was to take me back to town.

At the Mark Hopkins I dropped off my briefcases and met my wife, who had been staying with friends on Belvedere Island while I worked at the convention. We walked across the street to the Fairmont Hotel where the party for my original group was being held. Through all the vicissitudes on the long trail that led to the convention we had looked forward to this night. Here were forty men and women who had just helped write a page of history. They had every right to be proud, every reason to celebrate. But as I entered the room where the party was already in progress I encountered one of the gloomiest scenes I have ever witnessed.

Practically everyone in the room, men and women alike, were crying or fighting back bitter tears. I knew that the sources of their grief were many. My failure to get the National Chairmanship was perhaps the least, though it seemed symbolic of all the blunt rebuffs they had suffered. The main wellspring of their sorrow, however, was the defeat that loomed ahead. Every person in that room had struggled and worked against ostensibly insurmountable odds for nearly three years to obtain the Republican Presidential nomination for Barry Goldwater. Now, in the uncompromising words the Senator had flung out during his acceptance address, they had correctly sensed that all of their efforts, and the efforts of countless people across the land, were being thrown away. Most of them had seen it coming for months. But they had hung on, working all the harder, in the hope that somehow things would be changed. The Senator's speech was the final proof that nothing would change.

I knew that they would recover from their disappointment. They would continue working in whatever way they could for the Senator right down to election day. But I knew too, as they did, that it would be work expended in a lost cause. Theodore H. White, in his book *The Making of the President 1964,* was later to write of me, "He had misjudged his boss as much as his boss had misjudged him."[3] The same applied to every person in that room at the Fairmont Hotel that night.

I stayed on at the party until it broke up. Then my wife and I drove across the Golden Gate Bridge to Belvedere. Two days later we left for a vacation in Hawaii without my having seen the candidate again. It wasn't until two weeks later, when we returned home to Rye, New York, that I found a letter from Senator Goldwater waiting for me. It was dated July 21 and it read:

Dear Clif:
    You had already left the hotel when I tried to reach you the morning following the acceptance speech, so I didn't get a chance to tell you face to face the deep debt that I feel in my heart for your wonderful efforts during the entire campaign.
    It was you who got this whole thing started and it was you who led the team on to victory in San Francisco. I hope you have had a very fine vacation and are ready to go back to work, because we want to get started on a number of things immediately that will require your continued attention.
    I have about given up on getting a vacation and am spending a few days at my apartment here in Washington, locked up away from the press and the public, but I still would like to get away for about 10 days of sleep before starting again on this great challenge. As soon as you are back in Washington, Clif, I want to visit with you so please let me know when you are available.
    With best personal wishes,

                                         (Signed) /Barry/
                                         Barry Goldwater

Needless to say, I did get in touch with the Senator. In the end I went to work for him as national director of the Citizens for Goldwater-Miller. But the events of that campaign are outside the purview of this book. It is my purpose here to show how a relatively small group of citizens banded together and mobilized millions of people in a successful effort to nominate a conservative candidate for President of the United States, an enterprise that the majority of political experts considered quixotic.

In telling this story, the many and complicated reasons underlying Barry Goldwater's defeat for the Presidency will become apparent. But that is only a subsidiary aspect of this tale. The main goal is to prove that there was—and still is—an opportunity in the 1960's for men of goodwill to join together in this nation and, through a tremendous expenditure of talent and will, through dedication and fortitude, accomplish the impossible.

[3] Theodore H. White, *The Making of the President 1964*, Atheneum Publishers, New York, 1965, p. 205.

CHAPTER 2

THE PAST IS PROLOGUE

IN TRACING THE COURSE of a historical event, it is often difficult to identify the precise moment when the chain reaction which ultimately brought about the event actually began. Frequently, some obscure, seemingly minuscule incident, a chance meeting, or an unreported clash of personalities serves as the catalytic agent which first touches off the hidden molecular action in the capricious test tube of time. As we shall see in this book, many forces and factors—and literally millions of people—were to become involved in the intricate chemistry of the great Republican Revolution of 1964. Some historians will undoubtedly date the beginnings of the movement which forged this revolution to Senator Robert A. Taft's defeat at the national convention of 1952 or even back to 1912 when Theodore Roosevelt's Bull Moose movement opened the first great split in the Republican Party. But for all practical purposes the seed for Barry Goldwater's victory in San Francisco's Cow Palace was planted four years before at the 1960 national convention in Chicago.

Although chance must play a role in shaping history as well as our own lives, in the main men control events just as they do their personal destinies. Senator Goldwater's sudden ascent to national prominence at Chicago in 1960 was no more an accident than his nomination in San Francisco in 1964. Many were involved in this initial effort. But the two men who spearheaded it were Gregory D. Shorey Jr. and Roger Milliken. Shorey was then state Republican chairman in South Carolina. Milliken, a prominent textile manufacturer, served as the party's

Finance Chairman in the same state. Later, both were to help found the original *ad hoc* group which, under my direction, quietly worked for sixteen crucial months behind the scenes to nurture the organization that publicly blossomed out in April 1963 as the National Draft Goldwater Committee.

As Greg Shorey recalls, the first link in the chain of events leading up to Goldwater's dramatic appearance before the Chicago convention was forged in the fall of 1959 when he invited the Senator to speak at a dinner in Greenville, South Carolina. Both at the dinner and on a state-wide television program he arranged, Shorey introduced Goldwater as his choice for the 1960 Republican Presidential nomination. The Senator certainly didn't take Shorey very seriously at the time. But dozens of people at the dinner—and hundreds more who saw the television program—did.

The response to Shorey's announcement was so encouraging that he and Roger Milliken decided to ask Goldwater to come to Columbia, South Carolina, to address the state Republican convention in March 1960. The speech the Senator gave on that occasion unwittingly won him the unanimous support of the more than five hundred Republicans at the state convention. Before the day was out the South Carolina delegation was pledged to support Goldwater for the Presidential nomination. Not wishing to appear like a political orphan in his own home state, the Senator then got Arizona to back him as a favorite son, intending all the while to throw his support to Richard Nixon at the national convention.

Meanwhile, other forces were already projecting Barry Goldwater into the national spotlight. His smashing victory when he was re-elected Senator in 1958 over concerted and well-financed opposition from organized labor had caused many people to look upon him as the natural successor to the late Senator Taft as the leading Republican conservative. In 1959 he had become ranking minority member of the Senate Labor Committee, a post that won him national attention in his running debates with labor leaders and their spokesmen in the Senate. In addition, his position as chairman of the Senate Republican Campaign Committee since 1954 had brought him into contact with hundreds of party workers in almost every state.

The Senator had also become the hero of thousands of young people who had heard him speak on college campuses throughout the country. An expanding group of conservative intellectuals, headed by William F. Buckley Jr., L. Brent Bozell, Russell Kirk and Frank S. Meyer had helped give currency to his ideas. A newspaper column he had begun for the *Los Angeles Times* in January 1960 was being syndicated in scores of newspapers by that summer. And in the spring of the same year his book, *The Conscience of a Conservative,* was brought out. Written for him by Brent Bozell, then a *National Review* editor and an authority on the Constitution, it was privately published by Clarence Manion, former Dean of the Notre Dame Law School and former official in the Eisenhower Administration. Although not even reviewed at publication by many leading newspapers and magazines, the book suddenly became a runaway best seller.[1]

Thus, by the time the Republican national convention opened in Chicago in July 1960, a rather large group was pressuring Goldwater to make a run of it against Nixon. No one really believed he could defeat Nixon for the nomination. But there were some who thought he could win the Vice-Presidential spot on Nixon's ticket. At the very least his supporters believed a show of Goldwater strength would help guarantee a less Liberal Republican platform.

The Senator, however, discouraged all attempts to convert him into a bona fide candidate. He insisted that he was nothing more than a favorite son waiting for the propitious moment to deliver his committed votes to President Eisenhower's obvious heir, Dick Nixon. Patiently, he pointed out to his overly enthusiastic adherents that Nixon had the nomination sewed up and was obviously in such a strong position that he could pick whomever he wanted as his running mate. As a result, South Carolina's Greg Shorey wound up as the somewhat lonely chairman of the Goldwater for President Committee at Chicago.

Somewhat unrealistically, Goldwater still thought he might wield some influence over the formation of the platform. He came to Chicago armed with a relatively brief "statement of principles" which he hoped would be incorporated into the final draft. When he presented it to the Platform Committee he received a standing ovation and though his statement was not adopted it served to strengthen the hand of the conservative majority on the Committee who were being pressured to carpenter planks of a more Liberal pattern.

Roger Milliken and Mrs. A. Dabney Barnes of South Carolina managed to win two important points in the Platform Committee. Milliken was able to hammer into the business and labor planks wording that strongly supported the free enterprise system. Mrs. Barnes skillfully nailed down a moderate civil-rights plank that would be acceptable to most Republicans—and a good many Democrats—in both the North and South. Quoting from a book that favored a more moderate approach to civil rights, Mrs. Barnes drew violent opposition from Liberal members of the Platform Committee. "Nixon could never agree to that," they argued. Then they demanded to know who had written the book she was

[1] By 1964, *The Conscience of a Conservative* had sold more than 3,500,000 copies.

using. Calmly, Mrs. Barnes held up her copy. The author was Richard M. Nixon. The lady from South Carolina won the day.

But this victory proved illusory. The Platform Committee had virtually completed its work after a long, grueling week when on Saturday, July 23, Dick Nixon made his fateful pilgrimage to Governor Nelson A. Rockefeller's apartment in New York. At the end of a seven-hour meeting, Nixon flew to Chicago to dictate the more radical platform planks—including one on civil rights—that Rockefeller had demanded as the price for his support. The reaction was instantaneous—and dangerous. Members of the Platform Committee and other delegates promptly branded Nixon's meeting with Rockefeller "the sellout on Fifth Avenue." Barry Goldwater probably spoke for the majority when he angrily denounced the Nixon-Rockefeller pact as "the Munich of the Republican Party."

Even those of us who were working closely with Nixon, as I was at the time, were bewildered. Neither Leonard Hall, Nixon's campaign manager, nor any of the others inside the Nixon camp had any inkling that our candidate would capitulate to Rockefeller. Certainly there was no reason for him to do so. We had the delegates and Nixon knew it. Rockefeller controlled the New York delegation and a scattering of support in other states but he had no more chance of upsetting the Vice President in the 1960 convention than Barry Goldwater did. Ironically, by forcing the issue with Nixon over the platform, Rockefeller not only alienated the numerically preponderant conservative wing of the Republican Party but contributed substantially toward making Barry Goldwater the real hero of the Chicago convention. This was surely the last thing in the world Rockefeller intended. But it soon became apparent that his intransigence had come home to roost.

The pressure on Goldwater to oppose Nixon now began to build up in earnest. For the next three days he was besieged from every side. But the Senator knew his position was hopeless. With only 27 votes committed to him in Arizona and South Carolina, he doubted if he would get as many as 100 on the first ballot. He set a minimum of 300 votes firmly pledged to him by Tuesday night before he would make a move. He knew his hot-eyed supporters couldn't round up half that many and he was right.

On Wednesday morning, Senator Goldwater strode into the Chicago hotel room where the South Carolina delegation was holding its final caucus before the balloting began that night for the Presidential nominee. Goldwater politely thanked the delegation for its support. Then he announced that he had just released Arizona from its favorite-son commitment and was now releasing them so they could cast their ballots for Nixon.

The delegates were dismayed. Several urged the Senator to reconsider. Roger Milliken and Robert F. Chapman, who later succeeded Greg Shorey as state chairman, asked Goldwater to hold South Carolina and Arizona, which was also pledged to him, so that at least his name could be placed in nomination. They pointed out that he would then have to make a withdrawal speech to the convention and this would give him and the conservative cause he represented invaluable nationwide television exposure.[2] Persuasively, they argued that he owed it to conservatives to make himself and his philosophy better known, particularly to the doubting millions in the Northeast.

Reluctantly, Goldwater acquiesced. I doubt if he would have done so had he not still been smarting under the disillusioning impact of the Nixon-Rockefeller agreement. Now, however, in the speech the South Carolinians wanted him to give, he saw a chance to provide a conservative counterbalance to the GOP's so recently accelerated drift to the Left.

That night Senator Goldwater handled his chance beautifully. I was working in the Volunteers for Nixon headquarters, which were housed in an air-conditioned trailer off to the side of the convention floor in Chicago's cavernous International Amphitheater. I remember well the tremendous demonstration unleashed when the Senator was nominated by Governor Paul Fannin of Arizona. And I recall the hopeful anticipation that gripped the crowd when Goldwater later mounted the rostrum to make his speech. But when he asked that his name be withdrawn from nomination, a great groan of disappointment descended from the galleries, swept across the convention floor and echoed in the homes of millions of Americans watching the proceedings on television.

Delegates who only a few days before had arrived in Chicago believing they had no alternative but to act as rubber stamps for the nomination of Richard Nixon joined that night in the spontaneous protest against Goldwater's withdrawal. Reacting to the deal Nixon had made with Rockefeller, they now lent their voices to the chorus that rose and swelled to a deafening "No!" Repeatedly, that single word reverberated from the highest beams of the Amphitheater and simultaneously disclosed the depth of the decades-old division between conservatives and Liberals in the Republican Party.

On the closed-circuit television set in the Nixon trailer, Senator Goldwater's face appeared in a tight close-up. I could see that he was moved. But when he raised his hand to plead for silence, he faced his

---

[2] Two similar television appearances at the 1956 Democratic convention— one in seconding Adlai Stevenson's nomination, the other in conceding defeat for the Vice-Presidential nomination to Estes Kefauver—had started John F. Kennedy on his way to the 1960 Presidential nomination and ultimately to the White House.

task unflinchingly. There was grateful applause from the staunch Nixon forces when he announced that he was releasing the Arizona delegation and urged that they cast their ballots for Richard Nixon. And there was solemn attentiveness when he issued his memorable call to Republican conservatives to rally behind the party.

"This great Republican Party is our historic house," he said. "This is our home.

"Some of us do not agree with every statement in the official plat-form of our party, but . . . if each segment, each section of our great party were to insist on the complete and unqualified acceptance of its views, if each viewpoint were to be enforced by a Russian-type veto, the Republican Party would not long survive."

He cautioned conservatives not to let the coming election go to the Democrats by default, describing the opposition as "a party which has lost its belief in the dignity of man, a party which has no faith in our eco-nomic system, a party which has come to the belief that the United States is a second-rate power." Then he added:

"This country, in its majesty, is too great for any man, be he con-servative or Liberal, to stay home and not work just because he doesn't agree. Let's grow up, conservatives! If we want to take this party back, and I think we can some day, let's get to work!"

In the ensuing campaign that autumn, Senator Goldwater demon-strated that he was one politician who could practice what he preached. As Dick Nixon later said, "No one worked harder for the Nixon-Lodge ticket than Barry Goldwater." The Senator set an enviable example for conservatives—and for all Republicans—by traveling almost constantly up and down the land, delivering no less than 177 speeches on behalf of Nixon and Lodge. And unlike some other Republican leaders who could scarcely hide their desire for a Nixon defeat in order to further their own ambitions, Senator Goldwater was a deeply disappointed man when Richard Nixon lost to John F. Kennedy by a microscopic .16 per cent of the popular vote in the closest Presidential election in this century.[3]

The Senator's disappointment was easily matched by my own. In that hectic 1960 campaign, I had worked eighteen to twenty hours a day— and sometimes more—as director of organization in the Volunteers for Nixon-Lodge. No politician should complain if he has lost an election in a fair fight. But after the balloting, as I watched the mounting evidence of widespread vote frauds in reports coming across my desk in Wash-ington from Illinois, from Missouri, from South Carolina and from Texas, I became convinced that Richard Nixon had *not* been beaten fairly in his

---

[3] Kennedy's margin was 118,550 out of a total of 68,335,642 cast.

fight for the nation's highest office. I asked my people in the field to carefully check out these reports and then I talked with our campaign manager, Len Hall. I got the impression that after our talk Hall made a tentative decision to contest the election returns in questionable states.

The following day I took off with my wife for a long-promised vacation in Puerto Rico. While there I received more reports from my field directors. In Illinois, they said that flagrant vote thefts by the Democratic machine in Cook County (Chicago) had thrown that state's twenty-seven electoral votes to Kennedy. Far from losing Illinois by less than 9,000 votes as the official returns claimed, the reports said there was proof that Nixon had actually carried the state by some 50,000 votes.[4]

But by then the fight had gone out of Dick Nixon. In Puerto Rico I learned that he had refused to challenge the announced election results. I tried to reach him by phone to urge him to change his mind. But he had already firmly closed the door and my phone message went unanswered.

In failing to contest the returns in Illinois and other states, Nixon handed the Democrats their exceedingly doubtful victory on a silver platter. It is a decision I'm sure he has come to regret deeply many times since—and not merely for reasons of personal ambition as so many people profess to believe. I have known Dick Nixon long enough to testify that whenever it came to a choice between his own ambitions and the national interest, the latter always took precedence. His refusal to disclose information about U.S. plans for ridding Cuba of its Communist dictatorship during his televised debates with Kennedy stands as proof of that. I believe he rejected advice to contest the 1960 election largely on the grounds that it might further divide the country at a critical period in history. But if he could have foreseen the sweeping social and political revolution that has come to pass in the years since, I am certain his decision would have been quite different.

Several weeks after Nixon's defeat six men met with Senator Goldwater in a room at the Jefferson Hotel in Washington. All six had some

[4] In a story on Chicago's Mayor Richard J. Daley, entitled "The Last Dinosaur Wins Again," the *Saturday Evening Post* (April 11, 1964) reported: "The 1960 election, in which the [Daley] machine carried Illinois for President Kennedy by 8,858 votes, featured widespread accusations of crookedness. More than 600 election workers were charged with fraud. Only one was convicted. 'The charges couldn't even be investigated thoroughly,' says Mrs. Marie Suthers, Republican minority member of the Chicago Board of Election Commissioners. 'Mr. Daley's organization controls the pollwatchers, election officials—everything'."

The New York Times Magazine of September 11, 1966, in another story on Mayor Daley ("A Minority Objects, But Daley Is Chicago") said: "John F. Kennedy frankly called Dick Daley 'the man who got me elected'."

experience in politics and two of them—Stephen Shadegg of Arizona and William R. Spear of Nebraska—had been Republican chairmen of their home states. Roger Milliken, who by then was a member of the National Committee from South Carolina, was representative of the new breed of Republicans fast rising in the South. Charles Barr was an oil company executive from Chicago. Dick Herman, president of an Omaha trucking firm, had helped Senator Carl Curtis in his campaign for re-election the preceding fall. And G. R. Herberger, a Minnesota businessman who spent his winters in Arizona, had long been active in GOP finance operations.

Steve Shadegg, who for years had been Goldwater's strong political right arm and had managed his two successful campaigns for the Senate, had called the meeting with a view toward getting a head start on engineering the nomination of the Senator for President in 1964. Ostensibly, however, the discussion centered on how the Republican Party could best be revived in the wake of the Democrats' razor-thin upset. But when the talk turned to the 1964 Presidential race, Senator Goldwater shook his head and cut the others short. He insisted that they focus on the selection of a new chairman for the Republican National Committee since it seemed likely that Senator Thruston Morton of Kentucky would shortly resign from that post. In the end, Goldwater decided he would back Ray Bliss, the able and resourceful Republican state chairman in Ohio.

It is significant that two of the men who attended this meeting—Roger Milliken and Charles Barr—became members of my *ad hoc* group. At the time, however, neither they nor any of the other members of our pioneer cadre could possibly have foreseen the formation of this unprecedented movement which was to command so much of our time and effort over the next four years.

In the months that followed, countless citizens in many parts of the country similarly found themselves casting about for a way to breathe new life into the Grand Old Party. Among them was William A. Rusher, the erudite publisher of the conservative fortnightly, *National Review*. Bill was an old friend of mine and our political alliance dated back to our days in the New York State Young Republican organization which he served as chairman during my term as president. A World War II Air Force captain and graduate of Princeton, he had practiced law in New York after taking his degree from Harvard Law School and in 1956 had become Associate Counsel to the Senate Internal Security Subcommittee before joining *National Review*. Bill Rusher is that rarest of all combinations, an intellectual with a sure instinct for both business and practical politics.

There was a move afoot early in 1961 to place me in either the number one or number two spot on the Republican National Committee and tacit commitments had been made by some of the Nixon forces to support this effort. In January, Rusher went to Washington to obtain Senator Goldwater's help, only to find that the Senator was already committed to Ray Bliss.

While in Washington, Rusher ran into Congressman Carroll Reece of Tennessee in the lobby of the Metropolitan Club. Reece, once a diehard supporter of Senator Taft and in his own region as much a symbol of Republican conservatism as Senator Goldwater, was getting on in years and obviously ill.[5] But Rusher was amazed, in fact, as he puts it, "appalled," when the aging Congressman indicated whom he intended to back at the next Presidential nominating convention.

"Bill," asked Reece, "can anything be done with Nelson Rockefeller?" When he recovered from his surprise, Rusher replied that he didn't think anything at all could be done to deflect Rockefeller from the patently Liberal course he had set for himself. But he saw that his words had little effect on the venerable Congressman. For Rusher, this was a sobering and saddening experience. When we talked it over later in New York, we both perceived that Carroll Reece, like so many other people in the Republican Party, was grasping for a straw—*any* straw—that they thought might keep the party afloat on the storm-tossed political seas of the 1960's. It was one more piece of evidence to support what Rusher and I and several others were even then beginning to detect: namely, that a leadership vacuum existed within the Republican Party.[6]

This vacuum loomed much larger than the normal state of uncertainty that is to be expected after a party suffers a defeat in a Presidential election. To me, it appeared to have taken on the frightful dimensions of a yawning abyss, an abyss which separated the two seemingly irreconcilable camps of modern Republicanism. On the one side of this abyss stood the Liberals, or as some prefer to call themselves, the "moderates." All too many of them had drifted into this camp out of sheer opportunism —to get themselves elected to office or to perpetuate and advance their positions once they had gotten a toehold in office. There were some, of course, who had purer motives. But for the most part they had bought the Liberal line simply because it had proved successful for the Democratic Party and they hoped it would for them.

On the other side of the abyss were the conservatives. With few exceptions, I knew from personal experience that they were men and

[5] Congressman Reece died not long after this.

[6] It is a strange coincidence, but one of these others was General Douglas MacArthur. In a letter to Senator Goldwater dated February 3, 1961 he wrote, "I am watching with growing hope and enthusiasm your political strategy. A great vacuum exists that you can fill. Never let up and never flinch. Dramatic and startling events lie just ahead."

women who had deliberately taken their stand in this camp through honest conviction. This doesn't mean that they hold identical political beliefs on every issue. But they do hold certain truths to be self-evident. They know that the growth of big government must inevitably lead to a serious curtailment of the rights of the individual. In the accelerated whittling away of the Constitution they see a movement to establish in our nation a government of men and not of laws, a movement which will ultimately bring a bureaucratic dictatorship. They are aware, to a far greater degree than most of our citizens, that the cancerous growth of international Communism, which has fed for decades on ignorance and appeasement, must one day be checked if this nation is to endure.

There are, I know, many Liberal Republicans—and a good many Democrats, for that matter—who are also mindful of the imminence of the Communist threat to our survival. But in the late 1950's and early 1960's the majority of these Liberals were increasingly leaning towards some sort of vague accommodation with an international conspiracy that in their more perceptive moments they know is America's implacable enemy.

For my part, I had resolved the question of which camp of the Republican Party I belonged to long before 1961. In one way, I suppose the question had really been resolved for me during World War II when I served as a captain and lead navigator in a B-17 flight wing in combat missions over Germany. Watching my friends being shot down in flaming bombers almost every day, I made a private vow that, if I were lucky enough to get home alive, I would do whatever I could as an individual citizen to prevent another era of appeasement that would lead to a third world war.

However, I must confess that when I returned home to upstate New York and started teaching at Cornell University, my broader philosophical motivation was for a time subordinated to other seemingly more practical considerations. I soon became caught up in learning the intricate techniques of politics. After an unsuccessful primary campaign for a Congressional seat in 1946, I settled down to building a base in Ithaca and Tompkins County, branching out from there into state and national politics.

In 1948 I went to my first Republican national convention, to work for the nomination of Governor Thomas E. Dewey, and I continued working for him in the Presidential campaign that followed. By 1952 I was Acting Executive Secretary of the New York State Republican Committee and that same year I went to the national convention as a delegate pledged to Dwight D. Eisenhower.

Two years later I underwent one of those painful reappraisals that most of us go through at one time or other in our lives. At this point,

I was facing a decision as to whether I should return to teaching at Cornell, which I had left in 1950, and complete work on my Ph.D., or remain in politics. After several months of serious thought I arrived at two conclusions. First I decided that it was in politics, and not in education, that I could have the greatest immediate impact upon the society in which I live. Second, and more important, I came to understand more clearly than I ever had before that, if our society is to be preserved, each of us must accept his full responsibility as a citizen of a free country. To do this requires a grasp of the fundamental fact that it has been our Constitution and the free enterprise system which transformed America, during a relatively short span of history, from a hopelessly undeveloped wilderness into the greatest and most powerful nation the world has ever seen, a nation which has given its citizens far greater freedom and opportunity than any other country on earth.

Underlying this conclusion, I will admit in all humility, was my belief that our free society had to be predicated upon a fundamental faith in God. I do not mean this in any narrow sectarian sense. But history has shown that when a people or a nation becomes indifferent to God and turns its face against the traditional values that foster a belief in the worth of the individual, then that nation must one day be cast into chaos. Out of this an authoritarian form of government inevitably arises.

To some it may seem farfetched, perhaps even hypocritical, to cite religious beliefs as justification for a career in politics. But again, I think that history demonstrates that politics more often than not decides whether religion is even permitted to freely exist in a given society. Rome might never have become completely Christian without the conversion of the Emperor Constantine. And certainly Christianity itself will not endure in any meaningful form if the modern world surrenders to atheistic Communism. It is politics, then, that to a very large degree determines whether a society is to maintain its belief in God and in the dignity of the individual, or whether it will turn, as Oswald Spengler so pessimistically predicted, to a Caesar.

There were no Caesars on the American horizon in 1954. I felt reasonably sure, as did most citizens, that President Eisenhower and the Congress would continue to preserve our Constitutional system against both internal and external pressures. But as the father of two children, I felt that I had a responsibility to quietly enter and work in the conservative camp of my party in order to help insure the continuation of the democratic republic for which so many of my comrades-in-arms had given their lives a short decade before.

THREE MEN IN MANHATTAN

THROUGHOUT THE SPRING and early summer of 1961 I began to sense an incipient uneasiness abroad in the land. As a public affairs consultant to a number of industrial firms I traveled a good deal, and I found that many people were disturbed, as I was, with the drift of events, particularly in the international arena. The Kennedy Administration's failure to provide air support for the Cuban freedom fighters during the disastrous Bay of Pigs invasion in April appeared to be a deliberate sacrifice of men who had been trained, equipped and encouraged by our government to attempt the liberation of their country from Fidel Castro and Communism. In Laos, the State Department was pushing for a *rapprochement* with Communist forces, a move which could only serve to foster the aggressor's designs on South Vietnam and all of Southeast Asia. And despite stepped-up Communist terrorism in many other parts of the world and the long record of Moscow's broken agreements, the Administration seemed to be edging toward a policy of increased faith in the Kremlin's empty promises by planning an ominous series of concessions to the Soviets in the critical area of disarmament.

A scant six months after the inauguration of John F. Kennedy, the press was beginning to take cognizance of the public's growing dissatisfaction with the Administration's foreign policy.

As early as May the voters in Texas had shown their misgivings by electing a conservative college professor, John Tower, to the U.S. Senate seat vacated by Lyndon B. Johnson. Tower, whose victory came on the heels of the Bay of Pigs fiasco, was the first Republican that Texas had sent to the Senate since Reconstruction.

Tower owed his election, at least in part, to the active support he received from Barry Goldwater. It was not surprising, then, that the June 23, 1961 issue of *Time* should describe Goldwater as "the hottest political figure this side of Jack Kennedy."

In substantiation, *Time* noted that "no Republican is more in demand. Since March, Goldwater's Washington office has received more than 650 written invitations for the Senator to put in an appearance, plus hundreds of telephone requests. Goldwater's mail runs to a remarkable 800 pieces a day. Goldwater's political credo, *The Conscience of a Conservative*, has sold 700,000 copies in little more than a year . . . (and) visitors crowd around Barry Goldwater's fourth floor suite in the Old Senate Office Building hoping to earn a passing handclasp or a hastily scrawled autograph."

All this checked with reports of the Senator's growing popularity that I was beginning to receive from many parts of the country. But the paragraph in the *Time* story that caught my eye was one which quoted Goldwater's reply to the question as to whether he hoped to run for President.

"I have no plans for it. I have no staff for it, no program for it and no ambition for it," *Time* quoted Goldwater as saying. I made a mental note of this revealing statement, but in doing so I confess that I discounted the importance of the Senator's lack of desire for the Presidency. It wasn't until much later that I realized what a serious detriment this would prove to his candidacy.

Meanwhile, on July 10, 1961, Bill Rusher went to Washington. A month earlier, at the Young Republican biennial convention, the candidates our YR friends and successors had backed were defeated for the first time, and Bill wanted to make certain that all our fences were up and on the mend so none of our friends would be too disheartened by this unexpected loss. One of the men he went to see was Congressman John Ashbrook of Ohio, who had been our candidate for national chairman of the Young Republicans in 1957 and had used that office and several terms in the State Legislature as springboards for his election to Congress in 1960.

At lunch in the House Restaurant in the Capitol, Bill expounded on our thesis that there was a leadership vacuum in the Republican Party waiting to be filled. Nixon was down and out, Reece was dead, Rockefeller wasn't making much headway among rank-and-file conservatives whose support he needed to clinch the nomination in 1964. The people who had controlled the party for more than twenty years —the party pros to whom the press still paid homage—were in reality

on the shelf. They had not been through a national convention nominating fight since the Eisenhower-Taft battle of 1952 and they were
dreadfully out of condition. Moreover, it was doubtful if they could
whip themselves back into shape for 1964. Most of them were just plain
too old and too tired to answer the bell for another round.

"If we held a meeting of our old Young Republican group," Rusher
observed, "it would probably comprise about the third or fourth largest
faction in the Republican Party."

Ashbrook, a big blond man with a deceptively easygoing manner,
allowed as though that might indeed be the case. Later, he took Rusher
to his office and pulled open a file drawer. There, state by state, were
files on all the contacts he had made around the country during the
two years that he had been national chairman of the Young Republicans.

"These people still know me," Ashbrook remarked. He said no
more than that but the fleeting glimpse Rusher had of those files started
the wheels churning in his always quick and perceptive mind.

Three days later Rusher and I had lunch in the Tudor Room of
the Commodore Hotel above New York's Grand Central Station. When
we sat down at our table two old friends waved at us from across the
room. They were Bill Pfeiffer, the former New York state Republican
chairman, and Tom Stephens, a Dewey man who had served as President Eisenhower's appointments secretary. Bill, Tom and I had worked
together a decade earlier on the first Eisenhower campaign. But we
had found ourselves on opposite sides of the fence in 1958 when I had
managed the campaign of State Senate Leader Walter Mahoney for the
gubernatorial nomination against Nelson Rockefeller.

"What do you think they're up to?" Rusher asked, knowing full well
what my answer would be.

I smiled. "They are plotting nothing less than the election of Nelson
Rockefeller as the next President of the United States."

"Then I think we may have a way to thwart them," Rusher winked.
He then told me of his meeting with John Ashbrook and of the files
he had been shown in John's office. I admitted that I had files of my
own which included not only the names of my Young Republican and
regular party contacts but a number of very able people I had come
to know and respect through my industrial public affairs courses. We
talked of the possibility of merging the Ashbrook-White files and starting a nationwide organization committed to the nomination of a conservative candidate, or at the very least the drafting of a conservative
platform, at the 1964 convention. But we went no further than that.

Not long after this I went to Washington and had a long talk with
Charlie Barr, the Chicago businessman who had attended the little

meeting with Senator Goldwater at the Jefferson Hotel after the 1960 election. A large, heavy-set man with quiet blue eyes, Charlie was originally a Kansas farm boy, and he would like you to believe that he still has hayseed in his hair. But few people have ever put anything over on Mister Barr. I knew he would give me an honest reading on the plan that was beginning to take shape in my mind. When he said nothing to discourage me, and indicated that he would help in any way he could with the operation I had broadly outlined, I decided that maybe the plan was not too farfetched after all.

I felt, and Barr agreed with me, that the grassroots support for a conservative candidate in 1964 was spreading rapidly. This in itself was a phenomenon. Seldom in our history have large groups of voters started thinking in terms of a Presidential campaign a full three years before the nominating conventions. You can always find a few politicians who are looking ahead to the next campaign—or even two or three campaigns hence. But as I had discovered in my travels during the first half of 1961, the possibility of fielding a conservative in the 1964 Presidential race was being talked up by people who had never even taken an active interest in politics before.

A lot of interest I had encountered was focused on Barry Goldwater. But other conservatives were being mentioned too—or men the people hoped or believed were conservatives. However, this incipient conservative groundswell needed direction and organization. Without it, the chances were that the hopes of all these people would be dashed by the relatively small group of men who had controlled every Republican national convention since the Willkie bandwagon was manufactured out of well-financed press-agentry in 1940. The plan that my friends and I were beginning to formulate in this summer of 1961 was designed to give the people, including the rank-and-file party workers who had been ignored for so many years, a full voice in the nomination of the next Republican Presidential candidate.

On August 1, I again met Bill Rusher in New York for lunch. I told him that our embryo plan had received Charlie Barr's tacit blessing and that I was now ready to go. However, I cautioned him that with the 1964 convention three years away, it was still much too early to start an overt movement for any one candidate. I felt that at this juncture our sole aim should be to make certain that people who believed as we did about the fundamental issues confronting the nation would be delegates to the convention.

We both thought we knew who the candidate should be, but we had lots of time to settle on this. "After all," I said, "we may find that if 1964 looks like a strong Democratic year, it might strengthen the conservative movement more if we throw the nomination to a Liberal."

Bill winced at that, though by the time the lunch was over he had swallowed it. But I suspect he went back to the office with a slight case of indigestion.

A little later in August, I flew down to Washington again, this time to see John Ashbrook. After some preliminary discussion, we sat down in his office and drew up a list of the people we thought we could count on for help in all fifty states. However, we both agreed that this list needed a good deal more culling before we could safely use it. John promised to come to New York within the next month so we could meet with Bill Rusher and carefully sift our combined list, which at this point ran to several hundred names.

By the time Congressman Ashbrook came up to New York on September 7, the world situation had taken two more turns for the worse. The Communists had erected the infamous Berlin Wall in mid-August without the United States or its allies lifting a finger to protect their treaty rights under the Four-Power Agreement on Berlin. And on September 1, the Soviet Union had callously broken the nuclear test ban moratorium with the first of a series of multi-megaton explosions obviously aimed at overcoming America's nuclear superiority and terrorizing the free world. These events gave a sense of urgency to our all-day meeting, which began before lunch at the University Club and ended in Bill Rusher's apartment on East 37th Street well after 10 P.M.

Using the combined list of names that Ashbrook and I had previously drawn up in Washington and adding a number of others Rusher threw in, we plunged into the task of selecting the people who were to form the hard core of the nationwide political organization which was ultimately to capture control of the Republican Party for the conservative camp.

I won't pretend that our sorting-out process was an easy job. We had to carefully assess each individual in terms of his position in the party, his past and present allegiances, his capabilities and potential, and most important, his ability to keep his mouth shut if backed into a corner. Of necessity, from the very outset this had to be what the press was later to call a "clandestine" operation. If word leaked out that a group of relatively young men was planning to mold the Republican Party into an effective conservative force in America, we would either be laughed out of existence before we were fairly started, or "exposed" to the public as a cabal of sinister plotters.

Thus, we had no alternative but to make as certain as we possibly could that every man we invited to join us was, first, ideologically and philosophically committed to our cause, and second, could be completely trusted. All three of us suffered regrets that evening that many of the people with whom we had worked closely in the past—and who were still our friends in the best sense of the word—could not be included because they leaned, in varying degrees, toward the Liberal wing of the party.

Early in the evening, we devised what we thought would be a sufficiently acid test for membership in our founding group. All three of us had to vouch for each individual before we tapped him. However, we soon had to abandon this formula as too restrictive, since there were very few people on the master lists whom all three of us knew that well. In the end, we agreed that if any one of us was well enough acquainted with an individual to guarantee him without reservation, then that individual would be invited to join.

About six o'clock we moved our little meeting from the University Club to the Black Angus restaurant, an austerely pine-paneled steak house on 50th Street between Third and Lexington Avenues.

In a corner booth, we again got down to the business at hand. By the time we had finished dessert and coffee we had settled on twenty-six people—including ourselves—as the founding fathers of what later turned out to be the first authentic Presidential nomination draft in the history of American political parties. The last thing we did was to set a date—October 8—for the group's first meeting. Then we divided up the final list on the basis of our personal relationships with the people we planned to invite. I drew most of the names, probably because I had been around a few years more than Ashbrook and Rusher and had naturally come to know more people in politics.

It was a balmy late summer evening when at last we emerged from the Black Angus. Bill Rusher suggested we take a stroll down Lexington Avenue to his apartment on 37th Street, and go from there to the campaign headquarters of Ed Nash, a young friend of ours who was running in the primary election being held that day. Nash was seeking the Republican nomination to New York's City Council against the Liberal incumbent, Stanley Isaacs. He was considered an outlandish heretic because he had campaigned as an out-and-out conservative in Liberal John Lindsay's so-called silk-stocking Congressional district. However, Ed had avoided locking horns with Lindsay. Instead, he had concentrated his fire on his opponent, Isaacs, and had plastered brave signs all over the eastern part of midtown Manhattan proclaiming "Isaacs Can't Win." I remember John Ashbrook had a fit of laughter when we encountered one of these signs on a lamp post as we walked down Lexington Avenue. In fact, he thought the message so funny that he removed the sign and stuffed it in his briefcase with the remark, "I might want to try this one against my opponent in the next Congressional race."

The primary polls had closed more than an hour earlier and the returns were already coming in when we arrived at the Nash campaign headquarters. The early vote count revealed how brashly optimistic Ed had been. Isaacs was way out in front and he eventually won with about 58 per cent of the vote. But this did nothing to dampen the enthusiasm of the young people in Ed Nash's headquarters that night. With some justification, they were claiming a moral victory for Ed and their enthusiasm surpassed that of many an election victory party I've attended. The whole affair was genuinely festive, and the crowd perversely cheered every change in the vote tally as it put their man further and further behind. I'm sure the thought never crossed anyone's mind that they ought to be commiserating with "good old Ed," who was the target of much goodnatured back-slapping and the recipient of endless congratulations.

We stayed on at the Nash party until John Ashbrook was forced to leave to catch his plane back to Washington. On Lexington Avenue, John hailed a cab for the trip to LaGuardia Airport and we shook hands on the success of the venture to which we were now pledged to devote ourselves for the next three years. Then Rusher and I parted, Bill turning jauntily down the avenue en route back to his apartment and I heading up the street for Grand Central Station to take a train home to Rye.

CHAPTER 4

THE FIRST MEETING

AT TWO O'CLOCK on Sunday afternoon, October 8, 1961, twenty-two men assembled in a conference room at the Avenue Motel on Chicago's bustling South Michigan Avenue. For a whole month I had been carefully planning this meeting. We had chosen Chicago because it is accessible to all sections of the country by air and could easily be reached by car from most parts of the great Republican heartland, the Midwest.

Steve Shadegg has said, "In a very real sense, Senator Barry Goldwater was nominated for President by the men who met in Chicago thirty-three months in advance of the Republican convention."[1] Actually, I prefer to think that all we did was give direction and focus to a great grassroots movement. As columnists Robert Novak and Rowland Evans later noted, "Unlike the carefully constructed Kennedy campaign organization of 1960, the Goldwater boom is the closest thing to a spontaneous mass movement in modern American politics."[2] However, in issuing the invitations to this first meeting, neither John Ashbrook, Bill Rusher nor I spelled out its specific purpose. On the phone, Senator Goldwater's possible candidacy was never mentioned. We asked for no commitments. We made no promises. We simply called each man on the list we had drawn up in New York and told him that we were

[1] Shephen Shadegg, *What Happened to Goldwater?* Holt, Rinehart and Winston, New York, 1965, p. 44.
[2] *New York Herald-Tribune,* June 13, 1963.

getting a group of friends together to talk politics. We said that the three of us felt it was important enough for them to be there—and they came.

Of the twenty-six men we invited, all but four showed up, and these four—prevented for compelling reasons from reaching Chicago that Sunday—all attended our subsequent meetings. The twenty-two at this inaugural session came from 16 states. Although there was a certain homogeneity in the group there were also many differences in background, personality and individual interests.

They were for the most part young men. The average age was about forty, and one was only twenty-eight at the time. Most were veterans of World War II, and with one or two exceptions they were all college graduates. There were two Congressmen among them and three Republican state chairmen, but most of the others held no position of real influence in the Republican Party.

Despite the propaganda that later flooded the country about the high-powered "money men" who had conceived and engineered Barry Goldwater's nomination, this was not a noticeably affluent group. Except for two or three of us, we were all men who worked for a living, and one even had to borrow money for plane fare to Chicago. All of us, incidentally, came at our own expense.

Bill Rusher and I were the only New Yorkers. There were three from New England—David Nichols of Maine, Gerrish H. Milliken of Connecticut, and Roger Allen Moore of Massachusetts. Dave Nichols, a taciturn Downeasterner with a Cheshire-cat smile, was then Republican state chairman of Maine.[3] Gerrish Milliken was a wealthy textile manufacturer active in Connecticut politics. Roger Moore, who was twenty-eight at the time, was the junior member of the group. A proper Bostonian with a delightful sense of humor, Roger is a graduate of Harvard and Harvard Law School and is now president of the Beacon Hill Civic Association, counsel to the Massachusetts Republican State Committee, and chairman of the board of *National Review*.

The large Midwest contingent came from a total of seven states. John Ashbrook was the only Ohioan present and Charlie Barr was the sole representative from Illinois. But there were three members of what we came to call "the Indiana gang": Congressman Donald C. Bruce, a former Indianapolis newscaster who later served as chairman of the American Conservative Union; Robert E. Hughes of Greenwood, Indiana, who had been our candidate for Young Republican national

---

[3] At the time, David A. Nichols was, in terms of seniority, the third ranking Republican state chairman in the country. Ray Bliss of Ohio, now the Republican National Chairman, was the ranking state leader, and Mel Engels of Montana was number two. Nichols is now Maine's Republican National Committeeman.

chairman in 1961 and was then State Treasurer of Indiana; and Robert Matthews of Indianapolis, a former Indiana state Republican chairman and one of the ablest politicians I have ever worked with.

Wisconsin contributed two key men to this founding group—Leonard E. Pasek of Appleton, a businessman friend of mine whom I had met through my public affairs courses, and Sam Hay, a Milwaukee industrial relations executive who had become interested in politics only a few years before and with amazing speed had soon become Milwaukee County Republican chairman.

Our man from Kansas was Ned Cushing, a young bank president from the small town of Downs in Osborne County and more recently Republican state finance chairman. He was another of our Young Republican friends, having served as national YR chairman from 1959 to 1961.

From the great state of Iowa came John Keith Rehmann, a young businessman who had also worked with us in the Young Republican movement for some years and had become vice chairman of the Iowa delegation to the Republican national convention in 1960.

Nebraska sent us a rising young lawyer named Charles Thone, a former YR state president who had risen rapidly to become Republican state chairman and was now a member of the National Committee. Charley won the nomination for Lieutenant Governor of Nebraska the following year, but was nosed out by his Democratic opponent in the November election by 8,000 votes out of about three-quarters of a million cast.

There were five gentlemen from the South at the meeting, three of whom were from South Carolina. We had met these three earlier at the 1960 national convention: Roger Milliken, brother of Gerrish and chairman of the board of Deering, Milliken, Inc.; Greg Shorey, who was still Republican state chairman; and Robert F. Chapman, a Spartansburg businessman who succeeded Shorey as state chairman the following year. Rounding out the Southern delegation were two young businessmen who had worked for me on the Volunteers for Nixon-Lodge in 1960—Speed Reavis Jr. of Little Rock, Arkansas and James H. Boyce of Baton Rouge, Louisiana. Jimmy Boyce was the only Democrat at the meeting, though I am happy to say that he finally got religion and switched his registration later on.

Up from Texas came the only Southwestern representative to the meeting, Dr. Robert Morris, the former chief counsel of the U.S. Senate Internal Security Subcommittee and at this time president of the University of Dallas. A reflective attorney, Bob Morris became an outstanding leader of the conservative movement in America. He had seen, at firsthand with the Senate Subcommittee and earlier as a

Naval Intelligence officer, how Communist agents and their dupes incessantly bore from within in their untiring efforts to destroy our democratic society and pervert the foreign policy of the United States government.

And last, but by no means least, from the Far West came Frank Whetstone, a big, congenial bear of a man out of Cut Bank, Montana. Frank was an old and very close friend of mine; it is worthy of note that our friendship had survived the fierce battle in the 1952 convention, when I was aligned with the Eisenhower forces and Frank remained a hardnosed Taft adherent right down to the bitter end. Frank is the publisher of the *Cut Bank Pioneer Press,* a weekly newspaper which his father had founded. Both Frank and his dad, who served as a Republican National Committeeman from Montana, have been active in politics all their lives. They have brought to their town practically every GOP Presidential candidate of the past thirty years. In fact, I venture to guess that no town of comparable size anywhere in the country has had more prominent political figures visit it than Cut Bank, which boasts a thriving population of 4,539.

At this meeting in Chicago, I presided as chairman and presented a preliminary blueprint of the plan Ashbrook, Rusher and I had conceived. There was a completely free and open discussion, and very early in the game everyone agreed that our principal goal should be to re-establish the Republican Party as an effective conservative force in American politics. Some of us felt that to a considerable degree the party had performed that function all through the eight Eisenhower years. But we all recognized that the Republican emphasis had been shifting more and more away from traditional American principles. We all felt that if this trend was permitted to continue it would eventually bring about the end of any meaningful two-party system in the United States. In its place there would ultimately be established a monolithic state, with at best two factions, erroneously labeled Republican and Democrat, going through the motions of fighting a rubber-stamp election every four years for control of an all-powerful federal government.

Although there was unanimous agreement on making our principal goal the thwarting of this Orwellian prophecy of the Big Brother state, several people thought we should also start right off by gearing our efforts toward Senator Goldwater's nomination in 1964. I repeated what I had previously said to Bill Rusher, that it was still much too early to tie ourselves and our program to any specific candidate. In the end, everyone concurred. However, the group assigned me to a committee to seek an appointment with Senator Goldwater and inform him of what we were attempting to do. The feeling was that the Senator, as the leading conservative figure in the nation, should not be kept in the dark about our efforts to promote the conservative cause within the Republican Party.

At no time did I underestimate the magnitude of the task we were setting for ourselves. I probably didn't have to spell out the difficulties for most of these men, but I warned them that there would be powerful and ruthless forces aligned against us and that we had a long, tough road ahead. I pointed out that the people who had controlled the Republican Party for more than two decades, although they might be old and tired and somewhat disorganized, would fight us tooth and nail every inch of the way once they discovered what we were up to.

We knew that many of this Old Guard would be backing Governor Rockefeller for the nomination. I had had personal experience opposing Rockefeller when I worked for Walter Mahoney's gubernatorial nomination in 1958 and I was well aware of the tremendous resources the Governor could throw into this battle. All I asked was that anyone who felt he had to switch sides be honest enough to tell us that he was going the other way.[4]

At this point, Frank Whetstone got up and stood there for a moment glowering at the others, looking for all the world like a gigantic frontiersman who had accidentally put on a business suit.

"I want to remind you guys that less than three years from now we are going to be on the firing line in a national convention," he said finally. "I've been through these things before and I know some of the rest of you have too. Now, I can trust Clif White and I can trust myself. But what I want to know is where the rest of you s.o.b.'s will be when we get down to that final ballot."

This little speech resulted in every man there pledging to stick with us to the very last no matter how intense the heat became at the 1964 convention. Frank was to repeat this performance at almost every meeting after that, and I must say it was effective. If anyone else had done it, he might have been laughed out of the room. But no one, I'm sure, thought of laughing at Frank Whetstone.

Near the end of the meeting, someone moved that I be assigned the responsibility for establishing and implementing a program aimed at achieving our ultimate goal. The motion was carried unanimously and I agreed to take on the chairmanship of the group. However, I told them bluntly that I would regard this post as merely temporary unless they showed me that I could count 100 per cent on their support.

"I've sat in too many hotel rooms and won too many elections in meetings like this only to discover on election night that we hadn't

---

[4] Not one member of this original group defected.

won after all," I said. "It's easy to sit around here and talk and get one another steamed up to the point where you become convinced you can lick anyone in the world. I'm not about to pledge myself to this job on the basis of this one meeting. What I'm going to do now—and what I want all of you to do—is to go home and give this business a lot of serious thought. I think we ought to meet again here in Chicago in about two months. If at that point you have thought this thing through and decided that we have something feasible, something that you're sure has a good chance of success, then we will go, but not before."

It was 5:30 in the afternoon when we adjourned. Someone reminded me that this was the day of the fourth game of the World Series between the Yankees and the Cincinnati Reds. "Do you know something?" he grinned. "All afternoon not one of those guys ever even asked who was winning the ball game."

"Who did win?" I asked.

"The Yankees, dammit."

I smiled and I suppose it was the same rather smug, forbearing smile that all Yankee fans have smiled down through the years since the days when Babe Ruth and Lou Gehrig and Bill Dickey terrorized the American—and the National—Leagues with their big bats. Until recently.

It was a good omen. My team had won and here we were in Chicago getting ready to field another team in that greatest of all American games, politics. It was a game that in recent years had become much more serious for me, for the country, and for the world. But as I boarded the plane at O'Hare Airport for the flight back to New York I had a feeling that we were putting together a winning combination that might well capture the pennant race at the Republican national convention in 1964 and perhaps even the political World Series that would follow in November. I had come away from that first Chicago meeting reinforced in my judgment that, like the Yankees, my team was composed of real pros.

CHAPTER 5

THE SENATOR LISTENS

IT WAS ALMOST six weeks after the first meeting in Chicago before I finally got to see Barry Goldwater. There was some little difficulty arranging an appointment, perhaps because the Senator didn't know me very well at the time. Although I had run into him occasionally at Republican dinners and other functions, we had only had two previous opportunities to really talk. The first was in 1955. In the spring of that year Bill Rusher came back to New York from a Young Republican meeting in Colorado with a glowing report on a promising junior Senator from Arizona who had been one of the speakers. As a result, we invited Goldwater to address our New York State Young Republican convention later that year at a resort hotel in the Catskills. One of my friends met him at the airport and brought him to my room before he checked into the hotel.

We spent about a half an hour talking politics and political issues. I recall that I was impressed by his forthrightness and obvious integrity. Three years later, in 1958, I stopped by his office in Washington to inform him that I was going to Arizona to do some work and had some ideas which I would try to implement that might be of some help to him in his campaign for re-election to the Senate that fall. He was most courteous, as he always is, and thanked me for my interest in his campaign.

These two chats hardly qualified me as a close friend of Senator Goldwater's, so I was not surprised when I failed to receive a response to my request for a meeting after telephoning the Senator's secretary, Edna Coerver, whom we were all to come to know and respect in the next few years. Finally Bill Rusher tracked the Senator down in his home in Phoenix. On November 9 Bill sent him a special delivery letter urging him to meet with me and several other members of the group we had gathered together in Chicago, all of whom knew Barry Goldwater much better than I. He mentioned John Ashbrook, Roger Milliken, Charley Thone and himself as the other likely members of our little delegation. In view of the events climaxed by the Goldwater nomination at the Cow Palace nearly three years later, it is worth quoting a few passages from this letter; for it must stand as some sort of tribute to Bill Rusher's clairvoyance and to the determination of our whole original group.

Dear Senator Goldwater:

I am sending this letter to you Special Delivery at your home in Phoenix, because a development is taking place which I think is potentially of the utmost importance, and which rather directly concerns you.

Briefly, a number of us who started out together in Young Republican politics, and who are now all active in major ways in the senior Republican Party in various states around the country, realized two or three months ago that collectively we represent a by no means negligible fraction of the national GOP. . . .

The group that met in Chicago on October 8 has set some serious goals for itself, and for the Republican Party. It constituted itself a permanent (though informal) committee for these purposes, and elected my old friend and political ally Clif White (about whom I have spoken to you previously) as chairman and, hopefully, full-time coordinator of the whole project. Given his experience and ability, this insures that the whole thing will not just fade away, as such projects sometimes have a tendency to do.

The whole committee meets again in Chicago on Sunday, December 10. Meanwhile, it wants a small delegation of its members to meet with you, to outline to you the plans of the group. . . . I would not bother you about this, as I think you know, unless I were convinced that it represents the beginning of the most serious *professional* effort in almost a decade to turn the Republican party into a *more* conservative channel. . . . I hope you enjoyed your vacation, and that you are ready for the exciting year ahead—and the perhaps still more exciting ones that lie beyond it. With all good wishes to you and to Mrs. Goldwater, I remain,

Yours cordially,
William A. Rusher

The Senator responded quickly. He got in touch with his Washington office and asked them to arrange the meeting Rusher had suggested through me. Poor Edna Coerver, who had lost my phone number, spent the better part of a weekend trying to hunt me down. As luck would have

it, the date we settled on—November 17—turned out to be an impossible
one for Rusher, Ashbrook, and Milliken to be in Washington. Thus, in
the end only Charley Thone and I went. Charley flew in from Nebraska
and we met at the Senator's office on the fourth floor of the Old Senate
Office Building.

Charley had gotten to know Barry Goldwater quite well when he had
been Senator Roman Hruska's administrative assistant a few years before,
and the Senator was genuinely glad to see him when we entered the office
shortly after nine o'clock. Goldwater was wearing a colorful Western
vest with Navajo symbols on it under his suit jacket and he seemed
cheerful and relaxed behind his desk. He chatted amiably with Charley
about the political situation in Nebraska, where Charley was thinking
of taking on Fred Seaton in the gubernatorial primary. Then Charley
tossed the ball to me, saying that I had a report to make.

I proceeded to outline the conclusions of the discussion at the meeting
in Chicago, and I told him a little about some of the people who had
participated. As I've mentioned, Goldwater knew several of them well
and he appeared to be quite favorably impressed by the group we had
gathered together.

I explicitly stated that we had not formed the group to work for his
candidacy, nor for the candidacy of any other individual. I said we felt
that any decision we might make about a candidate should wait until
after the 1962 Congressional elections. In the meantime we would concentrate on setting up an organizational vehicle and on finding people
within the Republican Party around the country who agreed with us
that the party should be forged into an effective conservative instrument.
This, I said, was our primary goal.

Senator Goldwater, who had listened attentively throughout, broke
in at this point.

"This," he said, "is the best thing I've heard of since I became active
in the Republican Party on the national scene. I wish you fellows a lot
of luck." He hesitated a moment, then he asked: "Is there anything
I can do to help you out?"

"We'd appreciate any suggestions or thoughts you might have as to
how we might best develop our program," I replied. "And we'd like to
keep in touch with you. Perhaps you could have your secretary send us
your speaking itinerary for the next few months so we'll know what
states you're going into. That way I can ask our people in those states
to contact you and I hope you'll be able to see them when you go in and
advise them about other people you know there who might be predisposed toward our objectives."

The Senator agreed to do this, and we chatted some more about the
national political situation. Governor Rockefeller's name came up and I

was a little surprised that Goldwater seemed to feel that the Governor had the 1964 nomination all but sewed up and that there was no one on the horizon who might head him off. When I looked back on it later I thought it was strange that Barry Goldwater appeared to be acquiescing in Nelson Rockefeller's nomination. But as the months wore on I learned that Rockefeller was even then spending considerable time assiduously courting Goldwater.

The rest of our conversation revolved around the 1964 party platform, in which the Senator seemed more deeply interested than the possible Presidential nomination. In retrospect, this too was odd. It is an axiom of American politics that the candidate has the final say about the platform he runs on. Nixon, even while bowing to Rockefeller's demands, rather conclusively proved this in 1960.

Before we left his office, Senator Goldwater told me to call him personally if I had any problems he could help solve. Although I did not abuse this open invitation, there were, of course, a number of times during the ensuing three years that I telephoned him when I thought a matter warranted his attention. I must say that I have never dealt with any man in public life who was more accessible than Barry Goldwater. When I phoned I was usually put through to him immediately. If he was out, he would return my call as soon as he got back or checked with his office. The longest I ever had to wait was one afternoon in 1962 when I phoned his office in Washington only to find that he had left on a plane for a speech in San Francisco. Less than four hours later—apparently right after he had landed on the Coast and telephoned his office—the Senator returned my call.

As we were departing, the Senator walked us to the door. He shook hands and again wished us good luck with our project. Charley Thone and I left with the distinct impression that the Senator was happy to have found some allies. In the past he must often have felt it was a rather lonely struggle to steer the Republican Party onto a more conservative highway. It had been a most cordial meeting and, we both felt, a constructive one. The man who had become the symbol of the conservative cause in America had given us much encouragement—and even a pledge of his support and help. This did not, of course, extend to his own possible candidacy. The Senator obviously acquiesced in Nelson Rockefeller's candidacy, though it was an attitude which neither of us then took very seriously. But Charley Thone and I agreed that our talk that morning had achieved what we had hoped. Barry Goldwater had given us a green light to go ahead with our program.

On the eve of our group's next meeting, December 10, I flew to Chicago to meet with some of the people already assembling at the

Avenue Motel. It was a cold and stormy night, and a few hours after my jet liner landed at O'Hare the airport was closed to traffic. A number of our friends, including five from the first meeting, were unable to get into Chicago. Many, however, kept right on trying through the night. I remember that Sam Barnes, an old friend of mine who had been Republican chairman of Orange County in southern California, called me at the motel about two o'clock in the morning to report that his flight from the Coast had been forced to land in Cleveland, but that he would keep fighting to get on through to Chicago.

The next morning dawned cold and gray, with high winds still whipping in off Lake Michigan, but somehow Sam Barnes got in. So did ten others we had added to our group since the original meeting. Among them were two men who were to play key roles in our Texas operation— Tad Smith of El Paso, who was then Republican state chairman, and Albert E. Fay of Houston, a member of the Republican National Committee.[1]

The other new additions, several of whom had been invited to the first meeting but couldn't make it, included Donald J. Nutter, a World War II bomber pilot who had been elected Governor of Montana in 1960; John M. Lupton, a former advertising executive from Connecticut who was then in the State Senate; William G. McFadzean, a Minneapolis businessman whom I had met through one of my public affairs courses; Edward O. Ethell, a Colorado public relations man who had been Republican chairman of Jefferson County and at this time was administrative assistant to Senator Gordon Allott; John Tope, a steel company executive in Birmingham, Alabama, and a former Young Republican national chairman from 1949 to 1951 when he lived in Detroit; and attorney Sullivan Barnes of South Dakota, another former YR national chairman (1953-55) then working for ex-Governor Joe Foss in the American Football League.

In all, there were twenty-eight men present when we gathered that Sunday morning in the same motel conference room we had used the first time out. I had had private talks with most of them the night before, and by breakfast that morning I had determined that they all had thought this business through as I had suggested. Every one of them was ready to go. Thus, we wasted no time discussing the feasibility of the operation outlined at the first meeting. Instead, we got right down to the job of determining how we were to implement our program.

I opened the meeting by giving them a full report on the conference Charley Thone and I had had with Senator Goldwater. Then I presented a budget for our first year's operations, which were to consist primarily

[1] In addition to being a very competent politician, Al Fay is also a champion sailboat captain.

of a nationwide search for conservative Republicans we could recruit to help win control of the 1964 convention.

In view of the tremendous task we had cut out for ourselves, the budget I proposed—$65,000—was laughably low. If Nelson Rockefeller had learned about it, I'm sure he would have sneered us right off the political map—*his* map, at least. But I felt we could get along on $65,000 for the first year because I knew that most of the people in that room, and the thousands of others around the country who would be in sympathy with what we were doing, would be willing to volunteer their time and efforts to our cause with no thought of financial remuneration.

The budget covered only bare essentials: a small office in New York, a secretary-assistant, my travel expenses, and my salary since I was going to have to devote full time to this operation from there on in. I pegged the salary at $24,000 for the year, which was a rather substantial cut over what I had earned from my own business during the preceding year. The group unanimously approved the budget, although several told me afterwards they thought it was unrealistically modest. Roger Milliken then agreed to take the post of finance chairman, at least temporarily. Specifically, he promised to raise the first $30,000, a promise he promptly made good.

I had brought a map to the meeting that illustrated my proposal to divide the country into nine regions for our organizational effort. I told them that any politician who alleges that he can manage all fifty states himself is out of his mind. Since I hadn't taken leave of my senses, I knew I was going to need help. I then proposed nine people to serve unofficially as part-time regional directors for that first year. Each would have the responsibility of ferreting out and marshaling conservative Republicans in the states comprising his region.

I reminded them that our primary goal was to build delegate strength for the 1964 national convention. The only way we could realize this goal was by mobilizing the grassroots and thereby in effect introducing a broader application of the democratic process into the Republican Party. To accomplish this, each one of them would have to familiarize himself thoroughly with the statutes and by-laws governing the selection of delegates in his states. I announced that we were going after delegates in *every* state. No matter how hopeless the situation might look in any given state, we would fight to win at least a few delegates to our side.

To achieve this goal, I urged the group to begin organizing conservatives at the precinct, district and state levels immediately. Then I bore down on the crucial area that most people concerned with nominating a Presidential candidate tend to overlook. Two years before each national convention, precinct caucuses are held in virtually every state to name precinct, community and county committeemen. In most cases the committeemen then serve through the spring meetings two years later at which delegates are picked for the state conventions, or the candidates for national delegate posts are selected to run in the primaries. Our job would be to assure the selection of conservative precinct committeemen and committeewomen in 1962 and 1963 who would then have a major voice in picking delegates dedicated to our principles in 1964.

I made the further point that the large majority of delegates to the national convention are picked from Congressional districts. Usually the Governor or the state convention is empowered to appoint a small number of bonus delegates based on the success the party has had in electing candidates to Congress and the U.S. Senate. But all the other delegates come from the Congressional districts, where two delegates are named, or elected in primaries, in each district. This made it imperative for us to have strong Congressional district organizations with firm roots at the precinct level. And it behooved us to move toward forming those organizations now.

I knew that we would have deep and extensive silent support in every state of the Union. Many precinct and district committee members, even in the supposedly Liberal Northeast, were basically conservative. Often they had been forced to cover up their philosophical beliefs to keep peace with the powers who dictated party policy and candidates. The controlling faction, almost invariably a remote and lofty minority, played the game solely from considerations of what they conceived to be expediency. Sometimes this game included tacit agreements with the Democrat bosses, which in effect meant surrendering to the opposition party certain offices, specific districts, whole cities and counties, and, in the South, entire states and regions.

The committee people were frequently aware of these arrangements. But there was very little they could do as individuals to counter them. Some had quit politics entirely, disgusted by the sham battles they were forced to engage in. Too often they were replaced by party hacks, office holders who were permitted to keep soft jobs in the local, state and even federal government in exchange for not indulging too seriously in building an effective Republican organization. I felt we had a good chance of knocking out a large number of these hangers-on and replacing them with people interested in something more than soft political jobs.

Many of the older professionals in the GOP had lost touch completely with their grassroots. They were too intent on taking orders from above to notice what was happening right under their noses. The Democrat bosses were guilty of this too. But their machines were so massive and so well oiled, particularly now that they had the immense federal patronage back in their pockets, that they stood in no immediate danger. The Republican pros, on the other hand, were sitting ducks. Having lost the federal government, controlling only fourteen statehouses and but a small handful of the big city halls, they had very little to offer in the way of patronage. Thus they did not have much in the way of a club to use to beat the troops into submission. In short, the situation was ripe for revolt.

The revolt would in most instances be best directed at the precinct, municipal, county and district levels. It would manifest itself there long before it was even noticed on the state and national planes. However, we had no intention of inciting insurrection where it wasn't necessary. Wherever possible we would try to work through present officials of the Republican Party. One of our first tasks, I told the group, would be to determine exactly which officials in each state would be with us and which against us. Those who would give us reasonable assurance of their support at the national convention should have our full backing. Those who would not we would deal with as gently as possible so as not to open up any more divisive splits than would be necessary. If any of the second group held high office, we would probably have to support them while bringing pressure to bear from the party workers they depended upon to wage their campaigns.

In addition, I instructed the group to find civic leaders, who did not necessarily have to be in positions of leadership in the party, who would work for and support our effort. We would concentrate on finding people within the party's auxiliary organizations, such as the Young Republicans and the Women's Federation, who were predisposed to work with us. And finally, we were to become better acquainted with the members of the National Republican Committee so that we could build a group within the Committee to help get our people on the platform and other committees at the national convention.

All of our efforts would be devoted to winning as large a majority of delegates as possible for our candidate at the 1964 convention. Our objective would be to win the nomination for him on the first ballot. However, all our plans, at that time and right on through to San Francisco, would be predicated on the likelihood of a contested convention and the possibility of fighting for our cause through a number of ballots.

We spent considerable time debating whether we should give our little *ad hoc* committee a formal name. So it would have some identification among ourselves and those we would be working with, and for lack of a better name, the others decided to call it simply "the Clif White group." Although we were not a secret group in any sinister sense of the word, we had no intention of inviting publicity at this time. However, I felt then, and still do, that the press would most probably have ignored us even if we had asked reporters to attend our meetings. At any rate, there was absolutely no point in seeking publicity until such time as we decided to support a candidate. Meanwhile, there were certain advantages to our collective anonymity. At least we would present no visible target to potential opponents and unfriendly members of the fourth estate who would be only too happy to have a go at shooting us down before we got into orbit.

The meeting lasted all day, with only a short break for lunch. At the end of the afternoon, when we were getting ready to adjourn, Governor Nutter got up and asked if he might say a few words. He had not said a thing all day, although it was obvious that he was taking in everything that went on.

"I can't tell you how impressed I am with what you people have done here today," he said. "I don't have to spell out for any of you the dangers that confront America at this period of history—or the risks that each one of you is assuming in supporting a cause like ours, a cause which we all know is aimed at only one thing and that is the preservation of this nation. I am proud that you have included me in your group, and I hope that you will let me see this thing through with you, regardless of what my association with you and this cause might mean to my political future in the State of Montana. What you people are attempting to do is far more important to the future of this country than the political future of any one man, certainly more important than my being re-elected Governor of Montana."

The meeting broke up right after that. But I don't think anyone who was there will ever forget Don Nutter or the message he brought to us that Sunday afternoon in Chicago. Only a few weeks later Governor Nutter was killed in the crash of a National Guard plane in the mountains of Montana. But his words were to sustain us all in the trying months and years ahead.

CHAPTER 6

SUITE 3505

IMMEDIATELY FOLLOWING our second Chicago meeting, the members of our group repaired to their home states to begin the quiet hunt for allies. Since I was now charged with coordinating and directing this effort on a full-time basis, I spent the remaining weeks of 1961 winding up my business affairs and setting up a headquarters for our nationwide operation. I found a small two-room suite of offices on the thirty-fifth floor of the Chanin Building at the corner of 42nd Street and Lexington Avenue, purchased two desks, some chairs and file cabinets, rented a water cooler and went to work.

A day or so after I moved in Bill Rusher dropped by. The directory in the lobby bore the name "F. Clifton White and Associates, Inc." But I had not had any name printed on the door of the office, which simply carried the number of the suite—"3505." This prompted Rusher to ask what I intended to call the new offices.

"Just Suite 3505," I shrugged.

Rusher laughed. "I think that's a great no-name. It'll be a while before anyone penetrates that cover."

Bill's jest turned out to be an accurate prediction. It was almost exactly a year before the press caught on to what we were cooking up in that two-room office. But if reporters had come calling before that they would not have been much impressed. Suite 3505 was an unpretentious headquarters that belied the seriousness of our effort and the far-reaching effects it was to have. There were none of the trappings of the "well-heeled political machine" that so much of the press later detected. In fact our poverty, which the press subsequently refused to believe, showed rather starkly in 3505. The furniture was almost all secondhand. There were no rugs on the floor, no drapes on the windows. Like good conservatives, we were determined to live within our means, though before long we very nearly had no means to live within.

Shortly after Senator Goldwater's nomination, Bill Rusher wrote an article for *National Review* in which he briefly told how the Draft Goldwater movement began, carefully refraining from naming names.[1] Recalling the impoverished state of our operation in 1962, he wrote:

It is amusing, in retrospect, to contrast the modest little suite in the Chanin Building with the elaborate five-story town house at 22 West 55th Street near Fifth Avenue from which the Presidential ambitions of Governor Nelson Rockefeller were even then being promoted by a well-paid legion of speech writers, researchers, advance men and big-time political operators. Already Republican state chairmen and other major political figures from many states were being flown to New York City and ushered into the gubernatorial presence for a warm handshake, a personalized version of the famous grin, and murmured assurances of fond rememberance when the inevitable came to pass. It is unlikely that Suite 3505—had anyone known of its existence—would have caused anything but mirth.

Joe Kane, an old Boston political pro, cousin of Joseph P. Kennedy and advisor to Jack Kennedy in his first campaign for Congress in 1946, used to observe that it took three things to win an election. Said Kane: "The first is money and the second is money and the third is money." If we had believed this precept in 1962, our little group would have tossed in the sponge before we started.

But what we lacked in money we more than made up for in faith, know-how and just plain hard work. And we were fortunate at the outset in acquiring an invaluable asset in the person of Miss Rita Bree. Rita had been a successful businesswoman in New York, having been insurance manager for an investment trust company. She had also been active in politics, serving, among other posts, as chairman of the Young Women's Republican Club of New York.

Bill Rusher convinced Rita she should at least consider joining our new operation as an all-round girl Friday and coordinator of women's activities. We had two lunches together just after the Chicago meeting in December and at the second one Rita asked me where I thought we would be at the end of 1964. I knew that we were asking her to give up a secure position, but I refused to paint any glowing picture of the future.

[1] *National Review*, August 11, 1964.

Instead, I told her that I really didn't know. "But," I said, "I do know that I have a son, and I would like to leave him with what my father left me. It wasn't money. It was an opportunity. And I feel that unless someone makes the effort now, that opportunity won't be there for my son."

Rita now says that this finally convinced her to come aboard at 3505. Needless to say, it involved a considerable risk on her part. As the months wore on and the risk loomed larger, I'm sure Rita must have regretted her decision many times. But like the courageous Connecticut Yankee she is, Miss Bree never displayed any sign of discouragement. She simply kept working away and her example did much to buoy all of us up during the low ebb that almost left our operation stranded high and dry midway through 1962.

As soon as we had our little office organized, with Rita Bree to keep the wheels turning while I was away, I started the nationwide search for people who could help us build delegate strength for the 1964 convention. Early in January I took off for Oklahoma City where the Republican National Committee was meeting. It was the first of countless trips I was to make over the next two and a half years. All told, I was to travel more than a million miles during that period, which must be something of a record even among today's peripatetic politicians.

In Oklahoma City, my friend John Thomas arranged a meeting with John W. Tyler, the National Committeeman from Oklahoma. This was the beginning of an effort to create a unified conservative caucus within the National Committee, an effort that continued right down to the national convention in San Francisco. Roger Milliken, who was also on the National Committee, delivered a check for the funds he had collected on our behalf. It was enough to keep us in business for the next four months.

Senator Goldwater turned up at this National Committee meeting too. In an informal speech he made a moving appeal for greater Republican harmony, an appeal he was to repeat in vain many times during the next two years. "It doesn't help," he told the Committee, "to have our members characterized as Western Republicans, or Javits Republicans, or Rockefeller Republicans, or modern Republicans. Nor does it help when some of our detractors get into a particularly vengeful mood and refer to some of us as Goldwater Republicans. We've got to get together and decide just what we are."

Throughout the remaining months of that winter I was constantly on the go. Wherever I went I was encouraged by the enthusiasm and determination of the hundreds of conservative Republicans I met. Many were political neophytes, but they were eager and willing to learn. And I was happy to give them my primer on how to build an organization from the precinct on up and how to plan the selection of delegates from their districts and states.

In many states, I was able to help bring these amateurs into closer contact with old political friends I had acquired over the years. Most of the people in both these categories were relatively young. Only a very few could be considered wealthy. But virtually all had been successful in their fields and professions. The newcomers often brought refreshing new approaches to politics and during the next three years they introduced many innovations to a field that is frequently saddled with tired old slogans and methods.

There were many instances in which I was able to encourage people to plunge more deeply into politics. In Shreveport, Louisiana, I had a long talk one night with a civic-minded oil man, Charlton H. Lyons. He now claims it was this talk that started him down the political trail in earnest. Within a year he was a member of the Republican National Committee. The year after that he became state GOP chairman. And in between he ran for Governor, making one of the strongest showings any Republican had ever achieved in Louisiana.

On this same swing through the South and Southwest I landed in Houston, where Texas Republicans, after a century of playing the role of political outcasts, were exuding a new aura of confidence. I addressed a luncheon group that Al Fay and Tad Smith had gathered. That night I had a productive planning session with Jimmy Bertrand, then GOP chairman of Harris County. I went away with the feeling that Texas was one state I would not have to waste much worry on.

The next day I hit Jackson, Mississippi, where the Southern Association of Republican State Chairmen had assembled for a weekend conference. At LeFleur's Restaurant I outlined my plan to Charley Klumb and Wirt Yerger, who was until recently Mississippi state chairman. Wirt asked how many delegate votes I thought we could win for a conservative candidate like Goldwater at the 1964 convention. I went down the list state by state and then gave him my projected first ballot total. After the convention, Wirt wrote me a letter in which he said, "It is amazing to me how accurate your predictions were at that time." Out of the 1,308 votes cast for all candidates at San Francisco thirty months later, the projection had come within 20 of Goldwater's ultimate total.

Everywhere people welcomed me warmly. Even those I had never met before went far beyond the usual requirements of courtesy to help me deliver my message in their communities and states. In Wisconsin, one housewife took a whole day off to drive me hundreds of miles when I was unexpectedly stranded without transportation. On another occasion bad weather grounded my plane in St. Louis on a flight to Tulsa and I had to take a train via Kansas City. It was four o'clock in the morning when the train finally pulled into Tulsa, but there was John Thomas waiting for me at the station. In Minnesota, Bill McFadzean and Bill Bennett, two young businessmen now working with my group, took turns driving me up and down the state for three days. It was on this same Midwest tour that I first met J. D. Stetson (Stets) Coleman, the Chicago candy manufacturer who was to become one of the stalwarts of the Goldwater organization both nationally and in the three states where he maintained residences—Illinois, Florida and Virginia.

The coming 1962 elections were on the minds of many at this point. We saw in them a chance to test conservative strength at the polls as a prelude to our 1964 campaign. In Denver, I conferred with a group Ed Ethell rounded up. Even at this early stage they had plenty of problems.

Jean K. Tool, the resourceful and tough-minded Colorado state Republican chairman, was already beating the drums for Nelson Rockefeller. Tool had picked a political newcomer, John A. Love, as his candidate for Governor. Our group felt Love was a strong candidate with no personal Presidential preference though he might be influenced by Tool. Fortunately they had an outstanding young conservative Congressman in Peter Dominick to oppose Democratic U.S. Senator John A. Carroll, an old-line Liberal. I marked this race as one to watch.

Meanwhile, I urged the Colorado group to get cracking on precinct and district organization. Tool was obviously banking on getting Love elected Governor so they could deliver the state's 18 delegates to Rockefeller. But the grassroots sentiment in Colorado was strongly conservative, and I knew if we could get our people onto the precinct committees, or strengthen those who were already members, we could thwart Mr. Tool's handsome plan.

Twice during this period I flew to Washington to report to Senator Goldwater. His enthusiasm for our operation seemed to be growing as I brought him fresh evidence of the conservative groundswell that was beginning to build up in all parts of the country. But at no time did we discuss his possible candidacy. When I saw him on April 5 he still appeared primarily interested in the shape of the 1964 platform. With this in mind, I met that same day with Senator Tower of Texas and asked him to help in formulating plans for the platform; plans which, as we shall see, came to fruition in San Francisco.

Toward the end of the following week we held the third, and in some ways the most important, meeting of our original group. This time we gathered at a secluded hunting lodge in the woods of northern Minnesota. Although it was already springtime in Washington, the wooded hills around the lodge were still covered with snow and the air was crisp and very cold.

I had been in Kentucky the early part of the week and had flown back to New York to spend a day with my family before taking a plane to Minneapolis-St. Paul on Thursday night, April 12. This was the day that Roger Blough, chairman of U.S. Steel Corporation, made the announcement that his company was going to raise its prices. That move led the Kennedy Administration to crack down violently on the steel industry, and in the process it openly revealed the alarming extent of the federal government's power over private business. Two newsmen who had covered certain aspects of the steel price increase were routed out of bed before dawn by FBI agents who had been ordered to investigate the pricing "plot." A few days later, after President Kennedy had made the famous remark that his businessman father had "always said that businessmen were a bunch of s.o.b.'s," Roger Blough and the chief executives of the other steel companies were forced to capitulate.

My plane landed shortly before midnight at the Twin Cities airport where I ran into Charley Klumb and Wirt Yerger, who had flown up from Mississippi for our meeting. They ribbed me all the way up to the lodge about scheduling a meeting in such a cold and out-of-the-way place. A number of others were even more unhappy about having to travel into the north woods, but I had good reasons for holding the meeting there. I wanted the members of our group to get to know one another better, not only as fellow politicians but as friends. I decided that by being together in a place where they would be isolated from contact with the outside world for two whole days, they would develop confidence in one another and in the group. Of course, it *could* have had the opposite effect. But I felt that I knew my team well enough to predict their reactions, and fortunately I was right.

Even Bill Rusher, who was rather outspokenly opposed to having a meeting anywhere outside a large metropolitan city that could be easily reached from New York, fell into the spirit of this weekend bivouac in the Minnesota wilds. He later admitted the setting had had the desired effect of cementing the ties that bound our group together and turned it into a cohesive and tremendously effective team.

About thirty people showed up at the lodge (all but a few of whom had attended our two Chicago meetings), so some had to be put up in cabins away from the main building. Rita Bree was the only woman in the group, and thus the only one to have a cabin all to herself. The two Mississippians, Charley Klumb and Wirt Yerger, shared a cabin with those incomparable cosmopolitans, New Yorker Rusher and Bostonian Roger Allen Moore. When they arrived the temperature inside the cabin was below freezing, and Wirt still laughs when he recalls the president of the Beacon Hill Civic Association huddling in front of the fireplace trying desperately to get a fire going and brew a pot of coffee.

The following morning we had a meeting of the group's executive committee, which at that time included Rusher, Moore, Charlie Barr, Al Fay, Charley Klumb, Bill McFadzean, Dave Nichols, John Rehmann, Tad Smith, Frank Whetstone and myself.

Later, on the big glass-enclosed porch of the main lodge with a bright sun glinting on the snow outside, the entire group assembled for our first formal session. I brought them up to date on my activities in the field and reported that my extensive travels over the past three months had confirmed our original hunch that there would be no dearth of people willing to work for the cause. However, in some key states it was proving rather difficult to convince people of the need for starting their organizational activities now. With primaries and state conventions being held in practically every state that spring, the politicians were busy focusing on these and on the important local, state and Congressional races coming up in the fall. This was understandable, of course. And I reminded the members of our group that they should increase their areas of influence within the Republican Party by taking an active hand in helping select candidates and by working in the autumn campaigns.

I set December 30, 1962 as the target date for having a man in each state who would supervise the selection of delegates. By early 1963 we planned to have a citizens' organization set up to pave the way for the formal unveiling of our candidate before the Presidential primary campaigns began in January 1964. In each state, I wanted an outstanding chairman for this citizens' group, plus a state finance chairman and women's leader. By mid-1963 I hoped to have a contact or leader in every county and Congressional district. At Suite 3505 Rita Bree was already keeping a separate book for each of the fifty states so we could fill in the names of our leaders at every level as we acquired them.

Charley Thone had prepared a detailed report on exactly how delegates to the national convention are selected. As I have mentioned, the selection process varies widely, and we spent many hours going over the rules and regulations indigenous to each state. I charged the regional directors with the job of mastering these rules for all the states in their territories and with making certain that our state chairmen would be thoroughly acquainted with them when the time came.

We broke for dinner that first night, but immediately afterwards got back to work. Several members of the group gave presentations on ideas and programs that had worked out particularly well in their home cities and states. Sam Hay, the Milwaukee County chairman, demonstrated a bubble-shaped car top that he had invented. It was a sign frame that could be kept in a car trunk or quickly snapped onto the roof where it could withstand winds of up to 70 miles per hour if a candidate happened to arrive on a particularly gusty day. We later used Sam's invention in many parts of the country during the 1964 campaign. Items like this might seem like pure gimmickry, not worth the attention of a group planning the nomination of a Presidential candidate. But attention to even the most minute details at an early stage can save many precious hours during a campaign.

After these demonstrations we called it a day, though many of the fellows stayed up far into the small hours talking or playing poker. These all-nighters nearly mutinied the next morning when shortly after 6 A.M. Frank Whetstone ran a miniature fire truck with a screaming siren through the corridors of the lodge and out around the cabins to rout everyone out of bed. It was lucky for Frank that most of them managed to recover their good humor at breakfast, with the solacing aid of gallons of steaming coffee.

We worked all through that day, a Saturday, concentrating on the critical caucus and convention dates that would be coming up over the next two years so we could focus on the important dates in our districts and states and begin building our organizations toward them. Then we discussed the mechanics of the national convention itself.

At least a third of the fight in winning a convention depends on understanding its techniques and tactics, rules and procedures. But there are not too many opportunities to gain this kind of vitally needed knowledge. Presidential conventions are held every four years and Young Republican conventions every two. Fortunately, practically every member of this original group had convention experience. Our people included every YR national chairman (except Charlie McWhorter and Leonard Nadasdy) of the previous 14 years. Most had been delegates to Republican national conventions as well. This group actually had more practical convention experience at that time than any other team in either political party.

I wound up that day with a brief pep talk. "All we need to do," I said, "is get into that convention with a halfway decent break. We don't even need a majority of the delegates with us. If we can come within shooting distance of a majority, I'm convinced we have the know-how and the people to turn the tide in our favor. If we stick together and work like blazes for the next two years there isn't another team in the Republican Party that will be able to lick us in July 1964."

This was our last night at the lodge and we all stayed up late after dinner. I remember that about 2:30 in the morning one of the fellows asked: "Clif, you don't really think this is going to work, do you?"

I said, "Of course I think it's going to work. If I didn't, I wouldn't be in it."

He shook his head slowly. "I think you're out of your mind. You're never going to do it. I'm with you, and I'll be with you right down to the wire. But let's not kid ourselves. We can't stop the gang that's been running this party for the last twenty-odd years. We just don't have the muscle to beat them. Or the money."

"Money, no," I laughed. "But muscle? If by that you mean determination and savvy, we've got plenty of muscle."

Actually, I felt even then that this young gang of ours had a lot more political muscle than any of them realized. As subsequent events were to prove, their strength continued to grow and eventually it developed into more than enough to win the nomination for Barry Goldwater. I also believe that if the strength and conviction and knowledge of this group and of the people they rallied about them could only have been given a more important role after the convention, the election on November 3, 1964 would have been a lot closer than it was.

CHAPTER 7

VALLEY FORGE

THE SIX MONTHS that followed our meeting at the Minnesota hunting lodge developed into an almost constant struggle for survival. Bill Rusher has aptly called it the Goldwater movement's Valley Forge. Our biggest problem during this period from the spring through the fall of 1962 was money, or, more accurately, the lack of money.

The funds that our finance chairman, Roger Milliken, had raised early in the year were all but gone by the end of April. Thereafter, we did not know from month to month whether we could even keep our little office open. Everyone in the Republican Party, including the members of our group, was getting ready for the fall campaigns. Their resources were being plowed into local, legislative, gubernatorial and Congressional races. No one seemed willing to divert a dollar into an uncertain Presidential nomination campaign still two years away. It was costing us from four to five thousand dollars a month just to keep our modest operation going. But after April contributions seldom equaled expenses.

I tried to keep traveling since this was the only practical way we could reach out and get people sympathetic to our cause actively interested in building organizations in their areas and states. But by midsummer there were times when funds simply were not available for a trip to the West or the South or even closer to New York. I fell back on the telephone, making long-distance calls instead of taking a plane to see people in Texas or Illinois or on the West Coast. But there is just so much you can do on the phone. When you are trying to start something as vital as the nomination of a Presidential candidate your presence is demanded. People naturally want to see and talk to the men they are going to work with in such an effort before they will commit themselves. Moreover, not only did it become difficult for me to travel, but later on in the summer I often thought twice before picking up the phone and making an important toll call.

I was never able to get a permanent finance chairman to take over when Roger Milliken's commitment ran out. And I will have to confess that in those days neither I nor most of the other members of our group had had much experience in raising funds. It was the one phase of politics I had never taken to very kindly. It was somehow repugnant for me to have to ask people for money. But I did have some friends who came through, usually just in the nick of time, and the rest of the group did the best they could.

Bill Rusher returned from an extended tour of the Far East early in June and resumed his role as a one-man Greek chorus, lending a sympathetic ear to Suite 3505's financial problems. He enlisted his friend Ralph Bachenheimer to write letters to people asking for funds and a number of them later responded. Meanwhile, we survived the month of May largely on the strength of efforts made by Gene Perrin and Ty Gillespie in Michigan. They scampered around the state and held several luncheons, managing to dredge up $2,535 to keep us afloat that month. This money all came in small contributions of $100 or less. Some gifts were as small as $10, and we were grateful for them. Every little bit helped, and I'm sure those $10 contributions represented as much or more of a sacrifice for some donors as many a larger gift.

In June, which was a very busy month in other ways, our finances reached low ebb. Only $300 came in for the whole month, once again from the Perrin-Gillespie operation in Michigan. We were hard pressed to pay the rent and there were several costly trips already scheduled that I just had to make. I started dipping into my family savings to pay the bills. By November I had put about $6,000 into the operation. This meant that we had to hold down expenses drastically at home. But never once did my wife complain. She realized, as I did, that the whole future of our family, and particularly of our children, might well be involved in this effort. Cutting a few corners at home seemed a small price to pay to achieve something that ultimately might have great national significance and conceivably be the key to the preservation of freedom for our children and for their generation.

The contrast between our hand-to-mouth operation and the activities of the people we knew we would have to fight for control of the Republican Party was etched starkly by a tragic accident that occurred during this period. An airplane bound for California crashed in the waters off Long Island after taking off from a New York airport. Among those killed was a man who was working for one of the *sub rosa* candidates actively aiming at the 1964 Presidential nomination. Some $70,000 in cash and traveler's checks were found in the man's baggage. We knew this was just a small part of the money his candidate was able to draw on for his campaign.

In some states, we were hampered in our own fundraising by the ineptitude of regular Republican Party finance organizations. A classic case occurred in Pennsylvania. Shortly after our Minnesota meeting, one of our people in Pittsburgh visited a wealthy friend to see if he would give us a contribution. His friend reacted angrily. "The Republican Party will never get another cent out of me," he scowled. Then he explained why.

During the 1961 election campaign, he had advanced the party a loan of $10,000 which it promised faithfully to pay within thirty to sixty days. Now, more than six months later, he had just that day received a check representing a refund on a postage meter used in the campaign as "partial payment" on the $10,000. The amount of the check: $1.92. He never collected another cent.

Despite our difficulties in raising funds, things were looking up for Republicans, and particularly for conservative Republicans, on a number of other fronts. Early in May, Senator Everett Dirksen of Illinois and Congressman Charles Halleck of Indiana demanded a Congressional investigation into the Agriculture Department's relationship with a Texas wheeler-dealer named Billie Sol Estes.[1] The Administration tried to drown the episode in syrupy explanations. But before the case ran its course three Agriculture Department officials, including two Assistant Secretaries, were belatedly dismissed for accepting "gifts" from Estes. In addition, three Democrats in Congress, including Senator Ralph Yarborough of Texas, admitted receiving campaign funds from him. And the body of Henry Marshall, another Federal official connected with the case, was exhumed in Texas, where he had died in 1961 with five bullet holes from a bolt-action rifle. Marshall had been declared a suicide. The coroner now changed the ruling to "probable murder." The Billie Sol Estes case, though never completely aired, focused public attention on Democratic corruption during an election year.

On June 7, conservative Republicanism received another, and quite different, shot in the arm. Congressman Melvin R. Laird of Wisconsin,

[1] Credit for exposing the Billie Sol Estes case should go to Oscar Griffin, a courageous young editor of the Pecos, Texas, *Independent*. It was Griffin who first disclosed that the Estes gang was selling mortgages on non-existent fertilizer storage tanks in the Southwest.

Chairman of the 1962 Congressional Joint Committee on Republican Principles, issued a declaration of party policy that echoed many of the principles conservatives had been espousing for years. Nor was the Joint Committee stacked with conservatives. In fact, it included such leading Republican Liberals as Senator George D. Aiken of Vermont and Senator Kenneth B. Keating of New York.

The hardhitting declaration hammered away at the Democratic Administration for showing "little understanding of, or concern for, institutions that buttress freedom at home." It further charged that the Administration "has demonstrated neither the wit nor the will to meet effectively the assault of international Communism on freedom." Several Lincolnian passages could have come right out of Senator Goldwater's new best-selling book, *Why Not Victory?*

"The world cannot permanently endure part Communist and part free," the declaration said. *"In foreign policy, the overriding national goal must be victory over Communism through the establishment of a world in which men can live in freedom, security, and national independence. There can be no real peace short of it. An active strategy aimed at victory does not increase the risk of nuclear war. Weakness and irresolution on the part of the United States . . . are more likely to bring the world to hot war than are strength and firmness."* (Italics added.)

As a seemingly deliberate counterpoint to this forthright declaration of Republican principles, President Kennedy delivered a commencement address at Yale University four days later in which he attacked the conservative "myths" that bigger and bigger federal government abridges individual freedom and that federal deficits create inflation. And on the same day the State Department finally brought off a coup opposed by conservative Republicans and Democrats alike—the "neutralization" of Laos under a coalition government in which the strongest single force was the Communists.[2] As events were to prove, this move led directly to what the conservatives had warned would happen. Far from being neutralized, Laos became the scene of further Communist aggression and North Vietnamese troops and supplies increasingly infiltrated South Vietnam by coming over the Ho Chi Minh Trail running through Laos.

Another historic event in this same month of 1962 stimulated far more conservative sentiment at the grassroots level than any of the foregoing. On June 22 the Supreme Court issued its famed school prayer decision. People who had never considered themselves conservatives—indeed, many to whom this label was still a dirty word—suddenly found

---

[2] President Kennedy and Premier Nikita Khrushchev had agreed to support the "neutralization" of Laos at their summit meeting in Vienna a year earlier.

themselves protesting against this latest flagrant attack upon traditional institutions by the Liberals on the Supreme Court. Unwittingly, the Court had gratuitously handed the conservative cause an issue with which almost all Americans could sympathize. Unfortunately, it became just one of many issues which were not properly articulated in the 1964 Presidential campaign. But in 1962, and on into 1963, the decision to ban school prayer helped rally many new recruits to the conservative banner.

Meanwhile, I kept pushing ahead with our organizational drive. I made several trips to Washington in an attempt to secure the card files of the Nixon delegates to the 1960 convention, an attempt which ultimately proved successful. While there I would usually meet with James Day, a young Washington attorney who had been office comptroller for the Nixon-Lodge Volunteers and later was to hold a similar post on the National Draft Goldwater Committee. Jim had his ear to the ground in the capital and kept me faithfully posted on developments there.

Whenever possible, I made speeches before luncheon and dinner groups, always driving home the need for steering America back to its traditional road of individual liberty and responsibility. Frequently these talks proved fruitful. People would come up to the speaker's table afterwards and volunteer their help. I met a number of men and women in this way who later became stalwarts in our 1964 nomination campaign. One whom I met at a Rotary luncheon in Charleston, West Virginia in May 1962 was former U. S. Senator Chapman Revercombe. He became a key man in the Goldwater movement in what then appeared to be a strong Rockefeller state and was elected as a delegate to the national convention.

To keep in contact with the far-flung members of my group I periodically sent them confidential memorandums. I never signed these memos, and they bore no return address or any other clue as to the source. Only our members knew where they came from and what they meant. I will confess that I goaded the group on unmercifully, urging them to fulfill their assignments. And I never let them forget that time was running fast. In one typical memo dated May 29, 1962 I concluded:

1964 is just around the corner. 1963 is practically here. We never have time to do all of the preparation necessary to achieve a maximum effective political organization. Let's not kid ourselves into thinking that we have lots of time. We must stick to our agreed-upon schedule and get these things accomplished in an orderly fashion. If we do this, I have no serious concern as to our ability to be successful.

Towards the end of May I made another swing through the South on the first leg of a trip that was to carry me clear across the country and back. Greg Shorey met me at the airport in Greenville, South Carolina, and at lunch he and Bob Chapman filled me in on the situation in their state before we conferred with other Republican leaders that night. The next morning I was in Atlanta and from there I took off for Birmingham. John Tope was waiting when I got off the plane and on our way into town we stopped at a ball field where a Little League softball game was in progress. John hailed a man out of the crowd he wanted me to meet. It turned out to be Harold Dean, Birmingham County Republican chairman, who was already out beating the bushes for potential delegates in Alabama.

At a meeting later that day in Birmingham we talked future strategy with John Grenier, who was then preparing to step into the state chairman's job, and Jim Martin, an oil distributor (*not* a wealthy oil man, as the press came to describe him) who was getting ready to take on veteran Democrat Lister Hill in the fall campaign for Hill's seemingly secure seat in the United States Senate. Charley Klumb came in from Mississippi for this meeting and briefed us on the political scene in that state.

The next day I set out for Phoenix, Arizona. Plane connections were not too good and after several lengthy layovers en route we finally landed in Phoenix about 3 A.M. As usual there were friends at the airport to meet me, even in the middle of the night. This time it was Ralph Staggs, Mericopa County Republican chairman, and George Leiphart, who had worked with me in the Nixon-Lodge campaign. Conservatives were not hard to find in Barry Goldwater's home town, though not too many years before Phoenix and the whole state of Arizona had been Democratic strongholds. We talked with a number of these Republican converts the following day, and before I left Staggs agreed to start making arrangements for a Southwestern regional meeting of our group later in the summer.

The next stop was Los Angeles. I got there on the Sunday before the California primary and found the state in an uproar. The Republicans were involved in another of those recurrent internecine struggles that have caused such bitter dissension within our party through the years. This one resulted from the head-on clash for the gubernatorial nomination between Richard Nixon, who was striving for a political comeback after his 1960 defeat, and Joseph Shell, the former University of Southern California football star who is now a successful oil company executive.

Nixon had returned to California to find many of his oldest supporters there deeply disillusioned by his 1960 campaign. Many of these people, including A. C. (Cy) Rubel, former chairman of the giant Union Oil Company of California, were now backing Joe Shell in the primary race.

Shell was a conservative and an aggressive one. But Nixon had absorbed even more punishment from the strong Liberal Republican forces in the state. An ancient enemy, former Governor Goodwin J. (Goodie) Knight, had started sniping at him even before the primary campaign began. Knight had been planning a comeback too, and had his sights firmly set on his old office in Sacramento. Illness forced him to withdraw from the primary race and his Liberal supporters were thrown into a quandary. Now, faced with a choice between backing their old antagonist Nixon or the far more conservatively inclined Joe Shell, many of them decided to support Nixon in the primary. But they later cut his throat in the general election against the Democratic Governor, Pat Brown. Party loyalty among too many Liberal Republicans is not even skin deep, as the 1964 Presidential campaign was to demonstrate so clearly. You either play it their way, or they play for the other side.

Sam Barnes, who was on Nixon's side in the primary battle, painted the whole dreary picture for me in vivid colors as we drove from the Los Angeles airport down to his home on Balboa Bay, one of the many beautiful spots on the California coast. In meetings with our California people over the next few days we discussed possible solutions to the unbelievably complex political problems that existed in the state, problems that were likely to persist and even multiply well into 1964 no matter what the outcome of the Nixon-Shell fight that Tuesday.

There wasn't much we could do at this stage. If Nixon won the primary and went on to victory over Brown in November he would be a strong contender for the Presidential nomination again in 1964. He was not the nominee most of us now had in mind as our first choice, though we had all backed him to the hilt in the past. On the other hand, if he took the primary we naturally wanted him to win the general election. Unlike the Liberals who were aching to finish off Dick Nixon forever, we would support him right down the line that fall. I've always believed that with our two-party system this is the only way you can play the game, no matter how many bitter pills you have to swallow over the years. It's the way the Democrats play it, which accounts for the success of a party embracing a much broader spectrum from right to left than can be found anywhere in the GOP. The Liberals within our Republican Party are for the most part really conservatives compared with the far-Left extremists in the Democratic camp who call themselves Liberals. If Republican Liberals—and, yes, some conservatives too—would follow this one example of the Democratic opposition our party, and the nation, would be in an immeasurably stronger position today.

On the day before the 1962 California primary I visited the Nixon headquarters in Los Angeles and chatted with some old friends. The following day Sam Barnes and his wife took me to the Orange County headquarters in Santa Ana. Before the primary vote started coming in we drove over to a hotel in Newport for dinner and ran into Dick Nixon's younger brother, Don, in the restaurant. Then we went back to Santa Ana to spend the rest of the evening watching the election returns. We stayed there until the outcome was assured. Dick Nixon won handily, but Joe Shell nonetheless made a creditable showing, and I remember going to sleep that night hoping that the wounds opened by their primary fight would heal before November.

Flying home to New York the next day, June 6, I again mulled over the uncertain situation in California, which I knew would be a key state in the 1964 pre-convention and election campaigns. The problems we had discussed during my stay were still unresolved. Nixon had promised repeatedly during his campaign that he intended to serve out a full four-year term as Governor if he won the nomination and the election. We could only hope that if he did win in November, the 1964 convention would take him at his word and not pressure him into running again for the Presidency. He had carried California against Kennedy in 1960. As Governor, he could help carry it again for the Republican Presidential candidate in 1964. And I knew Nixon would throw his full support behind whoever was nominated. He is that kind of Republican.

After a few days in New York I again took off for the West Coast, this time for Seattle and the summer meeting of the Republican National Committee. Our embryo conservative caucus was beginning to shape up. After the National Committee's regular sessions ended the following day we met in an empty banquet room at the Olympic Hotel. This was the first time I had met Ann Eve Johnson, the attractive and charming National Committeewoman from Arizona. Senator Goldwater later named her as director of women's activities on the Goldwater for President Committee after he announced his candidacy in January 1964. Among the other National Committee members attending our caucus that night were Mrs. Norma Currier of New Hampshire and Mrs. Hazel Barger of Virginia.[3] Several state chairmen were also on hand, including one of the members of our original group, Dave Nichols of Maine. We all agreed that the conservative movement within the party was beginning to show surprising strength and we debated ways of increasing that strength.

Governor Rockefeller's organizers were much in evidence at this Seattle meeting of the National Committee. George Hinman and his New York cohorts were busy throwing parties and arranging private powwows in an attempt to round up supporters for what they confidently expected would be Rockefeller's 1964 blitz. Hinman and his group had every right to be confident at this time. The polls all placed the Governor

[3] As it ultimately developed, Mrs. Barger did not support Senator Goldwater's nomination at the 1964 convention.

well out in front of the pack of GOP Presidential possibilities. And I was somewhat dismayed to find a number of old-line conservatives openly backing the Governor. One of these was my old friend Mitchell Melich, then National Committeeman from Utah. Mitch had been a staunch Taft man at the 1952 convention and I had assumed he would be with us. But Hinman, who was a polished political operator and well liked in the party, could now count Mitch Melich among his converts.

I have never believed in letting political differences interfere with old friendships, and on Wednesday morning when the National Committee meeting ended I was delighted to join Mitch and his family for the windup breakfast in the Space Needle restaurant at the Seattle World's Fair. Riding out on the monorail, Bruce Chapman, publisher of *Advance,* a magazine put out by young Republican Liberals, was distributing copies to the passengers. Glancing through my copy, I was interested to see an article by that redoubtable Pennsylvania "moderate," Senator Hugh Scott. In it he emphasized that conservatives are by no means extremists and went on to say that "True conservatives and true liberals have no great breach with the moderates." I took some comfort from this. Perhaps the ancient factionalism that had torn the Republican Party might yet be buried. I certainly hoped then that this was the case, but it turned out to be a withered and sadly forlorn hope by 1964.

After the breakfast, an informal affair at which the Melichs and I even more informally celebrated my birthday, I went back to the hotel to meet with some of the people attending the National Legislative Leaders' Conference that was to open in Seattle the next day. At this session I established valuable contacts with a number of Republican state legislators who later wound up on our team.

At the end of the week, I flew back to New York. On Wednesday, June 20, I lunched in Manhattan with the president of a corporation which had been one of my business clients. He hinted that he wanted me to join his firm in a responsible position. Later this became a firm offer at a salary substantially more than I could ever hope to make in politics. It was tempting, I will admit. Our operation was rapidly running out of funds and I didn't know how much longer we could hold it together. But in the end I turned down the offer. There were times during the next two years when I seriously regretted this decision, and I'm sure my wife regretted it even more. At that point, however, I felt it would be close to treason to desert my friends in the group and the cause we were all working so hard to advance.

The next day I was flying West again, for I had agreed to run a workshop on national politics at the Montana state Republican convention in Helena. When the plane touched down at Great Falls I immediately spotted a broad giant waving to me from the little crowd at the airport.

It was Frank Whetstone, affable and smiling as always. We had a good chat on the drive to Helena and stayed up half the night with some of Frank's Montana cronies at the hotel. John Wold, the Wyoming state chairman, who in 1964 ran for the U.S. Senate, came in to help out with the workshop the next morning. We were beginning to build a solid nucleus for our operation in the West and the workshop and meetings we had on this trip won us some important supporters. That night I met with Governor Tim Babcock of Montana, who had moved up from Lieutenant Governor when Don Nutter of our original group was killed in the plane crash a few months earlier.[4] I laid out the whole plan for Governor Babcock and was much heartened to find that he was thinking along the same lines we were. Later, Frank Whetstone and I got together with Mel Engels, the Montana state chairman, who was also in our camp.

John Wold and I took off at dawn the following day in a small chartered plane, flying a winding course down through the mountain passes on the way to Billings where we were to catch a commercial flight. It was a beautiful, sunny summer morning, and as we flew over those rugged Montana mountains I thought of my grandparents, who had settled in that country nearly a century before. My grandfather was a first sergeant in a volunteer regiment from upstate New York during the Civil War. When he was mustered out after the war he and my grandmother went West in a covered wagon, eventually ending up on a mining claim near Billings.

My mother, who died in 1952, used to tell the story of how one day when my grandfather was away on business a tough-looking hombre showed up at the gate in front of their adobe house and started unloading gear from his pack horses. Grandmother called the children into the house and then went down to the gate. Politely, she asked the man what he wanted. "I'm coming in here," he scowled. "This is my claim." He took one step toward the gate and found himself looking down the barrel of a cocked Colt revolver Grandma had been holding under her apron. "If you lay a hand on that gate, I'll have to shoot you," she said evenly. The man looked up from the Colt into Grandma's eyes and decided he wasn't coming through that gate after all. She kept him covered until he got his gear loaded and galloped off toward town. Then she came back in the house and spent the rest of the afternoon nursing a bad headache.

I had other family associations with this part of the country. My father grew up in Madison County, New York, and after graduating from business college he followed the westward movement. He got no further than Billings, where he met my mother. After they were married he took

---

[4] Governor Babcock was elected in his own right in 1964.

her back to Earlville, a town of about 1,200 in Madison County, where I grew up and lived until after I got my degree from Colgate University, six miles away in Hamilton. On the plane I remembered that my own wedding anniversary had been the day before, June 22, and that several thousand miles were separating my wife and me.

At Billings, John Wold and I caught our flight. He got off at Cheyenne while I continued on to Denver where I was to board an eastbound plane for New York. En route, I picked up a newspaper and was much encouraged to read former President Eisenhower's speech at a Washington dinner the night before that was sponsored by the Republican Campaign Committees of the Senate and House. Ike had taken the Democratic Administration apart piece by piece, lambasting the "sophistication" which excused using "the FBI, the Internal Revenue Service, the Defense Department, the Justice Department, as well as the White House" to control private business and coerce individual citizens.

"The principles we [Republicans] follow," said General Eisenhower, "are . . . founded in an unshakable faith in the people of our country. It is this faith that makes us cleave to Constitutional government, that leads us to maintain a diffusion of power, to respect the checks and balances on the national level, to work for strong, effective government on lower levels, and always to keep government as close as possible to home and community.

"It is likewise our faith in the individual that incites us to be vigilant sentinels of liberty. As such we fight, as against a plague, the whole host of national planning and spending schemes that would destroy the enterprise and individuality of our people."

Ike was beginning to sound like Barry Goldwater! Yet a week later, when party leaders gathered under a big blue-and-white striped tent on the Eisenhower farm at Gettysburg and unveiled two new organizations called the All-Republican Conference and the Republican National Citizens' Committee, the press widely interpreted it as an Eisenhower move to head off the incipient conservative revolt within the party and lay the groundwork for the nomination of a "moderate" in 1964.

The press did have grounds for painting the All-Republican Conference in rather Liberal hues. The 100-man group, which was to have worked with the National Committee in shaping party policy, was indeed top-heavy with left-of-center Republicans. Senator Goldwater, who did not attend the Gettysburg meeting, wrote National Chairman William E. Miller a scorching letter saying the Conference would only serve to give a larger voice in party affairs to "the same people who caused most of our present party troubles. Most of those named as leaders of this new group contributed to the divisive tactics of the 1960 campaign," Goldwater charged. He added that they were the same people "who were responsible, in large part, for policies of the Eisenhower Administration which ran counter to the traditional principles of the Republican Party and the counsel of regular party leaders."

Not surprisingly, Eisenhower felt called upon to defend the new organizations and for a while I was afraid he and Goldwater were going to engage in a running debate. Fortunately, their incipient feud simmered down as the 1962 campaign neared and it sputtered out before any real damage was done. Actually, I have always believed these two men were very close philosophically. It was Ike's inexperience with politics that led him to rely on the advice of Liberals during his first years as President. As the years went on he came to see that he was really more in tune with the conservatives, but by then it was too late to reverse the trend his many Liberal advisers and Cabinet members had set in motion. One incident will serve as proof of this.

In 1957, Barry Goldwater was the only member of the United States Senate to vote against the Kennedy-Erwin Labor Bill, which was ballyhooed as an effective curb on racketeering and other abuses within certain segments of organized labor. Actually, it was a toothless and inoffensive piece of legislation drafted by the McClellan Committee, which Robert F. Kennedy was then serving as Chief Counsel, making certain that the bill which bore his brother's name would not create enemies for Jack among the more powerful union leaders. Jimmy Hoffa's Teamsters, already expelled by the AFL-CIO, were, of course, fair game. But the Kennedys did not want to ruffle the feathers of the bigger birds.

By contrast, Goldwater had openly tangled with Walter Reuther during several years of rough-and-tough hearings before the Senate Labor Committee.

Reuther was a sacred cow in Congress in those days, as he is now. Few elected representatives of the people dared challenge him. But when Barry Goldwater did, he received thousands of letters from rank-and-file members of the United Auto Workers supporting his stand and criticizing Reuther's dictatorial rule of the union. His battle with Reuther made Goldwater the UAW hierarchy's number one target for political execution in the 1958 Congressional elections. It has been estimated that COPE—the AFL-CIO's political arm—dumped $500,000 into Arizona to defeat him. COPE also demonstrated that it was perfectly willing to stoop to any tactic to do this, and two of its hired hands were caught distributing political smear literature linking Barry Goldwater with, of all things, the Communist Party. But despite all this the Senator won reelection handily in normally Democratic Arizona.

For some reason, President Eisenhower had tacitly supported the Kennedy-Erwin Bill and he was frankly miffed by Goldwater's lone dissenting vote. One day when Goldwater was visiting the White House, the President asked why he had opposed the bill, which still had not passed the House. Characteristically, the Senator laid his opinion on the line. He told Ike that he considered the bill a fraud. It would not, he said, remedy any of the abuses within the labor movement unearthed by the McClellan Committee. Then he spelled out why.

For the first time, the President understood the implications of the new legislation. He immediately started a thorough study. Then, armed with facts and figures, he made one of his relatively infrequent television speeches to the nation strongly denouncing the Kennedy-Erwin Bill as wholly inadequate.

In one of the fastest turnabouts in its history, the Senate soon there-after voted down the bill, 95-to-2, and passed the much stronger Landrum-Griffin Act instead. When people ask what effect a small conservative group in the Congress can have, I am reminded of how one man, Barry Goldwater, stood alone against the whole United States Senate and finally, with the enlightened help of President Eisenhower, turned the tide on an important measure.

Perhaps this incident also explains why Dwight Eisenhower refused to participate in the frenzied stop-Goldwater movement within the Republican Party in 1964, although the pressures exerted upon him to do so would have easily swayed a man of lesser principle.

On September 27-28 our conservative phalanx underwent its first test of strength. This came at the twelfth biennial convention of the National Federation of Republican Women in Phoenix. But it had been building up for many weeks. The Federation's nominating committee, under the chairmanship of Miss Marian Smith of Arkansas, had met in Chicago in advance of the convention and picked a slate of new national officers. In the past, the Federation had almost automatically elected the slate the committee chose. But this time the slate was lacking in balance and in addition several states with the largest Federation membership had been rudely disregarded.

By this time there was quite an active group of knowledgeable and widely respected Republican women leaders in the conservative camp. For the most part, they operated entirely on their own, with a minimum of guidance from our group. But in this instance they were kind enough to clue us in on what they were up to. Right after our group's meeting in the Minnesota wilds, Rita Bree had flown to Washington where the annual Republican Women's Conference was being held. Armed with the names of women leaders our team had given her, she contacted a number of them and arranged a *sub rosa* meeting at the Jefferson Hotel. I had then flown in to brief the women on what we were doing and find out their plans for the Phoenix convention.

Two members of the GOP National Committee, Mrs. Katherine Kennedy Brown of Ohio and Mrs. Ione Harrington of Indiana, started making phone calls around the country to see whether there was sentiment for fielding opposition to the official slate. They enlisted the aid of Mrs. Lucille Hosmer, president of the strong California Women's Republican Federation, Mrs. Roger Flaherty and Mrs. Maxine Charlton of Ohio. Together they rounded up considerable support for their revolutionary effort, and when the convention opened at the Hotel Westward Ho in Phoenix they were ready to act.

On Thursday morning, September 27, Miss Smith presented the Nominating Committee's slate to the assembled delegates. At this point our girls swung into action. They surprised the convention by offering four opposition candidates from the floor. They did not oppose Mrs. Dorothy Elston of Delaware, the regular candidate for president. But they nominated Mrs. Dorothy Camp of Iowa and Mrs. Constance Armitage of South Carolina for vice presidencies; Mrs. Martha Whitehead of Indiana for secretary and Mrs. Jean Leveton of Oregon for treasurer. The balloting was conducted at prearranged polling places, not on the floor of the convention, so the conservatives had time to do some more quiet electioneering before the actual vote.

On Friday one of the convention speakers was Mrs. Patricia Hutar of Illinois, then national co-chairman of the Young Republicans and one of our staunch allies. Pat fired up the delegates with a fighting speech in which she warned that the two greatest threats to freedom in our time are world Communism and "ourselves." Elaborating on the latter, she said, "It is the threat of indifference and declining initiative . . . the threat that the spark of fire we call individualism will be extinguished in a sea of regimentation."

Two hours later, when Mrs. Dolores Kiser of Colorado, chairman of the convention elections committee, gave her report, the four conservative insurgents had all been voted into office and the Liberal candidates roundly rejected. We had passed our first big test with flying colors.

As a bonus, the Federation adopted a series of hardhitting resolutions that had a marked conservative flavor, though I'm sure many of the women who did not regard themselves as conservatives wholly subscribed to them too. One resolution urged Congress to take legislative action to void the Supreme Court's school prayer ban. Others struck out against federal aid to education and Medicare. The foreign policy resolution charged that "The President has filled important policy-making positions with men who fail to understand the threat of Communism." Still another forecast the passage a year later of the Nuclear Test Ban Treaty, taking the Administration to task for its disarmament policy. It pointed out that the Director of the U.S. Arms Control and Disarmament Agency, William Foster, had declared that President Kennedy was ready to incur "desperate risks" to assure such a treaty and urged that United States disarmament negotiators "cease offering dangerous concessions to the U.S.S.R."

All in all, it was a stunning performance. Unluckily, I was unable to be in Phoenix to share this triumph. Right up until that week I had planned to attend the convention. But when the time came to purchase plane tickets there just was not enough money in the till at Suite 3505 or in my sadly depleted savings. It was a choice between my going or Rita Bree attending the conference as a representative of the New York State Women's Federation. Since Rita was a delegate, the choice was not too difficult to make. But it placed me in a rather embarrassing position with Senator Goldwater. Earlier I had called his office in Washington to see if we could fly out to Phoenix together. The Senator agreed and all the arrangements were made. Then I was forced to cancel my plane reservations and forego the chance to confer with him on the flight west.

When Rita Bree ran into Goldwater in Phoenix the first thing he asked was, "Where's Clif?" He said he had been looking for me on the plane. Rita replied that "other commitments" had kept me in New York. This was certainly not a fib. At this point I had a *lot* of "other commitments"—practically all of them to our creditors.

Even short trips to cities near New York placed too much of a strain on our overextended budget that fall. At one point I was ready to give it all up before my family became insolvent. Rita Bree and I had lunch with Bill Rusher in the Commodore's Tudor Room where the whole project had started only a year before. I told Bill we would have to fold the tent, that the decision had been made, and we were just paying him the courtesy of telling him before anyone else. Rusher argued against the decision so persuasively that I finally agreed to hang on just a little longer if Rita would stick it out too. Rita promised to see it through for another month and we returned to work at 3505 that same afternoon.

As the month wore on, there was no improvement in our financial situation. Just as I was beginning to think that our whole operation was about to be submerged in a churning sea of debt, several friends came to the rescue. Robert R. (Randy) Richardson, an old friend from Georgia, arrived in New York and temporarily moved his desk into Suite 3505 to begin his successful ventures in the publishing industry. In effect, Randy was sharing the rent, which took one worry off my shoulders. In Phoenix, Rita Bree had corralled some help from Ralph Staggs. Out in the Midwest Stets Coleman and R. Crosby Kemper pitched in with some welcome funds. And a group of my New York friends— Ed Lynch, Bill Middendorf and Jerry Milbank Jr.—also came through with generous contributions, enough to keep us going until after the November elections.

We never did approach the $65,000 I had estimated we would need for that first year. At the end of November, nearly twelve months after our second Chicago meeting, we had collected a total of $43,195. But at least we were able to keep the creditors from slamming a padlock on the door of Suite 3505. And, with more and more people dropping into our office from various parts of the country, this was psychologically vital. If we had collapsed at this point for lack of funds we might never have been able to launch our Draft Goldwater Committee the following spring.

CHAPTER 8

THE DISTANT DRUMS

As THE 1962 CAMPAIGN officially opened on Labor Day, both major political parties were striving to keep public attention focused on the vital state and Congressional contests. But the distant drums of the 1964 Presidential race were already thundering, setting up a distracting din that all but muffled more immediate concerns. There is no doubt, of course, that the popularity of an incumbent President has a direct effect upon the outcome of elections at all levels. And as John F. Kennedy openly acknowledged, his popularity was beginning to slip.

After taking soundings around the country, *U.S. News & World Report* ran a story that indicated how far the President actually had slipped, even among members of his own party.[1] After mentioning that Kennedy had been elected in 1960 by a minority of the votes cast (49.72 per cent against Nixon's 49.55 per cent), that article went on to say:

More and more often, in Congress and outside, among Democrats and Republicans, this question is being asked: Is there a chance that Republicans may win back the White House in 1964? Could John Kennedy turn out to be a one-term President?

Republicans are more hopeful than at any time since November, 1960, that the answer will be "yes." Democrats, once supremely confident that the answer would be "no," now are beginning to wonder.

Almost at the same time, Barry Goldwater's stock started to rise. In September, an Associated Press poll of delegates to the 1960 Republican

[1] *U. S. News & World Report,* August 6, 1962.

national convention put Goldwater out front as their choice for the nomination in 1964. The poll by no means indicated that the Senator had the nomination within his grasp. But among the delegates who responded it placed him well ahead of Nelson Rockefeller and Richard Nixon.[2] Since many if not most of these people would again be casting their ballots at the '64 convention, it was obvious that Goldwater already had a substantial hard core of support on which to build.

From Tad Smith in Texas came the results of another poll, this one taken among delegates to the Republican state convention in Fort Worth on September 18. Goldwater was the choice of no less than 1,115, or an overwhelming 78 per cent of the Texas state delegates. Nixon, Rockefeller and Romney were all so far behind that they were barely distinguishable figures on the Texas political horizon. The three of them scraped up a combined total of only 316 votes in Fort Worth, Nixon getting 147, Rockefeller 90 and Romney 79. It was apparent that only an unforeseen catastrophe could keep us from corralling the 56-member Texas delegation, fifth largest of the lot.

Although most of the press refused to take Goldwater's candidacy seriously even after the Texas convention straw vote and the Associated Press delegate poll, a few perceptive reporters were beginning to believe that the Senator might have a chance. In one mid-summer story Lyle Wilson, the highly respected Washington columnist of United Press International, did not mention Goldwater by name. But everyone knew whom he had in mind when he described what kind of candidate the GOP needed for 1964. Wilson underlined the indisputable fact that with "me-too Republicans in command, the Republican Party since 1940 has lost 13 of 17 national elections." He went on:

What the Republican Party needs more than a promise to be anybody's party is a commitment to a set of courageous political principles that clearly distinguish it from the Democratic Party.

The Republican Party also needs a blood transfusion to fire it up to the degree required to enable a Republican national convention to function with the courage of the party's conservative convictions . . . [and] in addition the GOP needs Presidential nominees who are clearly distinguishable from Democratic Presidential nominees.

To this I murmured a fervent "Amen." And even through the sporadic rumbling created by the 1962 campaign I could hear the echoes in

---

[2] Of the 1,331 delegates to the 1960 convention, 687 stated their choice in the AP poll. Goldwater was the choice of 264. Rockefeller trailed with 203 and Nixon was a poor third with 137. George Romney, who was running for Governor of Michigan, polled 32 votes, and a variety of favorite-son and other candidates had a scattering of negligible support.

millions of American homes. Barry Goldwater, however, was still turning a deaf ear. In reply to a letter from Wirt Yerger remarking on the heartening results of the Associated Press delegates' poll, the Senator wrote on September 19:

I have never sought the nomination, as I have told you many times. I have many reasons, but I wouldn't put money and organization last and neither of these has reared its ugly head.

The Senator was aware, of course, that our group was striving desperately to supply him with an organization, though we still had not discussed this with him in terms of his own candidacy. Money was another matter. But I was convinced that it would follow if only we could first lay a firm foundation for the organization. Most political professionals will tell you that this is putting the cart before the horse. They claim an organization simply cannot be built without money. Our group was flying brazenly in the face of this political commandment and Barry Goldwater knew this as well as we did. This probably explains his apparent refusal to take our effort very seriously at that time. And as I struggled to pay the rent each month on Suite 3505, I could hardly blame him.

There were occasions when the Senator sounded a bit testy about the party's preoccupation with the 1964 Presidential race. As chairman of the Republican Senatorial Campaign Committee he was obviously having a difficult time trying to get people to keep their noses glued to the 1962 grindstone. In a letter to Mrs. Clare B. Williams, chairman of the Republican Women's Conference, he laid it flatly on the line.

"Too many Republicans," he said, "are worrying about 1964 when 1962 should be our supreme and only goal. If the New Frontier is to be stopped, which it has to be, the election of a Republican House of Representatives in 1962 will accomplish this and the strengthening of the Republican forces in the Senate will certainly aid. . . . Let's win big in '62, then we can worry about '64."

This was typical of Goldwater. With him, the interests of the Republican Party and of the nation always came first. He would go all out in support of any Republican, including Senator Jacob Javits in New York or Senator Thomas Kuchel in California, as he did in 1962. This may explain why in 1964 he was so deeply hurt when the Javitses and the Kuchels, and the Liberal wing of the party generally, rejected him publicly and bitterly, thus setting off the countervailing reaction on his part that was so unfortunately reflected in his acceptance speech at San Francisco.

Early in September, the campaign shook off its summer doldrums and began heating up in an alarming manner. To his everlasting credit,

Senator Kenneth Keating of New York disclosed that the Russians were mounting a large-scale missile build-up in Cuba. On September 4, President Kennedy denied this, saying there was absolutely "no evidence of any organized combat force in Cuba from any Soviet bloc country [or] of military bases provided by Russia." He acknowledged that anti-aircraft missiles had been installed, but flatly denied "the presence of offensive ground-to-ground missiles, or of other significant offensive capability either in Cuban hands or under Soviet direction or guidance." Nine days later he felt constrained to add that the stepped-up Russian military shipments to Cuba "do not constitute a serious threat."

Thereafter, while Keating, Barry Goldwater and other Republican leaders kept warning that missiles were being brought into Cuba in increasing numbers, the President simply ignored the issue. As *Time* reported early in October, so far as Jack Kennedy's campaign speeches were concerned, "Cuba might as well have been on another planet."

The American people, however, were visibly disturbed. Former President Eisenhower echoed their growing concern with the New Frontier foreign policy in a mid-October speech in Boston. He reminded his audience that during his eight years in the White House "no walls were built, no threatening foreign bases were established," and went on to denounce the Kennedy record in foreign affairs as "too sad to talk about." This was much more than mere campaign oratory. Ike, in common with millions of other citizens, was plainly worried.

The Administration was worried too, but for somewhat different reasons. The threatening rumblings from the Communist bastion ninety miles off our shore had rudely awakened the slumbering voters. The Democrats were striving desperately to lull them back to sleep, but all across the land people were beginning to stir. By the middle of October, the pundits were predicting a Republican revival at the polls come election day.

The White House made a last attempt to kill the Cuban missile issue. In a speech at Indianapolis, President Kennedy on October 13 heaped scorn on "self-appointed generals and admirals who want to send someone else's sons to war." This was a pointed slap at Indiana's veteran Senator Homer Capehart, who had previously suggested a blockade of Cuba, or an invasion if necessary, to force removal of the missiles that were being prepared in Cuba for a possible nuclear attack on the United States.

The following day McGeorge Bundy, Special Assistant to the President for National Security, issued a statement that must stand forever as a classic in the art of managed news.

"I know," said Bundy, "there is no present evidence and I think there is no present likelihood that the Cubans and the Cuban government and the Soviet government would in combination attempt to install a major offensive capability. So far, everything that has been delivered in Cuba falls within the categories of aid which the Soviet Union has provided, for example, to neutral states like Egypt and Indonesia."

Bundy blandly made this statement several hours *after* a U-2 recon- naissance plane had taken photographs of medium-range missile sites in the San Cristobal area of Cuba—*and a full five days after U.S. Intel- ligence had secured photos of an "offensive capability" in the form of Soviet IL-28 bombers based on Cuba.*

It was a desperate effort to feed the American public a gigantic sleeping pill. And it is possible that if the people had swallowed it, the pill might well have had the same lethal effect as an overdose of bar- biturates. But the effort failed. By now the voters had swallowed more than enough of the Administration's brand of patent medicine. They were openly skeptical. Quite suddenly John Fitzgerald Kennedy realized this dangerous fact. Simultaneously, he was presented with incontro- vertible photographic evidence of Cuban missile sites, evidence that he could no longer ignore.

The President had seen this evidence nearly a week before. But he had continued his political campaign tour in spite of the rapidly escalat- ing crisis. Then, pleading a cold, he cut short his tour in the Midwest and hurried back to Washington. After a round of worried conferences at the White House, he went on television the night of October 22 and officially acknowledged that the Russians had introduced missiles into Cuba. He announced that he had ordered an air and sea "quarantine" of offensive military equipment to the island and declared that the launching of a nuclear missile from Cuba against any nation in the Western Hemisphere would require "a full retaliatory response upon the Soviet Union."

From the Democratic Party's standpoint, the timing was perfect. The election was barely two weeks away and just four days before the voters trooped to the polls the President reported that the missile bases were being dismantled and that "progress is now being made toward restora- tion of peace in the Caribbean."[3]

As they have always done in times of crisis when the nation's security is threatened openly, the American people rallied behind the President. Thousands of Democrats who had been in rebellion against his foreign

[3] The United States never obtained hard-and-fast proof that the Soviets removed all their ballistic missiles from Cuba in 1962. In May 1963, the Democrat-controlled Senate Preparedness Subcommittee reported that U.S. Intelligence officials "readily admit that, in terms of absolutes, it is quite possible that offensive weapons remain on the island concealed in caves or otherwise."

policy were brought back into the fold by his seemingly forceful stand. The Republican tide that had been running stronger with each passing day in October suddenly ebbed.

On November 6, the biggest non-Presidential election turnout in history brought nearly 54 million voters to the polls. When the smoke cleared the next morning, the Democrats claimed a victory and President Kennedy said he was "heartened" by the results. Actually, the election was a stand-off, and though many Republicans were disappointed that the party had not done better, the GOP had turned in a respectable showing against terrific odds in a time of national crisis. We failed to capture control of the House of Representatives as had been confidently predicted prior to October 22. At that time even Democrats like President Kennedy's friend, Senator Smathers of Florida, were saying that "a lot of Democratic heads will roll in November unless something is done about Cuba." But we did pick up two additional Congressional seats to bring the Republican total in the House to 176.

Most significant from the standpoint of my 1964 strategy, Republicans had scored solid gains in the Democrats' once solid South. All seven incumbent GOP Congressmen in the South won re-election, and the party added five new House members from that region: William Brock of Tennessee, James Broyhill of North Carolina, Edward Foreman of Texas, Edward Gurney of Florida, and Gene Snyder of Kentucky.

Nor were these gains won on the basis of "segregationist" campaigns, as so much of the press charged. Practically all of the Republican Congressional candidates in the South were running against outright Democrat segregationists, and they deliberately sought to play down the race issue. A case in point was the brilliant and reasoned campaign my friend Jim Martin conducted in Alabama against the veteran Democrat, Senator Lister Hill. Jim came within a whisker of capturing the seat Hill had held for five terms, and incidentally paved the way for his election to the lower House of Congress in 1964.

In addition, Republicans scored a net gain of some 150 seats in State Legislatures, probably because the Cuban missile crisis had less impact on these races than on contests for federal offices. Some of these victories came in the South, where Republicans had not served in most state legislative bodies since Reconstruction.

The United States Senate, however, was another and sadder story. Republicans suffered a net loss of four seats in the upper house, dropping our already weak minority there to only 32 against 68 Democrats. One of these losses was particularly hard to take. Homer Capehart was narrowly defeated in his bid for a fifth term from Indiana, despite the fact that he had so bravely sounded the alarm on Cuba in that state, once considered a safe preserve for the GOP.

Nonetheless, conservative Republicans did fairly well overall in Senate contests. In Colorado, Peter Dominick swept to a tremendous victory over incumbent Senator John Carroll, a Liberal Democrat, downing Carroll by nearly 50,000 votes out of the 600,000 cast. In Wyoming, Milward Simpson also scored an impressive win and in Kentucky, Thruston Morton soundly whipped the former chairman of the Americans for Democratic Action, Wilson Wyatt.

It was the gubernatorial elections, however, that commanded the most attention in 1962, and for the most part Republicans had done well in key races. Nelson Rockefeller won re-election in New York, though by a substantially reduced margin, due in large part to the 142,000 votes siphoned off by David H. Jaquith, a lifelong Republican running on the new Conservative Party ticket. In Pennsylvania a one-term Congressman named William Scranton pre-empted an eight-year Democratic lease on the State House in Harrisburg. In Michigan a newcomer to politics, former American Motors president George Romney, put an end to an even longer Democrat gubernatorial reign. In Ohio a conservative Republican, James A. Rhodes, ousted an old New Dealer turned New Frontiersman, Michael DiSalle. Oklahoma elected Henry Bellmon as the first Republican governor in the state's history, and Montana voters returned my friend Tim Babcock to the Governor's chair he had occupied since the tragic death of Don Nutter of my original group.

But there was bad news from California. Dick Nixon had gone down to defeat, losing to Governor Brown by nearly 284,000 votes out of 5,727,000 cast. Stung not only by his loss, but by the way so many newsmen had stacked the cards against him, Nixon bitterly denounced the press and simultaneously announced he was retiring from politics. At a press conference in Los Angeles the morning after the election, he rang down the curtain with these words:

> The last play. I leave you gentlemen now and you will now write it. You will interpret it. That's your right. But as I leave you I want you to know—just think how much you're going to be missing. You won't have Nixon to kick around any more because, gentlemen, this is my last press conference.

Seemingly, the book was closed firmly on Richard Milhous Nixon's political career. In the wake of his defeat came a great wave of agonizing analyses of his loss and of the outcome of other election contests. But the most penetrating appraisal of all came from the brilliant pen of author Frank S. Meyer, an editor of *National Review*. Noting that this was the first election in American history "almost universally" discussed by the press in terms of "a conservative-Liberal confrontation," Meyer rightly claimed that it represented the "coming-of-age of conservatism." As further proof of this he added:

> Except in a few strongholds of ritualistic Liberalism, no serious effort was made to go before the voters with a sharp, clear Liberal position. This was in marked contrast to the conservative candidates, successful and unsuccessful, who everywhere pressed their positions as conservatives.
> The major last-minute factor in the election on the Democratic side, President Kennedy's Cuban démarche, was—on the surface—a conservative gesture. However craven the policy of the Administration may turn out to be and whatever further appeasement lies ahead, in the two weeks before election the image Kennedy felt constrained to present to the voters was shaped to conform a great deal more closely to the image of Senator Goldwater than to that of Adlai Stevenson.[4]

Almost immediately after the election the talk turned once again to the possible Republican Presidential nominees for 1964. Nelson Rockefeller was the man most prominently mentioned, but GOP National Chairman Bill Miller acknowledged that Senator Goldwater "certainly would be a contender." Coming from Miller in 1962, this was much more of a concession than most observers may now believe. The National Chairman was not then in our camp by any means. In fact, he appeared much more interested in promoting Goldwater for the number two spot on the ticket—under Governor Rockefeller.

"There are many areas of agreement between Rockefeller and Goldwater," Miller hinted to newsmen. I'm sure Barry Goldwater thought so too then, and, as I soon learned, this was one of the major stumbling blocks we were to run into in our attempt to persuade the Senator to consent to a draft.

---

[4] "The 1962 Elections: The Turning of the Tide," *National Review*, December 4, 1962.

CHAPTER 9

STRANGE HONEYMOON

THE POLITICAL HONEYMOON of Nelson Rockefeller and Barry
Goldwater began shortly after Richard Nixon's defeat in the 1960
Presidential election and was to continue unabated for nearly three
years. Rockefeller was the ardent suitor in this strange misalliance, but
Goldwater was by no means a reluctant bride. At the outset the two
men were drawn together by their mutual coolness toward Nixon; Rockefeller because he feared Nixon would be a contender again for the
Presidential nomination he wanted so badly, and Goldwater for a somewhat less selfish reason, namely his disenchantment with Nixon's losing
"me-too" campaign for the Presidency. Ironically, the fact that Nelson
Rockefeller had forced Dick Nixon into conducting a powder-puff campaign by engineering the 1960 "Munich of the Republican Party" did
not seem to dampen Goldwater's ardor for his new-found friend from
New York.

However, the success of Rockefeller's courtship of the Senator was
probably predicated on something more substantial than a shared dislike
for Nixon. The Governor's chief selling point was party unity. After
the 1960 election, party unity was an item that Barry Goldwater, like
many other Republican leaders, found irresistible. Realizing that this
was the Senator's soft spot, Rockefeller picked up the theme and played
it for all it was worth. To Rockefeller, of course, it was worth quite a
good deal. If he could keep Goldwater neutralized through 1964, it
would almost certainly win him the conservative support he needed for

the nomination and might well facilitate his long-planned move from the Governor's mansion in Albany to the White House in Washington.

On his part, Goldwater undoubtedly believed that he was beginning to wield an important influence over Rockefeller. He thought he had discovered hitherto hidden facets of the Governor's political philosophy. If he could lead Rockefeller to look at more issues through the conservative prism perhaps these facets would be strongly reflected in the 1964 Republican platform. The Senator was already convinced, as he had told Charley Thone and me at our very first meeting with him in November 1961, that Rockefeller had the nomination in his pocket. The polls all had him leading the other Republican Presidential possibilities by a mile. The Governor's divorce early in 1962, which many politicians had thought would eliminate him from consideration, had not appreciably affected either his standing in the polls or his gubernatorial race in New York.

To Goldwater, Rockefeller looked like a sure winner at the 1964 convention. That being the case, the Senator apparently concluded that the best he could do was strive to move Rockefeller away from some of the more far-out Liberal stands he had taken in the past and get him over onto more solid conservative ground.

There were other things that seemed to cement the Rockefeller-Goldwater friendship. Both were genuinely disturbed by the formation of the All-Republican Conference and the National Republican Citizens' Committee in June of 1962. As we have seen, Goldwater opposed these new groups because he felt they would only help lead the Republican Party down the same old road of me-tooism that had brought disaster in the past. Rockefeller thought they were designed to pre-empt the nomination for Richard Nixon, or failing that, George Romney, if either or both won their gubernatorial elections that fall. Thus, from somewhat different motives, Rockefeller and Goldwater found one more good reason for maintaining their tacit alliance.

By November 1962, I was naturally aware of the warming relationship between Goldwater and Rockefeller. I knew that they had been getting together privately from time to time, usually at the Governor's lovely Washington home out beyond Georgetown in the exclusive Foxhall Road section. George Hinman, the Governor's likable lieutenant, and Vic Johnson, staff director of the Senate Republican Campaign Committee which Goldwater headed, sometimes went along. But more often the meetings were tête-à-tête. This gave Rockefeller a better chance to turn on the charm in man-to-man talks.

As Bill Miller had noted just after the 1962 elections, Goldwater and Rockefeller seemed to find many areas of agreement. By this time the Governor had beguiled Goldwater into believing that he was really a conservative at heart. The Senator was going around telling people "Rocky's not such a bad guy. He's a lot more conservative than you think."

Despite the rather abrasive public portrait painted of him in 1964, Goldwater's natural gullibility has always led him to believe that most people are fundamentally decent if you can only get to know them. With this factor in his favor Rockefeller's conservative ploy might have continued to work. Certainly, the Governor was doing all in his power to reinforce his "conservative" image. With a confidential memorandum I sent to our original group in the fall of 1962, I enclosed a memo fired off by L. Judson Morhouse, Republican state chairman of New York, to his county chairmen on August 14, advising how they could woo the Conservative vote in Rockefeller's gubernatorial campaign. It is, I think, worth quoting here in full:

A number of you have requested some basic information on the Rockefeller Record which would show his "Conservative" side. The items listed on the attached sheets do show this and is [sic] being sent to you for your use in talking to people who feel the Governor is strictly a Liberal.

It must be used cautiously and should not be published because we do not want to emphasize the conservative side so much that we lose other votes.

Attached to this memo was a list of twenty-eight positions the Governor had taken, mostly on fiscal matters. This, of course, was before New York State was revealed to be in serious financial difficulties after four years of Rockefeller rule and before the Governor had rammed through his legislature a series of unpopular tax increases to bail out the depleted state treasury. Within a matter of months after Jud Morhouse circulated the above memorandum, the fiscal façade that enshrined Rockefeller's "basic conservatism" began to show revealing cracks and before long it crumbled entirely.

This was the interlude when Governor Rockefeller was publicly describing Barry Goldwater as "a great Republican" and a "sincere and dedicated" American. Nor was his flagrant flattery wasted. That fall I had another piece of intelligence that indicated Goldwater was succumbing to Rockefeller's blandishments.

After a Republican rally in Great Falls, Montana, Frank Whetstone cornered the Senator. They had always hit it off very well together, but on this occasion they got into an almost violent argument. Frank bluntly remonstrated with Goldwater for seeming to support Rockefeller and told him that he had a duty to run for the Presidency himself. The Senator got his back up and reminded Frank that "it is my political neck you want to put on the chopping block." Frank, only half in jest, stripped off his coat and invited Goldwater to settle the issue with him then and there. The Senator, never one to back down, started to take off *his* coat. But at the last moment the ludicrous nature of the situation forced him to smile and the two of them took a fit of laughing. Needless to say, they parted friends.

I was becoming rather concerned with Goldwater's growing enthusiasm for Rockefeller, when a few days before the 1962 election I received a letter from the Senator, who was then in Arizona. He said that he planned to be in New York on November 12 for a meeting at the Wings Club and suggested we get together. Two weeks before this letter arrived, on October 18, I had sent our original group a confidential memorandum announcing another meeting in Chicago the first weekend in December. "This meeting," I wrote, "will determine where we go—whether we are serious or dilettantes."

The Senator knew of this scheduled meeting since I had sent him a copy of the memo. I had made it a practice to send him copies of all my memorandums to the group in addition to giving him personal reports on our meetings and other activities. Thus I assumed he would want to discuss this upcoming meeting with me and I worked like the devil to prepare the agenda and program early so I would have it ready for him when he came to New York. When the day arrived, Rita Bree bound the rather thick program in a loose-leaf black book so I could take it to the Senator.[1]

That afternoon in the cab en route to my conference with Goldwater at the new Americana Hotel on Seventh Avenue and 52nd Street I was oblivious to the crowds that thronged the ever busy theatrical district. Not long before this the president of the corporation who had offered me that enticing job had renewed the offer, making it even more attractive. I was forced to reconsider my position, especially after so many months of raiding my personal savings to keep our political operation solvent. I had deferred a final decision until my meeting with Goldwater in the hope he might give me some clue to his plans. If I sensed that he was so completely captivated by Rockefeller that he would throw his lot in with the Governor and refuse to seek the Presidency himself, then I was prepared to take the job, give up politics, devote myself to business and hope that the nation's political direction would be set straight by others. I certainly never considered myself the indispensable man. I had simply wanted to do what I thought necessary to foster the conservative cause I believe in. But it was obvious now that without

[1] We made only one other copy of this book, the one I was to use later in Chicago.

a candidate our operation must soon collapse. And after weighing a number of other possibilities our group was fast coming to the conclusion that the *only* candidate we had for 1964 was Barry Morris Goldwater. No other conservative had come to the fore in the Republican Party and there just was not time to build anyone else with only a little more than a year and a half to go before the national convention.

When I arrived at the Americana it seemed a propitious sign that I found the Senator comfortably ensconced in the Presidential suite. He greeted me in his usual friendly manner and I smilingly told him, "You've sure stirred up the bushes these past few weeks."

"How's that?" he frowned.

"All those nice statements you've been making about Governor Rockefeller," I said. "You've been agreeing with him an awful lot lately."

"Well," he nodded, "it's true. We do agree on a lot of things."

I laughed: "Perhaps so, but your agreeing with him has sure kept me busy answering phone calls from a lot of your friends."

There followed some conversation about the election six days before. Then we sat down and went over the agenda for the Chicago meeting. The Senator skimmed through it pretty fast but he could see that it contained the state-by-state organizational chart I was recommending to the group, a proposed budget, a timetable for the state conventions and primaries to be held in 1964, and my estimates of how many Goldwater delegates we could expect to win in each state. I held my breath a little when we went through this forecast, but the Senator never batted an eye. When we had run through the black book he simply nodded and said: "This looks good. It's fine." Then he promised to read it more carefully the first chance he got.

We had a wonderful chat for about an hour after that. The Senator is a refreshing conversationalist and I think anyone who gets to know him enjoys his company. It was not hard to see why newspaper reporters all seemed to take to him in those days. Even Liberal writer Gore Vidal conceded, in an otherwise vicious attack on Goldwater in *Life,* that "people like him."[2] This, in Vidal's mind, largely explained

---

[2] One example of Vidal's goring of Goldwater will suffice to give the flavor of his *Life* article. "I have often thought and written," he wrote, "that if the United States were ever to have a Caesar, a true subverter of the state, 1) he would attract to himself all the true believers, the extremists, the hot-eyed custodians of The Truth; 2) he would oversimplify some difficult but vital issues, putting himself on the side of the majority, as Huey Long did . . . 3) he would not in the least resemble the folk idea of a dictator. He would not be a hysteric Hitler. Rather, he would be just plain folks, Will Rogers or Arthur Godfrey, a regular guy, warm and sincere, and while he was amusing us on television the stormtroopers would gather in the streets. . . . It seemed to me that Goldwater was perhaps such a man." By the end of the article the "perhaps" had been deftly erased and Vidal concluded by recom-

why the Senator was what he called "the country's most popular politician, after Kennedy." Actually, at this particular point in history, if Vidal had thought that last qualifying phrase, "after Kennedy," was entirely accurate, I'm sure he would not have felt it necessary to do such a thorough hatchet job on a junior Senator from Arizona.

It was Barry's likability, perhaps more than anything else, that frightened the Liberal community. Wherever he went, Goldwater was committing an unpardonable sin; he was making the once disreputable label "conservative" eminently respectable. To the Liberals, this constituted a threat of truly unthinkable dimensions, a threat which was to drive them to near hysteria by the fall of 1964. For three decades they had felt secure in the mistaken belief that the conservative political philosophy had been safely interred with Franklin Delano Roosevelt's first campaign for the Presidency, in which FDR had stood four-square on the Democratic Party's conservative platform, "a covenant with the people" pledging "a sound currency," "a federal budget annually balanced," and a "drastic reduction of governmental expenditures."[3] Now conservatism appeared to be rising from the grave, and the personification of its dreaded resurrection was the tall, tanned, likable man chatting amiably with me on that November afternoon in the Presidential suite of the Americana Hotel.

The Senator's brother, Bob Goldwater, joined us late in the afternoon and Barry started to dress for the Wings Club dinner. I rose to leave but before we said goodbye I mentioned to the Senator that I had a fine job offer, hoping that he might either advise me to take it if he thought our operation to promote his candidacy was futile, or discourage me from accepting it if he seriously intended to seek the nomination and thought I might be needed.

"I'd heard about that," Goldwater smiled in reply. But he said nothing else.

Somewhat awkwardly, I added: "Well, I just wanted to tell you so if you hear I've taken this job you won't get upset. I'll only take it with

---

mending to Goldwater "Cicero's warning to a fellow political adventurer, in a falling year of the Roman Republic." That political adventurer was, of course, Julius Caesar.

[3] The Democrats' 1932 platform promised to accomplish this "drastic reduction" by "abolishing useless commissions and offices, consolidating departments and bureaus, and eliminating extravagances to accomplish a savings of not less than 25 per cent in the cost of the federal government." President Roosevelt actually appeared to keep this platform pledge after his inauguration when on March 20, 1933 he signed into law the Economy Act of 1933, cutting the salaries of federal employees 15 per cent. The act was repealed by other New Deal legislation the following year after FDR had succumbed to the theories advanced by the Keynesian economists in his "Brain Trust."

the understanding that at the point this thing needs to move and needs my full time, I'll be able to leave it for a while."

Goldwater put his arm around my shoulder and laughed. "Clif," he said, "if I didn't have to worry about anybody else I deal with in politics any more than I worry about you, I'd have a pretty pleasant life."

With that we parted. I hadn't gotten the exact answer from him that I wanted. But he had certainly not said anything to discourage my belief that he would seek the nomination and, perhaps overoptimistically, I interpreted the tone of our whole meeting as a reasonably definite indication that he did indeed plan to run. I thought that his parting remark was not merely a compliment, but a pretty positive sign that he would want me around to help with his campaign.

On the train riding home to Rye that evening I mulled over this pleasant visit, searching for clues that might give me some even more definite indication of his plans. Perhaps I was searching too hard for things that pointed to him doing what we all wanted him to do. At any rate, I thought I had detected some cooling of his previously outspoken enthusiasm for Nelson Rockefeller. This was reinforced by an incident I'd heard about a few weeks earlier. It seemed that the Governor had asked Goldwater to come to New York during the recent campaign to appear with him at a dinner attended by some conservative-minded New York business people. But when Rockefeller had not only insisted on keeping the joint appearance secret but had asked his aides to prepare a statement for Goldwater to make to the press on his arrival in New York, the Senator called the whole thing off. He had always been his own man and he had no intention of letting Nelson Rockefeller and his high-priced press agents put words into his mouth for public utterance. It seemed to me that the honeymoon might be nearing an end. And since I had come to regard Rockefeller's Svengali-like hold on Goldwater as the biggest obstacle we had to overcome, I now felt we might well have cleared our highest hurdle.

Before the train slid into the station at Rye I had decided to tell my wife that I was again going to turn down the job offer and stick with politics, at least until after 1964. I knew she wouldn't exactly be deliriously happy with this decision but after some twenty years of marriage I also knew that I could expect a warm vote of confidence. Barry Goldwater had given me one such vote that day. With that, and the one I could count on at home, I was ready for the meeting in Chicago that would essentially determine the direction our operation would take from that time until the Republican national convention of 1964.

CHAPTER 10

THE "SECRET" MEETING

As THE DATE of our Chicago meeting neared I began to grow a bit apprehensive. Many members of the group had insisted upon inviting friends and political associates, some of whom were completely unknown to me. The list grew until fifty-five people had promised to attend and I wondered how we could possibly keep word of the meeting from leaking out with that many people gathered in one room. However, against this fear of a news leak I had to balance the more compelling need for broadening the base of our operation now that we were moving into a new stage.

Our group was not the only one in the Republican Party that had plans afoot. A few days after my conference with Senator Goldwater at the Americana Hotel, the *New York Herald-Tribune* ran a story out of Washington by Earl Mazo, who reported that "There will be a rash of Republican leadership meetings in the next few weeks to chart the party's future."[1] He did not mention our Chicago meeting, since he obviously knew nothing about it, but spoke of a "movement initiated by Senator Clifford P. Case of New Jersey for a cooperative arrangement among the party's moderate and liberal officials." Among the Republican leaders Mazo said Senator Case hoped to recruit were Governor Rockefeller, Governors-elect William W. Scranton and George Romney, and Senators Jacob K. Javits, Kenneth B. Keating, John Sherman Cooper and Hugh Scott. The Case "movement" had all the ear-

[1] *New York Herald-Tribune,* November 16, 1962.

marks of an anti-conservative coalition and I had no intention of letting it get the jump on our group.

The day before our formal meeting on Sunday, December 2 at the Essex Inn Motel on South Michigan Avenue, I flew to Chicago to confer with the members of the original group that had met for the first time fourteen months earlier in the Avenue Motel a few blocks away. I was able to report that in the intervening period I had personally visited twenty-eight states and had established useful contacts in fourteen more. Thus we had the nucleus for organizations in a total of forty-two of the fifty states. In some cases we were actively working with the regular Republican organizations as represented by the Governor, the state and county chairmen, and the National Committee members. In others, our embryo organizations were largely comprised of just plain dedicated citizens who had never played a large role in politics before but who I thought had great potential. During 1962 we had also succeeded in activating caucuses within the National Committee and the Young Republican organization. We had established close liaisons with the National Federation of Republican Women and other groups. We now had the card files on delegates to every Republican national convention from 1952 through 1960, and had begun to work with Senator John Tower with a view toward establishing a conservative caucus on the Platform Committee in 1964.

However, the most pressing matter we had to discuss in the group that Saturday night was the all-important question of the candidate. About twenty of us had gathered for this private session and although everyone attending the formal meeting the following day would have a chance to express his preference, it would be best to thrash this out among ourselves beforehand so we could go into the meeting with a recommendation. Actually, I found that just about everyone had already settled on Senator Goldwater. Indeed, most of our group had decided at the very first meeting the year before that he would be our man and had only withheld their specific support of him on my insistence that it was then premature. Our deliberations were therefore now centered on an alternate candidate if something should happen to remove Barry Goldwater from contention. Some of the group leaned towards Senator Thruston Morton of Kentucky, who had become very highly thought of during his tenure as Republican National Chairman. Senator Morton had won re-election handily the month before against an outspoken Liberal Democrat and ADA founder, Wilson Wyatt, and though he was not openly identified with the conservative wing of the Republican Party we felt he was basically sound. The Texans in our group plugged Senator John Tower as another alternative. But Tower had then served less than two years in the Senate; it was his first elective office, and the general feeling was that he would need more seasoning before he could make a strong race for the Presidency. Congressman Bill Miller was also mentioned, as were Senators Carl Curtis, Roman Hruska, and several others.

In the end, we concluded that we would have to face the question of another candidate only if it became absolutely impossible for Senator Goldwater to run. He was the only conservative Republican with sufficient stature and standing at that time to win any kind of broad-based support. There were other good and qualified men, but none had a national following even remotely comparable to Goldwater's. The hopes of the conservative movement were clearly focused on this one man. It was inevitable that he would be our candidate, as indeed he had tacitly been all along.

We tentatively decided at this Saturday night session to structure our expanded organization as a Draft Goldwater movement, provided the Senator concurred. By then I was certain he would, since he had raised no objections to our activities over the past year nor to the program I had discussed with him on November 12 in New York. A draft movement would have several advantages over an avowed candidacy. First, we knew that at this stage Senator Goldwater would not consent to a formal candidacy. Second, it would give him the freedom he needed to continue evangelizing for the conservative cause without seeming to promote his own political ambitions. Third, it would give our organization a full year before the primaries and state conventions started to continue rounding up delegates without involving the Senator personally in local and state Republican Party in-fighting. Fourth, and most important of all, our draft movement could mobilize thousands of volunteer workers for the 1964 pre-convention campaigns and provide focus and direction for the millions of citizens we knew were already solidly behind the Senator.

When we broke up about midnight we felt that we now had a solid basis on which to present the other proposals I had drawn up for consideration the next day. I felt we had put in a constructive night's work.

Promptly at 9:30 the following morning the expanded group started gathering in the Essex Inn's Park East Walk Room for coffee. In addition to those who had attended our first two Chicago meetings in 1961, there were a number of others whom I had met during my travels over the past year. They included two National Committeewomen, Mrs. Ione Harrington of Indiana and Mrs. Hazel Barger of Virginia; one more member of the National Committee, John Tyler of Oklahoma; the National Young Republican co-chairman, Mrs. Pat Hutar of Chicago; three additional state Republican chairmen, Peter O'Donnell of Texas, John Grenier of Alabama and Wirt Yerger of Mississippi; the Cook County (Chicago)

Republican chairman, Hayes Robertson; and the man who had given Senator Lister Hill such a rough run in Alabama the month before, James Martin.

Others attending a meeting of our group for the first time included: Congressman William Brock of Tennessee; Robert Carter of Colorado, an airline executive who had formerly been an assistant to ex-National Chairman Leonard Hall; Jack Whittaker of Ohio; Wesley Phillips of Oregon; John McClatchey of Pennsylvania; Randy Richardson of New York and Georgia; and several of my New York friends including Ed Lynch, Jerry Milbank and Bill Middendorf.

Two stalwarts who planned to be there were prevented by illness. Len Salliday, the GOP county chairman in Spokane, Washington, suffered a severe heart attack a few days earlier. Somehow, he managed to get to a telephone. He called me in Chicago to explain why he couldn't be there and to extract a promise that I would fill him in on the meeting as soon as it was over. Ralph Staggs, Len's Republican counterpart in Phoenix, also phoned. He had landed in the hospital with pneumonia and was running a temperature of 103. But he slipped out of his room and got to a pay booth down the hall so he could talk to me without the nurses interrupting. I promised Ralph I'd report to him when the meeting ended and then I left my room to join the group that was already assembling.

After the informal coffee hour, we all took seats around a huge U-shaped table in the Inn's Buckingham Court Room where the meeting was scheduled to start at ten o'clock. When everyone was seated, I walked over behind the little podium and called the meeting to order. Although I hadn't planned it, I decided that in view of the importance of the project formally beginning that morning, and its possible effects not only upon our personal lives but upon the lives of millions of our fellow citizens, it would be appropriate to open the meeting with a brief prayer for divine guidance in our deliberations that day. Then I opened the black loose-leaf book containing the agenda and the proposed programs which we hoped would wrest control of the 1964 convention from the small coterie of kingmakers who had ruled the Republican Party for so many years.

Very quickly we determined that the overwhelming majority of the people in attendance were in complete agreement with our group's principal decision of the night before, namely that Barry Goldwater would be our candidate for the 1964 Presidential nomination. Then I emphasized that, in my opinion, the Senator would not agree to become a candidate until he saw adequate financing and the energy of a full-scale professional operation behind him. With this in mind, I next presented my proposed budget for the long pre-convention battle ahead. It called for a total of $3,200,000 for the entire year and a half, with somewhat less than half—$1,275,000 to be exact—earmarked for the incredibly expensive primary campaigns we knew Goldwater would have to enter. I said I realized this was a considerable sum, but I pointed out that it would be just a drop in the bucket compared to the huge funds our opponents were prepared to spend on their own campaigns.

It should be noted that we budgeted only $75,000 for the convention itself. In view of the vast sums spent for individual candidates at previous national conventions of both the Democratic and Republican parties this might seem a hopelessly inadequate figure. But at no time did our group plan to buy delegates. In fact, we decided very early in the game that we would have no truck with purchasable delegates. Even if we had been of a mind to make financial bids for them, which we never were, we couldn't possibly hope to match the bids they would receive from others. A delegate who can be bought for any one candidate can be bought away by someone with a more enticing offer. We wanted only dedicated people whose convention votes would never be up for sale. And we knew that with very, very few exceptions these were the kinds of people who were aligned with our conservative cause. They were people of principle, and their principles were strictly non-negotiable.

Besides the primaries and the convention, the other major items in the budget were $725,000 for rental of headquarters in Washington, office equipment, mailings and travel expenses; and $437,000 for headquarters staff salaries. During 1963 the staff would include a campaign director, a public relations manager, a research director, three financial and fund-raising experts, five field men (one for each of the new regions), an office manager and six secretaries. In 1964 we planned to add two more public relations men, four additional research people, five field men and four secretaries. Although this was not a large staff when compared with the teams other candidates could field, I felt it would be adequate for our operation since we could count on more volunteer help than any Presidential aspirant had ever had in the past.

As for the organizational program itself, our main activity would continue to be making contact with Republican Party leaders and workers at the precinct, local, county, state and national levels. Through our Organization Committee we would also establish close liaison with labor, business, farm, professional and student groups, veterans' organizations, women's clubs, and ethnic groups.

It is worth noting here that we placed Negro organizations high on our list. We did this on the assumption that Negroes, like members of all other so-called minority groups, were above all else Americans interested in the future of their country. At that time we believed that Negroes would contrast the obvious sincerity of Barry Goldwater's interest in and sympathy for their legitimate aspirations with the patently phony play for their votes being made by many other politicians in both parties. We thought that the Negroes would reject the patronizing approach of the Left, which seeks to deal with them as a mass voting bloc, and that many of them would embrace the true equality of conservativism, which welcomes Negroes, like all other citizens, as individuals worthy of respect. Personally, I still hope that some day in the not far distant future the Negro community will awaken to the fact that white Liberals are merely using Negro support to promote their own socialistic schemes. One day the Negroes, in common with millions of their white fellow citizens who have bought the same glittering package, must become aware that these schemes can only lead to the eventual enslavement of all of us, white and black.

In addition to setting forth in some detail the Organization Committee's work with Republican leaders and special groups, the master plan called for the establishment of several other committees with certain clearly defined duties. Thus the Public Relations Committee would not only prepare pamphlets and issue news releases to the mass media; it would also cooperate with the people assigned to the special groups in drafting programs. The Women's Division would seek to expand the Senator's already considerable popularity among distaff voters. The Survey Committee would work with the private polling firm we planned to hire, again with emphasis on determining appeals to broader segments of special groups than the Republican Party had won support from in the past. The Research Committee would be charged with discovering and developing the issues that most concerned the public. And finally, the Strategy Committee, comprised of the campaign director, the chairmen of the four special committees and the head of the Women's Division, would have primary responsibility for waging a victorious nominating campaign. We hoped that the Strategy Committee would meet regularly with Senator Goldwater who, of course, would be commander-in-chief of the campaign —covertly during the draft movement stage, openly after he announced his candidacy.

During the all-day meeting at the Essex Inn, I set forth the basic formula for winning the nomination, and beyond that the election, that I had developed as the result of my travels and the reports I had received from our regional chairmen and other members of the group in the year we had been at work. Actually, the formula did not deviate in any important respect from the delegate-vote forecasts we had made fourteen months before. We still planned to work for delegates in every state in the Union. But we now knew more certainly than we had at the outset the states in which a conservative candidate would show the most strength.

To win the nomination, Goldwater needed 655 delegate votes. My goal was 700 votes *before* the national convention was called to order in July of 1964. To achieve this goal, we would have to start with 451 votes from what I believed were solid Goldwater states—Alabama, Arizona, Arkansas, Colorado, Florida, Indiana, Louisiana, Maine, Mississippi, Missouri, Montana, Nebraska, New Mexico, North Carolina, Oklahoma, South Carolina, Texas, Utah, Virginia and Washington. We hoped to add another 81 votes from states that were leaning towards the Senator— Georgia, Kentucky, South Dakota and Tennessee. There were three more states—Illinois, Iowa and Ohio—that in combination we believed would yield 142 more votes with extra-hard work. That would give us a total of 674 votes on the first roll call at San Francisco, enough to squeak by but too close for comfort. I wanted more of a margin, and I thought we could pick up the remaining 26 votes to hit my target of 700 from split delegations in states like Michigan, New Jersey, Pennsylvania and Connecticut. To provide even more insurance, we planned to enter Senator Goldwater in the California Presidential primary, which could produce a big 86-vote delegate bloc, in the event our opponents chipped off votes in states we were not too certain of winning.

Looking beyond the convention to the 1964 election, in which we then believed the Democratic candidate would certainly be John F. Kennedy, we felt this same formula contained the ingredients for Goldwater's Presidential victory. He would need 270 electoral votes to open the door to the White House. From what I then had good reason to count as solid Goldwater states, he would get 179 electoral votes. He could pick up 36 more from the states we thought were leaning toward him. And he would go over the top with 61 votes from the Republican heartland states of Illinois, Iowa, and Ohio. If we could add California's 40 electoral votes to these 276 he could win with plenty of room to spare.

We did not write off the big Northeastern states. But we had to be realistic. States like New York are for the most part private preserves of monolithic Democratic big-city machines. Liberal Republicans can occasionally loosen the machine's hold—if they act and sound enough like Liberal Democrats. But the Northeast was not conservative country. We hoped our candidate could ultimately convert enough Eastern votes to annex this errant territory, and indeed he seemed to appeal to thousands of people in Pennsylvania, New York and elsewhere. However, in the East thousands of voters are not enough. You need millions, and we did not yet have them.

To offset the probable loss of the big Northeastern states which had gone Democratic by overwhelming margins in the 1960 Presidential elections, we believed that Goldwater could carry all or most of the states, mostly in the Midwest and South, where Kennedy had squeaked by with less than 51 per cent of the vote. The tissue-thin margin of the Kennedy victory can be measured by the amazing fact that these latter states contributed no less than 121 of the 303 electoral votes the Democratic candidate garnered. Even if only half of these electoral votes went to Goldwater he would win provided we could hold all of the states, comprising 219 electoral votes, which Richard Nixon had captured in 1960. Fortunately, Nixon's margins had been generally greater in the states the Republicans won than Kennedy's pluralities in the states which the Democrats had taken, in some instances by flagrant fraud in the vote count.

Not everyone at the meeting agreed that Goldwater could hang onto all the 1960 Nixon states. California loomed as a bigger question mark than ever in the wake of Nixon's gubernatorial defeat of the month before. And some of the participants felt there was a real danger that any Republican candidate might lose Iowa, Maine, Ohio, Oregon, and Washington, all of which Nixon had carried. But the consensus of the group was that hard work on the part of the troops and a fighting campaign by the candidate could bring the Republican Party victory in 1964, especially now that the Democrat stranglehold on the once solid South was visibly loosening.

The 1964 Presidential election, and through it the return of the Republican Party to control of the federal government, was of course our ultimate goal. We were all thoroughly convinced that the only way to achieve that goal was to assure the nomination of a candidate who could capitalize on the conservative resurgence which was then beginning to assert itself so strongly in America. Therefore the nomination of the candidate we had selected, Barry Goldwater, had to take top priority in all our discussions that Sunday morning in Chicago.

Not all the reports submitted that day were optimistic about Goldwater's chances for capturing the nomination. For instance, Congressman Don Bruce of Indiana told us that many Republican leaders in his state, once a rock-ribbed conservative stronghold, were "lurching" towards Governor Rockefeller. Others similarly reported signs of growing Rockefeller strength.

But I warned that our operation must not take on the appearance of a "stop Rockefeller" movement. We were simply and solely out to promote the candidacy of Barry Goldwater. It was imperative that this be done through a positive program of selling the Senator both to the Republicans who picked the delegates to the national convention and at the same time to the growing numbers of Democrats and independents who were discovering the soundness of the conservative philosophy. I felt it would be a serious mistake to inject a debilitating note of negativism into our campaign.

What so many conservatives seem to forget is that their philosophical position is historically the most positive approach to government ever devised by man. Conservatives are against many things. But they are against them only because they correctly see the development of an all-powerful central state as the mortal enemy of what they are *for*—namely, maximum freedom for the individual without encroachment on the rights of others.

There is no more positive and progressive position than this, and indeed there never will be. Yet in our justifiable alarm, caused by the accelerated usurpation by the federal government of the rights of the individual citizen, we conservatives have somehow permitted ourselves to be cast mistakenly in the role of negativists. This is largely our own fault. The Liberal elements of the mass media have certainly aided and abetted the propagation of this gigantic misconception. But we have done precious little to correct the record by giving proper emphasis to the supremely positive aspects of the conservative position.

As events subsequently showed, our efforts to elect Barry Goldwater to the Presidency never degenerated into a stop-anybody exercise. It was the Liberals who frantically threw themselves into this assignment. Their battle-cry filled the land, rising to the shrill and often completely irrational screech of *"Stop Goldwater!"* They failed with this sad motto at the San Francisco convention only because the members of our group, and the hundreds of thousands of citizens they organized, had anticipated their strategy as far back as 1961.

During the afternoon at the Essex Inn, we broke up into smaller groups. The finance team went into a huddle while the organizational committee held a separate meeting.

When we re-convened the entire group, I presented our projected time-table for 1963. If Senator Goldwater concurred, we planned to unveil the National Draft Goldwater Committee on March 15. I set a tentative schedule of regional and state meetings between April and June to begin formally constituting Draft committees in the states.

During the summer and fall we would test the effectiveness of these committees in selected local elections coming up in November. And right after the elections we would try to get Goldwater to announce his candidacy so we could start work on the primary campaigns he must enter.

Only 16 states hold Presidential primaries, beginning with New Hampshire early in March and ending with California, New York, Nebraska and North Dakota the first week in June. It might not be necessary for Goldwater to campaign in all of them and I promised that we would pick our targets well, with a view toward maintaining the vital momentum we would need to carry us over the top at San Francisco and on into the election campaign.

Stets Coleman, Bill Middendorf and Jerry Milbank agreed to serve as trustees of the Finance Committee until a national finance chairman was found. And for the fourth time the group elected me as its chairman.

THE "SECRET" MEETING 101

They also instructed me to report again to Senator Goldwater. This time I was to inform him of our plans to launch the Draft Goldwater Committee publicly in March. I was to tell him that we did not request his overt approval but that we would have to have his pledge not to disown the draft or repudiate his own possible candidacy.

With these details settled, we adjourned. There was one item on the agenda in my black book that I had not had time to cover. I had wanted to brief the members of the group on how to respond if the press found out about the meeting and questioned them. Bob Morris had touched on it during the discussion that morning when he expressed his misgivings, which I shared, about keeping our deliberations quiet. But I let this chance go by and in the rush to adjourn, the briefing session was omitted. It turned out to be no great loss. These people were all pros. And the following day I found how well they could handle themselves when the pressure began to build.

CHAPTER 11

THE "PLOT" UNMASKED

BENJAMIN FRANKLIN is alleged to have said, "Three may keep a secret, if two of them are dead." The secret, if we may call it that, of the nationwide activities directed from Suite 3505 had been kept secure for almost fourteen months. And Ben Franklin's formula had proven faulty, a fact that I set down with some reluctance since Franklin was certainly one of history's foremost conservatives. In addition to the twenty-two men who had gathered in Chicago on October 8, 1961 to found our operation, dozens more had been added in the intervening months. Yet no hint of our activities had ever leaked to the press. Author-columnist Robert Novak has called our organization "one of the most remarkable clandestine operations in American political history."[1] But on December 3, 1962 the covert phase of the great Republican revolution came to an end. Perhaps predictably, it all came to light as a result of espionage on the part of a small group of somewhat paranoid Liberals.

The first evidence I had that there had been a "spy" in our midst at the Essex Inn came on Monday morning, less than eighteen hours after our Chicago meeting adjourned. About ten o'clock the phone rang in Suite 3505. It was Carl DeBloom, the able Washington correspondent of the *Columbus* (Ohio) *Dispatch*. Carl said he had picked up a rumor that Congressman John Ashbrook of Ohio had attended a meeting I was said to have held in Chicago the day before. It was obvious that Carl's

[1] Novak, *op. cit.*, p. 119.

informant had not provided him with any detailed information on the meeting. And I had no intention of enlightening him further. I did not deny that a meeting had taken place. But I refused to supply any details and in effect tossed cold water on its significance.

As soon as Carl hung up I placed a call to Senator Goldwater in Phoenix. I got him on the line immediately and told him that the press had wind of our Chicago meeting. Then I added:

"I don't know whether they'll be after you, but for my part, I'm playing it down."

The Senator picked up his cue without hesitation. "Fine," he said, "I don't know a thing about it." This was essentially true, since I did not report to him on the meeting at all over the phone. However, I did ask when he would return to Washington so I could give him a report.

"I'll be flying back after the first of the year," he replied.

"That's good," I said. "I'll give you the details on this meeting then."

No sooner had the Senator rung off than my phone buzzed again. This time it was Arthur Edson of the Associated Press. He was calling from the AP Washington Bureau to inquire about the meeting. I gave him the same story I had previously given Carl DeBloom, but Edson wasn't satisfied. He kept questioning me and it was obvious that he somehow had been filled in on a few of the more pertinent points we had discussed the day before. He also had a list of names. It included about a dozen of the people who had attended the meeting. I asked him who had given him the list but he refused to tell me and I knew he had to protect his source just as I had to protect the members of my group.

Edson wanted me to confirm that the people on his list had met with me in Chicago. I said that I didn't think I should do that. "These people are all friends of mine," I added. "I don't know what they may have told their bosses or their families about coming to Chicago, so I'm not going to publicly state that they attended any meeting with me, political or otherwise."

I have always tried to play fair with reporters. I realize that when one calls you on a story he is only doing his job. Moreover, I fully recognize the importance of a reporter's job in keeping the public informed. But after fourteen months of running an operation *sub rosa* to keep it from being shot down in infancy, I wasn't about to spill the beans now and risk having all our work go for naught.

At last, Edson got the message. He gave up trying to squeeze more information out of me and said goodbye. But I knew he would be back on the phone again if he got another lead. Meanwhile, I decided to call as many of my key people as I could reach to warn them that it looked as though the cat we had nurtured so carefully was about to escape from the bag.

Late in the afternoon Arthur Edson called back. He had talked with some of the people on his list and they had all referred him to me. He asked if I had changed my mind about talking. I said that I hadn't and he hung up again.

Finally, just before five o'clock, he called for the last time. He had managed to get some quotes from several of the people who had attended the meeting. From these sketchy statements he had put together a story which he now read to me in essentially the same words that appeared in the newspapers later that night and the following day:

A secret, highly confidential meeting of leading Republicans who want Senator Barry Goldwater of Arizona for President was held in Chicago Sunday.

Their objective is to get, as one put it, "an honest-to-God conservative Republican candidate for President"—and incidentally, to try to block the road for Governor Nelson A. Rockefeller of New York. . . .

Reports of what went on at the meeting vary considerably. One source said $250,000 was pledged as a starter toward a goal of $3 million . . .

At this point I interrupted Edson in his reading. "I only wish $250,000 had been pledged," I said. "If it had, I would be putting out a statement saying so."

Edson, of course, had his pencil poised to take notes at his desk in Washington and this quote went right into the AP story verbatim. Then he continued reading:

It is not clear what relationship Goldwater had to this meeting of his admirers. It was first reported that he told the originators that any such effort takes a lot of money—and, anyway, he's not running for the Presidency. . . .

There was more speculation along this line and the story ended with the list of names Edson had obtained. By the following morning the list had grown to seventeen, with two- or three-line background sketches of each individual named. With only a few exceptions, they were all members of our original group.

When he had finished reading me the story, Edson said: "Unless you have any comment that's the way the story is going to roll. This is your last chance."

I said I had nothing to add to what he already had, though I believe I tried, obviously without success, to convince him that the meeting had not been held to mount a "stop Rockefeller" movement, as his story had said. With that he hung up.

I knew that within minutes the AP wire would be carrying the story into every newsroom in the nation. In a few hours it would hit the streets in the bulldog editions of every morning newspaper, and it would roll on the wire in time for the early evening television and radio newscasts as well. It was front-paged from coast to coast all the following day. In New York, the *Herald-Tribune* headline followed the line I had anticipated: "GOLDWATER '64 BOOM: MOVE TO BLOCK ROCKY." In San Francisco, the *Examiner* carried Edson's scoop under a giant head at the top of page one: "SECRET MEET TO PUSH GOLDWATER IN 1964." In Cleveland, Chicago, Kansas City, New Orleans, Los Angeles and hundreds of other cities the story was essentially the same. Some played up the "stop Rockefeller" aspects of the Edson story. Others, enlarging on the esoteric nature of the "secret meeting" in re-writes of Edson's AP article, carried more sensationalized accounts. Virtually everywhere the play was prominent and many papers followed up with editorials and columns analyzing the meaning of our Chicago meeting.

But before the newspapers could get their stories into the linotype machines, radio and television were already carrying the news to the far corners of the country and the world. On Madison Avenue, an alert CBS newsman spotted Edson's story as it came off the wire and immediately called it to Walter Cronkite's attention. Cronkite picked up the phone and called his Chicago bureau. Since the AP didn't give the name of the motel where we had met, the CBS reporter in Chicago had to spend almost an hour tracking down the site of what already was being called our "secret meeting." He finally zeroed in on the Essex Inn after calling several dozen motels to inquire whether I had registered over the weekend. Then he called Cronkite back and reported that he had found the place and was on his way there with a camera crew.

When Cronkite opened his evening newscast an hour and a half after Arthur Edson's story moved on the AP wire he was able to lead off with his Chicago reporter standing in a room at the Essex Inn in Chicago. The reporter announced that this was where, a scant twenty-four hours before, "a group of prominent Republicans had met to plot a Presidential campaign for Barry Goldwater." It was an inspired, though somewhat overdramatized, piece of reporting. The Chicago reporter staged it so realistically, with the camera shooting past him to bring in the turned heads of some ringers he had corralled for the scene, that several of my people called that night to ask how, when—and above all why—the CBS crew had slipped into the room to televise our meeting![2]

That night the telephone at my home in Rye rang continuously until

[2] Actually, CBS shot the show in Charlie Barr's suite, which was next to mine at the Essex Inn, and not in the Buckingham Court Room downstairs where the big meeting was held. But this is a minor point and detracts nothing from the splendid job of news sleuthing that Cronkite and his CBS team did to add another dimension to Arthur Edson's notable scoop for AP.

well past midnight. And the next morning when I got to the office at nine o'clock Rita Bree was already frantically fielding calls. All at once it seemed as though the whole country had discovered Suite 3505. Most of the members of my team called to say that they were still being pressed by reporters in their cities for comment. Backed to the wall by the AP story and the CBS coverage, a few had issued statements on their own when reporters tracked them down.

John Ashbrook set the tone of these replies in a candid appraisal to the press. "The real purpose of the meeting," he said, "was an effort to consolidate the Republican conservative groups around the country to make sure we have a candidate in 1964. Of course, Senator Goldwater is the front runner."

Wirt Yerger, speaking as Republican state chairman of Mississippi, said forthrightly: "We're the conservative party, and we have got to have a conservative candidate if we expect to win."

Practically all members of the group who were questioned were asked why they had kept the meeting secret. Charlie Barr set the record straight on that. "The reason the meeting wasn't announced to the press," he said, "was that we wanted to let our hair down and discuss the various candidates. We were naturally afraid no one would be candid if they knew they would be quoted."

In Phoenix, Senator Goldwater played it straight, as he had assured me he would. About the meeting, the Senator owned that he had "heard something" about it. Then he said, "I still plan to run for the Senate two years from now." However, I was relieved to see that he added that it was entirely possible he might not seek re-election to the Senate "since things change and it's too early to be absolutely certain."

Some of the people at the meeting, because of their official positions in the Republican Party, were placed in an uncomfortable position as a result of the spotlight suddenly turned on our operation by the press. David Nichols found himself in a particularly tight spot in Maine, where the Liberal brand of Republicanism has been gaining ascendancy in the last decade as the Democrats there become ever stronger. As the *Portland Sunday Telegram* reported it a few days later, ". . . some GOP leaders here are downright unhappy" about their state chairman attending a conference of conservatives. To keep peace in Maine's already factionalized Republican family Nichols took the position that he was "not committed to anyone" for 1964. This was absolutely true. Dave Nichols never did commit himself to Goldwater. He attended our meetings, and I have reason to believe he was sympathetic to our cause, but he seldom if ever said anything in these sessions. And at San Francisco in 1964 he went along with Maine's support of Senator Margaret Chase Smith as the first woman to receive delegate votes for a Presidential nomination at a

Republican national convention. Actually, I suspect that one of the reasons Dave became involved with our group at the outset was that he had some hope of selling Senator Smith as Goldwater's Vice-Presidential running mate.[3]

Unfortunately, Nichols, in common with others in our group, was accused of sowing seeds of dissension within the Republican ranks because of his attendance at the Chicago meeting. I very seriously doubt if Dave or the others would have been subjected to accusations of this sort if they had attended a meeting designed to promote the candidacy of Governor Rockefeller or any of the other Liberal Presidential hopefuls in the party. Indeed, many Republican officials met with Rockefeller and his representatives during this same period and never once can I recall that any of them were accused of breeding discord within the GOP.

It wasn't long, however, before our whole group was similarly branded as potential wreckers of the party. The *New York Herald-Tribune,* whose president, Walter Thayer, was still suffering from the shock of Nixon's defeat in California, a defeat which temporarily deprived Thayer and his paper of a candidate, led the branding roundup with an editorial on Wednesday, December 5. Aghast at what it called our "conspiracy," the *Herald-Tribune* accused us of "bad timing, narrow motives and poor politics." Then it added, "The luxury of partisan bickering of the kind we have just seen in Chicago is political nonsense."[4]

Though the editorial made a feeble attempt near the end to apply its criticism equally to "conservatives as well as liberals," it left no doubt that the *Herald-Tribune* believed conservatives were the chief architects of Republican disunity. But at least the *Herald-Tribune* largely confined its criticism to the editorial page. The august *New York Times* accused us of "splintering" the Republican Party in the very first "news" story it carried on our Chicago meeting.

It has never ceased to amaze me that the oracles who shout the loudest in defense of "human rights" and "political freedom" invariably squeal like stuck pigs when people in the conservative camp gather together to exercise their rights as free citizens. We are called "conspirators"

---

[3] Even the Maine newspapers surmised this. The *Portland Sunday Telegram* was certainly close to the truth when it reported (on December 9, 1962) that "some observers think it likely Nichols attended [the Chicago meeting] in an effort to gauge the role Maine's U.S. Senator Margaret Chase Smith might play in the 1964 presidential sweepstakes. . . . Senator Smith . . . would be a logical choice, many say, as a running mate for either Senator Goldwater or Michigan Governor George Romney. It's true that Senator Smith's political convictions are far more liberal than are Goldwater's, but in the area of military preparedness both agree on the necessity of a strong national posture. And from a practical standpoint, Senator Smith's moderate liberalism might balance Goldwater's conservatism."

[4] *New York Herald-Tribune,* December 5, 1962.

because we refuse to pay proper obeisance to the Liberal pantheon and the dogma of the welfare state. Yet day after day these same sages prove to the world that they judge by a double standard which grants absolution to Liberals for committing the same "sins" of free assembly and political action.

At Suite 3505 that Tuesday after the story of our "secret meeting" broke, the phones kept ringing into the late hours of the night. CBS called twice during the day to ask if I would appear on Cronkite's news show that evening. But I explained that it was impossible for me to take time ·out for a taped interview. The other news media and my friends throughout the country were calling constantly and I had an obligation to stay at the office and answer their questions. The following morning the phone calls let up somewhat. I was rather surprised when CBS contacted me again. I asked if they thought they still had a story since this was Wednesday and the meeting had occurred on Sunday. The news editor thought it was still worth a try so I agreed to come up to the studio for a taping session.

Walter Cronkite did the interview and he was eminently fair with me, as indeed he has always been. I remember I flubbed one little word and when we were done Walter asked if I wanted to do the interview all over again. I said I didn't think he and his crew had to go to all that trouble to make me look good. But Walter insisted and we went through the interview once more, fortunately without a flub this time.

When I got back to 3505 after the taping the storm of phone calls had subsided appreciably. I managed to catch a train home to Rye in time to see Cronkite's newscast. He saved our interview for the windup and after I saw it on my television set I was glad I had gone through with it. As one of my newspaper friends is fond of saying, when a rooster is caught coming out of the hen house he might as well crow or he may be mistaken for a hen and wind up with his head on the chopping block. I didn't crow on Cronkite's program, but I did have a chance to put the Chicago meeting in its proper perspective. I think it helped subdue some, though obviously not all, of the criticism that was being leveled at us.

The following night I flew to Washington. The Republican National Committee was to open its mid-winter meeting at the Mayflower Hotel the next day and I wanted to test the reaction there to the great "exposé" of our Goldwater for President operation. On that night, the eve of the meeting, National Chairman Bill Miller was holding a reception in a small ballroom to the rear of the Mayflower's lobby. I was hardly through the revolving doors of the Connecticut Avenue entrance when people started to besiege me. All the way down the block-long lobby to the ballroom they stopped me every few steps. Prominent Republicans from all over the country whispered words of encouragement or grasped my hand warmly and let it be known with a smile and a nod that they approved.

When I got to the ballroom I was almost mobbed. I remember that it took me an hour and a half to get through the foyer and into the room itself. John Tyler, the National Committeeman from Oklahoma, grabbed me by the arm and said with a broad grin: "The next time you invite me to a secret meeting, Clif, I hope the devil you'll warn me to prepare a statement for the press beforehand so I'll have something ready when the reporters call the next day."

Bill Miller cornered me in the foyer and took me off to one side. I thought he might be a little worried so I hastened to reassure him that I wasn't going to do anything that I thought would hurt the Republican Party. "You can count on me to play this straight," I promised.

"I have no quarrel with you," Miller replied. "As long as it doesn't split the party, you've got every right to work for whomever you please."

This, of course, was the proper posture for the National Chairman to take. By the very nature of his job, he has to remain neutral in the selection of the party's Presidential candidate. But later many people, in and out of print, accused Congressman Miller of winning the Vice-Presidential nomination as a reward for playing ball with Goldwater. It may come as a surprise to these people but right up until the convention I never considered Bill Miller to be one of our team. In fact, there were times when I thought he was being rather too "neutral" on the side of some of the opposition candidates, though this may have been a somewhat partisan interpretation on my part.

The Chairman's party at the Mayflower that night buzzed with talk of our Chicago meeting. Even among the people I knew to be sympathetic —or long since cemented—to other candidates, it was the principal topic of discussion. I remember later in the evening, when I finally had gotten through the foyer and into the main room, Governor Rockefeller's chief strategist, George Hinman, approached with a twinkle in his eye. I suspected he had been upstairs in his suite "plotting" the Governor's nominating campaign with some of Rockefeller's key supporters as well as prospective converts who might be induced to climb aboard the bandwagon of the man who was still leading all the polls by comfortable margins.

"Clif, how in the world do you get all this attention and publicity for your candidate?" George laughed. "I can't get anywhere near as much for mine—and his name is Rockefeller!"

I laughed in reply, "George, you just have to get out of the habit of holding these little private caucuses and stage a secret meeting."

He almost broke up at that and so did several of the people standing with us. However, I sensed even then that for Hinman our "secret" meeting was really no laughing matter. Although we had certainly not intended it that way, the meeting, or more accurately, the burst of publicity that resulted from it, seriously slowed the rising momentum of Rockefeller's previously swift and smooth ride toward the nomination. As Bill Rusher later expressed it:

The meeting served one useful purpose. Rockefeller's journalistic chorus of trained seals had been prepared to hail his re-election as making him the inevitable Republican nominee for President in 1964; and, despite the rather less than sensational margin by which he was returned to Albany, they were bugling away industriously when—like a discordant tuba blast—the word broke from coast to coast that 55 disagreeable people had just caucused quietly in Chicago to lay very different plans for 1964. Somehow, Mr. Rockefeller's nomination never seemed quite so "inevitable" again.[5]

It was with a dawning awareness of this unexpected by-product of our Chicago conference that I returned to New York after a successful round of meetings in Washington that weekend. But there was one thing that still troubled me, and continued to trouble me for weeks afterwards. I couldn't quite fathom how the story of our meeting had so quickly leaked to the press, even though I had felt before we assembled in Chicago that it would be difficult to keep any political gathering of fifty-five people quiet for very long.

At first I thought that perhaps someone had slipped into Suite 3505 and made photocopies of the agenda in my black book. But I rejected this theory as somewhat outlandish, though much stranger things have happened in politics. I knew that no one from our original group had tipped Carl DeBloom or Arthur Edson. After all, the group had kept our secret for well over a year. I trusted all of them completely.

It wasn't until the spring issue of *Advance* came out two months later that we finally found out what had happened. This allegedly Republican "journal of political thought" originally was published by a group of superannuated students and ivory tower hangers-on near Harvard Yard in Cambridge, Massachusetts. Its second quarterly issue in 1963 carried a lengthy article by one George F. Hobart entitled "Inside the Goldwater 'Draft.'" In this story I emerged as a sort of semi-sinister plotter because it named me as "the chief organizer of the Goldwater movement."

But far more important, the article boasted that an *"Advance* reporter managed to be present" not only at the informal meeting on Sunday, December 2, but at the Saturday night session of what Hobart called our "governing board." The latter claim was obviously spurious. It was ap-

[5] *National Review*, August 11, 1964.

parently designed to plant a seed of mutual suspicion among the members of our original group and strike fear into the breasts of all members of "the Goldwater movement" that its innermost circle had been penetrated by those who chose to regard themselves as our enemies.

A close study of the article convinced me that this claim was pure psychological warfare. Although the story cited several of my confidential memos to the original group, there was nothing in these passages that an enterprising spy could not have picked up in conversation with any number of people who would have confidently accepted him as a trusted conservative during the pre-meeting coffee hour or at lunch. Nor was there anything in the story about our original group's actual deliberations on Saturday night, except as I had presented them to the larger meeting the following morning.

Reading the article, I realized that the *Advance* "reporter," who posed for some years as a dedicated conservative, had probably come equipped with a hidden tape recorder. The story faithfully reported the Sunday meeting in the sequence actually followed, and not as it was laid out in my agenda, from which I had departed at several points. Moreover, all the quotes were presented verbatim. On top of that there were several mistakes in the partial list of names of those who had attended the meeting, the kind of mistakes a typist transcribing a tape would make if she were not familiar with the people mentioned in a recorded discussion. Significantly, all the people named had been on the list Arthur Edson had read when he had called me from the AP Washington Bureau, although *Advance* had omitted many others.

If the *Advance* "reporter" had been a professional doing his job for a newspaper, wire service, television or radio network I could see some point to his effort. However, I will confess that I know of no instance where legitimate newsmen have used hidden tape recorders during interviews of private meetings, and I should think that most newsmen and editors would frown on such a tactic.

But the "reporter" in this instance was no reporter at all. He was a paid hireling of a small Liberal Republican faction which apparently believes it is *de rigueur* to employ electronic eavesdropping devices and Gestapo-like infiltration techniques to spy on a group of citizens meeting in private to exercise rights guaranteed to them by the Constitution of the United States.

However, in December of 1962 I lost little sleep over the knowledge that we had such a hireling in our midst. His adventure in espionage had backfired. In attempting to sink Goldwater's candidacy in an ocean of publicity, he and his employers had perversely succeeded only in giving added buoyancy to the movement they hoped to drown. Besides, I was rather relieved that our operation was at last out in the open. It had been something of a strain to keep it under cover all those months, and there had been occasions when I began to think our whole group was in danger of assuming a collective James Bond complex. Now we were free to operate in the open for Barry Goldwater's nomination— or so we thought for a brief few weeks. Then, from Phoenix just after the New Year, came some disquieting echoes of the Senator's old uncertainties about his willingness to seek the nomination. Commenting to a reporter on the schedule of 1963 priorities I had given the group at the Chicago meeting, Goldwater said: "I hope they won't go ahead on this timetable. I'd rather stay in a fluid position for the rest of this year."

And from some of my Western friends who visited with Barry over the Christmas holidays I received reports that he seemed to have shifted from a spirit of cooperation with our group to something approaching downright hostility. It wasn't long before I was to have concrete evidence of the accuracy of these reports and feel the rather sharp cutting edge of the Senator's new attitude.

BOOK TWO

THE DRAFT

CHAPTER 12

THE NON-CANDIDATE

ON MONDAY MORNING, January 14, 1963, I drove across Long Island Sound from Rye, parked my car at LaGuardia Airport and caught an early Eastern Airlines shuttle flight to Washington. I had a 10:30 appointment with Senator Goldwater at his office, our first face-to-face talk since our visit at the Americana before the explosion of the secret meeting in Chicago more than a month before.

The newly elected 88th Congress had convened five days earlier and I had been in Washington the previous week to attend a conference sponsored by the publication *Human Events*. Those two Gibraltar-like figures of conservative journalism, Frank Hanighen and James Wick, both of whom were to die within the next twenty-two months, had made these *Human Events* gatherings into semi-annual forums of American conservatism. At this conference it was obvious that the movement that they had fostered so long and diligently was at last coming into its own. Citizens had come in from all over the country, some of them battle-scarred veterans of the political wars but many more who were new-comers to politics. The publicity that followed our Chicago meeting had given them all a clear focus for our common goals.

As at the Republican National Committee's winter meeting in December, Goldwater's impending candidacy had been on everyone's mind and I had found myself in the center of a three-day marathon of private meetings explaining our strategy to people from California and New England, from Florida and Washington State, and from most of the states in between. It had been a reassuring and highly encouraging session and I discovered many new allies whom I knew we could count on to go back and work their hearts out for Barry Goldwater in their home states. Moreover, the overwhelming reaction in favor of our operation which these people displayed must certainly have gotten back to Senator Goldwater. I counted on it to strengthen our hand in the discussion I was to have with him that Monday morning.

When I arrived at the Senator's office, Edna Coerver told me that he was tied up in a caucus being held by the dwindling minority of Senate Republicans to organize their Policy Committee for the new session, but she expected it to be over within a few minutes. Edna escorted me into Goldwater's private chamber and left me there to await his return. For about ten minutes I sat alone in a chair in front of the big mahogany desk with Barry's photographs of his beloved Navajos staring mutely down at me from the walls. Then the door burst open and the Senator stalked in. He said hello and I could see that he was quite upset. He seldom shows anger as other men do. His face wasn't flushed and he didn't appear excited. But I had known him long enough now to be able to sense his moods, and it was immediately apparent to me that he was in anything but a good mood at that moment. He walked over to the little refrigerator in a closet near the door and poured himself a coke. Then he carried the glass around behind his desk and sat down.

"Do you know what my esteemed colleagues just did?" he asked, almost incredulously. "They left me off the Policy Committee."

I said I couldn't believe it.

"Well, dammit, they did," he replied. He was furious, as he had every right to be. To the country at large he was the best known and most highly regarded member of the Republican minority in the United States Senate. Yet his fellow Republican Senators had barred him from the innermost sanctum where the real decisions on the party's strategy in the Senate are made.

For eight years Goldwater had unselfishly served his party in the thankless job of chairman of the Republican Senatorial Campaign Committee, traveling hundreds of thousands of miles up and down the land raising money and winning votes for Republican Senators. Now this was his bitter reward. As Barry well knew, his ouster from the Policy Committee—and not long after this his forced retirement from the chairmanship of the Campaign Committee as well—had been engineered by Jack Javits and his small coterie of far-Left Liberals among the Senate Republicans. Javits had been working toward these twin goals for years. After the 1960 election he nearly succeeded in tossing Goldwater off the Campaign Committee. But at the last minute Margaret

Chase Smith had turned the tide in the caucus with a moving statement which brought most of the other Senators back into line.

"There is still substantial divergence in the views of Senator Goldwater and myself," the lady from Maine had said. "But I am opposed to his being ousted from the chairmanship for the very simple reason that I think he has made an excellent chairman. . . . He showed an ability and a determination to do everything he could to get every Republican Senatorial nominee elected regardless of whether he agreed or disagreed with the views of the individual candidate."

On this morning, however, none of Barry's friends had been able to halt the action that Javits & Company had spent years engineering. A few days later enough Senators had apparently suffered sufficient pangs of conscience—or recognized the potential political damage they had done themselves—to decide to reverse field and reinstate him on the Policy Committee, though of course at this moment neither Barry nor I could foresee this corrective action.

We discussed the Policy Committee ouster for some minutes and when he seemed to have cooled off a little I gave him a proof of an upcoming article Bill Rusher had written for *National Review's* February 12 edition entitled "Crossroads for the GOP." It elaborated on our strategy of holding the Midwest and mountain states and sweeping the South, and I suggested he read the article carefully when he had a chance. I then proceeded to give him the promised report on the decisions made in Chicago and the message the group had instructed me to carry to him. He listened for about five minutes and then he held up his hand and stopped me.

"Clif," he said, "I'm not a candidate. And I'm not going to be. I have no intention of running for the Presidency."

I managed what was probably a pretty bleak smile. "Well, we thought we would have to draft you."

"Draft, nothin'," he shot back. "I told you I'm not going to run. And I'm telling you now, don't paint me into a corner. It's my political neck and I intend to have something to say about what happens to it."

I saw all our hopes, all our efforts over the past year and a half, disappearing swiftly down the drain, and I guess I got a little edgy myself.

"Senator," I retorted, "I'm not painting you into a corner. You painted yourself there by opening your mouth for the last eight years. You're the leader of the conservative cause in the United States of America, and thousands—millions—of people want you to be their nominee for President. I can't do anything about that and neither can you."

"Well, I'm just not going to run," he repeated. "My wife loves me, but she'd leave me if I ran for this thing."

There wasn't much I could say to that. He was not only slamming the door in our faces but he had Peggy behind him to ram the lock home and throw the key away. After a few more minutes of desultory discussion, I got up, said goodbye with as much cordiality as I could muster, and left. The door shut behind me with a click that had all the finality of that scraping sound that a coffin makes when it is lowered into the grave.

I walked out of the Old Senate Office Building into a cold January wind and hailed a cab at the corner. I had intended to see several more people in Washington that day, but instead I went straight to National Airport and got on the first shuttle flight back to New York.

From LaGuardia I went directly to the Chanin Building and up to Suite 3505. As Rita Bree always puts it in recalling that afternoon, "We were like mourners sitting around a corpse." In fact, the atmosphere became so black that about three o'clock Randy Richardson gave up trying to work at his desk in the corner and left with the remark that "There's no point in staying around and attending a wake." At the door he paused and said softly, "Take my advice, Clif. Never run a reluctant horse."

Bill Rusher came in and asked how the meeting with Goldwater had gone. My reply was short but hardly sweet. "I'm going to give up politics and go back into business."

Rusher, who seldom shows that he is surprised at anything, looked as though he was about to lapse into a state of shock. "What did Goldwater say to our proposal for a draft?" he asked finally.

"It's no use," I replied. "He won't permit a draft. He said he wasn't going to run under any circumstances and that's that."

This was one of the few times I've ever seen Bill Rusher really discouraged. He kept pecking away at possible alternative courses of action, but in the end he came to see that you just couldn't take a grown man by the scruff of the neck and force him to run for President of the United States.

Late in the afternoon Bill Middendorf and Dick Herman, who was in town from Omaha, joined the wake. They commiserated with me for several hours. Middendorf kept saying that we'd find a solution somehow but Dick Herman urged me to tell Goldwater and all the rest to go to hell and just quit. I confess that's exactly what I felt like doing that day. But every time I'd bring myself to the point of deciding to really quit my mind would refuse to let me take that last step. I kept thinking of all those dedicated and enthusiastic people I'd met in the last few months on my seemingly endless travels around the country, and I couldn't bring myself to walk out on them without at least another try. Rusher went on home and Middendorf took the rest of us up to the

Union Club in the East Sixties for dinner to continue our mourning in a more convivial setting.

The next morning I dragged myself back to the office and got on the phone. For two days I stayed with it, calling as many members of the original group as I could reach to inform them of the Senator's apparently irrevocable decision. On Thursday, Stets Coleman flew to New York, and we met with Rusher and Herman at 3505 to determine whether there was any way at all of salvaging this seemingly hopeless situation. Stets volunteered to round up several of Goldwater's friends and beard the reluctant lion in his den. I had little hope it would do much good, but I agreed that it was at least worth the attempt.

Over the next two weeks I began to pick up echoes of something that gave me a clue as to why Goldwater seemed so hostile at our meeting on January 14. Politicians, like all ambitious people, gravitate to power, and ever since the press had trained the bright light of publicity on our efforts after the Chicago meeting a number of them had come swooping in to share the limelight. There will always be people who work on the theory that the only way they can move in on a successful operation is by cutting down the man who appears to be in the driver's seat. Apparently several of this type who had access to Goldwater had done a beautiful hatchet job on one Clif White in the hope of enhancing their own position with the man whose Presidential star was obviously rising. Among other things, they convinced the Senator that I was out to make money off him and, as a matter of fact, was already drawing down a "fabulous" salary for the job I was doing. Goldwater must have known that I wasn't living on air, but I don't think anyone had ever told him how much I was actually making, so he believed them. I had never troubled him with our financial problems because frankly I did not want to emphasize how poor we actually were. And I'm certain he never knew that I had been plowing my family savings into our operation.

The Senator was naturally sensitive about people using his name to build their own bankrolls. I know of several individuals who had done exactly that prior to this period so I began to understand a little better why he might have reacted as he did to me. But I could not fathom why he had barred the door against our whole group and against his own candidacy. If he had asked me to withdraw and turn the operation over to someone else, I would naturally have been disappointed but I would have done so without hesitation. Yet right on through to the convention and on into the 1964 campaign he never once made such a request and in fact told me that he wanted me to stay at several critical junctures.

When I learned about the very efficient hatchet work that had been done on me I was shocked. The people who had executed it had been posing as my close friends and loyal supporters.[1] However, I refrained from any attempt to strike back at them either then or later. You only demean yourself when you start wading into the dismal swamp of recrimination and in the long run you are usually better off ignoring the knives that bitter associates stick in your back. In politics as in any other endeavor, you must come to accept this sort of thing. In-fighting has been one of the favorite pastimes of the human race since the dawn of time and I suspect it will ever be thus.

Bill Rusher wrote the Senator a letter during this period urging him not to let all the effort that we had put into this project go to waste. He got the following reply:

Some things must be brought into perspective that very obviously were not made clear or, if made clear, were not understood in the months that have gone by. The first that I heard of any project was not in connection with my name, but in connection with a possibility of conservative strength at the 1964 convention for any purposes later to be decided upon.

At no time have I committed myself to anyone that I would seek the nomination, nor have I indicated that I would stand still for a draft, even though your letter is the first formal indication that this might be in mind. . . .

Any overt action at this time could do me irreparable damage, because I plan to run for the Senate in 1964 and do not want anything like this to happen. Clif is coming down sometime in the immediate future and you can iron out the areas of misunderstanding.

This new meeting the Senator alluded to had been arranged by Charlie Barr. Charlie, who was as close to Goldwater at this time as anyone in our group, was making a valiant attempt to straighten him out on my role. He set up an appointment for the two of us to see the Senator on Tuesday, February 5, and though I was very reluctant to submit to a repetition of the January 14 fiasco I finally agreed to go.

That Monday I was in Houston giving a speech, since I was still trying to make things look as good as I could, and that night I flew back to Washington to meet Charlie. In his hotel room he told me that he wanted to talk privately with Goldwater before I joined them the following morning. He suspected that there were some things Barry didn't know about our whole operation even though we had faithfully tried to report to him as often and as thoroughly as we could.

The next day I gave Charlie Barr a twenty-minute head start and then hopped a cab up to Capitol Hill. When I got to the Senator's office Edna Coerver told me he was still closeted with Charlie and I waited another ten minutes before they finally called me in.

[1] Needless to say, they were *not* members of my original group.

Charlie looked pretty grim but Goldwater was much more relaxed than he had been the last time. Luckily, there had been no crisis that morning as there had been before our January confrontation. Nonetheless, he didn't give us any reason to rejoice. He said he wanted to stay in the Senate. He couldn't see how he could run for both the Senate and the Presidency, especially in view of his outspoken criticism of Lyndon Johnson for seeking re-election to the Senate from Texas after accepting the Democratic nomination for Vice President in 1960. Besides, he had come to love and respect the Senate as the greatest forum on earth and he would like to stay there just as long as the people of Arizona wanted him to represent them.

I knew he was being entirely sincere in his affection for the Senate. And as late as 1965 I would see further evidence of this. Though I have never quite deciphered the intricate logic involved, Goldwater told one of our former Draft Goldwater Committee officers that the reason he had dumped Dean Burch as Republican National Chairman and backed Ohio's Ray Bliss for that post was simply that he planned to run again for the Senate in 1966 and apparently wanted to mend his national fences before he did.

Several times during our talk that morning he repeated that he definitely did not want to run for President and that he thought Peggy would disown him if he did. But he was not quite so adamant as he had been on January 14. I don't recall that he once said that he *would not run* even if we were able to get the Republican Party to draft him, which had clearly been his position the month before. But he came perilously close to it.

At one point, Charlie got a little blunt. "It's a free country," he told Goldwater. "We're free to draft a candidate if we choose and there isn't much you or anyone else can do about it."

The Senator smiled at this show of spunk. But he shook his head and said something to the effect that we'd find out what he could do about it if we pushed him too far. Wisely, Charlie let the matter drop there. We had agreed the night before not to pressure Goldwater to the point where he would stalk out on us and issue a Sherman-like statement to the press.[2]

We parted cordially with the Senator that morning, but Charlie and I left with the distinct feeling that we had accomplished absolutely nothing.

Outside, Charlie confided that the Senator had been much more vehement about not becoming a candidate during their private talk. "He

[2] General William Tecumseh Sherman, the man who said "War is hell" and proved it in his scorched-earth march through Georgia, was being boomed as a Republican Presidential candidate in 1868 when he cut the ground completely out from under his supporters with the statement: "I will not accept if nominated, and will not serve if elected."

was throwing cold water on the whole idea," Charlie said. "And he was throwing it by the bucketful—with ice cubes in it."

"Well," I observed, trying to find some small consolation for our unsuccessful efforts, "at least he didn't pull a Sherman on us."

Charlie obviously took no comfort from this. "You know what he told me," he shook his head incredulously. "He said: 'You guys are just a bunch of amateurs. I haven't seen one Senator, one Congressman, or one state chairman come out for me yet and I don't see how you can expect me to take this thing seriously.' "

This took me aback. "My God, doesn't he know that we've got a whole battalion of Senators, Congressmen, state chairmen and National Committee members working with us?"

"I told him that," Charlie said glumly. "He knows that Ashbrook and Bruce have at least forty members of the House lined up with them. And we must have at least half a dozen in the Senate besides Tower who will come out at the proper time. Besides, if he read the stories that were splashed all over the papers on that last Chicago meeting he'd know that we also have some very key state chairmen and National Committee people. I went all over that with him. But he still didn't seem impressed."

Over lunch, Charlie and I decided that the time had come to call another meeting of the group. To avoid any possible repetition of the "secret" meeting news leak we agreed that it should be a small meeting with no more than a dozen people attending.

We set the date for Sunday, February 17. Chicago would again be our meeting-place. But I asked Charlie to find another motel where we hadn't met before and where it would be easier to hide out.

I went back to New York that day and started rounding up the gang by phone from 3505. After I reported on the discouraging second session with Goldwater there were several who seemed reluctant to travel a thousand or more miles for yet another meeting. Peter O'Donnell, who would have to come all the way up from Dallas, at first declined my invitation. "I'm not going to attend the wake of the conservative movement," he said. I could hardly blame him for his refusal. But Tad Smith, whom I reached in El Paso right after Peter hung up, said he would try to get Peter to change his mind. I knew that Tad, who had hardly ever missed a meeting since the second one at the Avenue Motel in December 1961, would be there unless the state of Texas suddenly blew up and sank into the Gulf of Mexico.

The twelve days between the February 5 meeting with Goldwater and our parley in Chicago were filled with frantic efforts to hold our embryo organizations in the various states together as more and more people became aware that Goldwater was simply refusing to become a candidate. I was on the phone constantly, reassuring the people who called that we would find a solution somehow, though I have to admit now that I hadn't the faintest idea what the solution might be.

In keeping with my usual procedure of getting to all conferences beforehand so I could get the lay of the land, I flew into Chicago on Saturday night, February 17, and checked in at the O'Hare Inn near the airport. Charlie Barr had reserved a big conference room hidden away at the back of this big, rambling motel and I sat up with Frank Whetstone and several other early arrivals going over the ground we had won and lost since the "secret" meeting.

Early the next morning the members of what had essentially become the overall group's executive committee gathered in the conference room for breakfast. It was a cold, dreary day and we drew the drapes over the big picture windows overlooking the deserted swimming pool, as much to shut out the gloom of the gray skies as to keep any wandering reporters or hired spies from spotting us. In addition to Charlie Barr, Frank Whetstone and myself, the others attending included Bob Matthews and Bob Hughes from Indiana; Tad Smith and Peter O'Donnell from Texas; Congressman Ashbrook from Ohio; Andy Carter, who had flown all the way up from New Mexico; and, of course, the omnipresent Bill Rusher.

It was one of the gloomiest meetings I ever attended. We all sat around in chairs and on the big day beds drinking gallons of coffee and worrying away at our central problem—how to get Goldwater to run. We had already determined that he was our only possible candidate. We were firmly convinced that we could get him nominated if we could only find some way to keep him from blocking us completely. Every possible avenue was explored, but it seemed we had been down all of them before and had run into the same dead ends. Finally, after about an hour, the conversation subsided and there was an unusually long silence. It was broken after several minutes by Bob Hughes' Indiana drawl. "There's only one thing we *can* do," Bob growled. "Let's draft the s.o.b."

"What if he won't let us draft him?" someone asked. "He's already told Clif he wouldn't sit still for a draft."

"We'll draft him anyway," Hughes persisted. "I mean *really* draft him."

We had, of course, skirted this possibility a number of times since my January 14 meeting with the Senator. But for some reason we had never quite come to grips with it. We had all mesmerized ourselves into believing that you just couldn't *force* a man to seek the Presidency. But something in Bob Hughes' determined voice, and the earthy way he expressed his solution, suddenly made us all sit up and ask ourselves if we hadn't been rejecting what was obviously the only way out of our dilemma. Bob's words were like a jockey's spurs ripping the flanks of a tired stallion that was ready to fade in the stretch.

Hughes' idea caught fire at once. It was approved unanimously and we moved immediately to our next problem: how to put together a draft organization that Goldwater would not repudiate forthwith. The solution to this seemed to be to find someone of sufficient stature within the Republican Party to take the chairmanship of the draft committee, at least nominally, someone whom Goldwater wouldn't dare slap down publicly. Most of us thought a fellow United States Senator would be ideal. It was highly unlikely that Goldwater would kick another member of his beloved "club" in the teeth. After running down the list of conservative Republican Senators whom we had reason to believe were leaning toward Goldwater, we finally settled on Peter Dominick, the dynamic new junior Senator from Colorado. We had to admit, however, that we could not count on Dominick's accepting the job. Prudence dictated that we hedge our bet by having at least one alternate waiting in the wings in the event Dominick declined.

Someone came up with the idea of having a co-chairman ready to go with Senator Dominick if he said yes. That way, if Dominick said no, the co-chairman could step into the top spot alone. Either way, the boys insisted that they wanted me to stay in the driver's seat and steer the bandwagon we were building right into San Francisco. I recognized that this sort of ambiguous arrangement could create some problems. But I saw even more clearly that, given Goldwater's present attitude towards me, it had become impossible for F. Clifton White to front a bona fide draft.

During our discussion of possible co-chairmen, Charlie Barr, who was sitting next to Frank Whetstone, whispered something in Frank's ear. A few minutes later I noticed Frank get up and tap Peter O'Donnell on the shoulder. They left the room together and when the door closed behind them Charlie rose and made a strong pitch for Peter to be co-chairman or chairman of the Draft Committee, depending upon Dominick's decision.

Peter was really the obvious choice. He had been elected Republican state chairman of Texas in September and had formally taken over from Tad Smith two months later. An articulate and dedicated conservative, O'Donnell had chalked up an impressive record in a relatively short period in politics. Not yet 39, he had been a Naval officer in World War II. He was a Phi Beta Kappa scholar and had received his master's degree from the University of Pennsylvania's famed Wharton School of Finance. Then he had gone back to Dallas to carry on his family's successful investment business. He entered Republican politics as a precinct chairman in Dallas in 1956. Three years later he was elected chairman of the Dallas County GOP Executive Committee. In 1960 he masterminded the campaign for Nixon in that county, a campaign which resulted in a massive 60,000-vote plurality for the Republican Presidential candidate, the largest plurality Nixon won in any metropolitan area in the country.

A few months later Peter was managing John Tower's campaign for the Senate in Dallas County, and the vote he and his workers turned out helped send Tower to Washington as the first Republican United States Senator from Texas since Reconstruction. After serving a stint as Tower's administrative assistant in Washington, he returned to Texas to manage the campaign for the GOP gubernatorial candidate in 1962, Jack Cox. If it hadn't been for the Cuban missile crisis, Cox probably would have won. As it was, he gathered an unprecedented 46 percent of the vote, the biggest any Texas Republican had ever won in a race for governor since the post-Civil War period. And the Dallas County organization Peter had helped build scored a clean sweep for our party in the same election, sending two Congressmen to Washington and six state legislators to Austin.

As I pointed out that Sunday after Charlie Barr's "nominating speech" for O'Donnell, Peter was the ideal man for the top Draft post. As Republican chairman of the fifth most populous state in the Union, a traditionally Democratic stronghold that was now very decidedly shifting toward the GOP, he commanded the admiration and respect of Republicans everywhere. I couldn't see how Barry Goldwater—or any other leading Republican in his right mind—could possibly thumb his nose at Peter O'Donnell. Without a single dissenting vote, we then elected Peter chairman pro tem and co-chairman of the National Draft Goldwater Committee, which we constituted right then and there.

I asked Charlie Barr to go out and find our new chairman so we could inform him of his election. A moment later Charlie and Frank Whetstone, grinning like a couple of cats who had just swallowed prize canaries, escorted the bewildered O'Donnell back into the room. I went through a little ceremony of formally announcing to Peter the decision of the group's executive committee. He looked somewhat taken aback, which was certainly understandable. I told him that we wanted someone with his organizational ability and political know-how to work with Senator Dominick, if Dominick would agree, and that this was really our only hope of making the whole thing go.

"You mean," said Peter wryly, "that what you want is the Republican state chairman of Texas."

We all laughed at that, and then the door opened and a waiter started bringing in the lunch.

Someone said, "Thank you, Peter, for accepting. Now let's eat." But Peter didn't let us get away with it that easily. As soon as the waiter had departed, he told us that he wasn't at all certain he could accept. He asked for twenty-four hours to think it over before giving his final decision; and he promised to call me the next day when he had made up his mind. However, none of us in that room entertained any doubt whatever that Peter, given this clear call to duty, would accept. The meeting broke up soon after this and we all flew home on a wonderfully comfortable carpet of optimism, confident that if we played our cards right, nothing on earth was going to stop us from nominating and electing Barry Morris Goldwater as the thirty-sixth President of the United States of America.

CHAPTER 13

THE DRAFT BEGINS

"THERE'S NO GAMBLING like politics," Benjamin Disraeli once observed. And if this consummate Conservative Party politician of Victorian England could have been privy to the backstage decisions we made in 1963 to launch the National Draft Goldwater Committee, he would have agreed that our group was about to take one of the biggest gambles in the long history of the game. It was not enough that we faced extremely long odds in attempting to persuade a party that had been controlled by Liberals for twenty-four years to nominate a conservative as its candidate for the Presidency. On top of that we had selected a candidate who not only had no desire to become President, but who had indicated in unmistakable terms that he would not permit the nomination to be forced upon him. Yet life itself is the most gigantic gamble of all, and the best any individual can do is to make certain he has covered the bets on his most important decisions as intelligently and completely as he possibly can before he acts.

We took nearly two months to prepare the public unveiling of the Draft Committee because we wanted to be sure that all our bets *were* covered first. The biggest immediate risk we had to insure against as best we could was an outright repudiation of the Committee by Goldwater. Beyond that we had to put together a Committee which would attract the broadest possible support, both within the Republican Party and from the public at large, to reduce to manageable odds our chances of securing the nomination for the Senator in 1964.

Peter O'Donnell was as good as his word and telephoned me from Dallas within twenty-four hours after the O'Hare Inn meeting. He still seemed a bit reluctant to take on the co-chairmanship because of the press of his duties as state chairman in Texas. But I pointed out that he was the logical man for the job—perhaps the *only* logical man— and after about fifteen minutes he finally agreed to accept if Peter Dominick would serve with him as chairman.

The next step was to get to Senator Dominick. The earliest possible date that O'Donnell and I could jointly work into the Senator's schedule was February 28. Ty Gillespie flew in from Michigan to join us. The three of us trooped into Dominick's office on Capitol Hill at 9:30 that Thursday morning with high hopes that we would sign the Senator up within the hour. But Dominick, a thoughtful, handsome man with a firm grasp of the realities of political life, had several good reasons for turning us down.

The main reason, which certainly made a lot of sense, was that he was a freshman Senator. "I want to be a good Senator," he said quietly. "I want to get established here in the right way. And I don't think that freshman Senators ought to be making Presidents. It's just too presumptuous, and I couldn't blame my colleagues in the Senate for regarding it just that way."

Naturally we were all disappointed. But it was difficult to argue against the logic of Dominick's reasoning and we left without trying to engage him in a lengthy debate. Outside, I turned to O'Donnell and said: "Well, Peter, it's your baby. You'll have to go it alone." He said he wanted another few days to think it over. Dominick's refusal had changed the picture somewhat for O'Donnell and he naturally wanted time to see if he could bring it back into focus.

The following Wednesday, March 6, Peter flew to New York. He came up to 3505 and sat down in one of the beat-up old chairs in front of my desk. He indicated that he had just about made up his mind to go with us but wanted to make it clear that I would have to run the new Draft Committee since it would be impossible for him to devote full time to this thing with his other duties in Texas. If I would go along with the arrangement, he said we could definitely count him in.

I agreed readily and we settled on my title as National Director of the Draft organization. Then we joined Bill Middendorf at the Downtown Association for lunch. Bill had already consented to serve as one of the finance trustees with Stets Coleman and now we talked him into becoming Treasurer of the Draft Committee. A graduate of both Holy Cross and Harvard, Bill Middendorf had taken his master's degree in business administration at N.Y.U. He had gone on from there to a successful career in the investment business and a partnership in a leading Wall Street firm. His interests covered a broad spectrum and he had once been chairman of the Friends of the American Wing of the Metropolitan Museum of Art. More recently he had become involved in politics in Connecticut, where he was now a member of the state Republican Finance Committee. More than once, Bill Middendorf would prove to be the man who stood at the dike and prevented it from crumbling around our ears.

At lunch we discussed other possible officers and I took on the job of rounding out the official staff just as soon as possible. The next day I hopped a plane to Dayton to see Katherine Kennedy Brown, the National Committeewoman from Ohio. We wanted this great lady of the Republican Party to serve as co-chairman and woman's director of the Committee. But when I visited her in her gracious home that day, she felt that a younger woman should have the job.

In the end, with Mrs. Brown's backing, we were able to get Mrs. Ione Harrington, Indiana's able and popular National Committeewoman. Because of her position on the National Committee, there was some doubt whether Ione would publicly identify herself with our Draft Committee. But as it turned out, she had really made her decision more than a year before when she visited former Senator William Knowland in California and told him she was ready to go for Goldwater just as soon as something got moving. Again, we had made what everyone hailed as a logical choice, and as our draft campaign got underway it became more and more apparent, as we shall see in subsequent chapters, that Ione was a tremendous asset not only to our Committee, but to the Republican Party and the whole conservative cause.

The last post we had to fill was that of Secretary. Once again we struck it lucky. Ione had suggested we get a young housewife for this job and we didn't have very far to go from 3505 to find her. Fortunately, Mrs. Judy Fernald was right across the Hudson in Upper Montclair, New Jersey. I had met Judy when she was still a student at Syracuse University and just beginning to get active in the Young Republicans. Now she was the wife of our good friend Dave Fernald, the mother of two children, a past president of the Young Women's Republican Club of New York, and immediate past co-chairman of the National Young Republican Federation.

Several members of the group didn't believe we could get Judy because they were under the impression she was not completely sold on Goldwater. But I thought I had her pegged, and when I phoned to invite her to join the Draft Committee she accepted without hesitation. An attractive young woman with a winning personality, Judy added an even more youthful element to our already youthful official staff. Peter was 38, Bill Middendorf 39, and I was 43. Ione Harrington was somewhat older than the rest of us, but you would never have known this from the pace she set on the campaign trail.

Everyone agreed that the National Draft Goldwater Committee should eventually set up headquarters in Washington. But we were reluctant to commit ourselves to an office lease in the event Goldwater pulled the rug out from under us before we had rolled it out on the floor. We could continue to run the organizational operation out of Suite 3505. But we badly needed a Washington address. This problem was solved nicely with an assist from my old friend Herbert Warburton, a former Congressman from Delaware who had served as general counsel to the Post Office Department during the Eisenhower Administration. Herb set up an appointment for me with the Postmaster in Washington and I went over to the main District of Columbia Post Office and rented a box. I was rather surprised that the Democrats hadn't already taken a lease on this particular box, but they hadn't, and so we now had what we believed then was the most prophetic address in the United States—Post Office Box 1964, Washington, D.C.

On March 27 I sent the following confidential memorandum to our original group and to our other trusted allies around the country:

We have had some unavoidable delays in getting our project launched publicly. However, we are now rapidly approaching the date.

Will those of you who have not yet established in your minds who you think would be the best people to lead this in your respective states . . . please go to work on this immediately and submit those names to me as soon as possible? . . . I hope to send you a press release in the very near future. When you receive it, please make every effort to get it in your local newspapers and on radio and television.

Let me hear from you soon.

The following day, John Ashbrook rose on the floor of the House of Representatives and laid down an artillery barrage designed to soften up our Democratic opponents, who each day were doing a better job of softening themselves up with the voters via what John very aptly termed the Kennedy Administration's "frightening lack of economic horse sense coupled with the inept handling of foreign affairs." Then he accurately forecast the Democrat strategy, namely to build up Nelson Rockefeller in the hope the Republicans would nominate him in 1964.

The reason for this was being whispered more and more around Washington. And only two days before Ashbrook's speech it had broken into the headlines in the *Chicago Tribune*.[1] The story, written by the *Tribune*'s veteran Washington bureau chief, Walter Trohan, was succinctly summed up by the copy editor who wrote the head:

[1] *Chicago Tribune*, March 26, 1963.

KENNEDYS FEAR ONE MAN IN 1964 ELECTION— GOLDWATER

Trohan said that President Kennedy and his brother Bobby, whom he dubbed "the grand vizier of the New Frontier," feared Goldwater because they knew he would carry the South and make strong inroads against them in those Northern states which they had carried by such slim margins in 1960. This was the reason, as Ashbrook noted, that the Democrats were letting it be known that the toughest possible opponent they could face in 1964 was Nelson Rockefeller. If they could sell this line to enough Republicans, they could knock off Goldwater before he could get out of the starting gate at the San Francisco convention. And there was increasing evidence that the line was already being bought by a substantial number of influential Republicans.

Congressional Quarterly published the results of a poll it had taken during the week ending April 3, 1963 that underlined the effectiveness of the Democrat propaganda. Of 1,045 delegates to the 1960 GOP convention who replied to the poll, 673 said they believed Rockefeller was "likeliest to receive" the nomination and only 276 thought it would be Goldwater. But when they were asked whom they personally preferred, the results were quite different—361 for Rockefeller against 481 for Goldwater. Thus the delegates—many of whom would be casting their ballots again at the 1964 convention—clearly *wanted* Goldwater but indicated they would probably support Rockefeller because they still believed his nomination was inevitable. This theory of "inevitability," which had been dealt a severe blow by the publicity given our secret meeting in December, was beginning to gather steam again under the impact of the Democrats' shrewd "we fear Rocky most" campaign. The time had come to give this theory another swift kick. And five days after the *Congressional Quarterly* poll was published that is exactly what we did.

In keeping with my pledge to Bill Miller to play it straight, we first sent letters to him, to the Assistant National Chairman, Mrs. Clare B. Williams, and to all members of the National Committee and the Republican state chairmen. Dated April 5, the following notices went out from 3505 over the signatures of Peter O'Donnell and Ione Harrington:

There will be announced on Monday, April 8, the formation of a National Draft Goldwater Committee. The purpose is to provide the leadership and organizational vehicle for the millions of people in this country who have indicated an interest in the Senator's candidacy.

We know that because of your important position, you feel strongly about the future welfare of the Republican Party. It is imperative that we nominate a candidate for our Party in 1964 who can win. It is our firm conviction that Senator Goldwater is such a candidate, and that you will agree with us as the breadth and depth of support for him becomes apparent. While we have not consulted Senator Goldwater about forming this Committee, we think as the extent of his support develops, that he will accept his call to duty. . . .

If for some reason, you do not agree with us, we still look forward to working with you within the Republican Party to make our Party the majority in 1964. We will appreciate your counsel and advice at all times. Regardless of who secures the nomination . . . we anticipate working with you to defeat the Kennedy Administration in November 1964.

The Sunday after this letter was mailed I checked in at the Mayflower Hotel in Washington. Peter O'Donnell joined me at lunch and we spent the rest of the day preparing for the press conference the following morning. I had already decided to stay out of this because of Goldwater's apparent antipathy toward me at this time. But Peter and I went over together every conceivable question the press might hurl at him.

Early Monday morning, April 8, I went down to the room we had rented at the Mayflower for the press conference to make sure that everything was in order. Then, before the reporters and television cameramen started arriving, I took the elevator back upstairs to my suite. Half an hour later Peter, Ione, and Judy stepped in front of the cameras and assembled members of the fourth estate and the curtain officially went up on the first successful bone fide Presidential nomination draft in the nation's history.

O'Donnell and the two ladies did a magnificent job. Peter read our prepared statement and fielded most of the questions. He announced that the Draft Committee had been formed "to mobilize the tremendous, spontaneous enthusiasm for Senator Goldwater that is sweeping the country."

Peter predicted that in the anticipated race against President Kennedy, Goldwater would sweep the Southern states, carry most of the border states and the Midwest, plus the mountain, East Central and northern New England states. But he stressed that we were not writing off any state or region. "The key to Republican success," he said, "lies in converting a weakness (the paucity of Republican votes in the South) into a strength and becoming a truly national party."

He added that we fully expected a contest for the Republican Presidential nomination. But he pointed out that the 1960 fight for the Democratic nomination had strengthened the Democratic Party by attracting national attention to its candidates and the same would be true of the Republicans in '64. "We must not," he emphasized, "give up the advantages to be derived from a contest simply because cries of party unity are being raised.

"We think the American people want a clear-cut choice between the New Frontier of the Kennedys and Republican principles. . . . The opportunity for providing that choice is now open to the American people by the nomination and election of Senator Goldwater."

During the question period, O'Donnell conceded that we were starting our draft organization on a "shoestring." But he added that the Committee would provide a focus for the already considerable enthusiasm for the Senator's candidacy. This in turn would "generate adequate financial support."

One reporter tried to trace the origin of the Draft Committee to the secret meeting in Chicago. Peter admitted that both he and Ione Harrington had attended the meeting and that tentative plans were made there "to get something moving."[2] He also announced that the Draft Committee would stage a giant rally in Washington on July 4, whether the Senator consented to be there or not.

Asked if our Committee would accept support from the Birch Society, Peter replied that he was "not aware that the John Birch Society endorses candidates or parties."

The reporter protested that Peter had not answered his question. Peter then amplified our policy on the Birch Society, a policy we had previously hammered out: "I would say that we would accept the support of those people who believe in Republican principles of free enterprise, fiscal responsibility, sound government and a firm foreign policy."

"That's what Mr. Rockefeller says, too," the reporter observed.

"We accept his support," quipped Peter with a wry smile.

A gale of laughter swept the ranks of the newsmen, one of several times that Peter elicited friendly laughter. Another came when he was being questioned about the possibility of Goldwater seeking the Presidency and re-election to the Senate simultaneously in 1964. Peter said he didn't think Goldwater would do that. A reporter then asked him if he saw anything wrong with the Senator doing it.

"Yes," replied Peter. "I don't believe that a person should run for two offices at the same time." He paused, and in a pointed reference to Lyndon Johnson, who had done exactly that in 1960, he said he made this observation despite the fact that it might seem he was "speaking out against someone from my own state."

[2] Despite this, the *New York Times,* reporting on the press conference the next day, made it appear as if there was no connection between the Chicago meeting and the Draft Goldwater Committee. The *Times* said, "Another 'draft Goldwater' movement was mounted from Chicago late last winter, but apparently never got far."

When Ione remarked in response to a question that she thought Goldwater had wide appeal to women voters, Peter slyly injected, "As a candidate," and again brought down the house.

At another point, a newsman asked if we intended to pursue the Goldwater draft "regardless of what the Senator may have to say about this."

"Of course, we will be affected by what he says," Peter admitted. "But I'm an optimist and I think he will become a candidate."

"What if we go to him now and he says, 'I want it to stop.' Would you stop?" the reporter persisted.

Adroitly, Peter sidestepped a direct answer. "I would like to see what he says before I would comment on that," he said.

When the press conference ended, Peter, Ione and Judy returned to the suite where I had been hiding. They felt the press had handled them fairly. Now it remained to be seen what the newsmen said in print and over the airwaves—and, more important to us at this juncture, how Senator Goldwater would respond when they cornered him.

Later in the morning we heard that the Senator's office had firmly refused to comment on the Draft Committee and we suffered through some anxious hours. But in the afternoon the reporters tracked Goldwater to a reception given by the Republican Committee of the District of Columbia. Pinned down finally, he replied:

"I am not taking any position on this draft movement. It's their time and their money. But they are going to have to get along without any help from me."

In the Mayflower suite, the four of us breathed a collective sigh of relief. Our gamble had paid off. Goldwater had refused to deliver the knockout punch we had feared so long. We were in business at last!

We could get along without the Senator's help until the time came for a formal announcement of his candidacy. As Peter O'Donnell had told the reporters that day, this date would hopefully be soon after January 1, 1964, a long eight months away. We could put a lot of hay in the barn in those eight months. And with what we had already stored up during the past year and a half, I felt confident that we would have more than enough to start Goldwater down the road towards the Presidential nomination.

That afternoon and evening the birth of the National Draft Goldwater Committee was covered on virtually every radio and television newscast from coast to coast. It was extensively reported in the newspapers, making the front pages in many cities. In some cases follow-up editorials endorsed our move and Goldwater's possible candidacy.

Moreover, the strategy which I had planted at the Chicago meeting in December suddenly blossomed out in newspaper and news magazine stories. The pundits began counting electoral votes for 1964, and each time they placed the big Southern bloc of 128 votes in Goldwater's column and subtracted them from Kennedy's, a Goldwater victory seemed more plausible. Bill Rusher had been the first to expound this plan in print with his "Crossroads for the GOP" article in *National Review,* the same article I had left in proof form with Senator Goldwater during our unfortunate meeting on January 14. Now, in April, a story came out in *U.S. News and World Report* showing a projected 1964 political map of the United States that closely resembled the one I had used in Chicago and that we were getting ready to use again in our first Draft Committee pamphlet.

All this obviously had its effect upon Goldwater. If the Rusher article gave the Senator pause in January, the stories that now began to appear really convinced him to view our efforts more receptively. When he realized that he was not going to be struck dead by the lightning we hurled in his behalf on April 8, his attitude began to change. In an interview with Cabell Phillips, published in the *New York Times* exactly one week after the Draft Committee was announced, he opened the door an inch or two more:

I don't want the nomination. I'm not looking for it. I haven't authorized anybody to look for it for me. *But who can tell what will happen a year from now? A man would be a damn fool to predict with finality what he would do in this unpredictable world.*[3] (Italics added.)

In the little office on the thirty-fifth floor of the Chanin Building the Senator's words, muted and uncertain as they must have sounded to the world, were welcome music to our perhaps oversensitive ears. And the refrain that seeemed to herald Goldwater's active candidacy echoed and re-echoed across the land all through that spring and summer and fall.

To describe the startling change between the mood that prevailed within our group after my January 14 meeting with Goldwater and the mood from April 8 onward, Bill Rusher recently borrowed an analogy from Beethoven. "The only thing I can think of that adequately expresses it," he reminisced, "is the change from the third to the fourth movement of Beethoven's Fifth Symphony. The third movement ends very quietly, down to just a few flickering strings. And then all at once they begin to flicker a little higher, and you get the feeling that something is going to happen. Then, the next thing you know, there's a tremendous crescendo building from the orchestra. That was the difference between January and April of 1963."

[3] *New York Times,* April 15, 1963.

CHAPTER 14

THE WOMEN

THE STORY of what came to be called the Goldwater movement is really the story of countless thousands of Americans who gave themselves unselfishly to a cause, not just to a Presidential campaign. Of all those who devoted themselves so unstintingly to this cause, without any thought whatsoever of possible political rewards, no other single group was as dedicated and hardworking as the women of this country.

Barry Goldwater's appeal to women was not merely that of a handsome, masculine personality whose wit and integrity came across well on television. His appeal called up far deeper responses from his many admirers. It touched the consciences of the nation's mothers and grandmothers, the co-eds, the stenographers, the girls working behind counters in shops and department stores. These women saw in Goldwater a man who would preserve the civilization and society they felt slipping out from under them. The women of America have labored valiantly to help build this society, a society which, if preserved, promises an even brighter future for their children. And many of them perceived the threat to this society long before their husbands and fathers and brothers did. As Victor Hugo once observed, "Men have sight, women insight."

Goldwater's popularity among the women came through with unmistakable clarity in the first big test of the Senator's strength within Republican ranks that followed the official announcement of the National Draft Goldwater Committee. This was the three-day Republican Women's Conference at Washington's Sheraton-Park Hotel held from

Thursday through Saturday, April 25 to 27, 1963. Ione Harrington, Judy Fernald and Rita Bree had been planning for this event even before our April 8 press conference. On April 18 they sent invitations from Suite 3505 to the chairwomen of all the state delegations asking them and the members of their delegations to "stop by for a visit" at the Draft Committee's hospitality room in the Ambassador Suite of the Sheraton-Park.

The girls then rounded up a team of hostesses from among the most prominent Republican women leaders they could recruit. They included Mrs. James A. Reed, widow of the former United States Senator from Missouri; two vice presidents of the National Federation of Republican Women, Mrs. John Camp of Iowa and Mrs. Norman Armitage of South Carolina; two other officers of the Federation, Mrs. Joe Leveton of Oregon, the treasurer, and Mrs. John A. Whitehead, secretary; and two Republican National Committee members, Mrs. Floyd W. Lee of New Mexico and Mrs. Louis G. Rogers of North Carolina.

The night before the conference opened we worked through until nearly 5 A.M., decorating the suite, setting out campaign literature and laying in huge supplies of coffee, chinaware and silver from the hotel kitchen. Just inside the door was a table piled with Goldwater buttons and bumper stickers, our new brochures, and reprints of the *U.S. News* story and Rusher's *National Review* article, "Crossroads for the GOP." We had to scrounge all over Washington for suitable pictures of our candidate. Finally, we found a larger-than-lifesize photograph of him in his Air Force jet pilot's uniform and helmet and placed it right outside the door. No matter which way you looked coming along the third floor corridor there was Barry Goldwater, the dashing pilot, smiling at you in welcome.

Judy and Rita grabbed a few hours' sleep in their room adjoining the suite after I went back to my hotel. But even before they were dressed next morning the women were knocking at the doors trying to get in to beat the anticipated rush when they formally opened at nine o'clock. For the next three days there was a constant human traffic jam in the suite, often overflowing into the corridor outside. Mrs. Reed and the other hostesses poured coffee in an unending stream. It became quite a knotty logistics problem to keep the coffee urns filled and the cups cleaned in order to serve each new wave of women that descended upon the room.

Goldwater never came near the hospitality suite. But when he arrived at the conference on Friday to make a speech following talks by House Leader Charles Halleck and Senate Republican Leader Everett Dirksen, the women went wild. Joseph A. Loftus faithfully reported the scene in the *New York Times* the following day:

Senator Barry Goldwater captured the women's votes before he uttered a word. The women knew he was at the door waiting for the entrance signal, and when the chairman said she had a few announcements first the women moaned their impatience.

When the Presidential possibility finally appeared they whooped it up. The lobby of the Sheraton-Park suggested that the three-day conference was more like a Goldwater party. Every pillar held Goldwater posters with directions to the Draft Goldwater suite.

By contrast, the Rockefeller hospitality room, doubling as the headquarters of the New York women's delegation, appeared deserted and forlorn. It was up one flight of stairs from our Ambassador suite and several of our curious friends poked their heads in the door and came back down to report that except for a few hostesses the Governor's suite was virtually empty.

Although this was a women's conference, a surprising number of Republican males showed up too. Some of the gals brought their husbands up to the suite and a lot of prominent GOP leaders and members of Congress were drawn by the tremendous sustained excitement that prevailed from early morning to past midnight on the third floor. Senator Tower, Congressman Ashbrook, Congressman John Rhodes and a number of our other friends from Capitol Hill came down to visit and I remember that John Tower had one devil of a time extricating himself from the crowd so he could get back to work. Peter O'Donnell and some of the other men who were working with us were there a good part of the time, and I stayed with it all the way through.

Peter and I were engaged in continual conferences with National Committeewomen and others who were prospective delegates to the 1964 convention. We had a small private sitting room off to one side of the suite and the ladies kept coming all day and halfway through the night to pledge us their support. They were all eager to get to work, and the most common remark I recall them making was, "Thank God someone is *doing* something. This is what we've been waiting for all these months."

These were all women not only prominent in the Republican Party but active civic leaders in their communities and states as well. There were scores of people who would listen to them with respect in their home towns and we knew they would carry the message of Goldwater's obvious popularity back with them to thwart the shallow soundings of the professional pundits. They could report to all their friends about our Draft Committee and its plans. And, most important, they could go home with our address, Post Office Box 1964, in their handbags to give them and their friends a central place to communicate with and from which they could obtain campaign materials and guidance.

Even on Saturday afternoon, hours after the conference had officially closed and while we were taking down the decorations, the women kept coming by the suite to say goodbye or introduce a friend we hadn't met before. When we finally shut down, Ione and the girls counted more than a thousand signatures and addresses in their guest books. And on top of that, a great many of these women had dropped donations into the gold-painted water bucket one of the girls had set up on a table by the door. The kind of operation we had at the Sheraton-Park for three days can run into a lot of money and Bill Middendorf had been a little concerned about how we were going to pay for it out of a treasury we had barely started building. But the donations in the bucket were nearly enough to cover all our costs—for the rental of the suite and adjoining rooms, for the decorations, and for what must have been enough coffee to send the Mississippi River flooding over its banks from St. Paul all the way down to New Orleans.

In all my years in politics I had never before seen anything quite like the enthusiasm and spontaneity, the wonderful spirit of hope and dedication, that prevailed at that 1963 Republican Women's Conference. If we had ever entertained any doubts that we had not only a just cause but a potentially winning candidate, they were completely eradicated by those three exhilarating days in April.

When it was over we were all totally, but happily, exhausted. Rita and Judy had literally been captive in the hospitality suite for nearly seventy-two hours. They had had to sneak their meals in their bedroom next door, and I suspect they missed more meals than they ate. Their feet were raw and aching from standing sixteen hours at a stretch, but Judy had taught Rita a new trick. During her two years as national co-chairman of the Young Republicans, Judy had learned that the way to keep your ankles from swelling at marathon political receptions is to change your shoes as often as possible. Both girls had come equipped with several extra pairs so at least they were in better shape than some of the other poor women who hadn't been prepared.

The Women's Conference was an important turning point in our fledgling drive to build momentum for Barry Goldwater's nomination. Until then Nelson Rockefeller had been far ahead in all the polls. We knew that the Senator had the support of thousands of Republican workers. But we were also entirely cognizant of the fact that a majority of these same people were reluctant to declare themselves publicly for a conservative and, as many of them had indicated in the *Congressional Quarterly* poll, they were resigned to accepting a Liberal candidate again in 1964.

This conference marked a vital change in the party workers' attitude. The women were leading the way in the shift from covert approval of Goldwater to overt endorsement. Subterranean support can be helpful.

Indeed, it is sometimes necessary to keep certain supporters of a candidate well hidden even through a first ballot on the convention floor. But too much of this kind of support breeds a reluctance in others to declare themselves and no candidate can hope to be nominated without a preponderance of open and enthusiastic approval from the party workers and the voters they influence.

The contagious enthusiasm generated by the conference spread across the country. Women became the leaders in the Goldwater petition drive. In Minneapolis, Mrs. Marion Pritchard gathered an amazing 750 signatures within a few weeks for the Valley Forge Citizens for Goldwater operation. In Columbus, Ohio, Mrs. Marion Livingston came up with nearly 500 more, and Mrs. Margie B. Ross of Cincinnati accounted for nearly 400. Miss Lorraine D. Yerkes of Palm Beach, Florida, got a group of friends together and in a few days rounded up 500 signatures. Thousands more were obtained in this manner by women in every state.

Ione Harrington and her team did not rest on their laurels after the April conference. For the next six months they traveled constantly, attending every important state and regional Republican women's meeting that was held. Ione, Rita, Judy, Maxine Charlton of Ohio, Patricia Hutar, the Young Republican national co-chairman, and their friends fanned out across the country, winning new Goldwater adherents wherever they went.

I will always be deeply grateful to all these women for the very real sacrifices they made in behalf of our mutual cause. I don't believe Barry Goldwater or any of the people in the small circle around him ever fully realized how much Ione, and the hundreds of other women who helped her, really gave up to promote his candidacy. Mrs. Harrington, who is not a wealthy woman, served all through the campaign without any salary and there were thousands like her who also worked for the Senator as volunteers.

For many months Ione lived out of a suitcase. She rotated her wardrobe, wearing one set of dresses and suits for a week while the other set was being dry-cleaned. Her home is in Chesterton, Indiana, nearly one hundred miles from Chicago's O'Hare Airport, and there were many times when she landed at O'Hare in the middle of the night, walked to her car in the cavernous parking lot, and drove all the way home alone, sometimes through the fierce storms that lash our Midwestern states.

Late one night Ione and Maxine arrived in Scotts Bluff, Nebraska, for a regional Republican women's meeting that was to open the next day. Our Draft Committee in Washington had called ahead that evening to alert the Goldwater chairman in Scotts Bluff that the girls were on their way. But when he met Ione and Maxine at the airport he told them that they were a day early. Until he got the call from Washington, he had been under the impression that they were coming in the following day. He was sorry, but the hotel was filled and he didn't know where they were going to stay. It was midnight by then and he said it was too late to start hunting another place out on the prairie.

Ione and Maxine thought the man was joking and they drove blithely on to the hotel. The night manager verified the Goldwater chairman's report. There were no rooms available. The girls finally convinced him that they weren't fussy about where they stayed. Reluctantly, he put Maxine in some sort of sample room and then took Ione all the way up to the top floor.

There was a tiny room there with just one single bed and the manager warned Ione that she would be staying there at her own risk. The room was leased by the airline they had just flown in on so that the pilots could catch a few hours' sleep between flights. He said they were often in the habit of arriving about two or three o'clock in the morning, and since they had their own keys they usually went straight up to the room. Ione had no choice. She said she would take her chances and if a pilot did show up she would just have to bail out and try to sleep the rest of the night in a chair in the lobby. The manager shrugged, put down her bag and left. Luckily, no one did pop into the room and Ione had it to herself for the rest of the night. But she slept fitfully, half listening for the key in the door that would signal her eviction.

The next morning when Ione and Maxine came downstairs the Goldwater chairman met them for breakfast. He said he had gone ahead on his own and made arrangements for the Goldwater operation at the women's conference. For a hospitality suite, he had rented the ballroom on the main floor.

"Wait till you see it," he said proudly. "It's beautiful. It has an eighty-foot bar, one of the finest in the West. I've hired two bartenders, if you think two will be enough. And the boys are bringing a truckload of liquor in this afternoon."

Neither Ione nor Maxine are Prohibitionists. But they had alarming visions of what the matronly delegates to the conference would think about the wild—and terribly wet—party the Goldwater people were tossing for them in this tough western Nebraska cowtown.

As gently as possible, Ione informed the chairman that the liquor order would have to be canceled. The bartenders wouldn't be serving anything stronger than coffee over that gorgeous eighty-foot bar for the next two days.

The man was horrified. No one in that part of the country would think of serving anything so inhospitable as coffee at a political meeting, he insisted. But Ione stood her ground and when the conference opened coffee, not whisky, was served in the Goldwater ballroom.

Despite this apparent handicap, Ione and Maxine staged a successful smaller edition of the April Washington conference. Their suite was jammed from morning to night with enthusiastic Republican women aching to get to work for Barry Goldwater. Congressman Ed Foreman of Texas flew to Scotts Bluff to make a speech for Goldwater and the delegates welcomed him with prolonged applause and loud cheers.

By the time Ione and Maxine wound up their stay there, it seemed that they had not only won the women's conference but the whole town of Scotts Bluff as well. They captivated everyone at the hotel, and even the manager, the elevator boys, the waitresses and the kitchen help were sporting the big Goldwater buttons the girls pinned on them. When they left, the Goldwater chairman drove them out to the airport. Before he put them on the plane for Denver he confessed that if he hadn't witnessed it, he wouldn't have believed that they could run such a successful party without hard liquor in that part of the world.

Ione and her girls were not only effective campaigners; they were, as I have already indicated, darn good soldiers as well. Uprooted from their homes for weeks on end, barnstorming endlessly about the country, gracefully handling the thousand and one problems that inevitably came up, I never once heard any of them really complain. And sometimes, in the face of unusual stress and very real danger, they were much more calm and courageous than many men I have known. One plane flight with Rita Bree sticks in my mind.

Rita moved down to Washington to serve as Ione's executive assistant early in the summer of 1963. On Friday night, October 4, Rita and Tom Van Sickle, my own executive assistant, were flying back to New York with me on a shuttle flight to attend an important meeting the next morning. Over LaGuardia Airport I became aware that we had been circling for an unusually long time. Finally the pilot's voice came in on the intercom, informing the passengers that when he had lowered the landing gear his instrument panel failed to show that the wheels were locked in place. He said that the landing might be a little rough, as obviously it would be if the wheels collapsed under us when we touched down. He instructed us to fasten our seat belts as tightly as possible, remove our shoes, and bury our heads in the pillows the stewardesses were already passing out.

I remember Rita asking me, just as calmly as if she were seeking advice on how she should have played a bad hand at a bridge party, if there was a chance the plane might catch fire if we crash-landed. I said no, I didn't think so, knowing darn well I was lying in my teeth as I looked past Rita through the window at the wing containing hundreds of gallons of high-octane gasoline.

The pilot's voice came in again, explaining that he was going to take

a pass at the runway at high speed so that if the landing gear did fold up
he could gun the plane back up into the air again. I was sitting in the
middle and I made sure Tom and Rita got their heads down between
their knees with the pillows against the seat backs in front of us. Then
we started to go down. We must have hit that runway at 200 miles an
hour and I felt the plane swerve as one of the tires blew under the
tremendous weight and pressure. But the landing gear held fast and
although we used up all but a few yards of the runway before we
screeched to a halt we landed safely. When I lifted my head out of the
pillow I could see the red lights on the fire trucks and ambulances
swirling around us outside.

Rita sat up, smiling happily, and started to applaud. Everyone on the
plane joined in, paying tribute to the pilot and his crew for bringing us
down in one piece. When we started to get up, Rita asked me why I had
fibbed to her.

"What do you mean?" I asked.

"When I asked about the danger of fire," she smiled. "You knew
darn well we were sitting right on top of the gas tanks in that wing."

Tom and I laughed, and I confessed that it might have gotten a little
warm in there if we hadn't been so lucky.

Rita made her second trip west of the Mississippi that year when she
flew out to Montana with Patricia Hutar for a Republican Women's
Federation meeting. Everywhere they went that summer and fall they
could see, as I could too, that the women of America were rallying to
the Goldwater banner in droves. I remember going through San Francisco before we set up a Goldwater Committee for the state of California.
Mrs. Bobbie Vargis and a group of other ladies took me downtown to
a headquarters they had rented on their own hook and I was amazed to
find about thirty or forty volunteers working away there, mailing out
materials, manning a battery of phones, arranging neighborhood meetings to drum up support for the Senator. They asked me to speak and I
gave a little talk, thanking them for their efforts. After that they always
called me with their problems and we became great friends. When the
Draft Committee was disbanded in January 1964 and the Goldwater for
President Committee took over under Denison Kitchel, these San Francisco women telephoned me and said they were going to wrap up their
operation too. But I managed to convince them that they should stay in
business and they kept on going through the California primary, the
convention, and right down to November 3, 1964.

I feel that some day the women of this country will play a major role
in turning the tide against America's great drift towards socialism. It was
the women who largely saved Brazil in March, 1964 when that country
was teetering on the brink of a Communist dictatorship. In São Paulo

alone, more than 600,000 women, carrying rosaries, prayerbooks and religious banners, staged their historic "March of the Family with God Toward Freedom." And in Rio de Janeiro a petite, 90-pound ex-school-teacher and wife of a retired Army doctor mobilized the Campaign of Women for Democracy which helped convert thousands of people in working-class slums who had previously supported the Communist-riddled regime of President Joao Goulart.

The United States is not now in immediate danger of a Communist takeover and therefore the threat to our freedom is not so apparent. The immeasurably more subtle design of the Fabian Socialists and their unthinking allies who are currently pushing America closer and closer to socialism has thus far gone undetected by the overwhelming majority of the voters. However, the millions of women who backed Barry Gold-water in 1964 may one day re-group and, with the help of other millions of their sisters who have blindly continued to support the Democratic Party, they may yet rescue Constitutional government in this land.

CHAPTER 15

OUT AHEAD

DURING THE FIRST four days of May 1963 a series of events, some predictable, several entirely unforeseen, catapulted Barry Goldwater from the underdog position he still held at the end of April into the unexpected role of front runner for the Republican nomination. There is a question whether this combination of fortuitous incidents alone would have accomplished this feat, a feat which the press and the pollsters professed to find so surprising. Certainly, without the great grassroots groundswell that had been a-building behind the Senator for more than two years, he would not have been in a position to take the lead. Nor would this groundswell have grown large enough to put him out ahead if it had not been for the simmering reaction against the policies of the Kennedy Administration. Then, too, the underground organizational drive which our group had conducted for eighteen months, climaxed by the unveiling of the National Draft Goldwater Committee, undoubtedly helped create a sense of hopeful confidence and serious intent regarding Goldwater's candidacy, particularly among large numbers of Republican leaders and workers.

At the end of April, the Gallup Poll gave Nelson Rockefeller a long lead as the choice of Republican voters for the 1964 Presidential nomination. But he had slipped from 49 per cent in February to 43 per cent and Goldwater was gaining ground even faster than the Governor was losing it—up from 17 per cent in February to 26 per cent in April. The Senator obviously had a long way to go. However, none of the other

GOP hopefuls had moved an inch. George Romney seemed to be trotting on a treadmill, with 13 per cent in both February and April. Bill Scranton had dropped one point to 7 per cent during the same period. And Oregon's Mark Hatfield trailed even farther behind the field with a minuscule 2 per cent.

There was one man Gallup didn't even bother mentioning—Richard M. Nixon. However, I still counted Nixon a formidable factor, despite his defeat in the 1962 gubernatorial contest in California and the bitter farewell to politics he had delivered at his "last press conference." Any man who had won more than 34 million votes in a Presidential election and lost by an almost invisible margin would have to be considered for his party's next nomination. How the pollsters could write him off was beyond me, unless they simply had not included his name on the list of possible candidates for whom they had asked the people to state their preference. I did not believe Goldwater would have to face Nixon in the primaries and state convention contests. But I could foresee a swing toward Nixon if Goldwater and Rockefeller deadlocked the convention and in the early spring of 1963 such a deadlock appeared well within the realm of possibility.

Then, on May 2, Nixon virtually removed himself from contention by announcing that he was giving up residence in California to move to New York where he would enter private law practice. In so doing he abandoned his traditional political base in his home state. Moreover, to further decrease his chances of even getting into the ball game for the 1964 nomination, Nixon moved his family into an apartment at 810 Fifth Avenue—right next door to Governor Rockefeller's Manhattan apartment, the scene of the inexplicable "sellout" of 1960. To many observers this seemed to indicate that Nixon had decided to plant himself firmly in Rockefeller's camp, though I happen to know that this was not the case. The selection of the apartment really had no political overtones. Desirable apartments in midtown New York, particularly along Fifth Avenue, are always at a premium. This one happened to be available, Pat Nixon and their two daughters fell in love with the place and the view of Central Park from the windows, and Dick decided to take it. But to the people who still had hopes of securing the 1964 nomination for Nixon it was an unfortunate move from every standpoint.

Coincidentally, on the same day Nixon disclosed this move, there was a coming-out party for George Romney in Washington. It was held at the home of J. Willard Marriott, the motel chain owner, and my informants told me that Len Hall and his financial lieutenant, Cliff Folger, had helped make the arrangements. It was surely more than just another social affair. It was timed to coincide with a speech Romney was giving at the National Press Club and while he was in town he also held a press conference. During the latter he was at some pains to explain that the Marriotts' party was *not* a launching pad for his candidacy. "I want to keep a purely private affair from turning into something it isn't intended to be," the Governor told reporters. "I am not a candidate for President, and I am not going to become one."

This was the standard disclaimer one might expect fifteen months before a national convention from any man being mentioned as a Presidential possibility. None of us in the Draft Goldwater movement took Romney's statement very seriously. In our book, he was still a force we would have to contend with. A dynamic personality and forthright speaker, George Romney made a big hit with the press corps in Washington on May 2. And we were not the only ones who detected the beginning of a boom for the man who within a brief five months as Governor of Michigan had already established an enviable record by winning a referendum for a new state constitution in a head-on clash with the Democratic machine.[1]

While in Washington, Romney gave our candidate an unintentional boost. Still a little naive in the unfamiliar matters of political protocol and the often absurd significance attached to who-calls-on-whom-and-where, Romney paid a call on Goldwater in the Senator's office on Capitol Hill. It was supposed to be a private meeting, but somehow the reporters got wind of it and were already waiting when Romney arrived. Nothing of any moment was discussed during the meeting but naturally some members of the press thought the Governor was currying favor with Goldwater, particularly since he had requested the appointment in the first place. There was some speculation he might be seeking Goldwater as a Vice-Presidential running mate and this added a new dimension to the incipient boom for Romney.

But to our surprise the Romney boom was immediately deflated by a pot shot from a most unexpected source. The *Detroit News,* Michigan's largest and most influential newspaper, fired off a blistering editorial the day after the Governor's debut in the nation's capital roundly criticizing him for casting covetous glances at the White House when he still had a mountain of problems piled up in a state that had been ruled for many years with hopeless ineptitude by the Democrats. "Come home, George," the editorial ordered, "and let's get on with the chores." Since the *Detroit News* and its editor, Martin Hayden, had been among the first, and certainly the most important, backers of Romney in his gubernatorial race, he obviously could not afford to alienate them. Besides,

---

[1] The vote in the April 1, 1963 referendum on the Michigan Constitution, which Romney had pushed as founder of the Citizens for Michigan organization even before he ran for Governor, was 810,000 to 799,000 in favor of it.

I have no doubt that Romney's prime concern lay in doing a good job for the State of Michigan. So the Governor went home, and though he popped up again briefly in Washington less than a week later for a dinner in honor of Senator Goldwater, thereafter he kept his nose to the legislative grindstone in Michigan, where the difficulties he encountered over tax reform kept him out of national politics for more than a year.

With Romney apparently safely nailed down in Michigan and Nixon out of the way, this left only Rockefeller as a major contender to oppose Goldwater for the nomination. Then, two days after Nixon disclosed his impending move to New York and less than twenty-four hours after the *Detroit News* summoned Romney back to Michigan, came the bombshell that blasted all the New York Governor's carefully laid plans for 1964.

On May 4, Nelson Rockefeller married Mrs. Margaretta Murphy, who a month earlier had divorced her first husband, Dr. James S. Murphy. There had been no prior public announcement of the marriage and it burst upon the political world as a complete surprise.

Oddly enough, I received my first word of Rockefeller's remarriage indirectly from Senator Goldwater's office. Peter O'Donnell had established liaison for our Draft Committee with the Senator through Senator Tower, Congressman John Rhodes and others. By a rather roundabout route, I learned that Rockefeller had telephoned Goldwater at his Washington apartment that Saturday afternoon to personally inform the Senator of his marriage to Happy Murphy less than an hour before.

They had taken their vows at a private ceremony on the 4,000-acre Rockefeller estate in Pocantico Hills along the Hudson near Tarrytown. Goldwater apparently was even more amazed than I was when I later heard the news. He stammered his congratulations to the Governor into the phone and, of course, wished him luck. But when he finally hung up the receiver he just stood there in his living room and shook his head in stunned disbelief. The man he had thought all along had the 1964 nomination all sewed up had just surrendered his claim to the candidacy.

The impact of Rockefeller's remarriage was almost immediately reflected in the polls. George Gallup's organization made a hasty survey of Republican voters within the next few days and Rockefeller's stock had already plummeted 14 points to 29 per cent while Goldwater's zoomed from 26 to 40 per cent. Romney reaped a slight gain too, moving up from 13 to 16 per cent in the period between Gallup's April survey and the one ending May 7. But it was Goldwater who took the commanding lead. As Gallup noted in his analysis of the poll published later in May:

Not since the spring of 1952 (during the Taft-Eisenhower battle) has a conservative Republican been in so strong a position in Gallup Poll surveys as Senator Goldwater is currently. . . . Among the all-important Independent voters, the pattern of a Rockefeller loss and a Goldwater gain parallels the situation among Republican voters since the remarriage.[2]

It was on this note of Goldwater's zooming popularity that my original group gathered for a private meeting at the Mayflower Hotel in Washington the night before the big $1,000-a-plate Republican fundraising testimonial dinner for Senator Goldwater. This was the first meeting at which Peter O'Donnell had presided as chairman, and he handled the transition from my previous chairmanship with grace. We shared the honors equally, each of us giving major reports, and I was slightly embarrassed when the group decided again to give a vote of confidence in my leadership.

Again, we ran down our state-by-state list of potential Goldwater state chairmen. We decided to go ahead with these appointments as quickly as possible, taking care, of course, to make doubly sure we had the right people with us who would not only work hard for the Senator's candidacy but do their utmost wherever possible to preserve Republican unity. Bill Middendorf reported that he was pushing ahead with the fundraising operation, and Stets Coleman had set up a meeting for the following night with George Humphrey, the former Secretary of the Treasury, and several others to see what help they might give us. Although Bill was willing to continue as treasurer of the Draft Committee, he insisted we get someone who was nationally known to serve as finance chairman. We hoped to solve this problem at the meeting with Humphrey and his friends.

The testimonial dinner for Goldwater at the Sheraton-Park the next evening was a huge success, both from our standpoint and from that of the Republican Party at large. The money raised went a long way toward filling the sadly depleted party coffers, and in exiting from the chairmanship of the Senate Republican Campaign Committee Barry proved once again that he was the most successful fundraiser the party had. It also clearly demonstrated that the Senator's popularity lay not only with the rank-and-file as the polls showed, but with the business community as well. This was most important because more and more of the really big contributors had been drifting over to the Democrats. In the wake of President Kennedy's steel pricing victory over U.S. Steel's Roger Blough just a year before, many influential men in the business-financial world had discreetly cast their lot with the Democrats while still maintaining nominal membership in the GOP. It takes strong leaders

[2] George Gallup, Director, American Institute of Public Opinion, Princeton, New Jersey, as published in the *New York Herald-Tribune*, May 26, 1963.

to hold out against the rising threat of federal reprisal against their businesses, and there are not many left who have the guts of a George Humphrey and the relatively small circle of financial men who openly supported Barry Goldwater in 1963-64.

Virtually all the prominent Republican leaders paid public tribute to Barry Goldwater at this dinner. Even Nelson Rockefeller sent a warm and friendly telegram from Venezuela where he was honeymooning with his new wife. George Romney gave a brief speech that was well received, but unluckily he injected the one sour note of the whole evening.

Shortly before the dinner, when Romney entered the Sheraton-Park ballroom, a group of newspaper photographers tried to get him to pose for pictures with Senator Goldwater. Probably because of his experience five days before when reporters besieged him outside Goldwater's Senate office, Romney refused. Within minutes everyone in the place learned that the Governor of Michigan had declined to be photographed with the guest of honor. Romney realized too late that his spur-of-the-moment decision had caused an ungracious tempest in the GOP teapot. He tried to rectify this later on by posing for photographs with the Senator, but some columnists subsequently made a mountain out of this infinitesimal molehill anyway.

Before the dinner got under way, Peter, Bill Middendorf, Stets Coleman, Jerry Milbank and I had headed separately for a room way out in one of the Sheraton-Park's new motel wings where we met with George Humphrey and his friends, Douglas Stewart, the chairman of Quaker Oats, and Charles White, the former chairman of Republic Steel. When we were all assembled, Peter and I both emphasized the necessity of getting substantial financial support so we could build the Draft organization into a powerful force that would be ready to go for Goldwater in every state when we moved into the primary campaigns and state convention battles eight months hence.

It was an impassioned plea, and I thought we were getting through to these gentlemen. But when we had finished speaking, George Humphrey said he didn't think we ought to get going just yet. He thought it was much too early to start and that we really wouldn't need large sums of money until after the first of the year at which time we all hoped Goldwater would become an open candidate. I will confess that this was one of the few times during the whole long struggle that I became irritated and noticeably impatient. I have always had a great respect for George Humphrey. But I was on the verge of asking him how the devil he could say it was too early to start when we all knew that Rockefeller had been going since right after the 1960 election and that the Kennedy clan had begun its work to put Jack in the White House more than four years before and had poured an estimated $10 million into building him toward that goal.

Peter O'Donnell must have detected my annoyance. Just as I was about to read the riot act he got up. "Thank you very much, gentlemen," he said. "We certainly appreciate your coming here and we will keep in touch if we have anything new to report."

I have always been grateful to Peter for interrupting me that night. In the heat of debate, I might very well have alienated George Humphrey and these other men, all of whom proved to be valiant warriors for the Goldwater cause a year later. In retrospect, I can better understand Humphrey's reaction to our plea. Organized pre-convention nominating campaigns are not new to American politics. But they had been given a whole new dimension by the Kennedys, who had started the drive to nominate Jack Kennedy a full four years or more before the 1960 Democratic national convention. Most people did not yet realize that the Kennedys had set a precedent which serious Presidential candidates in both major parties are sorely tempted to follow.

In this age of pollsters and big television build-ups, political strength must be solidified through national organizations, not mere coalitions of local Tammany-type machines. This is far more true for the Republican than for the Democratic Party because the GOP does not control a single really effective big-city machine today. It has some passable, and a few good, organizations in several cities, most notably Dallas and Indianapolis. But none of them exert the ironfisted control of the Democratic bosses in Chicago, New York, Philadelphia, Pittsburgh and the other great metropolitan centers. Thus, increasingly, the GOP will have to learn to live with extra-party national organizations like our Draft Goldwater Committee which draw their strength from the grassroots. If it discourages these organizations, it will not be able to hang in in the battle against the big-city bossism that is tied tightly to the monolithic super-party the "benevolent" welfare-state Democrats have centered in Washington.

Despite the rejection of our appeal to Messrs. Humphrey, White and Stewart at the Sheraton-Park, we managed to keep afloat financially in the months that followed. Peter O'Donnell brought in Frank J. Kovac, the aggressive young former executive director of the Republican National Finance Committee, to serve in a similar capacity with our Draft organization. Kovak did a good job and the money we received through the Goldwater petitions we circulated helped greatly. But it wasn't until the latter days of the Draft phase that we finally secured a finance chairman. He was Daniel C. Gainey, a Minnesota businessman and former Republican national finance chairman. Dan did such a tremendous job in cooperation with Bill Middendorf that he was persuaded to stay on in the Goldwater for President Committee that took over in January 1964. He must share a large part of the credit for lifting the financial burden from our shoulders as we got into the grueling work of the delegate countdown in the six hectic months before the convention.

The morning after the Goldwater dinner, I met with Len Hall in his suite at the Sheraton-Park. Len and I were old friends, going back to my days as a county chairman in upstate New York when he was a Congressman from a district on Long Island. We had traveled on Dwight Eisenhower's campaign train across the state in 1952. Later, when Len was National Chairman, we kept in touch and he had been one of the people who brought me into the Citizens for Nixon-Lodge when he managed Dick Nixon's campaign in 1960. Len was staying neutral in 1963, but I think he had about given up on Nixon's possible candidacy for '64 and I knew there was no love lost between him and Nelson Rockefeller. He had opposed Rockefeller in the three-way fight for the gubernatorial nomination in 1958 when I had managed Walter Mahoney's campaign, and although he had faithfully supported the Governor ever since he was not a member of his establishment. After the party at the Marriotts', the press believed Len was locked in with Romney. But Len Hall is basically a conservative and I had hopes of bringing him over into the Goldwater camp.

My conversation with Len that morning ranged widely over the political landscape. I could see he was impressed by the fresh evidence of Goldwater's increased strength and I hinted that I thought it would be a mistake for any politician to swim against the tide and back Romney or some other dark horse. I told him that our Draft Committee was going to unveil good, solid organizations in every state by the end of the year. He could see we were off and running, and it wasn't necessary to paint any detailed pictures for this old pro.

Len Hall stayed neutral right down to the convention, though I know he was under considerable pressure to throw his support to the "stop Goldwater" movement that was jerry-built in desperation in the spring and early summer of 1964. I don't know if the talks he and I had from time to time had anything to do with his neutral stance. Perhaps Len just wanted to sit that one out anyway. But I was perfectly satisfied with his position of neutrality and we never tried to pressure him into joining our team, though we would have been grateful if he had.

Besides, in May of 1963 it began to be obvious that we would not lack for public support of Barry Goldwater by leading Republicans. Traditionally, most politicians wait at least until the election year before coming out in the open for a Presidential candidate. But with nearly eight months remaining before 1964 bowed in, a number of prominent

GOP figures publicly announced that they would back Barry for the nomination. Among them were Senator John Tower of Texas and Senator Carl T. Curtis of Nebraska.

Tower, of course, had been openly identified as a Goldwater supporter as early as 1961 when he successfully ran for Lyndon Johnson's old seat in the U.S. Senate. But now he began to take to the road to stump for Goldwater's nomination. In May he invaded Nelson Rockefeller's home territory and delivered a persuasive speech for Goldwater before the New York Young Republican Club at Churchill's restaurant in Manhattan's financial district. He stated flatly that the Senator would make the best candidate because he "would state the Republican case most forthrightly." A number of the more than two hundred young people in the audience were proudly wearing Goldwater buttons. Needless to say, Rodman Rockefeller, the Governor's son, was not one of them. But Rodman did venture a question after Tower's speech, asking him how Republicans in Congress could increase their effectiveness and perhaps come up with a more constructive policy to counterbalance Democrat programs.

"We are striving to form a unanimity of policy," Tower replied. "Right now it may seem negative but it is really constructive—like stopping a runaway horse."

The next day Senator Curtis announced his support of Goldwater. "I intend to do everything in my power to bring about his nomination and election," Curtis said. Since he would almost certainly be a delegate to the national convention I put a double check next to his name on my list of potential delegates and added a similar check next to Nebraska, which I now had good reason to hope would produce 16 votes for Goldwater at San Francisco.

When I got back to New York the weekend after our round of meetings in Washington, my wife and I, with our daughter Carole, drove up to the New York Military Academy at Peekskill to visit our son Kip. It was a beautiful Sunday in the Hudson Valley and we had a great day together. It was also one of the last weekends I was able to spend with the whole family for more than a year. The time had come to hit the road again and help the state organizations we had built get ready for their separate debuts as affiliates of the National Draft Goldwater Committee.

On Monday morning I went back to 3505 to start winding things up there before I took off. We had found an office in Washington, at 1025 Connecticut Avenue off Farragut Square, and after June 1 this would be our Draft headquarters. Even after the announcement of the Draft Committee in early April, my New York office had continued to be the focal point of our organization for nearly two more months. Jim Day and our other friends in Washington picked up the mail each day at Post Office Box 1964 and sent it to us on a plane. Thus, all of the early correspondence and the petitions were funneled into 3505, and all of the plans and strategy continued to radiate out from there.

But now it was time to move. Suite 3505 had served its purpose. I refused to give it up entirely, although some of the other officers of the National Draft Committee urged me to do so many times. Later on, I was glad we kept it. Our rather shabby little hideout continued to serve as the communications center for the Goldwater movement in New York, New Jersey and Connecticut. Rita Bree left to join Ione Harrington in Washington but Mrs. Patricia Sprague, the charming former president of the Young Women's Republican Club of New York, took over the office and ran it with dedicated efficiency on a volunteer basis. I became a rather shadowy figure to Mrs. Sprague and her volunteers. Although they fielded my phone calls and handled a good deal of my correspondence they seldom saw me. I remember returning after one particularly long absence and receiving a loud round of cheers as I entered.

Psychologically, it was important to keep 3505 operating. It was a little island of conservative political action in an otherwise vast sea of regimented Liberalism. Our allies in megalopolis were cheered by the knowledge that the lights burning long after dark high up on the face of the Chanin Building above fabled Forty-second Street represented a lonely beacon for our cause in the nation's largest city.

CHAPTER 16

IN ORBIT

ONE OF THE STRONGEST issues Barry Goldwater had going for him in the spring and early summer of 1963 was Cuba. The flimsy façade that had shielded the actual outcome of President Kennedy's allegedly firm stand on Cuba from the American voters during the October 1962 missile crisis was beginning to show alarming holes. The Administration was still claiming the "eyeball to eyeball" confrontation with Russia's Premier Khrushchev as a major victory in the Cold War. But many of the same voters who had cast their ballots for the Democrats in the belief they were standing behind their President during a national crisis saw now that the "victory" was a hollow one at best.

Russian troops and technicians were still based in Cuba in large numbers. The Communists continued to use the island as headquarters for their massive infiltration of Latin America. Cuban freedom fighters attempting to mount guerilla warfare against Castro were turned back in their boats by United States naval patrols. And in May, the Senate Preparedness Subcommittee, dominated of course by Democrats, issued a thoughful report which disclosed that America's top intelligence officials could *not* guarantee that Soviet missiles had been removed from Cuba because the Administration had surrendered its initial insistence on on-site inspection by reliable observers.[1]

---

[1] There have been many subsequent reports to substantiate the Subcommittee's grounds for doubt. One such report came in August 1964 from Fidel Castro's sister Juanita. After she defected from her brother's Communist

More and more there were guarded reports of a "deal" between Kennedy and Khrushchev. The President was said to have promised the Russians a privileged sanctuary on Cuba and the dismantling of U.S. missile bases abroad in exchange for the evacuation of Russian missiles on Cuba. Substance was given these reports when the United States did in fact dismantle its Thor and Jupiter intermediate range missile bases in Turkey, Italy and the United Kingdom. Moreover, the halting by U.S. warships of the vest-pocket invasions by anti-Castro guerillas lent added credence to the "privileged sanctuary" aspect of the reported deal.

The day before we unveiled the National Draft Goldwater Committee, Senator Goldwater issued an incisive indictment of the Administration's Cuban policy during a national television program.[2] He accused Kennedy of "doing everything in his power" to keep the flag of the Cuban exiles "from ever flying over Cuba again." He said the United States should support the exile invaders and clamp a tight economic blockade on the Communist bastion in the Caribbean. If these steps failed to oust Castro and the Russians from their island fortress, he proposed a "multilateral effort" with the other members of the Organization of American States to drive them out by force. He indicated, however, that he didn't have much hope that this would occur because he felt the Administration was "too frightened" to hold to a firm policy on Cuba.

Goldwater received some surprising support for his stand. The late Senator Clair Engle of California, a Liberal Democrat, did not agree with all the points Goldwater made. He said diplomatic efforts should first be stepped up to get the Soviet troops off the island. But if these efforts failed, Engle added, the United States should "just go in there and get them."

Nelson Rockefeller, in an April 9 news conference in Washington, hinted broadly that he was afraid the Kennedy Administration was guilty of following an appeasement policy with regard to Cuba although he "hoped it wasn't." Asked if he thought there was a "possibility of some secret arrangement between the President and Mr. Khrushchev on the matter of holding back the freedom fighters in Cuba," the Governor echoed the uncertainty that was beginning to trouble many citizens.

"Well," he replied cautiously, "I have no idea. But maybe Mr. Khrushchev will release some more of the correspondence and we will find out."

Rockefeller took some lumps from segments of the press for these remarks. The *Washington Star* accused him of "trying to smear the

---

fortress, Juanita Castro told a Brazilian newsman, "In Cuba there are long range ballistic missiles which are well camouflaged."

[2] ABC's "Issues and Answers," April 7, 1963.

President by expressing a 'hope' that he is not an appeaser." And the *New York Herald-Tribune* suggested in an editorial that he was engaging "in a contest with Senator Goldwater to see who can throw the most matches into the most inflammable material."

The *Herald-Tribune*'s appraisal, which was probably made before the editorial writer had enough hard evidence on hand about the Cuban situation, was manifestly unfair to both Goldwater and Rockefeller. No doubt the Governor was purposely cultivating conservative support in those days as the editorial implied. But I doubt if that was his motive in this instance. A careful study of his statements and writings should convince the most hardshelled anti-Rockefellerite that the Governor has been reasonably consistent in supporting a firm U.S. policy in foreign affairs. And, in essence, that was what he was doing when he criticized the Administration for its vacillation on Cuba.

To the nation at large, however, it was Barry Goldwater who was identified as the leading spokesman for the fast-growing group, in and out of government, who felt the national security was being jeopardized by John F. Kennedy's Cuba policy. This accounted in no small measure for the vast number of rank-and-file Democrats who began during this period to support our Draft Goldwater Committee and the other Goldwater groups that suddenly started proliferating across the country.

In Texas, Peter O'Donnell and his friends conducted a series of highly successful "resignation rallies." During these meetings thousands of disenchanted Democrats renounced the party that had deserted them and pledged themselves to the Republican Party by promising to switch their registration. But the large majority of the Democrat disaffections elsewhere were accomplished quietly, in most cases by individuals who didn't even bother to change their party affiliation. In Pittsburgh, a beauty shop owner who had been a lifelong Democrat secured nearly 1,000 signatures on petitions urging Goldwater to run for President. He confessed that he converted many of his customers while they were captives under his dryers and then sent them out armed with petition blanks to help him build his signature total.

As soon as the Draft Committee was announced we gave top priority to these petitions. Peter O'Donnell moved fast and had more than a million printed within the first few weeks. Each petition had a space for ten signatures, and unlike those circulated by other Goldwater organizations, we asked $1.00 from each signer. There was a psychological, as well as a financial, benefit that accrued from this. If a person was willing to donate money, even such a small sum, to the Goldwater movement, the chances were pretty good that he was not signing merely to accommodate a friend. More likely he was committed, at least to some degree, to the conservative cause the Senator represented. This was proved later on when we got into the primary campaigns. The names of the overwhelming majority of our vast volunteer army came originally from the more than one million signatures accumulated on petitions.

We recognized at the outset of the Draft movement that the other, smaller Goldwater groups that had already started springing up could present a major problem. Most of them were formed by political amateurs, but they were hard-working amateurs and their enthusiasm could be channeled into useful work that would produce delegates and votes. Unfortunately the leaders of these groups, with some notable exceptions, chose to regard themselves as competitors rather than allies of the National Draft Goldwater Committee.

Shortly after the Draft Committee was unveiled I flew to Phoenix to negotiate with the leaders of a group that called themselves the national "Goldwater for President Committee." This group was preparing to issue charters to local Goldwater clubs all over the country. Since they were based in the Senator's home town, many people in other states assumed that the Phoenix committee had Goldwater's personal blessing and the committee did little to disabuse them of this notion.

There were many fine people connected with this Phoenix operation. But none of them had any real experience in national politics. Some were alleged to be members of the John Birch Society. When word of this got out, they reorganized and a Democrat named Jay O'Malley took over the helm.

It was with O'Malley's predecessors that I conferred in April 1963. I warned them that any public identification of the Senator's backers with the Birch Society could do irreparable harm to his candidacy. We had already established a hard-and-fast policy within the Draft Goldwater Committee not to appoint members of the Society to leadership positions at the national, state, or local levels. It was not that we believed the Society was in some way "subversive" or "Fascist." For one thing, a true Fascist believes in a strong central government. As nearly as I can tell, the Birchers are vehemently opposed to strong central government.

However, President Kennedy, apparently inspired by the notorious Reuther Memorandum outlining an all-out attack on the "right wing," had lashed out at "extremists." He left little doubt that one of the groups he was aiming at was the John Birch Society. The mass media had immediately picked up the theme, and indeed some segments of the press were pushing it even before he did. For a time, much of the press seemed to regard the Birchers as a far greater threat to America than the Communists. Newspapers, magazines and TV screens were filled with exposés of the Birch Society.

The Society's founder and leader, Robert Welch, had invited much of this criticism himself by making the ridiculous, indeed libelous, charge that former President Eisenhower was a conscious tool of the Communist conspiracy.

In fairness, however, I must state that we had much less difficulty with Birch Society people than many of our group anticipated. As the Goldwater campaign progressed, most of them seemed to accept quietly the fact that any public display of Birch support for the Senator would hurt his chances. When they worked for him, as many of them did, they did so unobtrusively and made no attempt to capture leadership posts so far as I could tell.

At the time, I thought the meeting with the Goldwater group in Phoenix had accomplished nothing. Perhaps I was right. But not long after this most of the Birch Society people resigned from the group and O'Malley assumed the leadership. We never were able to work out a fully cooperative arrangement with him, but his reorganized committee did a good job at the grassroots, particularly in the Western states.

Another group we tried to bring under the Draft Committee tent was the "Citizens for Goldwater" group headquartered at Valley Forge, Pennsylvania. It was run by a young insurance executive, Robert Yarnall, who had considerable help from his attractive and capable wife Polly. Bob Yarnall had access to a printing press and he had thousands of Goldwater petitions printed under the imprint of his Citizens organization. There were spaces for fifty names on these petitions and the signers were not required to contribute anything.

At the peak of the disillusionment with the Kennedy Administration's Cuba policy, the Yarnalls had gathered in many thousands of signatures, particularly in traditionally Democratic areas of Pennsylvania. I wanted to get these names and addresses for our Draft Committee and also see if we could somehow mesh gears with their mailing operation. John McClatchey invited me up to his home near Philadelphia and the Yarnalls came over to see us. I met with Bob Yarnall a number of times after that, and ultimately he promised to deliver his lists to our Washington office in exchange for several thousand dollars he needed to get the names off the petitions and into a card file. I don't believe we ever did get all the names, but he sent us a large number and we reached many people through this Valley Forge list.

The main thing I wanted to do with regard to these other Goldwater groups was to get them working with us so we would all be going in the same direction and not duplicating efforts. It caused confusion when two or three Goldwater organizations popped up in one conmmunity, all claiming to be *the* group and displaying a charter from a "national office" to prove it. I spent an unconscionable amount of time trying to get them to at least accept the Draft Committee's guidance, but with only limited success.

The month of May, when Goldwater took the lead in the polls over Rockefeller, saw merely the first stage of what then seemed to be his orbital flight toward the White House. By June the Goldwater movement was bustin' out all over like a brilliant galaxy exploding in space. Early in the month I flew to the West Coast, working my way northward from Los Angeles to San Francisco, Portland and Seattle. Everywhere people were clamoring to climb aboard our Draft Committee. We did not want to dampen their enthusiasm, of course, but in some cases it was necessary to urge them to slow down just a little so we could put together the best state draft organizations possible before we gave them a full head of steam.

I caught a jet back from the Coast in time for the formal opening of our new national Draft office in Washington. For two months I had been trying to keep out of the public eye as much as possible so as not to inhibit the Senator's growing feeling of friendliness toward the Draft Committee. I had not seen him since our disappointing February 5 meeting with Charlie Barr. And I had no intention of attempting to see him until he wanted to see me.

But my attempt to stay out of the limelight again proved futile. The publicity explosion after the December secret meeting in Chicago made it all but impossible for me to keep the press entirely off my trail. As early as April 30 Richard Bergholz, political writer for the *Los Angeles Times*, wrote a lengthy story about my travels and activities, including what he called "a series of hush-hush meetings" with Goldwater supporters in Phoenix. How Dick Bergholz found out about my attempt to get the Phoenix group under the Draft tent I will probably never know, but it is of course a political reporter's job to know what's going on on his beat and you can waste a lot of energy tracking down his sources, so it was an exercise I seldom indulged in. Other stories followed his, and by June we all knew it was becoming ridiculous to try to hide me any longer. When the second Draft Committee brochure was published about this time my photograph was prominently displayed along with Peter O'Donnell's and pictures of the other officers of the organization. And it was decided that I should be on hand to meet the press when we opened the Washington office on Monday, June 10.

We had actually moved into this office ten days earlier. But it took us that long to get it into presentable shape for the opening, although the staff and a large group of volunteers were working sixteen or more hours a day while the renovation went on.

The opening was quite a gay affair. Ione, Peter and I shared the ribbon-cutting ceremonies, and the press and television people were present to duly record the event. We had a little party and took the visitors on a tour of the suite and got quite a lot of newspaper and TV coverage out of it. I had to laugh the next day when I read some of the stories. A few of the reporters gave somewhat colored accounts of our "lavish, $1,000-a-month suite" and although by comparison with Suite 3505, which none of these newsmen had ever seen, our Connecticut Avenue diggings probably would have appeared lavish indeed, by any other standard they were in fact rather austere. The suite was on the ground floor of a venerable apartment house that a few years before had been converted into an office building that has since been torn down. I remember we were always having trouble with the plumbing, and once the pipes in the ceiling burst and drenched the room where several secretaries worked. But they were rather large offices, though they became crowded as we expanded, and they were conveniently located in downtown Washington between busy Farragut Square and the Mayflower Hotel. Jim Day found the place for us and it worked out so well that we kept this office operating right through to November 3, 1964. Perhaps it was a coincidence, but in the preconvention days the national Rockefeller for President office opened across the street and after the conventions the Democrats moved their Scientists and Engineers for Johnson-Humphrey headquarters into the offices vacated by Rockefeller's team.

The same week we opened the Washington office, Goldwater's nomination stock, which had been rising steadily since early May, took another sudden spurt upward. Dick Nixon, cornered on June 12 at Idlewild Airport just before he and his family boarded a plane for a long European vacation, conceded that Barry Goldwater was way out front. "Among professional politicians, Senator Goldwater has the lead, and they have more influence on nominations than anyone else," Nixon said. This was a rather left-handed concession, which implied that Goldwater might still lack popular support. But as Nixon knows well, the professionals never get behind a candidate unless they have taken some careful soundings among the rank-and-file.

That same day Senator Goldwater met former President Eisenhower at a Washington luncheon. The event, honoring Eisenhower, was sponsored by the Effective Citizens Organization (ECO) which a group of us had formed in the mid-1950's to get more businessmen interested in politics and was now headed nationally by Charlie Barr. Ike grinned as he shook Barry's hand warmly and remarked, "Maybe this will stop those reports that I'm trying to put a knife in your back."

The following afternoon the GOP leaders of five Northeastern states and the District of Columbia began a two-day meeting at Cherry Hill, New Jersey, and when it ended a *New York Times* headline proclaimed: GOLDWATER GAINING IN NORTHEAST, REPUBLICAN STATE CHAIRMEN SAY.[3] According to the *Times*, the chairmen made no

[3] *New York Times*, June 15, 1963.

secret of the fact that the Senator "has gained considerable support" in their states. Even Craig Truax of Pennsylvania admitted that Goldwater had won "many friends" in the Keystone State.

David Broder, then the political writer of the *Washington Star* (and now on the *Washington Post*), journeyed to Hershey, Pennsylvania that week to cover a Republican workshop attended mostly by other Easterners. After talking with many of the people present, Broder reported:

"A surprising number—considering the scarcity of strong conservatives in the group—indicated a willingness, if not an eagerness, to see the nomination go to Senator Goldwater."

By contrast, Broder wrote, the attitude of the party leaders and workers at the workshop towards Bill Scranton and George Romney "was one of apathy."

A few hours before the Cherry Hill meeting convened, Charlie Barr escorted Hayes Robertson, the powerful GOP chairman of Cook County (Chicago), Illinois, to a private meeting with Senator Goldwater in Washington. When the press got wind of it more headlines followed. The Goldwater bandwagon was obviously shifting into high gear. *Time,* in its June 14 issue, stated flatly, "If the Republican national convention were to be held today, Goldwater would almost certainly be its presidential nominee."

Basking in the warm spotlight of predominately favorable publicity, Barry was beginning to thaw. He was still saying it was "too early" to decide whether he would run, but he told a *Time* reporter, "There are a lot of things I have to consider." If he refused to seek the Presidency, he said, "I have to face the question of whether I'm letting down conservatives, particularly the young people."

On June 17 he gave further indication that he had moved a long, long way from the adamant position he had taken when I had last talked with him on February 5. In an interview with a United Press International newsman he said:

I don't want this nomination but it may be forced on me. If I'm put in the position where I have to take it, I won't be a reluctant tiger. I'll get out and fight.

With the Senator now holding such a commanding lead and obviously warming to the idea of his candidacy, I decided the time had come to start doing some spadework for the primary election battles that lay ahead. A few days after we opened the Draft Committee office in Washington I flew to New Hampshire and spent two days traveling around the state meeting with Republican leaders. In Concord I had dinner with Doloris Bridges, the attractive and charming widow of the late Senator Styles Bridges. We hoped to get Doloris as a Goldwater delegate in the primary.

I also visited Bill King, the GOP state chairman. I told Bill that we would do nothing to add to the already heavy load of problems he had inherited from the bloody state primary battles a year before. He indicated he would have to stay neutral and I understood his position completely. There was no point in pouring salt on old wounds by forcing commitments in New Hampshire.

The Goldwater clubs that had been organized in the state for some time were straining at the bit to start the primary campaign now, a full eight months before the March 10 election. Tom Phillips, a Dartmouth student who headed the Young Americans for Freedom in New Hampshire, arranged a meeting with the club leaders who wanted to announce a state Goldwater committee. I told them that we had a good chance of getting Senator Norris Cotton, a moderate Republican and the party's strongest votegetter in the state, to head up the Goldwater forces in the primary, but we would not make any formal move until Cotton was ready to go. In the meantime, I urged them to concentrate on building strong town and precinct organizations.

One of the club leaders protested that they had already done that. I said fine, but could he show me a card file of every voter in his own township that indicated whether each one was pro-Goldwater, anti-Goldwater, for some other candidate, or what-have-you? He said no, but that they were working on that now. I said that this was great, and when they had such a file for every town and city in New Hampshire to let me know and we would announce a state Draft Goldwater Committee. I didn't want to discourage them, but they were relative newcomers to politics. They had a lot more homework to do and I wanted to give them some practical assignments. We never did get a statewide card file, although I'm sure some of these people did go home and start to work on one for their own towns.

At the end of the following week I went to Denver, where the Republican National Committee was meeting for the first time since Barry Goldwater took over the lead. Our Draft Committee threw a party at the Brown Hotel for Senator John Tower, who was acting as a sort of ex-officio stand-in for Goldwater. The suite was so packed with people the party overflowed into the corridor outside. At one point when I left for a few minutes I literally couldn't get back into the room when I returned.

The Rockefeller team, under George Hinman and Fred Young, an old friend of mine who had recently been named state chairman of New York, also had a party going. I dropped by for a visit and I was at once elated and somehow saddened by the aura of defeat that permeated their suite. George Hinman even told a reporter, "I am not depressed about the current situation. I don't think we can appraise it now." But it was perfectly obvious that Rockefeller's men had good reason to be depressed.

Peter O'Donnell attended a special meeting of the GOP state chairmen held in conjunction with the National Committee Conference. When he emerged from the meeting the reporters asked him if he had detected much Goldwater sentiment. Peter replied that there was widespread support for the Senator among the state chairmen and somehow his remarks were mistakenly interpreted as meaning that Goldwater's candidacy had been formally discussed in the meeting.

The next morning Ray Bliss of Ohio, who had presided as chairman, rose at the National Committee meeting and rapped Peter's knuckles for suggesting that the state chairmen had discussed Presidential candidates. Peter, who was not in the room at the time, had not meant to suggest anything of the kind. But as one newsman later noted, Bliss was rebuking O'Donnell with "unusual vehemence," and I got up to go find Peter so he could straighten things out.[4]

On the way out, I bumped into John Tower. I told him what had happened and he said he would reply for Peter in case I couldn't get him down there fast enough. When Bliss finished speaking, Tower gave him our answer and later on in the day Peter set the record straight too. He said he had only been referring to his own personal discussions with his fellow state chairmen when he said many of them were leaning towards Goldwater. If anyone doubted this was true, all he had to do was ask the chairmen themselves.

There was a move made in Denver to begin organizing a block of convention delegates around the favorite-son candidacy of Senator Gordon Allott of Colorado. This may not have been Senator Allott's idea. It was probably Jean Tool's, and Tool, the Colorado state Republican chairman, was a staunch Rockefeller man. However, we quietly managed to nip the plan in the bud. It proved to be one of the many grossly inflated trial balloons that were quickly deflated by the soaring rocket of Goldwater popularity.

This caper, however, was the beginning of a spreading favorite-son movement which Jack Steele of the Scripps-Howard newspapers correctly called "an effort to slow down a Republican stampede to Goldwater." But Steele, whose apparent personal prejudice against Goldwater showed more plainly as the 1964 campaign proceeded, was way off base when he wrote that the movement "unquestionably has slowed the

[4] Jack Steele, *New York World Telegram and Sun,* June 24, 1963.

Goldwater boom." It had no effect whatever, despite the fact that Ray Bliss, Jean Tool and some other powerful Republican chieftains pushed hard for it at Denver, and a few days later Governor Scranton eagerly tossed his hat into the favorite-son ring.

Columnist Robert Novak, who covered the Denver meeting, was one of the first to detect what was happening within the GOP. In his joint column with Rowland Evans on June 24, Novak wrote:

The fact that Senator Barry Goldwater is so far in front for the Republican Presidential nomination is proof of a little-understood transformation in the party's power structure.

This transformation, exhibited dramatically here during last week's Republican National Committee meeting, is nothing less than a quiet revolt. The aggressive post-war club of conservative young Republicans from the small states of the West and South are seizing power, displacing the Eastern party chiefs who have dictated Republican policy and candidates for a generation.

It was some time before the press in general confirmed this assessment. Many newsmen still didn't grasp the meaning of the new movement even at San Francisco. Or, perhaps, they simply didn't want to grasp it.

CHAPTER 17

THE MODERATE EXTREMISTS

FOR A DECADE and a half the Young Republicans have played a vital role in the affairs of the senior GOP. Unlike the Young Democrat organization, which has always been a pallid and impotent tool of the Democratic National Committee, the Young Republicans are essentially independent. Instead of parroting a line laid down by the parent party, they have consistently exerted a powerful influence upon Republican policies and principles. Many of today's GOP leaders came up through the YRs and thus have a proper respect for the views of the younger people who have followed them into YR leadership positions.

Moreover, the last three Republican Presidential candidates—Dwight Eisenhower, Richard Nixon and Barry Goldwater—all proved themselves first in tests within the Young Republican organization before they received their nominations. This is not to say that any one of them would have been denied the nomination if they had not passed these tests, but there is little doubt that they would have found the going substantially more difficult if they had failed.

The election of a friendly YR national chairman at the biennial convention held the year before the Republican national convention has become a tell-tale barometer for GOP Presidential nominations. In 1951 my friend Herbert Warburton ran as an ally of the forces that later backed Eisenhower. Herb defeated a **YR** Taft candidate, thereby handing the Ohio Senator his first defeat in a major pre-national convention test. In 1959 Ned Cushing, who later became one of the steadfast members of our original Goldwater group, campaigned for **YR** national chairman as a Nixon supporter, warding off a bid by the Rockefeller forces to seize control of the Young Republicans and start a Presidential boom for the New York Governor. And in 1963, Goldwater partisan Donald E. (Buz) Lukens and his backers helped pave the way for the Senator's 1964 nomination by whipping a desperate and frenzied gang that was trying to bolster Rockefeller's sagging political fortunes.

The YR national convention held in San Francisco the last week of June 1963 proved prophetic in many ways. For one thing, it gave us an accurate foretaste of the desperation tactics the so-called moderate wing of the GOP would indulge in before, during and after the 1964 nominating convention. For another, it revealed once again the alarming predilection of powerful segments of the press to completely distort any event in a manner which makes conservatives appear like uncivilized thugs while casting the "moderates" in the role of gentlemanly martyrs. And finally, it foreshadowed the tragic deepening of the suicidal split within the Republican Party that led to Lyndon Johnson's landslide victory over Barry Goldwater on November 3, 1964.

The stage was set for the unseemly series of events that embarrassed the whole Republican Party in San Francisco from June 25-28, 1963 by the incumbent YR national chairman, Leonard Nadasdy, a press agent from Wayzata, Minnesota, elected in 1961 and widely regarded at that time as a Nixon supporter. Nadasdy had been jockeying for two years to keep control of the national YRs for his Liberal friends in the senior party. He realized that he could not hope to accomplish this in a head-on clash with the predominantly conservative forces in the YRs. He freely admitted beforehand that a poll of the more than 1,400 delegates and alternates to the San Francisco YR conclave would show that at least 75 per cent were for Senator Goldwater. So he seized upon the ploy of running an avowed conservative, whom he believed his Liberal peers could control, to succeed him as national chairman.

The heir apparent Nadasdy picked was Charles R. McDevitt, 31, a lawyer from Boise, Idaho. McDevitt had been Nadasdy's campaign manager at the 1961 YR convention in Minneapolis and since then had served as Nadasdy's appointed ally on the YR National Federation's executive committee. Nonetheless, with an eye towards the 1963 contest for chairman, McDevitt had continued to flaunt his "conservatism" by openly supporting such proposals as the Liberty Amendment, which seeks to abolish the income tax and remove the federal government from all areas where it is competing with private business.

I had a chance to size up McDevitt on May 10 when I had breakfast with him in Washington before my meeting with Len Hall. He seemed a nice enough chap, and it may be that he really was a conservative. But it was perfectly obvious that he was mesmerized by Nadasdy and his "moderates."

Edward Failor of Iowa and some of my other Young Republican friends quickly saw through Nadasdy's plan. They picked Buz Lukens, a native of Ohio who then headed the District of Columbia YR organization, to run against McDevitt. For several months they had been grooming Lukens for the race, but they had encountered some difficulty in getting the California YRs, headed by Robert Gaston, to go along with Lukens' candidacy. Gaston wanted a favorite-son candidate from California, more specifically himself. Without the support of Gaston's big California delegation, Lukens went into the YR convention a decided underdog.

The chances are that McDevitt would have defeated Lukens handily had it not been for the unbelievably crude tactics Leonard Nadasdy employed at the convention in his attempt to shove his candidate down the throats of the delegates. As so often happens when authoritarian methods are used, people rebelled against them and Nadasdy's carefully laid plans backfired. Ironically, however, many of the news accounts of the convention made a martyr of the man who had engineered his own and his candidate's downfall.

The "nightmare" that Nadasdy later told reporters he had gone through at San Francisco began on Wednesday, June 26, during the contest to select a national chairman of the college division of the YRs. M. Stanton Evans, the brilliant young editor of the *Indianapolis News,* later reported this event in a *National Review* article about the YR convention:[1]

Nadasdy had plunged into the campaign of Liberal-backed candidate Ward White of Cornell Law School against conservative Jerry Dickson (immediate past president of the University of Kansas student body) by attempting to control the makeup of the college Credentials Committee. Officials of the campus group rebelled, with the result that conflicting credentials reports were placed before the assembled college delegates; on two divisions as to which credentials would be accepted, the conservatives won. At that point, certain of defeat, the Liberal faction walked out, holding a rump meeting at which Nadasdy presided until a temporary chairman could be chosen.

[1] "Goldwater, Rockefeller, and the Young Republicans," *National Review,* August 13, 1963.

Nadasdy's role in the college election was but a mild augury of his behavior during the convention proper.

Nadasdy, who had arrived in San Francisco about a week early, had arranged a clever device for controlling the convention in the Sheraton-Palace Hotel. He had a master switchboard installed on the podium he would occupy as convention chairman. From this board, he could control all the microphones of the state delegations. If he did not want to give recognition to any individual or delegation all he had to do was flip a switch and cut off their mike. On top of that, he had hired a battalion of private policemen—who were promptly christened "rent-a-cops" by the delegates—to back up his handpicked company of sergeants-at-arms in enforcing his peculiar brand of "order" on the convention floor.

Despite these precautions, or more likely because of them, Nadasdy had some difficulty on Thursday ramming through an "unappealable" ruling in favor of granting the New Jersey delegation a disputed unit rule vote, thereby disfranchising a number of conservatives and locking up New Jersey's 21 votes for McDevitt. The conservatives, of course, saw what was coming and did not take Nadasdy's decision lying down. But when they tried to get hold of a microphone to register their protests they were often physically blocked by people who weren't even in their delegations, including, several reported, Nadasdy's rent-a-cops. If they did manage to get their hands on a mike, the chairman simply cut them off or refused to switch them into the public address system. Predictably, this caused a great deal of shouting and arm-waving from the floor as delegates fought to be heard. But in the end, Nadasdy's ruling stood.

That night the Young Republicans were given a respite from the convention battle when Barry Goldwater came to San Francisco to address them. All of the leading GOP hopefuls, including Rockefeller, Romney and Scranton, had been invited to speak, but only Senator Goldwater had accepted. A poll of the delegates taken that day disclosed that the Senator was the YR choice over Rockefeller by 8 to 1, over Romney by better than 16 to 1, over Scranton by a whopping 23 to 1. There were reports that the others did not wish to expose their obvious lack of popularity by risking personal appearances during the convention, although Governor Mark Hatfield of Oregon had been politely received when he delivered the keynote address the day before. However, Hatfield was really not in the running for the nomination and had much less to risk.

Goldwater was greeted at the airport by an enthusiastic crowd of young people and when he addressed his audience that night the ovation they gave him was deafening. Lawrence E. Davies reported the scene in the *New York Times* the next day:[2]

A packed crowd of 3,000 cheering delegates and guests nearly lifted the roof off Harry Bridges' Longshoreman's Hall at Fisherman's Wharf in showing its affection for the potential candidate for the Republican Presidential nomination in 1964.

The Senator gave them a fighting Republican speech in which he decried the cynical Democratic alliance of "phony Liberals" with "corrupt big-city machines whose job it is to deliver the bloc votes in the big Northern cities." He drew his loudest cheers when he lashed out against the Kennedy Administration's policy on Cuba, charging that the Soviet military occupation of that island represented a "dangerous defeat" for the United States. And even the few in the crowd who may have been antagonistic toward him listened thoughtfully when he pointed out that the Liberal Democrats "have not had a new idea in thirty years."

"Modern Liberalism is only a form of rigor mortis," he said. "The old, respectable, sometimes noble Liberalism of fifty years ago is gone for good."

When he finished speaking the crowd started a demonstration reminiscent of those usually reserved for candidates at national conventions. But while this was going on, someone cut the telephone lines at the Lukens campaign headquarters. Previously a saboteur had broken into the hotel room of the New Jersey conservative delegates and cut the wires of their mimeograph machine. The attempt to sever the conservatives' communications was apparently not going to be confined to the convention floor.

The next day, the moderate steamroller went into high gear at the Sheraton-Palace. Patricia Hutar, the outgoing national YR co-chairman, was by this time openly aligned with our National Draft Goldwater Committee. When she rose to give her farewell address to the Young Republicans an unbelievable cacophony of screams and shouts started emanating from the moderate-controlled college convention behind a thin partition off to one side of the floor. The screeching reached such a crescendo that Pat was unable to finish her speech and was forced to retreat from the platform.

At last, the time came for the balloting on the national chairmanship. Nadasdy ordered his sergeants-at-arms to clear the floor of all unauthorized persons. This order apparently applied only to Lukens people

[2] *New York Times*, June 28, 1963.

because the McDevitt campaign crew still had free run of the floor. A YR vice-chairman appointed by Nadasdy descended on Lukens' floor manager, who was sitting with his state delegation. Behind the vice-chairman loomed three sergeants-at-arms and two uniformed rent-a-cops with their open handcuffs at the ready. Nadasdy's man asked the Lukens manager if he would leave quietly. Since the floor manager was an accredited delegate to the convention, he refused to go. Luckily, before the cops could clap the handcuffs on him, someone produced a printed list of delegates which included the floor manager's name. He was permitted to remain. But whenever he tried to leave his state delegation he was followed and constantly harassed by sergeants-at-arms.

After much shouting and shoving caused by a repetition of the previous day's control of the microphones by the chair, the first roll-call vote was completed. Neither McDevitt nor Lukens had won a majority of the votes. But California's favorite son, Bob Gaston, rose to throw his state's big bloc of votes to Lukens. Nadasdy refused to recognize him. Instead, he tried to gavel the convention into submission and promptly declared McDevitt the winner.

At this point all hell broke loose. A phalanx of "moderates" tried to get McDevitt up on the platform so Nadasdy could raise his hand in victory. But they ran into a solid wall of delegates crowding around the podium pleading with Nadasdy for another roll call. Finally, Nadasdy admitted he had made a mistake and at once started another roll call. This time Lukens emerged with a clear majority.

Instead of proclaiming Lukens the winner, Nadasdy tried another stall. He started going back over the roll of states, asking the delegations if there was any change in their votes, while McDevitt's men roamed the hall in a futile effort to pressure delegates into switching. The only result was that more votes went over to Lukens as still more delegates rebelled against Nadasdy's tactics.

Under the by-laws of the convention, the YR national secretary, Carolyn Manchester of Portland, Maine, was supposed to announce the tally as soon as the roll call was ended. Nadasdy had kept her away from the microphone after the first round, but when Lukens had undeniably won on the second roll call, Carolyn attempted to make her announcement. As she stepped up to the mike, Nadasdy, his face flushed with anger, pushed her away and Carolyn fell to the floor. Pat Hutar and one of the other girls on the platform picked her up and somehow got her through the crowd and down the stairs. Fortunately, Carolyn wasn't hurt, just badly shaken up—and she was still clutching the official tally in her hands.

One of the many people who observed this incident was Robert D. Bell, chairman of the Young Republican Federation of Oregon, who had led his delegation to the convention uncommitted. In a letter to the editor of the *Portland Oregonian*, Bell replied to a column by *New York Herald-Tribune* columnist Rowland Evans that had given a quite different view of the convention proceedings:[3]

[Rowland] Evans would have the people believe that the key issue of the Young Republican convention was one of the "moderates" vs. the "extremists" and which philosophy was going to prevail. Actually the issue was justice vs. injustice. . . . The ruthless parliamentary tactics used by out-going chairman Leonard Nadasdy will be long remembered by this writer. . . .

As moderate Republicans, it did not take us [the Oregon delegation] long to see through the shoddy veil of deceit that [Nadasdy] was trying to draw over the eyes of the delegates present. . . .

According to Evans, out-going chairman Nadasdy, in trying to bring order to the proceedings, muttered to himself: "This is incredible." Observing from the floor chairman Nadasdy's entire handling of the convention, I concur, this was incredible. Incredible that an officer of a highly respected national organization would indulge in such shenanigans. Incredible that the tone of the convention was set by the fact that Nadasdy's organization hired private police to be present and also insisted upon reinforcements in the form of members of the San Francisco police. . . .

Strangely enough, the police were absent at the precise moment that the national YR secretary, Carolyn Manchester from Portland, Maine, needed them to protect her from the irrational outburst of chairman Nadasdy.

This session of the convention, which was scheduled to wind up in time for a dinner at 7 P.M., lasted until almost midnight. During an evening recess, Nadasdy disappeared and he failed to return to the chair when the balloting resumed for other national YR officers. From his point of view, this was probably just as well. The Lukens group picked up several other offices they had thought they had no chance for at all. Nadasdy's rout was complete.

However, Nadasdy was not content to let the matter rest. When he returned to Minnesota (as he put it, "still in a state of shock") he was interviewed by Gene Newhall of the *St. Paul Pioneer Press* and Mercer Cross of the *Minneapolis Tribune*. This was the version he gave Newhall:

Young Republican delegates identified with the arch-conservative John Birch Society, although a minority at the convention, tied it up with repeated appeals of chairman Nadasdy's rulings, he reported.

When outvoted, they moved for reconsideration and demanded numerous roll-call votes, he added.

"They were using the exact same techniques used by the Communists,"

[3] *Portland Oregonian*, July 6, 1963.

Nadasdy said. . . . In preparation for the 1964 senior party convention "we'll see this radical right running a slate of delegate candidates for Senator Barry Goldwater for President," Nadasdy said.[4]

He told Mercer Cross that Goldwater's speech had served only "to pour gasoline on the flames" at the YR convention. Then he added, "Unless the Senator starts getting some sane conservative people around him, he's going to have a very difficult time getting the nomination and being elected." He informed the *Minneapolis Tribune* reporter that the Birch Society people at the YR conclave were mostly from California, Illinois and Iowa, with a scattering from other states.[5]

When I read this, I sent a letter to Ed Failor in Iowa asking him for a report. By return mail I received the following memo from him:

We have no information as to the John Birchers from California. As it regards the delegates from Illinois and Iowa, this statement is a complete and total lie. Not one of these delegates has been or is now a member of the Birch Society. I have already received sworn affidavits from each Iowa and Illinois delegate to this effect. Moreover, there were no members of the John Birch Society included in any phase of leadership—at any level—in the Lukens campaign. Nor were any members of the Society knowingly consulted with regard to Lukens' campaign strategy.

Unfortunately, Nelson Rockefeller apparently accepted Nadasdy's version at face value without making any real attempt to get at the facts. The Governor waited more than two weeks after the YR convention ended. Then, on Bastille Day, Sunday, July 14, he let loose with a broadside attack against the victorious Young Republican group, the "unprincipled extremism of the radical right," and, although he did not mention him by name, against Senator Goldwater. Rockefeller's lengthy statement read in part:

No one could fail to be deeply disturbed by the proceedings at the recent Young Republican national convention in San Francisco. . . . every objective observer has reported that the proceedings there were dominated by extremist groups, carefully organized, well-financed[6] and operating through the tactics of ruthless, rough-shod intimidation. These are the tactics of totalitarianism. . . .
The leaders of the Birchers and others of the radical right lunatic fringe—every bit as dangerous to American principles and American institutions as the radical left—who successfully engineered this disgraceful subversion of a great and responsible auxiliary of the Republican

[4] *St. Paul Pioneer Press*, July 6, 1963.
[5] *Minneapolis Sunday Tribune*, July 7, 1963.
[6] Ed Failor estimates that $12,000 was spent on Lukens' campaign, about one-fifth the sum the opposition forces plowed into McDevitt's.

Party are the same people who are now moving to subvert the Republican Party itself. . . .

No Republican can stand by idly in the face of this threat. . . . One must be either for or against these forces. The time for temporizing is over.

In this same vein, the Governor lashed out at the "sinister" plan to have the Republican Party "write off the Negro and other minority groups . . . the great industrial states of the North . . . the big cities, and that it direct its appeal primarily to the electoral votes of the South, plus the West, and a scattering of other states."

Although I could hardly recognize it through this distorted prism, the plan Rockefeller referred to was of course my own, although for some weeks now the columnists had been incorrectly attributing it to Senator Goldwater. Never at any time had I suggested that the GOP "write off the Negro and other minority groups." On the contrary, at our December meeting in Chicago I had set up special committees to go after votes within these groups. Nor had I suggested that we "write off the great industrial states of the North and big cities." From the very outset, I had told our original group that we would *not* write off any state or region, and that we would go for delegates—and votes—in every state of the Union.

Nonetheless, we had to face political realities. I recognized that any conservative candidate—even a dedicated integrationist—would have great difficulty making inroads in the North, although up to this time Senator Goldwater had been amazing us all by the growing popular support he was winning in the Northeast. This region, as I have noted before, is largely controlled by the Democratic big-city machines. In a Presidential election even a middle-of-the-road Republican stood a good chance of getting clobbered in these states, as Dick Nixon discovered to his everlasting dismay in 1960. The only hope the Republican Party had of counterbalancing this tremendous handicap was to win the Southern states. And the GOP was already growing by leaps and bounds in the South without emphasizing the race issue at all, as Jim Martin's senatorial campaign against segregationist Democrat Lister Hill had proved in Alabama only eight months before Rockefeller issued his statement.

As I told the press the day after Rockefeller's declaration, our Draft organization was conducting a national, not a sectional, campaign. The *New York Times* cited our map, which projected a Goldwater victory over Kennedy by the Senator's winning the South but failing to take the big states in the Northeast. I pointed out that this did not mean we were "writing off" these states. It simply reflected, as the *Times* correctly quoted me as saying, "states which have a history of going Republican over the last several Presidential campaigns, plus the South, which is the area where, in the 1962 Congressional elections, the Republican party made its greatest gains."[7]

Actually, we were trying to make the Republican Party into a national party for the first time in its history. Aside from the vindictive period of Reconstruction when radical Republicans installed carpetbaggers and others in political office in the South with the aid of occupation troops, until now there had never been a viable Republican Party in that region. But in the twisted semantics of our age, it was somehow morally wrong for Republicans to aspire to political power in Southern states but of course perfectly all right for Democratic segregationists to continue their reign and help keep Democratic administrations in control of the federal government.

No one on our National Draft Goldwater Committee, not even our staunchest supporters in the Deep South, ever suggested Senator Goldwater run on a segregationist platform. If they had, I'm positive the Senator would have angrily rejected the idea. Goldwater had always had a deep sympathy and understanding for the plight of the Negro in America.

The Goldwater department store in Phoenix was, under his management, among the first in the Southwest to hire Negroes. As a member of the NAACP he had backed a successful move to desegregate the Phoenix schools. When he was chief of staff of Arizona's National Guard he had helped bring about the desegregation of all Air National Guard units in the state. Although he no longer belonged to the NAACP, he was still a member of the Urban League, which is also dedicated to the advancement of Negroes. And his record on civil rights legislation in the United States Senate was certainly far better than that of Lyndon B. Johnson. Only a few weeks before Rockefeller delivered his declaration, the Senator said he would offer an amendment to the Kennedy Administration's civil rights bill that would have denied unions practicing racial discrimination recourse to the National Labor Relations Board.[8] And a week before that, the *New York Times* had frontpaged a story under the headline "GOLDWATER GIVES LIFT TO PROSPECT FOR A RIGHTS BILL" when he lined up with Senator Dirksen's position on the pending legislation.

Rockefeller's ill-timed statement was the desperate act of a fast-falling candidate grasping for one last hold at the cliff he had leaped from himself. But in going down, it appeared as if he was determined to take the whole Republican Party down with him. Ultimately he succeeded, with

---

[7] *New York Times*, July 16, 1963.

[8] Ironically, Goldwater had already prepared this amendment when Rockefeller opened up on him. He introduced it and several others on the floor of the Senate on July 16, 1963.

some notable assistance from the other "moderates" in the pre-convention struggle of 1964.

The following day, which may yet go down as the bluest Monday in Republican history, the *New York Journal-American* set the tone of the headlines that flashed across every newspaper in the country:

ROCKY DECLARES WAR ON GOLDWATER

Immediately many prominent Republicans leaped into the fray. The two Senators from New York, Jack Javits and Ken Keating, were joined by California's Thomas Kuchel in vigorous defense of Rockefeller's position, which heaped more hot coals on the already blazing fire. However, even Keating admitted that Goldwater was, as he put it, "on the side of the angels" when it came to civil rights and was "way ahead" of President Kennedy on this issue despite Rockefeller's charge that Goldwater wanted to "write off Negroes."

In Frankfurt, Germany, Dick Nixon's comments on the Rockefeller statement were widely interpreted as a slap at Goldwater when they were taken out of context. Nixon was quoted by UPI as saying that "the extreme right wing is behind Senator Goldwater now." But in many printed accounts his qualification of this remark was lost in the linotype shuffle. He had hastily added, "But I do not think he [Goldwater] is one of them and I am sure he must regard them as a liability just as I do."

Senator Carl Curtis of Nebraska rose on the floor of the Senate to defend his good friend and colleague from Arizona. He charged that Rockefeller had been out to "smear" all conservative Republicans as extremists in a wild attempt to save his own political neck. "It is my considered judgment," Curtis said, "that a man who would take such desperate and destructive measures against his own party in a gamble to gain some temporary personal advantage has already forfeited any claim to loyalty from any part of the party organization." Then, with a warning that today has the ring of a fulfilled prophecy, Curtis added:

If we of the party allow such desperate opportunism to cloud the chances of all Republicans in 1964 we shall deserve what we get. . . . The whole ticket from top to bottom must not be brought into jeopardy because a small handful of willful men find this to suit their personal advantage.

Congressman Robert Taft, Jr., who was the obvious choice of Ohio Republicans to run for his father's old Senate seat in 1964, said that Rockefeller's attack on Goldwater "may have served more to build up than to quell" disunity in the GOP. Governor Hatfield of Oregon, although he was known to be leaning toward Rockefeller's candidacy, issued one of the strongest statements of all. "Our party," said Hatfield, "is in no position to incite political mayhem by ruthless intramural attacks which only lead to fratricide."

Goldwater was himself stunned. Rockefeller's statement was a rude end to the political honeymoon and ripening personal friendship he had been enjoying with the Governor for two and a half years. Rockefeller's main theme during those intimate breakfasts out on Foxhall Road had been the vital need for party unity. Now that carefully nurtured unity lay in a shambles, destroyed perhaps irrevocably by the Governor's own hand. Goldwater felt betrayed. He suddenly discovered what any of us in the original group could have told him all along—Rocky was playing him for a sucker. "There'll be no more breakfasts," the Senator bitterly told his staff at the office Monday morning. "None at all."

This feeling of betrayal was accentuated by the fact that Rockefeller had sent him a telegram the day before the bomb was dropped saying that he was about to issue a statement dealing with "a common cause." The Governor's wire brazenly added that he hoped Goldwater would stand with him on the statement in the interest of party harmony. The telegram had arrived at the office on Saturday, when of course the Senator's staff was off duty. They found it waiting on Monday morning, along with a mimeographed copy of the statement Rockefeller had airmailed on Saturday with the full knowledge that it would not reach Goldwater until after he had issued it to the press.

The day after his opening roundhouse, Rockefeller deliberately rubbed more salt into the wound. In Massena, New York, he addressed a meeting of the New York State Society of Newspaper Editors and this time *named* Goldwater as the target of his attack. He said the prospect of the Senator's domination by extremists "should be of the greatest possible concern to Barry himself." He declared there was no doubt that there were extremist elements among Goldwater's supporters. "I have some concern," he said, "as to whether he may not end up the captive of these elements." Then, somewhat unctuously, he added: "I have great respect for Barry's patriotism and dedication to political principle and he is a personal friend of mine."

One of the editors present was overheard saying afterwards, "With a friend like that, Goldwater surely doesn't need any enemies." It was an old saw, but like many clichés, nonetheless true. And between July 1963 and the Republican convention one year later Barry Goldwater discovered, with understandably growing bitterness, that he had many "friends like that." If Rockefeller had been only one, his Bastille Day bombshell might well have turned out to be a long forgotten dud by July 1964. For the bombshell quickly burst in the face of the man who detonated it. Instead of halting his slide into the political limbo where he was to wander for nearly a year in lonely and frustrated solitude, his declaration of war on Goldwater quickly made Rockefeller an untouchable within the Republican Party. As Evans and Novak noted in their column three days after the bomb burst:

[The statement] seems to have failed to accomplish what many thought to be its major purpose: pumping new life into the Rockefeller Presidential candidacy, which has been in a state of near-death since the Governor's marriage two months ago.

The widespread suspicion persists, even among Republican moderates and some outright liberals, that the Governor's motives were not entirely selfless and they resent it.[9]

That same night John Tower, Frank Kovac and I sampled some of this resentment when we journeyed to Wilmington, Delaware, to address a fundraising dinner for our Draft Goldwater Committee. It turned out to be one of the most successful money-making affairs we had had to date. Obviously, there were still many influential Republicans, even in the Northeast we had been accused of "writing off," who weren't buying Rockefeller's party-splitting strategy.

More concrete evidence of Goldwater's growing support in the "great industrial North" followed. During this same month a poll of Republican county chairmen in Pennsylvania revealed that more than half of them favored the Senator even after Governor Scranton announced his favorite-son candidacy. In Ohio, despite Ray Bliss's assertion that Goldwater would hurt the GOP ticket there, a similar poll showed that Goldwater was the pick of county chairmen by a 3-to-1 margin. And in Illinois, no less than sixty-five Republican county chieftains backed Goldwater as against four for Rockefeller. Moreover, Hayes Robertston, the Cook County chairman, publicly announced his support of Goldwater and denounced Rockefeller's attack as "a baseless smear." Even among Republican governors Goldwater was given a wide 6-to-1 lead over Rockefeller in the nomination race.[10]

In spite of the deep personal hurt he felt over the Rockefeller assault, Goldwater at first chose to turn the other cheek. The day after the initial attack he issued a mild reply which simply denied that he intended to make any appeal based on racial or sectional considerations. "I have never had any theory of that kind," he said. "I am not for giving up anybody's vote. We Republicans have got to go after every available vote in the big cities and everywhere else." He added that he regarded

[9] *New York Herald-Tribune Syndicate,* July 17, 1963.
[10] *Los Angeles Times* poll, July 20, 1963.

Rockefeller's declaration as "just his formal declaration of candidacy" and nothing more. Nor was he alone in this opinion. Prominent Republicans of all political hues shared this view, as the columnists later noted.

The knowledge that his motives were widely suspect did not dissuade Rockefeller from escalating his divisive harassment of Goldwater. On July 17 he made the first of many attempts to euchre Barry into a knockdown television debate. When the Senator declined on the grounds that such a debate would only "have the effect of contributing to disunity in the Republican Party," Rockefeller piously expressed his regret. He added that a debate "would strengthen rather than weaken the party" and would "serve the public interest." This, despite the fact that less than a year before he had rejected an offer by his Democratic gubernatorial opponent, Robert M. Morgenthau, to debate the issues in New York.

A few days later Rockefeller stepped up his attempt to tie Goldwater to the "radical right" and challenged him to disown this group for the good of the country. The Governor joined Javits and Keating in expressing doubt as to whether he could in conscience support Goldwater if he became the GOP Presidential candidate. Soon after this he went one step further and said that he definitely would not back Goldwater unless he strongly repudiated the party's right wing, the same group he had been cultivating so assiduously himself a few months earlier.

In the face of these unremitting attacks, Goldwater remained remarkably patient. He refused repeatedly to strike back at Rockefeller and the Republican Left, and stated again and again that he would support any candidate the party picked to run for President, including Rockefeller. But he asked his critics to define what they meant by the "radical right." And finally, on August 6, he called upon all Republicans to "stop chewing on each other and start chewing on the Democrats." He pointed out that further internecine warfare within Republican ranks could only serve to aid the opposition party.

Rockefeller, of course, refused to let up. And what was worse, his rule-or-ruin tactics were picked up by an increasing number of other Presidential aspirants and their supporters as the nominating race progresssed and as the hue and cry against the vaguely defined radical right mounted to a crashing crescendo.

The thing that dismayed me most as the campaign wore on was how a growing number of true moderates, even many who had previously considered themselves conservatives, were drawn into the vortex of this controversy. Conservatives for the most part are by their very nature moderates in the true sense. But the "moderation" of Leonard Nadasdy and Nelson Rockefeller soon obscured the real meaning of that word.

And, far more serious, it split not only Republican voters, dividing them more rigidly into warring camps, but aided the Far Left in its ceaseless efforts to polarize the American people into two great irreconcilable factions. Only the future will tell whether the political battles of 1963 and 1964 carried this polarization beyond the bitter point of no return.

CHAPTER 18

RALLY IN WASHINGTON

ONE OF THE EVENTS that nudged Barry Goldwater closer to his ultimate decision to run for President was the Draft Goldwater Committee's mammoth rally at the National Guard Armory in Washington on July 4, 1963. In the beginning I was very skeptical about the rally. To my knowledge, no one had ever held one successfully before in the nation's capital on the Fourth of July. It is probably the worst day of the year to stage any kind of mass meeting in that city. As a rule, there is a mass exodus from Washington on this holiday. Congressmen and Senators scatter off to their districts and states to participate in parades and other patriotic events. And everyone else leaves town to escape the unrelenting heat that roasts the city to a shriveled turn every July.

However, Peter O'Donnell felt we needed something to dramatize our Draft movement and to convince the Senator that this was a serious effort based on broad popular support for his candidacy. Later, after Peter announced the rally at the Draft Committee's kickoff press conference on April 8, he had some moments of doubt. As the date neared, he seriously considered canceling it altogether.

Although I had opposed the idea of the rally at the outset, I felt we had now gone too far to call it off. I reminded Peter that we had already sent out extensive mailings advertising the rally and stories about it had appeared in newspapers all over the country. "If we cancel now," I said, "it will hurt us worse than if we hold it and fail to fill the Armory. We will have a good excuse for not drawing a big crowd on the Fourth of

July. But if we cancel out it will look like we are losing confidence—in ourselves and in our candidate."

Peter, who is one of the most perceptive politicians I have ever known, quickly saw that there was no way out. We simply had to hold the rally as scheduled. There was no alternative but to pull out all the stops and try to make it a success. Through some of my friends in New York we had hired "Rally Don"—Donald Shafto, a protégé of Marvin Liebman, the versatile New Yorker who had filled Madison Square Garden twice in recent years for Young Americans for Freedom rallies.

Peter had picked the Armory because it was the biggest indoor hall in Washington. But it had only been filled three times before—for Dwight Eisenhower's inaugural ball in 1957 and Jack Kennedy's in 1961, and for Billy Graham's Washington crusade. This didn't faze Rally Don. He moved into our office at 1025 Connecticut Avenue in May and just kept forging ahead with his plans. We were starting to build a pretty good mailing list through our petitions, and Don acquired some other lists. Thousands of invitations went out, with tickets enclosed, but we had no way of knowing how many people would use them.

Peter and I worked frantically through the month of June trying to get speakers. Barry Goldwater, of course, would not appear. If he did, it would be tantamount to announcing his candidacy. Neither he nor the Draft Committee were ready for that yet. We finally lined up Governor Paul Fannin of Arizona, Senator Curtis, Senator Tower and Congressman Ashbrook, our original group's man in Ohio. A group of Hollywood stars also promised to appear—Walter Brennan, William Lundigan, Chill Wills, and Efrem Zimbalist, Jr. We now felt we had a solid cast.

During the last two weeks in June, Peter brought most of his personal staff and a group of associates up from Texas. They pitched in and worked night and day with our Draft Committee staff and a growing group of volunteers. As July approached everyone was becoming more nervous—everyone, that is, except Rally Don, who plunged into an intensive promotion campaign Peter concocted for the District of Columbia area. We took a number of radio and TV spots and even plastered some billboards in northern Virginia with announcements about the rally.

On Wednesday, the day before the event, Peter, Ione Harrington, Judy Fernald and I drove out to the Armory to run through a quick dress rehearsal. Washington had been sweltering in the grip of a heat wave for more than a week and we almost melted inside the Armory, which had no air conditioning. When the rehearsal was over I remarked, only half in jest, that if the weather broke we would know that God was on our side. Nobody laughed. The searing heat wasn't exactly conducive to laughter. And we all had visions of tier upon tier of empty seats mocking us in that cavernous hall the following night.

The next day dawned clear and beautifully cool, with a fresh breeze blowing in off the ocean across the Eastern Shore and Chesapeake Bay and up through the Potomac Valley. Ione dropped by my office, smiling happily. "Clif," she said, "your prayer has been answered."

Even during the morning we had evidence that the rally was going to be a success. We had thrown open the doors of our Connecticut Avenue office for an all-day open house, and before ten o'clock droves of people had already started drifting in. They seemed to come from every state in the Union. They had arrived by car, bus, train and plane and they wanted to inspect the National Draft Goldwater headquarters before attending the rally. I remember meeting one young couple who had driven all night from Cleveland with their two small children. They planned to catch a few hours' sleep before they left the youngsters with a baby-sitter at their motel and went out to the Armory. But they wanted to drop by and say hello first and find out if there was anything more they could be doing for the Senator back in Ohio.

Rita Bree returned from lunch with a report that several busloads of young Goldwater fans had arrived from Massachusetts and were picketing the White House. They were joined by others, and one—Tom Duckworth of Washington—was photographed with a live monkey perched on his shoulder and carrying a sign, "Get the Monkey Off My Back, Jack." The pickets were passing out throwaways inviting passersby—presumably including some New Frontiersmen—to attend the rally.

About six o'clock those of us who were to appear on stage, plus a growing list of distinguished guests, assembled in the Colonial Room of the Mayflower for a buffet supper. Afterwards we all went out to the Armory. About thirty minutes before the rally was to start, I left the others in the Trophy Room on the second floor to see how the crowd was coming in. From the balcony where I stood, the hall appeared less than half filled. For a few seconds I had a hollow sensation at the pit of my stomach. Then I reminded myself that people didn't normally come to events like this until the last minute. Still, that Armory looked so empty I didn't see how it was going to fill up in a short half-hour.

Promptly at 8 P.M. the door to the Trophy Room opened and a group of Goldwater Girls whom Ione had outfitted in Western straw hats escorted us out onto the speakers' platform. When the crowd saw us coming a mighty cheer went up and the whole Armory seemed to shake. The place was packed. Normally it seated only 6,500, but somehow more than 9,000 people had jammed themselves inside and someone whispered that the fire marshals had closed the doors, leaving several thousand more stranded in the street.

The excitement was electric. We had at least equaled the crowd records set by Eisenhower, Kennedy and Billy Graham. Balconies were festooned with banners proclaiming "Brooklyn Backs Barry," "Wisconsin Goes All the Way with Goldwater," "Only Barry Can Carry Ohio," and so on. The Armory had all the trappings of a national nominating convention, and it sounded twice as noisy.

When we were all out on the stage the band struck up the national anthem and everyone in the hall joined in singing it. A Catholic priest, Father Edmund McCaffrey, offered the invocation, and Congressman James Battin of Montana led the crowd in the Pledge of Allegiance. Peter O'Donnell acted as the master of ceremonies, and I will always remember him stepping up to the rostrum with an armful of papers, including one of those long legal-size pads he was in the habit of jotting notes on. Peter gave the welcoming remarks and from the cheers he received you would have thought he was Barry Goldwater announcing his candidacy. He told them:

You and dedicated people like you in every state of the Union are beginning to write a new chapter in American political history. We are embarking on a great crusade together. This evening marks the first step toward our goal—*to put Goldwater in and Kennedy out.*

There are people here from forty-four states, including big delegations from New York, Pennsylvania, and very significantly, Massachusetts. This is proof positive that Kennedy does not have the big states signed, sealed and delivered, no matter what the corrupt big-city machine politicians tell the Kennedys.

The affirmative responses he got from the New York, Pennsylvania and Massachusetts sections when he asked each of them in turn, "Is that right?" resounded through the Armory. "The support you will receive from forty-seven other states," he assured them, "will make JFK a one-term President."

Then Peter quickly introduced the honored guests—not all by name since the list was much too long—but collectively by group, such as the nearly one hundred delegates and alternates who had gone to the 1960 national convention from more than thirty states, the score of Congressmen, the group of National Committee members, and the half-dozen or more state Republican chairmen.

Governor Fannin was the first speaker. To the crowd, more than anyone there he represented his boyhood friend, who that day was leading a Fourth of July parade back in Prescott, Arizona, riding a horse and dressed as a cowboy. They cheered the Governor after almost every sentence. And he wound up his speech with what ultimately turned out to be the theme of Barry Goldwater's campaign in 1964:

The time has come to give the American people a choice—and a chance to vote their consciences and their true convictions.

The time has come to put an end to the political confidence game which is undermining our free institutions and paralyzing the pursuit of individual happiness for 180 million Americans.

When he closed by saying that Barry Goldwater was the man to accept this challenge and lead this fight, the rafters of the Armory reverberated with a standing ovation for both Governor Fannin and his absent friend.

Efrem Zimbalist followed with a short biographical sketch of the Senator, and John Ashbrook's brief speech was pitched to the many hundreds of young people in the hall. Then came the sleeper of the evening. It was an address by Dr. Enrique Llaca, Jr., a Cuban captured at the Bay of Pigs whom Peter O'Donnell had met after Dr. Llaca had been ransomed some months earlier. Few people who heard Dr. Llaca that night could have failed to be deeply moved:

When we lost our freedom in Cuba, I vowed to fight to regain it, and I joined the Cuban Freedom Fighters. With the promise of support from the United States government, we landed at the Bay of Pigs. At the crucial hour the air cover we were promised was withdrawn and we were betrayed.

As a result of that betrayal, many of my comrades died, and the rest of us were thrown in a Communist prison. I was released because of ransom paid to Castro by the United States government. But mark this well, there will be no one left to pay *your* ransom, no one left to come to *your rescue*. There will be no second chance for Americans. America is the last hope for free men. Should America fail, freedom fails everywhere.

The crowd sat through Dr. Llaca's talk in solemn silence, the only time that evening that it was quiet for more than a few minutes. But it gave him a thunderous ovation when he finished.

Walter Brennan gave one of the finest performances of his long career during his short address—only he wasn't acting when he pleaded with the crowd to do their utmost for Senator Goldwater. My turn came right after this. Our political map of the U.S.A. was projected on a giant screen and I went quickly through my state-by-state forecast of the electoral vote for 1964.

"We do not write off any state or any area," I said in conclusion. Then, as an afterthought, I added, "However, I do feel in all honesty that I must list Massachusetts as doubtful."

Somewhere in the back of the hall a great shout went up. A large contingent from Massachusetts, many of them from the Boston Young Republican Club, leaped up and yelled, "No! No! We want Barry! We want Barry!"

Judy Fernald reported on the massive shift of the women's vote to the Senator and then Bill Lundigan and Chill Wills paved the way for a collection. We had not charged for tickets, and the rally was costing us nearly $59,000, so we had to defray our expenses somehow. We put a good dent in them that night and since most of these people took home petitions which they later returned with $1 for each signature, I think we eventually came close to breaking even.

Senator Curtis came next and his was one of the great addresses of the evening. He spoke eloquently of "the valiant—at times, lonesome —fight" that Barry Goldwater "has waged for those principles of freedom and a government of law that bring us together tonight." He vividly described how the New Frontier was establishing "bureaucratic dictator-ships" with "policies anchored in the strange philosophy that to im-poverish the nation is to guarantee its strength and prosperity." And he called the dismal roll of recent foreign policy failures "from the Berlin Wall to the jungles of Vietnam."

And finally, there was John Tower, delivering a rousing finale in which he reviewed Barry Goldwater's record as a Republican, as a Senator and as a man. "No one has worked as hard for his party," said Tower. "He has constantly been a team player. . . . He would not be a regional candidate, nor a pressure-group candidate, but a candidate for all the people. No other candidate of either party can command the intense loyalty and effort of so large a segment of the American citizenry."

The crowd was on its feet, cheering and chanting "We want Barry! We want Barry!" The demonstration that followed outdid anything I had ever seen at a national convention, and I knew there was not one hired hand in all that vast throng. On the contrary, these were people who had given up a holiday weekend to travel hundreds, and in many cases thousands, of miles at their own expense to urge the candidacy of a man they knew would not even be there.

Somehow we all got out of the Armory in one piece. Just outside one of my friends from New York grabbed my arm and asked me to say a few words to some people from our home state who had come by bus. He led me to the parking lot where the people were already sitting in the bus. I thanked them for coming and gave them a little farewell pep talk. Then my friend led me to another bus parked beside the first and I repeated my talk there. When he started to lead me to a third, I asked how many New York buses there were. "Forty-two," he beamed happily. At this rate I knew we would be giving talks all night and none of these tired people would get home until long after dawn. So I begged off and asked my friend to convey my thanks to all the New York delega-tion as best he could.

When I returned to the front of the Armory to find the car that was supposed to take several of our Draft group back downtown, I had to thread my way through a thin line of pickets representing the American Nazi Party. They were wearing brown uniforms with swastika armbands and carrying signs reading "Goldwater Supported NAACP" and "Goldwater Is a Race Mixer." Ironically, there were also some members of the Black Muslims on hand peddling pamphlets which purported to prove Goldwater was a segregationist. The happy stragglers coming out of the Armory ignored both groups, though I saw one knot of young people pointing in derisive disbelief at the "storm troopers" and having a good laugh among themselves.

Back at the Mayflower, I joined my son Kip in our rooms. I hadn't seen very much of him for almost two months and we sat up for an hour or two catching up on one another. Later on I went downstairs to get the early editions of the morning newspapers. Our rally had made the front pages. When I got some more papers the next day I had to chuckle over the wide disparity in the crowd estimates. The *Washington Star* placed the turnout at 8,000 and the *Baltimore Sun* cut us down to 6,000. But we got big headlines everywhere, even in New York, and in some cases they were banner heads at the top of page one. The *Washington Star* actually had two rally stories on the first page, one by Mary McGrory and the other by David Broder. One paragraph in the Broder piece particularly pleased Peter O'Donnell and me and the members of the original group:

The entire evening—from the first bit of oratory to the last button on the costumes of the Goldwater Girls—showed a professionalism surprising in a group that opened its headquarters less than a month ago.[1]

For weeks our Draft Goldwater Committee reaped publicity and public support from leading Republicans as a result of the rally. In Chicago, Charles H. Percy, the young president of Bell & Howell who was making a bid for the GOP gubernatorial nomination, predicted Goldwater would carry Illinois in the 1964 election and promised to support him.

Percy, who had been chairman of the Platform Committee at the 1960 convention, was considered a Liberal. But he knew that he would never get the nomination for Governor in Illinois if he opposed Goldwater. And he was not the only Republican Liberal who was shifting toward our conservative candidate, either out of necessity or from honest conviction that Goldwater was the best candidate the party had.

Arthur Krock, the veteran *New York Times* columnist and confidant of several former Presidents, wrote a prophetic story on July 6 comment-

[1] *Washington Evening Star*, July 5, 1963.

ing on the Goldwater boom and the counteraction it was producing within the Eastern wing of the Republican Party.

"The boom attained high visibility," wrote Krock, "with a wildly enthusiastic Fourth of July rally in Washington by citizens, predominantly youthful, from all parts of the country." He said the organized Eastern effort to deflate that boom "is less visible," but noted that one of the quiet strategies then gaining momentum was the "favorite-son gambit."

We had, of course, anticipated this plan months before, and we were already gearing to thwart it in a number of states. There was a move afoot to run Senator Thomas Kuchel as a favorite son in the California primary. But when we got finished building our volunteer army on the Coast I knew that the Senator would be too smart a politician to take us on.

Romney and Scranton were in somewhat stronger positions in their states. But at this time I was not ready to concede the entire Michigan and Pennsylvania delegations to them. Wherever possible we wanted to avoid fights that might split or weaken the party, but I felt we could work something out whereby Goldwater would get an equitable share of the delegates from both these states.

The favorite-son strategy is an interesting and legitimate technique in American politics. However, for it to have real meaning, it is essential that the party have a significant number of leaders who are considered Presidential candidates, and who are willing to submit themselves to their constituency as potential Presidential nominees. This was the case in the 1940 Republican Convention, when 11 names were submitted (where Wendell Willkie trailed until the fourth ballot and did not receive the required majority until the sixth), and in 1948 when seven names were presented at the Convention (and Governor Thomas E. Dewey of New York was finally nominated on the third ballot).

In 1963, the Republicans were at low ebb in their control of the governorships and the national legislative leadership was in such a state of flux that it presented a limited number of potential Presidential candidates. Even some of those who might have been considered potential candidates on a favorite-son basis were denying their interest in seeking the office, thus depriving their constituents of the opportunity of considering them.

The facts led me to believe that this technique was not going to be applicable in the 1964 nominating process. But the press and some commentators would undoubtedly speculate on the possibility that it would be used, and thus, perhaps for a limited period of time, would give some hope to those who looked to this technique.

Also, in the ten days immediately following our Washington rally the Goldwater boom, so excitingly dramatized by that event, was smothering the few favorite-son campfires that were being lit around the country. As *U. S. News & World Report* noted in the issue published the next week, some Eastern GOP leaders were suggesting that if 1964 looked like a Democrat year, "the big-city states might let the nomination go to Senator Goldwater without too much of a fight."[2]

Then, on Bastille Day, Nelson Rockefeller lowered the boom. From then on we knew we would have to fight every inch of the way to San Francisco, and although we were confident of the ultimate outcome, no one on the Draft Goldwater Committee welcomed a struggle that we well knew might tear our party apart.

[2] *U.S. News & World Report*, July 15, 1963.

CHAPTER 19

THE GOLDWATER SUMMER

BY THE END of August 1963, many of the people in our National Draft Goldwater Committee and in the state organizations we were rapidly forming believed that Senator Goldwater had the Republican Presidential nomination neatly wrapped up. I was optimistic too, but I knew that our toughest battles still lay ahead. I was perfectly willing to make predictions on how I thought each state would line up at the national convention. But I refused to count delegates until we could accurately determine how well the spadework we had been doing for nearly two years at the precinct and district levels would pay off.

Frankly, I was a little leery about bringing our candidate to a peak too soon. He was at the top of the heap now, almost a year before the San Francisco convention convened. But in the unpredictable world of politics almost anything could happen during that year to topple him from the pinnacle he occupied at that moment.

However, there seemed to be no way of holding back our people in the fifty states. They wanted to go—*now*. If you can hitch your sulky to a horse that wants to gallop before you can get him into the starting gate, it is a good idea to let him go when the gun goes off and hope that he can head the field all the way around the track. And in the summer of 1963 the conservative movement, prematurely turned out to pasture years before, was full of oats and ready to run. It needed a driver to steer its course. Barry Goldwater still refused to take the reins. Therefore, it fell to us in the Draft Committee to fill in for the Senator until he was willing to take over.

Our activities that summer were geared to maintaining the momentum of Goldwater's phenomenal rise. And to keep our Draft Committee rolling we needed money. Early in the summer we had taken on Frank J. Kovac, who had just finished three years as executive director of the Republican National Finance Committee. Young, aggressive, and exceedingly knowledgeable in his field, Frank never ceased to amaze me. By nature, I am not a fundraiser. As I have mentioned, I find it somehow repugnant to ask people for money no matter how worthy the cause. But I have never been with Frank Kovac when he showed any compunction whatever about asking for a contribution. He was a great fundraiser and his services as executive director of the Draft's finance committee proved invaluable.

Our really large contributors were a relatively small band. Many of them believed, as George Humphrey had in May, that it was still much too early to start. But there was no alternative but to go out and find the funds we needed to keep our Draft organization in business.

Kovac dragged me off on a series of tours about the country and as a team we proved fairly successful. At a dinner or luncheon, often arranged by a member of my original group or some of the people I had met during my 1962 travels, I would give an analysis of the political picture. Then Frank would come on with his pitch for funds.

I remember one swing we made through Florida in early August. We hit Miami, Fort Lauderdale and Jacksonville, in that order. In Miami, a goodly crowd turned out for a dinner. As soon as we arrived Kovac started buttonholing people. I didn't know it then, but he was lining up help for his fundraising speech.

Later, when he finished his talk, a half-dozen people leaped up and started pledging contributions. The first one started at $25 and they got it up to $100 within a few seconds. It was just like an auction. Everyone caught the fever. When the bidding lagged, Kovac would exhort individuals to join with others at their table and see how much they could raise.

I subsequently found out that Frank had coached the original bidders beforehand. These tactics proved quite successful and we raised nearly $12,000 on the Florida tour. To our Draft Committee this represented a substantial sum for two days' work.

Kovac was indefatigable. He kept pushing people in different states to organize dinners, luncheons and cocktail parties in order to raise funds. In Toledo, Roland MacNichol, Jr. set up a meeting which was most productive. In Detroit, Leonard Schoenherr, our Draft finance chairman for Michigan, staged a profitable dinner. Stets Coleman got a party going in Chicago. A. C. (Cy) Rubel, the California oil man, headed a group which put on a wonderfully successful dinner in Los Angeles at which Kovac and I spoke. Peter Hoguet and Ed Stephenson, whom we had met earlier at a dinner in Wilmington, Delaware, helped Frank set up a score of similar events through friends across the country.

A lot of fundraising activities were sponsored by free-lancers not connected with our Draft Committee. An Omaha housewife, Mrs. Truman Wood, conceived the "Gold for Goldwater" drive. A Texas businessman, Jay Ernest Stroud of Amarillo, dreamed up the idea of minting "Goldwater dollars." These and other similar "currencies" were checks or pledges made out to the Republican National Committee but payable only *after* Barry Goldwater was nominated in 1964. If another candidate won, the checks would be worthless. This naturally had a psychological impact upon the National Committee.

The demand for materials—Goldwater buttons, bumper stickers, literature and so on—rose to astronomical proportions that summer. There were virtually no materials out for other candidates of either party. But what little there was, their friends would have been happy to give away. The Draft Committee sold all its campaign materials and although it cost us considerable sums to produce them we nevertheless made some profit.

Goldwater bumper stickers blossomed on cars everywhere. One of the favorites was the chemical formula for the Senator's name—AuH_2O. They even appeared in foreign languages—French, Polish, Italian and, unbelievably, in Chinese!

Thousands of letters containing pledges and contributions poured into our Connecticut Avenue headquarters from so-called "little people." In Topeka, a mother and father held a conference with their two children and decided to cut corners on the family budget so they could send us $10 a month "from now until the time Barry Goldwater is elected President." A thirteen-year-old boy in California sent $5 he had saved out of his weekly allowance. We got several Social Security checks endorsed over to the Draft Goldwater Committee. A very small boy in Brooklyn sent us a card with three pennies taped to it. On the card he printed, "I say a prayer for Senator Goldwater every night." A young couple who said they were "going steady" wrote from St. Louis that they had given up their Saturday night movie dates and were watching television instead so they could send us $2 each week.

These messages did much to spur us on at the Draft office. I suspect that many of the volunteers who opened the mail quietly redoubled their efforts, as I know we did. No one ever complained about overtime. Twelve- and fourteen-hour days were standard for most of the staff as well as the Committee officers.

Some members of my original group, plus the Draft officers and a few others, had been formed into a Steering Committee for our organizing drive. Besides the officers, this committee included Senator John Tower, Congressmen John Rhodes of Arizona and John Ashbrook of Ohio, Bill

Rusher, Charlie Barr, Stets Coleman, Jerry Milbank and Peter O'Donnell's Texas associate, Arthur Wesley.

The first meeting of this group after the July 4 rally was held on Sunday afternoon, July 28, at our Washington headquarters. The chief order of business was the selection of state Draft committees. By this time we had already announced, or were about to announce, chairmen and co-chairmen in fourteen states. My job that afternoon was to run down all fifty states to review how we stood, first listing the states where chairmen were now appointed.

Peter O'Donnell voiced the fear that we were moving too fast in naming state chairmen. He felt that it would be better to pace ourselves more slowly so we could have a chance to get more prominent Republicans to head the state committees rather than lower-echelon office holders or political unknowns.

Peter had a point here, of course, but in some states we just could not afford to wait. Our people were pushing us to unveil the state organizations. In some instances other groups not aligned with our Draft Committee had already declared themselves to be the Goldwater state committee, or were on the verge of doing so. A few of these groups were controlled by members of the Birch Society, and Peter recognized that we could not afford their public identification with Goldwater.

In some states even our own people were growing so impatient that they refused to wait. They just took the bit in their teeth and galloped off. We had a perfect example of this in Oklahoma. At the Steering Committee meeting, Peter and I still had hopes of getting Governor Henry Bellmon as the state Goldwater chairman. But that month a thousand people met in Tulsa and virtually constituted the state Republican Party as the Goldwater organization of Oklahoma. This would have been great except that the state GOP chairman, Bill Burkett of Oklahoma City, didn't like it, though he said he was for Goldwater.

The issue in Oklahoma turned on whether to send a delegation to the national convention with specific instructions to vote for Goldwater. There was no law or any party rule covering this question. But at the July mass meeting in Tulsa, Burkett declared his opposition to an instructed delegation. Some people in the crowd tried to debate him on this point, but Burkett was adamant. When he insisted on having his way, a large group of the Goldwater partisans practically hooted him out of the hall. They wanted no part of an uninstructed delegation that would be open to bids from opposition candidates at San Francisco.

Burkett went home that night understandably feeling somewhat chagrined. But instead of realizing that his state was so overwhelmingly for Goldwater that he could not stop an instructed delegation, Burkett began a bitter fight to thwart the obvious wishes of the majority of

Republican—and a good many Democratic—voters in Oklahoma. There were probably not more than twenty people at the Tulsa mass meeting who sided with Burkett. But they were mostly people of some standing and influence in the Republican Party and they joined the state chairman in his battle.

Henry Bellmon, the only Republican ever elected Governor in Oklahoma's history, was at that time all but committed to Goldwater. He was one of the Senator's staunchest supporters at all the Governors' meetings and he was predicting flatly that Goldwater would win the nomination. However, Burkett and his friends convinced Bellmon that he should go along with them on the issue of an uninstructed delegation. This issue caused a serious split in the Republican Party, even though those who sided with Burkett were a relatively small minority.

The Governor, unfortunately, was caught in the middle. And so were my good friends John Thomas and Denzil Garrison, the latter then minority leader in the State Senate. John and Denny were close friends and early supporters of Henry Bellmon and they wanted him as the state Goldwater chairman as much as we did. But they recognized that we could not afford to have someone heading up the Goldwater committee who was committed to sending uninstructed delegates to the national convention. Denny Garrison was prevailed upon to take the job himself and he proved a providential choice. If it had not been for him and John Thomas, the Republican Party in Oklahoma might have disintegrated entirely. As it was, the deep divisions in the GOP ranks still dragged down the whole ticket there in 1964 as they did everywhere. However, Oklahoma Republicans registered a respectable showing in the election and the party is still a viable force in that state as the 1966 elections proved.[1]

Ironically, Senator Garrison found himself temporarily pitted against his friend Governor Bellmon in the struggle over the instructed delegation issue. But the tide was running so strongly for Goldwater in Oklahoma, and Denny's people had done their spadework at the district level so thoroughly, that the outcome was never in doubt. Garrison swept the six Congressional district conventions and had an even dozen delegates

[1] Goldwater lost Oklahoma by a 4-to-5 margin and Bud Wilkinson, the GOP candidate for U.S. Senator, was edged out by Democrat Fred Harris by only 21,000 votes out of more than 912,000 cast in this traditionally Democratic stronghold. Wilkinson, the immensely popular former coach of the University of Oklahoma's great football teams, should have been an easy winner. But the combination of the public climate that prevailed in 1964, the hopelessly inept national GOP campaign, and the deep split in the Oklahoma Republican Party doomed him to defeat. Bud Wilkinson might have overcome any two of these obstacles, but all three piled on top of one another proved an insurmountable barrier.

firmly instructed to vote for Goldwater even before the state convention on February 28, 1964 picked ten additional delegates-at-large.

In late October, prior to a critical Republican State Committee meeting that preceded the convention, Garrison sat down with Governor Bellmon at breakfast in the Mayo Hotel in Tulsa. They worked out a semantic compromise, and agreed to join in recommending that the controversial word "instructed" be dropped. Instead, all twenty-two Oklahoma delegates would go to San Francisco "pledged" to Goldwater. On such thin threads history often hangs. In this instance, the Republican Party in Oklahoma was saved, for a knockdown-dragout battle between Senator Garrison and Governor Bellmon in the state committee would have set the GOP back twenty years.

There were only two dissenting votes against the compromise in the state committee meeting at Oklahoma City. One was registered by a man named Jim Farley, who was obviously not a student of the former Democrat National Chairman of the same name.

It was this kind of strength the Goldwater movement developed in the summer and early fall of 1963, the strength that carried it through to victory at the national convention. There were simply too many people in too many states who, like John Thomas, Denny Garrison and their Oklahoma team, refused to be shaken, no matter how formidable the power arrayed against them. This was something neither the press nor any of the opposition candidates recognized until they got to San Francisco. Strangely, Senator Goldwater himself did not fully understand it either until after the California primary, and even then he did not accurately grasp the strength of the conservative cause. If he had, I think he would have waged a far different campaign in the fall of 1964.

The issue that more than any other firmly cemented these people to Goldwater in the summer of 1963 was the Test Ban Treaty. The Supreme Court prayer ban had won the conservative cause thousands of converts, and in recent months Cuba had added thousands more. But the Treaty of Moscow solidified the new converts and reconfirmed the beliefs of traditional conservatives that U.S. foreign policy had degenerated to the level of appeasement.

The country was forewarned that revolutionary steps were about to be taken in the field of foreign policy when President Kennedy made his famed American University speech on June 19, 1963 calling for an entente with the Soviet Union. But few people believed the U.S. would surrender its insistence on adequate inspection to enforce disarmament agreements. Then, within a month, came the Treaty of Moscow. As in the Cuban missile crisis, we had again waived foolproof inspection.

The actual signing of the treaty on July 25, 1963 followed by less than two years the Soviets' cynical abrogation of the tacit nuclear test moratorium initiated by former President Eisenhower. Photographs of American diplomats smiling at, and even hugging, Russian officials at the formal signing of the pact flashed around the world.

To his credit, President Kennedy submitted the treaty to the Senate for its approval. This was an improvement on Franklin Roosevelt's handling of the infamous Yalta agreement. But what followed this creditable action read like something out of Allen Drury's best-selling novel, *Advise and Consent*.

At the outset it appeared as though there would be considerable opposition to the test ban in the Senate. There were a substantial number of Senators in both parties, including some Liberals, who seriously questioned the wisdom of a treaty which failed to provide the United States with adequate insurance against a Soviet nuclear buildup. Then came the cleverest pressure campaign the Kennedy Administration ever mounted in the Congress.

The Senate was not asked to judge the test ban on its merits. Through the skillful use of propaganda, Senators who lined up behind the treaty were made to appear as though they were on the side of the angels and for peace. Those who stood against it were cast in the undeserving role of warmongers.

Expert witnesses were trotted out to support the Administration's contention that on-site inspection of Soviet nuclear installations was somehow no longer necessary. Even the Joint Chiefs of Staff were bludgeoned into line. Reluctantly they testified in support of the Administration's position, though it was plain that they had serious doubts. One old friend who saw General Curtis LeMay, then the Air Force chief of staff, emerge from the Senate hearing described him as "a beaten man."

There were a few witnesses who refused to bow. Foremost among this small but brave band were Admiral Lewis Strauss, the wise and prudent ex-chairman of the Atomic Energy Commission, and Admiral Arleigh Burke, the esteemed former Chief of Naval Operations who now guides the Center for Strategic Studies at Georgetown University. And Admiral George W. Anderson, another former Chief of Naval Operations, had told the Senate Preparedness Subcommittee as early as June 26 that he was opposed to any treaty banning tests in the atmosphere. The Soviets had won a clear lead over the United States in the development of high-megaton weapons when they broke the test moratorium in 1961. Any new ban on such tests would foreclose U.S. chances of overcoming the Soviet lead.

Admiral Anderson, a courageous exponent of keeping U.S. defenses strong, had already been informed by the Administration that he would be retired in midsummer, although he had been expected to serve another term with the Joint Chiefs of Staff. His opposition to the test ban undoubtedly hastened his departure.

General Thomas Power, chief of the Strategic Air Command, also held out against Administration pressures. Knowing that he was putting his career on the line, this doughty New York Irishman nonetheless testified against the treaty and in doing so decimated the arguments in its favor. Power was soon scheduled for early retirement, though he had been in line to succeed LeMay as the Air Force member of the Joint Chiefs.

Dr. Edward Teller had guided the development of the hydrogen bomb in an era when J. Robert Oppenheimer and others had fought bitterly against it, although Russia clearly had the capability of producing this weapon too. As much as any other man, Dr. Teller had saved the U.S. from that earlier threat of Soviet nuclear blackmail. Now, he testified that the Test Ban Treaty was "not a step toward peace, but away from safety and possibly a step toward war." He called Defense Secretary McNamara's judgment that the Soviets had not developed an anti-missile defense system an "undue exaggeration." And he disagreed flatly with McNamara that the U.S. could perfect a similar system without atmospheric tests.

Senators Goldwater and Strom Thurmond of South Carolina, both members of the Preparedness Subcommittee and therefore privy to information most of their colleagues did not have, led the last-ditch fight against the test ban. They were joined by Senator Richard Russell of Georgia, chairman of the Armed Services Committee; John Stennis of Mississippi, chairman of the Preparedness Subcommittee; and Frank Lausche of Ohio, the only Northern Democrat who stood firm against the Administration juggernaut.

Despite this powerful combination of leadership, opposition to the treaty dwindled under the inexorable pressure from the White House. In two weeks of debate, every Senator who *supported* the treaty confessed the fear that he might be tragically wrong. Goldwater struggled on against increasing odds. He attempted to get a rider attached to the Senate motion that would call on the Soviet Union to live up to its agreement to get its troops out of Cuba as a condition for U.S. acceptance of the ban on atmospheric nuclear tests. When this was beaten down 75 to 17, it was clear that the opposition was doomed to defeat.·

The final vote, on September 24, was 80 to 19 in favor of the ban. Thus, by an overwhelming margin, the Senate of the United States consented to the treaty and in effect advised the President that it was willing to share with him the risk that the Soviet Union would keep its word. This, despite the fact that the Soviet had broken its word scores of times in the recent past.

In a moving speech on the floor of the Senate five days before the roll-call vote, Barry Goldwater displayed once again the unswerving courage which had drawn millions of Americans to his cause:

I do not vote against the hope of peace, but only against the illusion of it. I do not vote for war, but for the strength to prevent it.

I have been told, as have others, that to vote against this treaty is to commit political suicide.

I will vote against this treaty because in my heart, mind, soul and conscience, I feel it is detrimental to the strength of my country.

If it means political suicide to vote for my country and against this treaty, then I commit it gladly. It is not my future that concerns me. It is my country—and what my conscience tells me is how best I may serve it.[2]

Thus was drawn the great overriding issue of the coming Presidential campaign. Goldwater had placed the security of his country and his people above all political considerations. He and the other Senators who fought the Test Ban Treaty saw clearly, as Winston Churchill had in the 1930s, that a free nation's only hope of peace lay in maintaining its military strength. But, like Churchill, they were branded by their opponents as irresponsible warmongers.

[2] See Appendix A for the full text of this speech.

CHAPTER 20

"MEET MISTER KITCHEL"

ONE MORNING in the summer of 1963 Congressman John Rhodes of Arizona phoned me at the Draft Goldwater headquarters. He said there was someone in town I should meet and asked if I could be at his office right after lunch.

As I entered Rhodes' office on Capitol Hill at two o'clock I noticed a small man with gray brushcut hair and a rather long face who had arrived almost at the same moment. We were ushered into the Congressman's chambers together and I realized that this was the man Rhodes wanted me to see.

"Meet Mr. Kitchel," Rhodes said. "Denison Kitchel from Phoenix."

Kitchel and I shook hands and we sat down with John at his desk. "I thought you two fellows should get together," John said, but he gave me no clue as to why. We launched into a general discussion about politics and somehow the question of national conventions came up. Kitchel wanted to know how they worked and I gave him about twenty minutes of my standard primer on handling conventions, in essence the same lecture I used in my workshop courses on practical politics. We chatted about forty-five minutes in all, and then Kitchel had to leave for another appointment.

I knew very little about Denison Kitchel then. I had heard of him for the first time some months before when Barry Goldwater had named him as his 1964 Senate campaign manager in Arizona. I was a little surprised that Steve Shadegg had not been appointed to that post. Shadegg had done a great job for Goldwater in his two previous Senate races. But it was rumored that he and Barry had fallen out when Steve made an unsuccessful bid for the Republican nomination to run against the venerable Democrat Senator and Goldwater's friend, Carl Hayden, in 1962.[1]

It wasn't until some weeks after our first meeting in John Rhodes' office that I learned Kitchel was moving to Washington. At the time I thought this was a little odd. If he was managing Goldwater's Senate campaign he would certainly be working on that in Arizona. I suspected right away the Senator might at last have definitely changed his mind about trying for the Presidency instead of seeking re-election to the Senate. We had had other indications of this decision that summer, but I was certainly pleased to have this new evidence to confirm it.

As time went on I picked up bits and pieces of Kitchel's background. He had mentioned at our first meeting that he was originally from Bronxville, not far from my present home in New York's Westchester County. He was a product of Eastern prep schools, Yale, and Harvard Law. After he got his law degree he migrated to Arizona in 1934, married into the family that built a lucrative copper mine business now controlled by the Phelps Dodge Company, and joined the Phoenix law firm that handles Phelps Dodge's business in Arizona.

Kitchel had served for a half-dozen years as general counsel to the Arizona State Republican Committee. But he had little chance to familiarize himself with the intricate national political picture, and his circle of acquaintances on the national scene was understandably limited. Once, in the early fall of 1963, he flew from New York to Washington on a commercial flight with Goldwater and one of Barry's Republican colleagues in the Senate. They sat in the little lounge area at the back of the plane and chatted about politics all the way down. When they got off the plane Kitchel asked the other Senator what line of work he was in.

To save him similar embarrassments, I prepared a large handbook for him—a sort of *Who's Who* in politics, with brief biographies of prominent Republican figures and others he might expect to encounter. He kept this book on his desk and made intelligent use of it. Whenever he got a call from a stranger, or had an appointment with someone he didn't know, he would flip the pages in the big black loose-leaf book and find

---

[1] Steve Shadegg denies this. He says Barry asked him after that to manage his 1964 Senate race but withdrew the request because Steve was acting as public relations advisor to a privately owned utilities system that was threatening to get into a fight with the tax-exempt Salt River Project utility in Arizona. For some reason, the Senator considered this a potential political liability, though Shadegg had been associated with the private utility off and on for over twenty years.

out who the person was. I had appended little notes indicating whether the people listed were friendly or antagonistic to Goldwater, or whether they had already lined up with some other candidate, and so on. At a glance, Kitchel could determine how he should handle each visitor or phone call.

My contacts with Kitchel were confined strictly to politics. I was never in his home in the Westchester Apartments where one of his neighbors was his old friend Barry Goldwater. Since Kitchel was reluctant to be seen at the National Draft Goldwater Headquarters, we usually met in the offices he took in September in the Carroll Arms Hotel, across the street from the Senate Office Building.

In his book, *What Happened to Goldwater?*, Steve Shadegg describes Kitchel as "a one-time ardent New Dealer" who switched his registration after 1950. Kitchel never discussed this phase of his life with me, but perhaps it explains why he got on so well with William J. Baroody, another former New Dealer who became a member of Senator Goldwater's inner circle about this same time.

As soon as he moved to Washington, Kitchel was taken in tow by Baroody. Aside from their former philosophical devotion to the New and Fair Deals, the two men ostensibly had little in common. Kitchel was dour, almost austere, whereas Baroody always made it a point to appear affable and indeed seemed to consider himself something of a comedian. At 48, Baroody was seven years Kitchel's junior. Of Armenian parentage, he had been educated in New England but not in one of the Ivy League schools Kitchel valued so highly. He had come to Washington many years before to work for the government under the Democratic Administrations and had become a specialist in Social Security matters.

In recent years, Baroody had built the tax-exempt American Enterprise Institute into a research service that was used by Congressmen and Senators of both political parties. In fact, Baroody went to some lengths, even after he became associated with the Goldwater campaign, to preserve the non-partisan image of AEI. On the wall of his office in downtown Washington he hung autographed photos of the most Liberal members of the Congress, including Hubert Humphrey, next to those of some of the most renowned conservatives. He delighted in the confusion this caused among reporters and others who visited him.

Until he became openly identified with the Goldwater campaign in 1964, Baroody had been almost esoteric about his work. He had established fairly wide contacts in the academic world, and used a number of professors, mostly economists, to do research for AEI on a free-lance basis. But very little was known about his many activities outside AEI.

The first indication I had that Baroody was to become part of the Goldwater operation was sometime in the fall of 1963. I had been using a research firm in Washington to do background studies on issues I anticipated were going to be used by the Democrats and Liberal Republicans against Goldwater. But one of the Senator's friends told me that Barry wanted all such work done by Baroody's American Enterprise Institute.

Not long after this, it was announced that Edward A. McCabe would be in charge of research for the Senator. A native of Ireland, McCabe was a Washington lawyer who had served as an administrative assistant to President Eisenhower and for a time had been a Congressional liaison man for the White House.

There was an elaborate plan at this time to feed all of the Senator's public statements on various issues into a computer. The idea was that when his opponents in both parties started clobbering him on certain stands he had taken, the research team would merely push a button, the computer would serve up the Senator's actual statements, and the distortions of the opposition would become immediately apparent. However, no one ever quite figured out how you could get the press to disseminate this vast store of information to the public.

In the long run, a candidate must project his own ideas as a campaign develops. The computer might help remind him of what he had said on a given issue three, four or five years before. But it is the candidate who commands the headlines, not the computer, and he must make his views known anew as he goes along and state them in such a way as to capture the imagination of the voters.

Kitchel, Baroody and McCabe became almost obsessed with research activities. None of them had any knowledge of, or respect for, political organization per se. I say this not to downgrade the function of research in a Presidential campaign. It can be of vital importance. But it is only one ingredient, and unless it is coupled with a practical approach to politics, seasoned with an understanding of people and fused with these factors into an effective, fighting force by a candidate who appeals to the voters, all the research in the world will fail to maintain the momentum of a campaign. Besides, research, if it is to be of any help at all, must be *used* by the candidate. Goldwater, particularly after he won the nomination, but even before, did not always use the information available to him. He knew his subjects well enough, but he fell into the fatal error of assuming that the public knew as much about, for example, high-yield nuclear weapons as he did.

In the autumn of 1963, Dean Burch came to Washington as Kitchel's assistant. Dean was 35, a Tucson lawyer who had served as an assistant state attorney general in Arizona and had spent four years as Senator Goldwater's administrative assistant prior to his return to Arizona in 1959.

Kitchel told me that Burch was coming in to "take care of the house-keeping chores" for him. When Burch came down to visit us I had our office manager at the Draft headquarters, Jim Day, get together with Dean and work out arrangements for the physical expansion of the Carroll Arms offices.

It soon became apparent that Kitchel, Baroody, McCabe and Burch were forming themselves into a tight little circle around Senator Goldwater. They socialized a lot together, and often with the Senator. I have been criticized by some of my friends for not trying to establish a closer social relationship with them and with Goldwater. But the fact is I was never invited in, and like most people I had no desire to force myself on anyone. I didn't feel snubbed or left out. I had more than enough to do keeping tabs on our budding Goldwater organizations in all fifty states and I felt that the most important thing was to do a good job. The socializing seemed trivial, though I realized it was necessary for a candidate to have a group around him with whom he could relax in easy camaraderie after a grueling day on the campaign trail.

I didn't see then that these men would eventually shut Goldwater off from the world around him, and that they would successfully freeze everyone else out. I'm sure that Kitchel and Burch, at least, did this from the best of motives. They probably wanted to protect the Senator, to keep him from being overtaxed by all the people who suddenly came swarming around him. Neither of them had ever been involved in a Presidential campaign. They were not forewarned that when a man runs for the highest office in the land, everyone wants to get his ear. Not everyone should have it, of course. But a candidate has to make himself accessible at least to the leading people who are supporting him in every state. He can accept or reject their advice as he sees fit, but he should listen to them. And the most important thing is for the candidate to make his own decisions on issues and other critical matters. He cannot delegate authority entirely if he is to provide proper leadership.

As 1963 waned and the nominating campaign got under way, even Goldwater's oldest and closest friends were walled off from him. This sort of thing happens to every man who runs for President. It happened to Nixon in 1960, and many prominent Republicans still blame his defeat on the small coterie who, in their desire to protect Nixon, shut out capable people who wanted to give him sound advice.

To a lesser degree it happened to Kennedy. The little group of Left-leaning professors and political professionals who surrounded him effectively insulated him from the more conservative elements in the Democratic Party. But they were shrewd enough to do this in such a way that the conservatives deluded themselves into thinking they were being given a fair hearing. The ADA gang let Jack listen to these people, and even incorporated conservative ideas into his speeches, in the confident knowledge that after the election they would be the ones who could call the shots on policy.

In addition, Kennedy had his brother Bobby, and other members of his numerous clan, who would patiently lend their ears to politicians laboring under the impression that to advise a member of the candidate's family was as good as advising the candidate himself. And more important, Bobby Kennedy and his kinsmen sorted out the advice they got and passed on to Jack whatever they thought would be of value.

Barry Goldwater, unfortunately, had no one with sure political instinct who could listen and act in his behalf. His own brother Bob had never been in politics and took no major part in the 1964 campaign. Kitchel was the man closest to the Senator. But Kitchel was forced to learn national politics as he went along and there was just too much to be learned in such a brief period.

Among those who found themselves on the outside looking mutely in was one of Goldwater's most trusted advisors, a man who had been generously helping him since his first Senate campaign in 1952. I will call this man Mr. X, because to name him might jeopardize his career, although he has been identified elsewhere under a pseudonym. Not even the Senator was aware that Mr. X had been shut out. Once he asked Charlie Barr why this man never called him any more. Charlie could have told him, of course. But by then Charlie was on the outside himself, having given up trying to pierce the impenetrable defenses of the palace guard.

One incident involving Mr. X that occurred in September of 1963 should have given us all ample warning of what lay ahead. He arranged a meeting in his hotel suite at Washington's Hay Adams between the members of Goldwater's embryo inner circle, of which he was then one, and William F. Buckley, Jr., editor of *National Review,* and Buckley's brother-in-law, L. Brent Bozell. Buckley's magazine had been one of the Senator's earliest and most effective supporters. More important, this publication had given an intellectual focus to the whole conservative movement that it had sadly lacked prior to the magazine's founding in 1955. *National Review,* as much as Barry Goldwater, had accomplished the impossible. It had made the label "conservative" respectable once again, particularly in the academic community.

Brent Bozell, like Buckley, is one of the recognized intellectual leaders of the conservative cause. He had in fact written Barry Goldwater's first best-selling book, *The Conscience of a Conservative.* There are some who say the Senator trusted Brent so implicitly that he never even read the manuscript of that book, which was an accurate distillation of Goldwater's past statements and speeches liberally spiked with pure 200-proof

Bozell. Instead, Goldwater passed the manuscript on to Steve Shadegg, and accepted Steve's approval.

The purpose of the meeting at the Hay Adams was to determine how Buckley, Bozell and their friends could be of service in the coming campaign. Bill and Brent had conceived the idea of gathering a group of leading professors and others to act as an advisory committee to the Senator. Unfortunately, Bill Baroody, who also attended the meeting, had already begun to move in his own stable of AEI professors for the same purpose. Buckley and Bozell knew Baroody, and indeed Brent considered him a friend. But they were somewhat surprised to find him at the conference in Mr. X's suite. Kitchel was also present.

As the meeting wore on, Buckley and Bozell found that every suggestion they made was being turned aside by Baroody, who seemed to be playing the role of devil's advocate for Kitchel. At last, Brent felt he had had enough. Politely but firmly he put Baroody in his place. The meeting broke up soon after, with nothing decided, but with a tacit promise that the idea for forming an academic committee would be considered.

The committee was eventually formed, under Baroody's auspices, but neither Buckley nor Bozell played any role whatever in the ensuing campaign, before or after the nomination. However, a few days after the meeting, the *New York Times* carried a most amazing story with a lead that went directly to the point: "[The] Goldwater for President ship has just repelled a boarding party from the forces who supposedly occupy the narrow territory to the right of the Arizona Senator." The story claimed that Buckley and Bozell had "cornered some Goldwater aides" and expressed their desire "to join the campaign organization . . . on the policy-planning level." Then the *Times* story went on:

Feeling that what their candidate needs least is more support from the far right, Goldwater advisers used an old political dodge. They played dumb. They just could not seem to understand what the *National Review* men were getting at. Mr. Buckley and Mr. Bozell reportedly emerged from the conference with no share of the Goldwater command and wondering if they wanted any.

It is not hard to imagine the reaction of the two principals when they read this story. It was plain that one of the other people in the room had leaked it to the *Times,* either directly or through an intermediary.

Brent Bozell telephoned Senator Goldwater personally to ask him about it. The Senator simply replied "Well, you don't think I did it, do you?" Bozell had not suggested that, of course, but he was understandably concerned that news of a confidential meeting could be fed to the press through the Senator's closest associates.

Buckley phoned Kitchel in California, and Kitchel said he had not talked about the meeting with anyone, let alone a reporter from the *New York Times.* I am sure this is true. I don't believe Denison Kitchel would have been party to this kind of treachery. And I know for certain that Mr. X did not do it, although he told one other member of Goldwater's Senate staff of the meeting. Tony Smith, who had been a newspaperman for years, had been around Washington too long to let a story like that slip out. Baroody, when asked, volunteered the belief that the room had been bugged. But this seems highly unlikely. The *New York Times* has not yet, to my knowledge at least, authorized its reporters to use secret recording devices.

Many people have asked me if I knew that Denison Kitchel had once been a member of the John Birch Society. The answer is no. I had no inkling of this whatsoever until I read the manuscript of Steve Shadegg's book early in 1965.[2] After the book was published in July of that year, Kitchel admitted that he and his wife, Naomi, joined the Society in 1960. But he said they quit within "ten days or two weeks" after he read *The Politician,* the book in which the Birch Society's founder, Robert Welch, characterized Dwight Eisenhower as a tool of the Communist conspiracy.

Kitchel, who is basically a moderate man, certainly would not have swallowed this rank distortion of Ike, and I'm sure he reacted exactly as he said. However, his short-lived membership in the Birch Society must go down as the best-kept secret of the 1964 campaign.

None of us knew it, but everyone associated with the Goldwater campaign was sitting on a truckload of political dynamite all the while Kitchel was in the driver's seat. In July 1965, Steve Shadegg's revelation caused only a minor flurry. But if Kitchel's former membership in the Society had been made known during the 1964 campaign it would have blown everything to smithereens. Kitchel's brief and innocent association would have been magnified beyond belief by an already hostile press, and we all would have been tarred with the "extremist" brush.

I believe Kitchel had an obligation, to the Senator and to all the rest of us, to step aside, or at least remain far enough in the background that he would not be publicly tagged as the leader of the Goldwater campaign. If the Senator was aware of his manager's past association, no matter how innocuous it actually may have been, discretion should have dictated that he appoint someone else to that important post.

If it seems that I judge too harshly, I must point out once again that in the irrational climate that prevailed in 1963 and 1964, the merits of Kitchel's Birch membership, or anyone else's, would *not* have been calmly and intelligently weighed by the press and the public. The hard realities of political life in that climate demanded that Denison Kitchel

[2] *Op. cit.,* p. 105.

take a very different course than the one he took in becoming Goldwater's campaign director.

Although I do not believe Kitchel had a hand in giving the story of Bill Buckley's and Brent Bozell's "boarding party" to the *New York Times* in September 1963, he nonetheless acquiesced in keeping both these men, and many more, out of the subsequent campaign. This was done, as the *Times* story accurately reported, on the flimsy grounds of their supposed connection with the "far right." Ironically, Buckley has been an outspoken critic of Robert Welch's conspiratorial view of recent history and, more recently, of the Birch Society itself.

Initially, the arrival of Denison Kitchel in Washington had no effect upon our Draft Goldwater operation. We sensed that Kitchel would come to play an important role in the campaign and at the behest of John Rhodes and others we established close liaison with his office in the Carroll Arms. But he rarely presumed to advise us in our continuing organizational drive.

On Labor Day, September 2, Barry Goldwater was in Williams, Arizona leading another parade and maintaining the position that he still intended to run for re-election to the Senate. That day Peter O'Donnell flew to Chicago to announce the formation of our Draft affiliate, the Illinois Volunteers for Goldwater. At a press conference in the Sheraton Chicago Hotel, Peter introduced John F. Milliken of Winnetka, the executive vice president and a director of Midland Casualty Insurance Company, as our state chairman, and Mrs. Laddie F. (Pat) Hutar, the immediate past national co-chairman of the Young Republicans, as the Illinois co-chairman. Then they had a reception and ribbon-cutting ceremony, attended by some of the state's leading Republicans, at the Illinois Volunteers' new office at 116 South Michigan Avenue.

The following day Tom Van Sickle joined us at our Washington headquarters as my executive assistant. Although he was only 26, Tom had served two years in the lower house of the State Legislature in Kansas and nearly three in the Senate. He had won his first election at the age of 21, as one of two Republican candidates who defeated opposition incumbents in the 1958 Democratic landslide that swept his state. Two years later he moved up to the Senate, again defeating a solidly entrenched Democratic incumbent.

Although he was threatened with a primary fight before he could run for re-election in 1964, Tom chose to join our Draft movement in Washington. He did this at a considerable sacrifice, taking a sabbatical from his law studies in Kansas and thereby deferring his career by at least a year. Tom not only lightened the heavy load I was then carrying by regularly putting in 16- to 20-hour work days himself, but he remained one of our strong right arms in Kansas and the whole Midwest.

On Sunday, September 8, I was back in Chicago again, this time for a Draft Steering Committee meeting at the O'Hare Inn. Fifteen members of the Committee showed up that morning and I couldn't help but contrast the aura of confidence that prevailed this time with the dismal mood of the meeting we had held in February at this same motel.

Peter O'Donnell presided and he underlined the pressing need for expanding our Washington staff. Despite all the publicity that had been cranked out of our office since June, we still did not have a press relations man. Peter wanted to retain a New York advertising and public relations agency to help. Charlie Barr opposed this on the grounds that we should not take a Madison Avenue approach to publicity matters.

The remaining state organizations were rapidly forming. Peter reported that Senator Tower was in California, where he planned to meet with former Senator William Knowland. John Rhodes had already urged Knowland to head up a California Goldwater Committee comprised of Congressmen, state legislators and others. We hoped that the Committee would represent all Republican factions in that strife-torn state.

I had just finished a swing through Wisconsin where Sam Hay had just gotten Wayne Hood to come out of political retirement to head up our state Goldwater committee. Wayne was one of the most highly regarded Republicans in the Midwest. He had been Wisconsin GOP state chairman in the early 1950s and later executive director of the National Committee. But after Senator Taft's defeat at the 1952 convention, Wayne gradually withdrew from politics, and since then had devoted full time to his family's manufacturing business in La Crosse. No one thought we could get Wayne to join us, but Sam Hay and an old contact of mine in Wisconsin had done the trick.

During a tour of Wisconsin the previous fall I had stopped off in Madison to see Tom Coleman, a former Republican state chairman and National Committeeman. I had written Tom from Suite 3505 to let him know that I was coming. But when I arrived at his plant office the receptionist told me he was in the hospital. I asked if I could see his son. While she was trying to locate the son in the plant, a taxi pulled up outside. Through the glass doors I saw an elderly man get slowly out of the cab. He had a heavy white blanket draped around his shoulders to shield him from the bitter cold. I ran to the door to help him inside and he grinned at me in sheepish recognition. It was Tom Coleman!

"All those doctors and nurses said I couldn't come," Tom growled. "But I told them I had an important appointment and nothing was going to keep me from it." He pulled on the hospital blanket. "One of the nurses threw this darn thing around me as I got into the cab."

I followed him into his office, the blanket still trailing from his shoulders, and his son joined us. We reminisced for a few minutes about Carroll Reece and some of our friends. He talked a bit about the 1952 convention, but all the bitterness he must have felt at Taft's defeat had long since drained away. I gave him a report of what we were doing out of 3505. When I was finished he smiled and said, "Thank God something is moving again. I was beginning to think the conservatives were dead forever."

I asked Tom's advice about a chairman for Wisconsin when we got ready to unveil our organization. He suggested Wayne Hood, the man Sam Hay and I had been thinking about too. I asked him if he would help us get Wayne and he promised he would. He kept his promise, as I knew he would, and when the time came Wayne Hood was with us. On February 4, 1964, Tom Coleman died. But to the very last he was full of hope.

At the Steering Committee meeting in Chicago I urged that we get a man working on physical arrangements for the San Francisco convention as soon as possible. The convention was still ten months away, but I had learned that 60 per cent of the available hotel rooms had already been reserved. The news media people and others had learned that you have to sign up early for space in a convention city and I was sure my friends who were working for Rockefeller had already surveyed the San Francisco scene as well.

Peter O'Donnell announced that we had formed a Youth for Goldwater Committee. Jim Harff of Wisconsin, former college chairman of the Young Republicans, would head it up, and Carol Bauman, an exceptionally able young woman, had signed on as executive secretary and would start work September 16.

The meeting, which had started shortly after nine o'clock, adjourned at three. Before I left, Charlie Barr gave me a detailed report on Nelson and Happy Rockefeller's disastrous invasion of Illinois the day before. They had flown out in the Governor's Convair for a Republican picnic at the Ogle County Fairgrounds in Oregon, Illinois. There was a little crowd of curious spectators at the Rockford airport when they landed and Rockefeller left his entourage to go off on a handshaking sortie.

Perhaps no one would have noticed that there were some important Illini among the missing if it had not been for Chicago's Lar Daly. For years Lar, invariably dressed in his red-white-and-blue Uncle Sam suit, had been a well-known political comedian. He had run for every office in the book, from dog catcher to President, switching parties as his fancy directed. Now, in 1963, he was attempting to enter the already crowded Republican primary for the Illinois gubernatorial nomination.

Lar was standing in front of the crowd and when Rockefeller shook his hand he yelled, loud enough to be heard clear back to Chicago, "I'm one candidate for Governor who's not afraid to be here!" The fixed grin on Rockefeller's face momentarily vanished. Hovering reporters started scribbling in their notebooks. And the incident was duly broadcast to the world that night.

Rockefeller probably had not expected two of the GOP gubernatorial candidates to show up. One, Hayes Robertson, the Cook County chairman, had openly come out for Goldwater weeks before. And Charles Carpentier, Illinois Secretary of State, although not yet overtly supporting the Senator, was nonetheless regarded as a conservative.

But Chuck Percy's absence must have really hurt. Not only had Percy backed Rockefeller during the platform battle at the 1960 convention; he was also a director of the Chase Manhattan Bank, which is controlled by the Governor's family. Rockefeller had counted on Percy as his key man in the Midwest. But as I have mentioned, Percy was already predicting Goldwater would get the nomination. Now his failure to welcome Rockefeller to his home state added to the accurate public impression that prominent Republicans were staying just as far away from Rockefeller as they could get.

When Rockefeller rose to speak at the fairgrounds he found himself facing a vast sea of Goldwater buttons. He made a brave try, as he always does, and gave the crowd a fighting conservative speech. He lambasted the Kennedy Administration unmercifully, and at one point shouted out, "We are not on the New Frontier. We are lost in the woods." The crowd applauded its approval, but it was plain to every politician there that the Governor had won no converts in this Goldwater heartland. Later, Robert Novak graphically recorded Rockefeller's visit to the fairgrounds:

There was a smell of political death about the day in Ogle County. It was like observing a political corpse who did not realize that he was dead.[3]

Rockefeller's dismal excursion into Illinois contrasted sharply with a visit Barry Goldwater had made to that same fairgrounds a month earlier. His appearance at the Ogle County Fair had not only attracted a huge and enthusiastic crowd but a host of prominent Republicans as well. Barry had surprised everyone when he introduced two other out-of-staters, former U.S. Attorney General Herbert Brownell of New York and ex-Postmaster General Arthur Summerfield of Michigan. Brownell and Summerfield had also served as GOP National Chairmen, and the significance of their appearance with the Senator in Illinois was not lost on the tiny group of uncertain Republican leaders in that state.

The New York Governor's debacle in Ogle County was still fresh in the public mind when, four days after Rockefeller's departure, Gold-

[3] *Op. cit.,* p. 224.

water came back to Illinois. Barry flew into Chicago on a commercial flight from Washington on Wednesday, September 11, to attend the 25th annual meeting of the National Federation of Republican Women. When he entered the hotel ballroom just before the dinner at which he was to speak, the women shook the chandeliers with their cheers. And, of course, all three of the Illinois gubernatorial candidates—Percy, Robertson, and Carpentier—were on hand to greet him.

Ione Harrington and her girls were there too, working away in the Draft Goldwater hospitality suite at the hotel. The turnout was excellent and we got hundreds more new signatures on our Draft petitions. A poll taken at the conference reflected Goldwater's strong appeal to women voters. Of 293 women polled, 262 said Barry was their first choice as the Republican nominee. The remaining 31 votes were divided among *all* the other possible candidates.

The afternoon before Goldwater's appearance, Ione gathered Pat Hutar, Judy Fernald, Maxine Charlton, Lucille Hosmer and Rita Bree into her own room to outline a plan she had cooked up. Mrs. Ann Eve Johnson, the former National Committeewoman from Arizona, also sat in.

Ione pointed out that there were 197 women delegates and 401 alternates at the 1960 national convention. If anything, we could expect even more women in the 1964 delegations at San Francisco. To make certain that Goldwater had an overwhelming majority of these distaff delegates, Ione had decided to adapt my regional plan to her women's organization. She intended to appoint six influential Republican women as regional directors. Their first order of business would be to establish contact with all of the 1960 delegates and alternates and report on which candidate they preferred. Special attention would be given to those who were not for Goldwater. If they could not be persuaded to support the Senator, then there would be no alternative but to find more dependable delegates to replace them wherever possible. Ione hoped to have the regional directors working within six weeks and would urge them to get their reports in by early January so we could determine where we would have contests coming up for the women's delegate seats.

The day they held this meeting I was in Colorado for the Republican Governors' Conference. After several decades of me-tooism, the number of GOP governors had dwindled to seventeen, barely half the number of Democrat state chief executives. Unfortunately, there was only a small handful of the seventeen we could count on to help Barry Goldwater get the nomination.

I arrived in Denver the day the conference opened and drove down to Colorado Springs for a meeting with three of the governors—Paul Fannin of Arizona, Tim Babcock of Montana and Cliff Hansen of

Wyoming. All were, of course, firmly in Goldwater's camp, and we discussed their strategy for trying to win, or at least neutralize, the other governors who were to attend the Denver conference.

I left at 1 A.M. and flew east to Michigan for a state Republican meeting on Mackinac Island. For some reason, the press predicted that I was coming into Michigan to attack Governor Romney and everyone expected an explosion at Mackinac. I'm afraid I disappointed them. My public position on George Romney, then and right on down to the convention, was simply that we were all for him—as Governor of Michigan. Instead of attacking him, I issued a statement urging all Goldwater supporters in Michigan to get behind Romney's re-election the following year. I said that I hoped eventually the Governor would support Goldwater for the Presidency, but this was another hope that went a-glimmering in 1964.

Our Michigan Goldwater Committee, under Creighton Holden and Ty Gillespie, was gaining strength with each passing day and the turnout at their hospitality suite on Mackinac Island gave added evidence of this. On top of that, a recent poll of Michigan's county chairmen showed that 70 per cent favored Goldwater.

Romney could see that if the trend continued he would not be able to control his own state delegation at the national convention. He was already having a great deal of difficulty, not so much with our Committee, but with another Goldwater supporter named Richard Durant. Although Durant admittedly had been a member of the Birch Society, he had for many years been chairman of the Republican organization in Michigan's 14th Congressional District, which encompasses the fashionable Grosse Pointe area just outside Detroit.[4]

In his desire to appear as a dedicated opponent of "extremism," Romney denounced Durant and a long and vicious battle ensued. It was some months later that Romney summoned me to a private conference in Lansing to discuss the Durant situation. He wanted me to join him in denouncing Durant but I refused.

George Romney is a very direct man, a quality I greatly admire. So it was not surprising that our meeting ended up almost in a shouting match. We stood in the middle of the room, jowl to jowl, and Romney kept repeating that Durant was a cancer in the Republican Party and ought to be read out of the party entirely.

I told the Governor flatly that Durant was his problem, not mine. "I

[4] Richard Durant's brother-in-law, Earl Heenan, had been a close friend of Captain John Birch in China, where Birch reportedly became the first American soldier killed by the Communists in the post-World War II era. It was this friendship that later led both Durant and Heenan to join the John Birch Society. Durant later resigned.

didn't put Dick Durant in Michigan," I said. "I didn't elect him a precinct committeeman. I didn't elect him a Republican district chairman. Your people here in Michigan did that. Now you will have to live with him."

Romney said that, since Durant was part of the Goldwater organization, we were perpetuating Durant's attacks on him by refusing to denounce Durant.

I denied that Durant was part of our organization. He might support it, which was his right, but he had nothing whatever to do with the state Goldwater Committee.

Later, when Durant sued the Governor for libel, I felt he had gone too far and I did repudiate him publicly. Despite this, Durant remained loyal to the Goldwater cause, and he was one of eight delegates from Michigan who voted for the Senator on the first ballot at San Francisco.

In that wonderful September of 1963 I could take all these problems in stride. Goldwater was soaring toward what turned out to be the zenith of his popularity, although at that time we had every reason to believe it would keep on ascending. In the middle of the month, the Gallup Poll had the Senator winning the nomination in a walk. In a contest between him and Rockefeller, he was favored by no less than 59 per cent of the Republican voters polled.. Moreover, his stock was still climbing with the independents too. A good, solid 56 per cent of these voters preferred Goldwater over Rockefeller.

But the big news from the Gallup Poll was that Goldwater was rapidly overtaking the man who had once been considered unbeatable—John F. Kennedy. In the Democrats' solid South he outpolled the President 54 per cent to 34 per cent. He still trailed Kennedy in other parts of the country. But we had more than a year to go until the election, and all of us in the Goldwater organization felt confident that at the rate he was then going he would overtake and pass Kennedy by November 3, 1964.

The reasons for the Goldwater surge were never more apparent than at the Dodgers' stadium in Los Angeles on Tuesday night, September 17. Nearly 50,000 people jammed the arena to hear the Senator that night. They punctuated almost every statement he made with applause and cheers and stomping feet.

At the end of his speech, he told them that he was flying back to Washington to take part in the debate on the Test Ban Treaty. A great groan of opposition to the treaty rumbled through the stadium. But when Goldwater reassured them that he was going to vote against it, the cheers that filled the night sky must have echoed all the way up the coast to San Francisco.

CHAPTER 21

THE PRODIGAL'S RETURN

IN OCTOBER, our National Draft Goldwater Committee had been in business for six months. Yet in all that time as the Committee's national director, I had not once talked with the man we were trying to nominate and elect President of the United States. In fact, I had had no personal contact whatever with Senator Goldwater since the last disappointing meeting Charlie Barr and I had had with him on February 5, 1963.

Then, one busy morning, a call came through our switchboard at the Draft headquarters in Washington. The caller asked for me and the young telephone operator, following instructions, inquired who was calling. The voice at the other end of the line said "Barry Goldwater." In her excitement, the girl almost pulled all the plugs out of the board trying to locate my line. The Senator had never phoned our office before and the staff was well aware of the fact that I hadn't seen him for many months.

I picked up the phone when it buzzed in my office and the operator almost punctured my eardrum with her shouting. "It's Barry Goldwater!" she yelled. "Barry Goldwater! He's on the line now!" I smiled and said, "Well, why don't you put him through?"

The Senator sounded in good humor. He must have caught a little of the by-play at the switchboard and he was still chuckling when I came on the line. "Clif," he said, "I'd like you to come up and see me."

"Fine, Barry," I replied. "When would suit you?"

"Right now, if you can make it. At my office."

I told him I'd be there in ten minutes and he hung up. I left the head-quarters immediately and caught a cab on Connecticut Avenue. The taxi dropped me off at the Old Senate Office Building and I took the elevator up to the fourth floor. Edna Coerver gave me a big hello and smile when I entered Goldwater's office and showed me right into the Senator's chambers.

Barry was sitting behind his desk. He got up as I came in and shook hands warmly. "How've you been, stranger?" he greeted me. "It's nice to see you."

When we finished with the amenities he sat down and waved me to a chair beside his desk. Kitchel and Mr. X were there too and they both appeared quite pleased. I confess I felt a little like the prodigal son re-turning home after having been away for a very long time. Barry looked tanned and fit and was obviously relaxed and in fine spirits.

"I don't know whether I'm going to go all the way on this thing or not," he said finally. "But if I do, I want you in it. So I thought it would be a good idea to clue you in now. We're going to ask you to do certain things. But for obvious reasons you have to stay with your Draft Com-mittee and operate that as you have been, without any identification with me."

I said that was fine. I was used to operating undercover. We could handle it any way he wanted. But I asked if he would call Peter O'Don-nell and let him know. Peter was still the chairman of the Draft Com-mittee and, though I didn't underline it because I was sure the Senator would appreciate my position, I knew that it might put me in an em-barrassing spot to start doing things for Goldwater without telling Peter why I was doing them.

Barry said he would call Peter and let him know. Then we chatted for five or ten minutes about the coming campaign and the people Goldwater wanted in key positions. Although he didn't come right out and say so, I got the definite impression that he wanted me to serve as his director of organization, or possibly co-director with Mr. X. Since I had had a good working relationship with this gentleman for many months, and had known him well for some years, I was delighted to learn that we would be working together on the Senator's campaign team. He and I left together that day and Kitchel stayed on to talk some more with Barry. I knew Mr. X had been pulling for me, and before we parted I thanked him for his support.

That afternoon Congressman Rhodes phoned me at the Draft head-quarters. He had been in Barry's office earlier that morning with Kitchel and Mr. X and he asked if the Senator had been in touch with me. I told him about the call and the visit with Goldwater. John was very happy. He said that this was something he had been hoping for for a long time. I knew he had been working in my behalf too, trying to offset the damage effected by the splendid hatchet job my "friends" had done on me with the Senator back in December and January after the secret meeting in Chicago.

Several days went by, and though I was on the phone with Peter O'Donnell three or four times he never indicated that he had heard from Goldwater. I thought perhaps the Senator hadn't been able to catch up with him, since Peter was traveling a good deal during this period. Once when he returned to Dallas he called his wife from his office to let her know that he would be home that evening. "Great," she said, "I'll put name tags on the children." They still laugh over that, but I know how Peter's wife and his three daughters must have felt during those days because my own family felt exactly the same way. Our families seldom saw us, and it was a big event whenever we were able to come home for a day or even a few hours.

Peter and I had a Steering Committee meeting coming up the first weekend in October in New York and I tried to make sure the Senator called him before that. I phoned Mr. X and asked him whether the call had been made. He said he didn't think so, and I impressed upon him that I felt it was essential to my continuing partnership with Peter that he be informed of the change in my status. I told him that I couldn't do this myself because it might appear that I had engineered the meeting with Goldwater. The last thing I wanted was for Peter to think I had pulled an end run on him. He had always been our Draft Committee's contact with the Senator, mostly through John Tower, and I saw no reason for that to change now.

An intelligent and unusually perceptive man, Mr. X. understood my concern completely. He asked where the Senator could reach Peter. I told him that I had just talked with O'Donnell at his Dallas office and he would be there the rest of the day. I gave him the phone number and he promised that he would see to it the Senator made the call.

On Friday night I got into New York with Rita Bree and Tom Van Sickle after the rather harrowing landing at La Guardia, and went straight to Suite 3505. After I had worked for an hour or so, my wife came in to drag me off to dinner. We dined with Rita and Tom, Ione Harrington and Judy and Dave Fernald. Then those of us who were on the Steering Committee adjourned to a suite at the Sheraton-East, the old Ambassador Hotel on Park Avenue at 51st Street. After the meeting I asked Peter if just the two of us could get together for breakfast the next morning and we set the time for eight o'clock.

I stayed overnight at the hotel instead of going all the way home and

Peter and I met in the coffee shop for breakfast. "Peter," I said, "did you get a phone call from Barry?"

He said yes, but he wasn't sure he knew what the Senator was talking about. "He called me up and said that he was asking you to do some special things. Maybe you can tell me what that means."

I said that I guessed it meant just that. I told him that the Senator had asked me to come up to his office and had said that he wanted me to do certain things for him but that I was to stay on as national director of the Draft Committee. At this point several other members of the Steering Committee came up to the table and sat down with us. Peter and I never had a chance to finish our talk and this led to some misunderstanding later on when I ordered a special poll at Goldwater's request. Ultimately, however, Peter and I wound up in much the same boat.

At this October Steering Committee meeting there was no longer any doubt that Barry Goldwater would, as he had put it, "go all the way." A story had recently leaked out that he had personally reserved the entire fifteenth floor of the Mark Hopkins Hotel in San Francisco for convention week when he had visited California during the summer. At our Sunday morning session, I reported that I was going to San Francisco myself the following week to complete arrangements for hotel space. This was one of the "certain things" the Senator's people had asked me to do, though I had been in favor of getting someone in San Francisco to work full-time on convention plans.

The finance committee reported that we had taken in nearly half a million dollars since the inception of the Draft Committee. Although our fund drive had bogged down in September, we still had about $125,000 in the bank, enough to carry us through to the end of the year. However, the finance men were rightly concerned that we weren't building a big enough war chest for the primary and convention battles after the first of the year.

We were all amused by a report in *Roll Call,* a Capitol Hill newspaper which had recently quoted an anonymous Goldwater backer as saying that the Arizona Senator had $7,500,000 in the bank and access to $17,000,000 more.

Ironically, our financial campaign had been inadvertently slowed by Goldwater himself. He was the main attraction at fundraising dinners for the Republican Party that fall and most of our potential contributors were kicking in for these instead of to the Draft Goldwater Committee.

One of the most successful of these GOP dinners was held in Hershey, Pennsylvania on the Thursday following our New York meeting. The Pennsylvania Republican organization was in critical need of money and Barry Goldwater was summoned to bail them out. Governor Scranton and the state Republican chairman, Craig Truax, knew that the Senator was the only party personality who could attract a really big crowd at a $100-a-plate dinner. Barry was happy to help them, as he had helped Cliff Case's GOP organization in New Jersey earlier and as he helped many other state Republican organizations that autumn.

It was a beautiful, warm, sunny day in central Pennsylvania when Barry landed at Hershey. More than 3,500 tickets had been sold for the dinner, pouring an unprecedented $350,000 into the state GOP's coffers, some of which must have been siphoned off indirectly the following year for Scranton's campaign against Goldwater. The ticket sale had gone so well that the dinner had to be held outdoors in the Hershey high school stadium under five gigantic circus tents erected for the occasion.

In order that the diners would all be able to hear the man they had each paid $100 to come and see, the GOP State Committee had rented the huge Hershey Sports Arena across the street from the stadium for his after-dinner appearance. This event was to be thrown open to the public.

By six o'clock a large crowd of people who had not attended the dinner were already milling around the main entrances to the stadium and the arena hoping to get a glimpse of Goldwater. Another and smaller group, comprising the leading Republicans and Goldwater supporters in Pennsylvania, were waiting for Barry at the Hershey Hotel just beyond the town.

The warm sunshine and the gorgeous flaming foliage of the autumn forests that covered the high rolling hills surrounding the lovely old inn contributed to the holiday spirit that prevailed. On the broad stone steps leading to the hotel's veranda Raymond Pitcairn, a Philadelphia attorney and one of the major shareholders in the Pittsburgh Plate Glass Company, was passing out our Goldwater campaign literature and some other items he had had printed at his own expense.

One of the latter was a mimeographed copy of a poll taken by the *Pottstown Mercury* among members of the Montgomery County Republican Committee a few weeks before. The poll showed that in this eastern Pennsylvania county the GOP committee preferred Goldwater by more than 4 to 1 over his nearest poll rival, Rockefeller, and by more than 12 to 1 over their own Governor, Scranton.[1] As a matter of fact, Scranton was far behind all the five other candidates named by the committee members. Nor was this sentiment peculiar to Montgomery County. It was an accurate reflection of the personal preferences of GOP leaders and workers in every section of Pennsylvania, with the possible exception

[1] The exact results of the Montgomery County poll were: Goldwater, 109; Rockefeller, 24; Lodge, 21; Nixon, 16; Romney, 13; Scranton, 9.

of Philadelphia. Even there, though, the party's candidate for Mayor was sounding amazingly like a Goldwater Republican that fall.

The Senator's plane was late that afternoon and, as often happened, he got way behind schedule. He had to cut short his visit with the people at the hotel in order to make a previously scheduled press conference inside the arena. The route from the hotel had been carefully mapped out in advance so that the Goldwater caravan would arrive at the back door of the arena.

Although Scranton had not been on hand to greet the Senator at the hotel, he had considerately arranged for a state police cruiser to escort the Goldwater cars to the arena.

An errant reporter who had come up to the hotel suddenly found himself without transportation to the press conference, and the state trooper escorting the caravan let the reporter ride along with him. As the little motorcade started down the hill, the trooper called in on his radio to report to the central traffic control car parked outside the stadium. He told control the motorcade would be arriving in about five minutes at the front entrance to the arena in compliance with his instructions from Governor Scranton's aides.

The reporter, who had been clued in on the route and had seen the big crowd in front of the arena, told the trooper they were supposed to go to the back door to avoid the crowd. "He's half an hour late for the press conference now," the reporter said. "If he gets tangled up in that mob at the front he'll have to cancel it entirely."

The trooper hesitated, but at the reporter's urging he finally stopped the car, got out and walked back to check with the Senator's car behind him. Bennett C. Chapple, the U.S. Steel vice president who was soon to be announced as chairman of our Western Pennsylvania Citizens for Goldwater, was in the car with the Senator. Ben verified the reporter's route. The trooper got back in the cruiser, and after winning a brief debate with his traffic control led the caravan to the arena's back door.

About a hundred newspaper, radio and television people were impatiently waiting for the Senator when he arrived. There had been plenty of time to test the public address system which the GOP State Committee people had set up. But when Goldwater climbed up on the stage and got behind the microphone, the system suddenly went dead. With the TV cameras whirring, he had to shout out his answers to the reporters below and they kept yelling for him to speak louder. The one question he had come to Pennsylvania prepared to answer wasn't asked until the press conference was almost over. Then the same reporter who had steered the state trooper straight coming down from the hotel popped it:

"If you should win the nomination, would you accept Governor Scranton as your running mate?"

Goldwater owned that it was a little early for that, since he had not yet announced that he would seek the nomination. But he had nothing but the highest praise for Scranton. In fact, he told a little story of how two Congressmen, Bill Scranton and Peter Dominick, then members of the Capitol Hill Air Force Reserve Squadron commanded by the Senator, had asked his advice before running for Governor and Senator in their home states in 1962. Goldwater said he had urged them both to run, and he was proud of the records these men had established since their election.

The press conference had to be cut short because the roast beef simmering in the big tents on the stadium's football field was beginning to get cold. After the dinner the Senator returned to the arena for his speech. Considering that the meeting was free, and that Hershey is only a scant fifteen miles from the state capital at Harrisburg where the bulk of Pennsylvania's more than 83,000 state payrollers reside, the crowd was rather disappointing.

The 3,500 diners who strolled across the street to the arena were joined by about 3,000 others, practically all of them Goldwater partisans who had come from all over the state. But the big arena was only a little more than two-thirds filled. The press, of course, took note of this and also quoted Pennsylvania Republican officials who piously proclaimed they couldn't understand the poor turnout because they had distributed "thousands of free tickets" for the Goldwater speech.

The affair that followed was, as many of the reporters also noted, one of the most bungled political events of all time. Long after the speeches were scheduled to start, the Lebanon High School band and other musical units kept parading endlessly around the floor of the arena while the guest of honor, the Governor, Senator Hugh Scott of Pennsylvania, and the other dignitaries sat twiddling their thumbs on the platform. But a large group of Goldwater demonstrators, waving signs and shouting "We want Barry!", were ushered off the floor by police when they attempted to occupy the space in front of the platform during one of the many lulls.

Next came some alleged entertainment. A large male chorus imported from Philadelphia by the State Committee sang a seemingly unending medley of dreary ballads. For their finale, "in honor of the Senator from Arizona," they picked "Bury Me Out on the Lone Prairie." But somehow it came out "Bury Me Deep in the Lone Prairie." Not content with this, the singers grabbed Goldwater by the arms and forced him to join them in this dirge—after first stripping off his jacket!

At last the speeches started. Hugh Scott led off with a series of puns on Goldwater's name which few people in the crowd found amusing. Then came Governor Scranton, to introduce the man who had just helped lift a heavy burden of debt from the shoulders of the Pennsylvania GOP. Scranton devoted his talk to a rather lengthy review of the accomplishments of his state administration. As L. R. Lindgren, veteran Harrisburg correspondent of the *Pittsburgh Press,* wrote in his story the next day, the Governor "carefully refrained from saying anything that might be construed as lending aid and comfort to the Goldwater cause."[2] In fact, he barely mentioned Goldwater until the last few seconds of his speech, and then it seemed almost an afterthought.

Goldwater bore all this with equanimity. The fact that the crowd gave him a five-minute welcome ovation probably helped quell the uneasiness he must have felt. Then he launched into a straight, down-the-line Republican speech. He praised Scranton's accomplishments in Pennsylvania and said he hoped the state would keep Hugh Scott in the United States Senate "for the rest of his life." He drew sustained applause when he urged that, regardless of the nominee and notwithstanding personal preferences, all Republicans should vote the party ticket to regain the White House in 1964.

The Senator drew his loudest cheers when he ripped into the Kennedy Administration's foreign policy, and posed the question many Americans were asking themselves in 1963: "Do the Russians vacate Cuba now— or a year from now, a few weeks before a national election?" He deplored the Kennedy clan's link to corrupt big-city machines and cited Philadelphia and Pittsburgh as two "horrible examples."

"Sever the links of political corruption that bind Washington to the bosses," he declared, "and decent men and women everywhere will have a chance—their best chance—to clean up the messes in their cities, towns and counties." He added that there was an "international implication" to bossism as well: "A party and an administration so beholden to the bosses must be prepared also to play precinct politics with the hopes of the whole world."

Unfortunately Goldwater's speech, one of the best he had made to date, came through the temperamental public address system terribly garbled. Not only did the people at the back of the huge arena have trouble hearing him, but even the men in the press section down front were at a loss to make out what he said. John Cummings of the *Philadelphia Inquirer* later remarked in his column:

Senator Goldwater disclosed a platform technique compounded of apparent sincerity of purpose and an evangelistic fervor that had his listeners hanging on every word.

Which is to say they hung on what he had to say if they could hear it.

[2] *Pittsburgh Press,* October 11, 1963.

And much of what they did hear rolled out in a jumble of sound that might have come from a man speaking with his mouth filled with marbles.[3]

On Saturday, two days after the Hershey rally, Goldwater flew to the West Coast to speak at the Western States' Republican Conference at Eugene, Oregon. I had come up the day before from San Francisco where I had made my preliminary survey for the national convention. Tony Smith, the Senator's press aide, and Karl Hess had also arrived ahead with the speech Karl had written for Goldwater to deliver at the conference. They had only one copy, and since Goldwater would give the speech at an evening dinner, I knew it would miss all the Sunday papers in the East and Midwest unless we could get it distributed to the press beforehand with a "hold for release" time on it. Tony agreed that this was what we should do and I had the speech duplicated and sent around to the reporters.

When this was done Karl and I left the motel where we were all staying and drove out to the University of Oregon campus to look over the building where the Senator was to make his speech. The building was locked and we had some little difficulty getting inside. But we finally found a friendly janitor who let us in and we satisfied ourselves that the arrangements made for the Senator's appearance that night were all in order.

That was the first time I had met Karl Hess. He became Goldwater's principal speech writer at this juncture and continued in this role right on through to the disastrous defeat of November 3, 1964. Karl was working for Bill Baroody's American Enterprise Institute when we met in Oregon. Baroody soon worked him into the key speechwriting spot where, between the two of them, and with much help from Denison Kitchel, they gradually came to control not only Goldwater's speeches but his every public utterance.

In the tight little group that Baroody, Kitchel & Company formed around the Senator, Karl Hess was called "Shakespeare." He was about 40 then. He had worked for *Newsweek* for a few years in the early 1950s and then had become a ghost writer and contributor to several smaller magazines. One of these was the old *American Mercury,* which had gone off the deep end politically in the mid-1950s.

While Karl, Tony and I were waiting for Goldwater to arrive in Oregon, Rockefeller tossed another challenge at the Senator to debate with him. He did this at the GOP Western Conference just before Barry came in, and the three of us talked it over in my motel room that afternoon.

I told Karl and Tony that if he accepted, I would quit. I had been

[3] *Philadelphia Inquirer,* October 13, 1963.

down that road with Nixon and had seen perhaps the most important Presidential election of this century literally thrown away when he accepted Kennedy's challenge to debate.

I reminded them that, like Kennedy with Nixon, all Rockefeller wanted to do was have Goldwater pick him up and rescue his falling fortunes via a series of televised debates.

The New York Governor had hit rock bottom. That week *U.S. News & World Report* had published the results of a national poll it had taken among Republican leaders.[4] Of the 209 GOP Senators and Congressmen responding, 56 per cent were for Goldwater as against a little more than 10 per cent for Rockefeller. Among members of the National Committee the percentage ratio was the same for Goldwater and only a little better for Rockefeller. And a resounding 71 per cent of the thirty-five Republican state chairmen who answered the poll were solidly behind the Senator. Only three were for Rockefeller. And just one backed Scranton.

Goldwater also saw through Rockefeller's ploy. When he landed at the San Francisco airport that day the reporters asked him if he would take Rockefeller up on his offer. He stuck by his guns and repeated that he would not "take part in any debate that would disunite the Republican Party." Then he climbed into a chartered plane and piloted it up to Eugene.

The speech he gave that night, Karl Hess's speech, was a good one. But like so many of his speeches from there on in, it fired up only his partisans. It seemed to leave almost everyone else cold. Part of this, of course, was the Senator's method of making a speech. He had never been a great orator. His delivery was rather flat, and he seldom displayed emotion, or even very deep feeling. This had been fine while he was still just "pooping around," as he phrased it, as a Senator from Arizona. In fact, his unemotional speeches and responses to questions in press conferences had probably enhanced his aura of reasonableness, and had kept the press from attacking him as a demagogue.

Until this time his audiences outside the Senate, with some notable exceptions, had been composed mainly of people who agreed with him. They would cheer any statement he made because he was saying what they felt every American politician should be saying. But now that he was moving out onto a larger stage before people of all political persuasions, he should have given some thought to changing his style. General Eisenhower, who had never been a public speaker prior to 1952, learned quickly under the tutelage of the former Hollywood actor Robert Montgomery during that campaign. But Goldwater was not a man who would

[4] *U.S. News & World Report,* October 7, 1963.

take kindly to tutoring of this sort, however obviously necessary it might be. To him it would seem phony, a stage trick that would make him feel he was pretending to be something he was not. So any elocution lessons were doomed to failure.

We saw another example of Goldwater's uneven and sometimes uninspiring speechmaking style in New Hampshire late in October. I was in the state twice that month. The first time, I was with Denison Kitchel to confer with the people who were going to lead Goldwater's primary campaign. On the second trip I went up to see what arrangements had been made for the Senator's first formal pre-campaign appearance. This was a dinner to dedicate the Styles Bridges' Chair in history at New England College and the stage had been carefully set a month beforehand.

On September 24, Senator Norris Cotton wrote a letter to his New Hampshire constituents in which he said:

I am for Barry Goldwater because he has fought courageously and unceasingly for a philosophy of government and a way of life to which this nation was dedicated and to which it must return if it is to endure.

I want my country to stand for something in the world, and I want my party to stand for something in the country. . . . The next election must not be a mere popularity contest. It must be a fight to the finish on basic principles. The people must be given a chance to make a choice. The Republican Party must have character, not just smooth sales talk. That is why I am for Barry Goldwater for President.

Although Cotton's announcement had not been unexpected, the unequivocal force of his statement jolted our Liberal opponents in both parties. Senator Cotton was a moderate and he had once voted for the censure of Senator McCarthy. Thus, he was considered a Liberal in certain quarters, on the Right as well as the Left. In my opinion his announcement accounted in large part for a sudden Goldwater surge in his basically moderate state.

The day before Goldwater flew to Concord for the October dinner, the *Chicago Tribune* released the results of a poll among New Hampshire's Republican voters.[5] A comfortable 58 per cent of them said they would vote for Goldwater in the nation's first primary. His nearest rival, Rockefeller, scraped up a scant 20 per cent. Since New Hampshire is a predominantly Republican state despite recent Democratic gains, it was apparent that Goldwater was starting to crack the moderate-Liberal bastion in the Northeast. This was more than I had counted on in my most optimistic appraisals of the Senator's chances.

However, our people in New Hampshire reported to me that the Sena-

[5] *Chicago Tribune,* October 23, 1963.

tor's speech at Concord was quite a letdown, though it did not immediately seem to affect his popularity with the voters.

The Senator was also beginning to show some susceptibility to a malady that has plagued many politicians—the old foot-in-mouth ailment. During a tour of Arizona with Stewart Alsop, he had casually let drop the remark, "You know, I think we ought to sell TVA."

After Alsop inserted this in a semi-facetious article in the *Saturday Evening Post*,[6] a Democrat, Congressman Richard Fulton of Tennessee, wrote the Senator in October and asked if he really meant that the federal government should put the Tennessee Valley Authority up for sale. Goldwater replied that he was "quite serious" about it. He explained that he felt TVA "would be better operated and would be of more benefit for more people if it were part of private industry."

Fulton, of course, released the letter to the press. It caused quite a flap, particularly in the states served by that federal power project. A group of Southern Republicans even visited Goldwater to protest. Having taken his stand, the Senator characteristically refused to budge. He told the Southerners forthrightly, "You either take Goldwater or you leave him."

Fortunately none of them took him at his word, and he later unbent to the extent of explaining his position on TVA more fully. He said he still meant what he had said about selling TVA. But he added, "this hardly means that I propose to abolish all TVA services." He said it would be much more economical and productive if TVA steam-generating plants and the fertilizer-production program, both of which cost taxpayers millions of dollars each year, were sold to private companies who would have to *pay* taxes on their profits. He pointed out that TVA returns to local communities less than 20 per cent of what it would pay in taxes if it were privately owned.

The Senator hadn't yet learned that when a man is seriously being considered for the Presidency people hang on his every word. A casual remark to a friend or confidant is one thing. The same remark dropped in the presence of a reporter—even a reporter you happen to be "pooping around" with on a friendly tour—may make the headlines next day.

Many reporters protect their sources. They realize that everyone makes slips and as a rule they will either ask a source to amplify his views on a potentially controversial point, or, if they feel the man wasn't entirely serious about it, they will let it pass entirely when they write their stories. Goldwater had had this kind of friendly protection in the past. But he could expect it no longer.

Early in November, Peter O'Donnell met with the Senator and handed

---

[6] "Can Goldwater Win in '64?", *Saturday Evening Post*, August 24, 1963.

him a confidential memorandum he had drafted. The memo took Goldwater to task for "shooting from the hip" and cited the TVA business. Peter said it was "an example of kicking a sleeping dog."

"But," O'Donnell added, "even if it is decided to kick the sleeping dog, your entire position should be spelled out at one time, rather than spread out over a period of days and weeks as the original statement is clarified, amended, or supplemented.

"A series of TVA-type statements could greatly weaken your position. For instance, TVA puts your supporters in an important area on the defensive. *We must continually be on the offensive in the fight for the nomination and the general election."*

Peter advised the Senator to steer clear of meeting sensitive issues head-on. He said it would be best to bear down on party unity and other "non-issues" to "keep your ammunition fresh" for the general election campaign. "If you spell out your position on all issues at this time," Peter stressed, "you will have fewer new things to say come next October. Also you will be presenting a nice, fat target to some group or other every time you take a stand."

Needless to say, Goldwater did not follow O'Donnell's advice. If he had, I believe it would have made the difference of hundreds of thousands, perhaps millions, of votes in November, 1964. But unfortunately, the only purpose it served in 1963 was to further estrange Peter from the Senator and his inner circle. Goldwater did not take kindly to advice. Moreover, Kitchel and the others regarded it as a sign of impetuosity and disloyalty for anyone outside their circle—and even some of those within it—to presume to offer advice this forthrightly.

One probable reason that the Senator ignored O'Donnell's warning was simply that, at the time, the TVA goof appeared to have done him no great damage. It might have lost him some votes in the area where a combination of federal propaganda and tax-supported low power rates had made TVA a sacred cow. But the rest of the country largely ignored the whole thing and it probably would have been soon forgotten if certain elements of the press hadn't kept it alive long after it should have died a natural death.

It has always puzzled me that so many members of the fourth estate— even those whom I consider my friends—will go out of their way time after time to magnify some point a conservative makes. Yet these same people conveniently forget embarrassing stands taken by Liberal Democrats. A case in point was Goldwater's stand on foreign aid. He advocated substantial cuts in this program, which has cost the American taxpayers more than $100 billion since the end of World War II. Next to the Test Ban Treaty, the issue with which the Senator was beaten over the head most in the fall of 1963 was foreign aid.

Yet in 1960 when John Kennedy ran for President the press never raised the issue of his fairly recent opposition to foreign aid. Kennedy had a long history of voting for healthy slashes in aid appropriations in the Senate.[7] As late as 1958 he cast his vote for an amendment to the Mutual Security Act which lopped $200 million from military assistance programs to foreign nations. At that time, the future President stated:

I do not think that we can afford in this country to raise the standard of living of all the people all over the globe who might be subject to the lure of Communism because of a low standard of living. I say it is impossible for us to think of raising the standard of living of all the low-standard countries of the world.

Kennedy's stand was then diametrically opposed to the ambitious foreign-aid programs like the Alliance for Progress which he pushed so fervently when he became President a few years later. But the press never went to any pains to point out this glaring inconsistency. There was no concerted attempt made to underline it even when Kennedy, in a slap at Goldwater and other Republicans who pressed for cuts in his aid bill, said, "I recall during eight years in the Senate from 1953 to 1960 consistently supporting the request [when] General Eisenhower was President of the United States."

It was only Barry Goldwater's occasional slips that fascinated large segments of the press in the latter part of 1963. It was the beginning of a long conditioning process that ended with the Senator being regarded by millions of Americans as an "irresponsible radical." But that autumn the Liberal camp was only just becoming aware that Barry Goldwater and the conservative movement represented a very real threat to their Establishment.

Within the Republican Party "stop Goldwater" drives were being born almost every day—and dying by nightfall. Dick Nixon was revived and, when that didn't take, Nixon came up with a dark-horse candidate of his own—General Lucius D. Clay, the former U.S. High Commissioner to Germany who was now with the Wall Street investment banking firm of Lehman Corporation. Overnight, the Clay boomlet quietly expired. Someone suggested George Romney again. But in November Romney

[7] As far back as 1951 Kennedy introduced an amendment to cut foreign aid by $85 million. On July 29, 1953 he voted to cut the Mutual Security Act appropriation by $50 million. On August 3, 1954 he stood in favor of the Long Amendment to the Mutual Security Act of that year, which cut foreign aid by half a billion dollars. On July 22, 1955 he voted against restoring a $420 million slash. On June 14, 1957 he voted for a $90 million cut. And on June 5, 1958 he approved the $200 million cut noted above.

suffered a crushing defeat on his tax bill at the hands of his Republican majority in the Michigan legislature and the Governor was out of the running for good. Drew Pearson, a columnist hardly noted for friendly feelings toward Republicans, made an attempt to resurrect Dwight D. Eisenhower as the 1964 GOP candidate but Ike quickly laughed that one off. It would of course have been unconstitutional.

A synthetic boom for Henry Cabot Lodge went a-glimmering when President Diem of Vietnam and his brother were murdered early in November in a coup that U.S. Ambassador Lodge had certainly done nothing to prevent.[8] It soon became apparent that for all his failings, Diem had been the only stable political force in that war-torn country. Some of the American press belatedly discovered that the Buddhists who had brought about Diem's downfall, with the tacit sympathy of Ambassador Lodge, were tools, or at the very least dupes, of the Communists. But by then it was too late. Diem was dead—and so was Henry Cabot Lodge, as a likely Presidential candidate.

More and more the Liberal oracles were touting Bill Scranton as the only hope of stopping the Senator. But Scranton's rating in all the polls was scarcely visible. Most voters outside Pennsylvania freely admitted they had never heard of him. And the overwhelming majority of the Republican county chairmen in his own state, along with Paul Hugus in Pittsburgh, personally preferred Goldwater.

There were very few political realists left who thought that anyone could keep Goldwater from taking the Republican nomination. Realizing this, Peter O'Donnell went with John Tower to see the Senator and handed him another confidential memorandum. Peter reviewed all of Goldwater's possible opponents for the nomination and eliminated them one by one. Only Scranton was left, and although Scranton did not have any chance of winning the nomination, it was obvious that he could split the party wide open if all the anti-Goldwater groups suddenly got behind him.

"Instead of fighting your way through all those primaries," Peter told Goldwater, "you can wrap up the nomination right now by getting Scranton to announce as your Vice-Presidential running mate. He will have nothing to lose and everything to gain. His term as Governor ends after 1966 and since there is no Senate seat up in Pennsylvania that year he will be out of the political picture for two long years. As the Vice-Presidential candidate in 1964, even if you should lose, he will have gained stature in the party and a name for himself in the nation. I think Scranton will look upon this idea as irresistible."

---

[8] The boom was later revived after Ambassador Lodge's victory in the 1964 New Hampshire primary.

Peter argued that a series of primary battles could only serve to divide the Republican Party even more than it already was. And he knew, as I did, that the primaries have much less effect upon the outcome of national conventions than is generally believed. We were already predicting we would have a minimum of 500 delegates. We were certain that we could add at least 200 to that figure before going to San Francisco: more than enough to win the nomination.

Goldwater had previously told Peter that he liked Bill Scranton personally. Moreover, the Senator believed that he and Scranton were not too far apart on many important issues. The Governor of Pennsylvania would serve to balance the ticket, both geographically and ideologically. As O'Donnell succinctly put it:

"You've got the nomination wrapped up. Now let's get Scranton and move on to the general election campaign. Kennedy has already started campaigning against you. There's no point in your dissipating your energies by campaigning against other Republicans for the next eight or nine months when you could be concentrating on Kennedy."

Goldwater listened politely to the arguments of O'Donnell and Senator Tower. But they knew they weren't getting through. When they finished, Goldwater said he was going along fine as it was and he didn't see any reason to push just yet. There would be plenty of time to decide on a Vice-Presidential candidate later on.

But if Barry Goldwater lacked a sense of urgency as the days dwindled down in November, Jack Kennedy did not. The young President clearly read the handwriting on the political wall. Beneath the brave smile and crackling witticisms he carried a new and weighty concern. His re-election in 1964, which he had once viewed with such surpassing certainty, was no longer by any means assured.

BOOK THREE

DALLAS: BEFORE AND AFTER

CHAPTER 22

HIGH TIDE

UNTIL THE AUTUMN MONTHS of 1963 the public interest in Barry Goldwater primarily centered on the growing likelihood of his winning the Republican Presidential nomination. Relatively little was said in the mass media about the possibility that he might also win the Presidency. When it was mentioned at all, any chance that he could beat John F. Kennedy was shrugged off as, at best, extremely unlikely.

However, for some months there had been a strong undercurrent of speculation in Washington that Goldwater might very well be able to upset JFK. The *U.S. News & World Report* article in April, revealing the strategy hatched eighteen months earlier in Suite 3505, brought to the public's attention the fact that there was an incipient doubt as to Kennedy's invincibility. The response to our National Draft Goldwater Committee, which based its appeal on the Republican opportunity to *win* the 1964 election, steadily heightened this doubt. And there is no question in my mind that John Fitzgerald Kennedy increasingly shared the uncertainty as the summer wore into fall.

Kennedy, a great believer in hitting his opposition early and often, actually began his campaign against Goldwater in late September of 1963. When the Senate ratified the nuclear test ban treaty by an over-whelming vote, the President hailed this action as an "historic step toward peace." But he knew that the roll-call count in the Senate did not necessarily mirror the sentiments of the voters. The many thousands who cheered Senator Goldwater's refusal to accept the Treaty of Moscow during his speeches in Los Angeles and elsewhere served as a warning signal to the President's sensitive political ear.

A few days after the Senate vote on the test ban in late September, Kennedy flew to Salt Lake City during a "non-political" tour of the West. Speaking before some 8,000 people in the great Mormon Tabernacle, the President took sharp issue with the foreign and defense policy ideas expressed by Goldwater. Rather incongruously, he charged that these ideas could only serve to "invite a Communist expansion."

Kennedy did not mention Goldwater by name. But it was clear to everyone that the Senator was his target. The Associated Press reported that same day:

Without question, Kennedy in this speech went farther than ever before toward challenging Goldwater. But he went beyond that and took issue with the whole political force often labeled the "radical right."

Clearly, Jack Kennedy was already on the offensive against the man he knew he would have to face in the 1964 election campaign. It is a tribute to his perspicacity that he knew this sooner, and with far more certainty, than many members of Barry Goldwater's own party. And it is a further tribute to his political foresight that he knew Goldwater was the one Republican who could possibly beat him.

Kennedy saw that his own popularity was slipping precipitously while Goldwater's was still steadily rising. On his flying tour of the West, the President had tangible evidence that he was losing touch with the voters. In Duluth, Minnesota, during the entire course of a thirty-minute speech he was not once interrupted by applause. The next day at Grand Forks, North Dakota, he spoke after receiving an honorary degree from the state university, and the audience was equally cool. In Cheyenne, Wyoming and Great Falls, Montana he encountered more disappointment.

Nor were the signs of his falling fortunes read only in the chilly crowd reactions in the West. That same week *Time* published the results of a state-by-state survey made by its correspondents. Not long before this, *Time* noted, most political experts figured Kennedy could win in a walk against any Republican in 1964. "Now," it added, "many are changing their minds." The survey indicated that at least one Republican, Barry Goldwater, "could give Kennedy a breathlessly close race." It also confirmed the accuracy of my own political map, although it placed a big question mark over Texas, which I believed we could safely claim.

"Kennedy could easily beat any other GOP candidate," *Time* conceded. "But against Barry Goldwater, he can only be rated even. . . . If Texas went for Goldwater, Barry would have 266 [electoral votes] with an excellent chance for picking up more than the necessary additional four [to make him President] among the Kennedy-hating unpledged electors of Alabama and Mississippi."[1]

Time was not alone in its appraisal of Goldwater's chances. In varying degrees, publications of all political persuasions soon were leaning toward this analysis. Even the faithfully Liberal *Look* ran a story entitled "JFK Could Lose."

At his press conference on October 9, the President conceded with refreshing honesty, "We are going to have a hard, close fight in 1964." As for Goldwater's chances of getting the Republican Presidential nomination, Kennedy said that "he has a long way to go, but I think he can do it." With this statement he abandoned the previous Democrat strategy of promoting Rockefeller as his toughest potential opponent. Unlike so many Republicans, Jack Kennedy was facing political realities squarely.

The *Chicago Sun-Times* Washington correspondent, Carlton Kent, observed that at this same press conference Kennedy was "apparently taking delight in stirring up the GOP political pot." Former President Eisenhower had recently been quoted as saying he wasn't entirely clear as to where Goldwater stood on major issues. Asked about this, Kennedy replied with a broad grin, "I don't think Senator Goldwater has ever been particularly deceptive. I think he has made very clear what he is opposed to and what he is for. I have gotten the idea. I think President Eisenhower will as time goes on."

It was a typically witty Kennedy reply. But as James Reston of the *New York Times* later noted in his column, "The President was light-hearted about the prospects of meeting Goldwater, but privately his associates are not so sure."[2]

The reasons for the Kennedy Administration's gnawing doubts were becoming more apparent with each passing day. On October 13, Eric Severeid stated in his column, "The Goldwater phenomenon has reached proportions far beyond anything most serious observers, especially those in the Eastern centers, imagined it could attain a year ago, and the phenomenon is just hitting its stride."

Goldwater's popularity was in the ascendant not only among what the Liberals loosely labeled the "far right." He was daily gaining strength among "regular Republicans," independents, Democrats, moderates in either party or in none, and even among a few of the more reflective members of the Liberal community itself.

The Democrats' once solid South had long since gone with the wind. The West and Southwest seemed virtually in Goldwater's pocket. A strong Goldwater tide was running along the California coast. Much of

[1] *Time,* October 4, 1963.
[2] *New York Times,* October 12, 1963.

the Midwest, particularly the big states of Illinois and Ohio, were considered Goldwater territory. And now his popularity was rising in the industrial Northeast that he had so recently been accused of writing off.

The reasons for this phenomenon, as Severeid aptly called it, were as many and varied as the makeup of the states and regions themselves. In New England, it was a combination of two things. First, there was the factor of respected leadership, as personified by Senator Norris Cotton, supporting a man whom the Left was stridently attempting to make voters believe was far out in right field.

Second, I believe that Barry Goldwater was beginning to appeal to the ancient and in many cases almost forgotten patriotic instincts of the people in those towns and cities which gave birth to the American Revolution. Nor am I referring only to those New Englanders who are Yankees by blood. There were thousands in that region of Irish, Italian, Polish and other heritages who responded to this same appeal. In so doing, they were merely harking back to a time when the proudest thing any citizen could call himself was simply an American.

Indeed, Goldwater's rousing of the dormant spirit of patriotism was the fundamental basis of his broad appeal in every section of the country. But each region had its own additional motives for supporting him. In the South it was not only civil rights. In fact, many Southerners found it hard to swallow Goldwater's stand on this issue. It was more his willingness to accept the South as a partner with an equal share in working out the nation's destiny that appealed to a group of people who for a century had been treated as poor and somehow undesirable relations in the American family. In the Far West it was the Senator's independence and individualism that drew voters in a region still imbued with the spirit of pioneers. In the Midwest it was his adherence to the same set of solid traditional values that had made that part of the country America's spiritual heartland. In the big cities like Chicago, Cleveland, Detroit, it was the growing resentment against the obvious excesses of certain elements in the civil-rights movement.

The National Draft Goldwater Committee had been aware of this resentment from the outset. We had learned of a private study conducted by Theodore Humes, a Pittsburgh economist and educator of Polish extraction. Humes had made an extensive tour of a number of cities to sample the voting sentiments of the so-called ethnic groups. Everywhere he went, Humes found the Polish, Slovak, Hungarian, Ukrainian and other groups of Eastern European origin in rebellion against the school bussing of their children and the threatened eradication of their old neighborhoods by "blockbusters"—the greedy real-estate speculators who were deliberately and systematically exploiting Negroes who wanted to buy homes of their own.

By November 1964 the "white backlash" was a seemingly dead issue, drowned in the great pounding wave of "peace vs. war" and buried under the comforting, illusory promises of the Great Society. But a year earlier when Humes made his soundings—and even many months later during the spring primaries—the backlash was a real and potentially vital issue. It was an issue we made no plans to exploit. But it was there nonetheless, and it was helping turn thousands in the "nationality" groups against the Kennedy Administration and the Democrat big-city machines.

At a Midwest Democrat conference held early in October in Madison, Wisconsin, many leaders of that party privately admitted that there was a great Goldwater groundswell in their cities and states. One reason for it, they confided, was the mounting Democrat disaffection within organized labor. This rebellion was most evident among the rank-and-file workers in many unions. But now it was becoming apparent among the union leaders as well. As early as September 16 prominent labor columnist Victor Riesel wrote:

For the first time since John Kennedy took over the White House there is an open break on the New Frontier's labor front over support of the President for re-election in 1964.

At least one influential labor leader has quietly been urging his colleagues to swing away from the Administration to the Republican Party. This unionist is Lee Minton, a national vice president of the AFL-CIO and president of the Glass Bottle Blowers Association and one of the most respected of the younger group in labor's 29-man high council. . . .

Riesel said that the Republican Lee Minton was leaning toward was Nelson Rockefeller. But, he added, Minton "does not appear to have any personal animus toward the Senator from Arizona—just policy differences on labor issues." The Teamsters' Jimmy Hoffa was another labor leader who was threatening to bolt the Democrats. Like Minton, he favored Rockefeller. But the rebellion of these and other labor leaders was based, for various reasons, on a deep dislike of Kennedy Administration policies. Faced with an election contest between Kennedy and Goldwater, rather than Kennedy and Rockefeller, they might well decide, as some labor men already had, either to support Goldwater or to sit out the campaign.

Summarizing the results of interviews with rank-and-file union people in various parts of the country, the *National Observer* reported that Goldwater would obtain a surprisingly large number of union votes in the race with Kennedy. Many union members told *Observer* correspondents that they felt Goldwater acted on principle, while most of the President's actions seemed to them to be politically motivated.

As early as August, COPE—the political action arm of the AFL-CIO —started training its guns on Goldwater in an effort to halt his deepening inroads among union members. A COPE newsletter dated August 17 ran a scare story under a panic headline: "If Goldwater Were President—Goodbye to Social Security, Jobless Pay, Minimum Wage, Progress." Tragically, this theme was soon picked up by some members of the Senator's own party.

The *Wall Street Journal,* commenting on the "wild arm-flailing at Barry Goldwater," tried to set the record straight. It acknowledged that the Senator "does have some controversial views." But, the *Journal* said, they are "hardly radically reactionary or recipes for panic. . . . Unless, perhaps, the panic is on in the camp of the political Liberals."[3]

By November, the panic had spread to the point where an abortive attempt was made to link Goldwater to labor racketeer Willie Bioff, who had been executed by mobsters in Phoenix in 1955. On a November visit to Pittsburgh, Goldwater said he had known Bioff as "Al Nelson." Further research disclosed that a federal court had granted Bioff permission to change his name to Nelson after he was released from prison in 1944. This was before he moved to Phoenix to escape gangland vengeance for testimony he had given which led to the conviction of other labor mobsters.

At a conference held by the Draft Committee on November 15 in Washington, many of our state chairmen reported that a goodly number of union members, and even a few individual labor leaders, had privately expressed interest in working for Goldwater's nomination and election. Some leading Democrats allied with labor were also moving in the same direction.

In Pittsburgh, the birthplace of modern unionism, a prominent Democrat told James Helbert, the astute political editor of the *Pittsburgh Press,* that "if the election was being held this year, Goldwater would sweep Allegheny County—and furthermore I would vote for him."

Allegheny County, which Pittsburgh dominates, is one of the most heavily industrialized areas in the United States. Since the days of Franklin Roosevelt and the CIO's revered president, Philip Murray, the alliance between the Democratic Party and labor had made it a virtually impregnable Democratic citadel. But now the same people who had kept the Democrats in power were shifting to Barry Goldwater and they included many members of the late Mr. Murray's own United Steel Workers Union.

Typical of these was the head of one of the biggest Steel Workers' locals in the Pittsburgh area. In a confidential interview with a *Fortune*

[3] *Wall Street Journal,* September 30, 1963.

reporter, this union leader vowed, "If the choice is between Kennedy and Goldwater, I will have to go for Goldwater, though I don't agree with all the things Goldwater advocates." Then he added thoughtfully, "But Scranton may hurt him around here. A lot of us went for Scranton in the governor's race last year, but Scranton has hurt all Republicans by raising the sales tax and some of the other things he's done. Still, Goldwater will do a lot better with the men down in the mills than any other Republican. They like his honesty. He's a straight shooter and the men like that."

Concrete evidence that in Allegheny County many union members were not afraid to vote for their convictions and against the solidly entrenched Democrat machine of former Pittsburgh mayor and Pennsylvania Governor David Lawrence was dramatically presented in the county elections on November 5. Two conservative Republicans were elected in the major contests—Robert W. Duggan as District Attorney and Judge Blair F. Gunther as County Commissioner. In a county where the Democrat registration edge is almost 2 to 1, this represented a resounding victory for the Republican Party.

At the Denver meeting of the Republican National Committee, Craig Truax, the Pennsylvania state chairman, had asked Peter O'Donnell to hold off the unveiling of a Draft Goldwater committee in his state until after the November elections. It was one of several such requests from Republican leaders that we honored faithfully, in the interests of party unity. But now that the elections were over we were ready to roll in Pennsylvania, where we had had a group organizing quietly for many months.

A week after the elections, on November 13, we announced the formation of our Draft affiliate, the Western Pennsylvania Citizens for Goldwater. Ben Chapple of U.S. Steel was named chairman and Ted Humes, the economist who had been doing the ethnic-group surveys, was appointed vice chairman. A well-known Pittsburgh citizen, Pressley H. McCance, headed up a strong 75-man advisory board which included as vice chairman the new County Commissioner, Judge Gunther, who was also head of the Polish National Alliance, and the young D.A.-elect, Bob Duggan.

At the last minute, just before the press conference Ben Chapple held at Pittsburgh's Penn-Sheraton Hotel, the Allegheny County Republican chairman, Paul W. Hugus, decided to add his name to the advisory board. It took courage for Paul to fly openly in the face of Governor Scranton's favorite-son candidacy. But as the most successful GOP chairman Allegheny County had had in more than thirty years, he could not have foreseen then that with this action he signed his own political death warrant. Within six months, as we shall see in a later chapter,

Hugus was driven by a vengeful state administration from his county chairmanship because he had dared to express his preference for a Presidential nominee other than Governor Scranton.

However, for the next nine days, until November 22, it did not appear that anything was going to stop Paul Hugus and the others in the Goldwater Citizens group from coming up with a winning "harmony slate" that would guarantee the Senator a substantial number of Pennsylvania's 64-man delegation, the third largest in the 1964 national convention.

Just two days after the Citizens group was announced, Goldwater came to Pittsburgh for a dinner speech before the area Harvard Business School alumni association at the Penn-Sheraton. The largest crowd ever to attend an event sponsored by this association turned out, thanks largely to the efforts of its former president, a young Gulf Oil executive named O. Henry Hoversten, who later became one of the most effective members of our Citizens group in Pennsylvania.

In his speech, the Senator struck out at government controls. "A free economy cannot flourish under the shadow of a sword clasped by a heavy-handed government, ready to slice off incentives to work, to invent and to earn," he declared. "Millions of new jobs are lost in the limbo of investments not made, risks not taken, enterprise not dared . . . because of the lack of confidence that becomes the reflex as the economy is regimented and regulated."

At a press conference beforehand he was asked why he was delaying the announcement of his candidacy. With a smile, he replied, "Why rush? I'm doing all right."

Nine days earlier, on November 6, Nelson Rockefeller had formally declared his own candidacy on NBC-TV's "Today" show. But despite this free national television exposure, the public hardly noticed. No one was taking the Governor very seriously any more.

An Associated Press poll of GOP state and county leaders released on November 2 revealed that only 56 of the 1,404 leaders who responded —or less than 4 per cent—thought Rockefeller would make a good candidate. Dick Nixon picked up even fewer votes—44—and all the others were out of sight. But an overwhelming 1,194—more than 85 per cent—voted Barry Goldwater the party's "strongest candidate" against Jack Kennedy. The Senator topped all other GOP hopefuls by wide margins in every state except New York, although even there he received nearly a third of the poll's votes.

None of this was lost on the dashing young resident of the White House. By October the whole Kennedy clan was on the move. Sargent Shriver managed to mix a lot of politics with his travels for the Peace Corps. Another Presidential brother-in-law, Stephen Smith, popped up in a dozen states from coast to coast. Ted Kennedy was trying to keep the political hatches battened down in New England. And in the Attorney General's office brother Bobby was drawing up plans for the campaign, plans which some said included dumping Lyndon B. Johnson as Jack's 1964 running mate.

The Kennedy strategy staff of Bobby, Ted Sorensen, Arthur Schlesinger and Kenny O'Donnell were meeting regularly. And they had added a new member to the team, Hubert Humphrey's friend Richard M. Scammon, Director of the U.S. Census Bureau who prior to 1960 was, of all things, an expert on Russian "elections."

At Democratic National Committee headquarters, symbolically located on Washington's K Street, a staff of ninety research experts and assistants were concentrating on assembling background files on Barry Goldwater. Their Goldwater dossier already weighed nearly forty pounds and the National Committee was periodically sending out special memorandums advising key Democrats how to cope with the Goldwater surge. In addition, thousands of pamphlets ripping away at the Senator and the conservative cause were beginning to flow from the presses and into the mails—along with an equal number of brochures and press releases extolling the virtues and accomplishments of President Kennedy.

In many of his speeches that fall, Jack Kennedy sounded surprisingly conservative himself. *Time* noted that he "seemed to be trying harder to invoke the conservationist image of Republican Theodore Roosevelt than the Democratic Party's openhanded patron saint, F. D. Roosevelt." But, the magazine added, he "seemed ill at ease in this guise—and his audience sensed it."[4]

Perversely, he insisted on pushing a number of projects that he must have known would deepen the growing antipathy toward his Administration. The Soviet-American wheat deal was one. Apparently not realizing that the Russians could use wheat to divert scarce grain into the manufacture of ethyl alcohol for missile fuel, the President wanted the United States to sell 150 million bushels of wheat to Russia on long-term credits. He argued that if the U.S. turned the deal down it would only convince the Russians "that we are either too hostile or too timid to take further steps toward peace . . . and that the logical course for them to follow is a renewal of the Cold War."

Obviously, the President had already decided that the Cold War had, in fact, somehow ended despite growing American casualty lists in Vietnam and continuing Communist subversion and terrorism in other parts of the world. By way of proof, he took yet another "bold step toward peace" and, against the warnings of many scientists and military experts, approved a United Nations resolution banning nuclear weapons in space.

[4] *Time,* October 4, 1963.

Once again, there were no firm guarantees that the Soviet Union could be made to observe the ban. But unlike the Test Ban Treaty, this agreement was *not* submitted to the Senate, a move which prompted Senator Goldwater to call it a "blatant usurpation by the Executive branch of the advise-and-consent powers bestowed on the Senate by the Constitution."

Of all the issues that threatened to damage the Kennedy Administration in November 1963, none was more potentially explosive than the eerie case of Otto Otepka, the State Department's downgraded chief of internal security. This strange affair, which to this day has never been entirely aired, first broke into the open when the Senate Internal Security Subcommittee found that William W. Wieland, a State Department desk officer, could not "escape a share of the responsibility" for Castro's rise to power in Cuba. Yet in the face of this President Kennedy defended a State Department decision to promote Wieland and told a press conference that this official had been cleared of any dereliction of duty.

However, Otto Otepka, who had conducted State's investigation of Wieland, told the Senate Subcommittee that he had not issued a clearance. In fact, he had recommended that Wieland be dismissed for "policy impedance" and for lying both to the Subcommittee and to officers of the Department of State.

Wieland was not fired, but in September 1963 Otepka was. The "evidence" against him pertained to his cooperation with the Senate Subcommittee. It had been secured under the direction of one John F. Reilly, a former Justice Department attorney and protégé of Bobby Kennedy.

When, in late September, the State Department upheld the firing of Otepka, the Internal Security Subcommittee and its parent Judiciary Committee registered a strong protest with Secretary of State Dean Rusk. But Rusk ignored them, and once again confirmed Otepka's dismissal. On November 5, the Subcommittee's vice chairman, Senator Thomas J. Dodd of Connecticut, disclosed that he had evidence that State Department officials had perjured themselves in denying that they had tapped Otepka's phone.

The next day Reilly and two subordinates sent letters to Dodd's Subcommittee in effect admitting that they had lied under oath. On November 18 Reilly and Elmer Hill, State's chief of technical services, were permitted to resign and Otepka's firing was delayed indefinitely.[5] But there was much, much more to this case that never came out. It included an apparent attempt by an Assistant Secretary of State to get Alger Hiss back into the State Department and the hiring, over Otepka's objections, of a number of persons, including one of the highest policy

[5] Reilly was rewarded with a $17,500-a-year job with the Federal Communications Commission a few days after the 1964 election.

officials in State, who had been previously judged security risks for various reasons.

The Otepka case threatened to cause a bigger split in the Democratic Party than existed within the GOP. Tom Dodd was not the only prominent Democrat who was deeply disturbed by the behavior of high State Department officials and the President's stubborn insistence on supporting their weird actions.

The assassination of Vietnam President Diem also worried many members of Jack Kennedy's own party. Diem's murder had not only eliminated Cabot Lodge from further serious consideration for the Republican nomination; it promised as well to turn many Democrats against their Administration. In its November 8 issue *Time* reported:

There could be no question that the U.S., in the policies and in the pressures it brought to bear, had effectively encouraged the overthrow of the Diem regime. Only a few weeks ago President Kennedy, appearing on a television interview with CBS's Walter Cronkite, argued that the winning of the war against the Communist Viet Cong would probably require "changes in policy, and perhaps in personnel" in the Diem government.

Undoubtedly all these issues, dimly understood as they may have been by most Americans, accounted in large measure for the frosty reception Jack Kennedy got wherever he went that November. Even in Philadelphia, which he had captured by an enormous vote in 1960, there was no cheering and very little waving from the people he passed along strangely deserted streets as he drove the dozen miles from the airport to Independence Hall for a speech. And inside that hallowed building he found himself addressing half-filled galleries, although local Democrats had distributed 10,000 free tickets—more than enough to fill the hall many times over.

More and more, leaders of his party were warning Kennedy that he was in deep trouble. Many of them had already written off the Deep South for 1964. Lyndon Johnson warned him that Texas was in danger of going too, and urged him to start stumping the state now in an effort to rebuild the crumbling Democratic political fences. The President and his advisers also decided to start campaigning early in Florida in an attempt to salvage that state's fourteen electoral votes.

At his last press conference before he took off on two flying trips to Florida and Texas, Kennedy openly displayed his frustration with the mounting rebellion against him in the Democrat-dominated Congress. Angrily, he lashed out at the Congress' failure to act on his tax-cut and civil rights bills.

In Florida that last week he again encountered cool receptions.

Speaking before the Florida State Chamber of Commerce in Tampa, he petulantly spanked the business community for opposing his fiscal measures. Later he drove to Miami. The crowds along his announced route were sparse and unresponsive. He ran listlessly through his speech on Latin American policy and the Miami audience listened unenthusiastically.

Flying back to Washington that night he went over plans with some of his campaign team for a fundraising extravaganza to be held in Washington in January. Then the next day he took off for Texas. This time he took his wife with him. It was the first public tour Jacqueline Kennedy had made with her husband since the death of their newborn son during the summer and her subsequent vacation in Greece. Her presence seemed to buoy up Kennedy—and the crowds. The receptions they received in San Antonio, Houston and Fort Worth were the warmest in many months.

On the morning of November 22 he addressed a breakfast meeting of the Fort Worth Chamber of Commerce. The ready wit which had begun to fade of late once again flashed through. The *Houston Chronicle* was in print that day with the results of a state-wide straw vote which showed Barry Goldwater leading him in Texas by 52 to 48 per cent. But no matter what he may have felt in the recesses of his soul, nothing in Jack Kennedy's demeanor that morning indicated discouragement or despair. Smiling happily, with his lovely wife at his side, he rode to the Fort Worth airport to climb aboard the Presidential plane for the short flight to Dallas.

CHAPTER 23

DALLAS

On the morning of November 22 I was in St. Louis working the Midwest regional conference of the Republican National Committee. Peter O'Donnell and I had sat up late the night before in my suite at the Sheraton Jefferson reviewing our present position and future strategy. Peter was concerned about Senator Goldwater's refusal to move on the appointment of a high-powered finance committee to build an adequate war chest. He was also disappointed that Goldwater had failed to act on the suggestion he and Senator Tower had made about securing Bill Scranton as a running mate to avoid further dissension in the Republican Party.

However, these problems seemed almost trivial that night. Barry Goldwater's popularity and political strength had soared higher and faster than either of us had any right to expect when we had formed the National Draft Goldwater Committee a little more than seven months before. There were a lot of small hurdles ahead, but we could foresee no major obstacles blocking the Senator's headlong drive toward the nomination. Moreover, the most recent nationwide polls showed him cutting deeply into President Kennedy's once commanding lead. O'Donnell and I both felt that a Goldwater victory over Kennedy was definitely in the making.

A few days before, Goldwater had made a tentative decision to formally announce his candidacy the following week. But Peggy Goldwater's mother had just died in Phoenix and the Senator and his wife were flying the body to Peggy's girlhood home in Muncie, Indiana the following day.

In view of this development, my primary concern was to determine the next possible date for the announcement. Goldwater would naturally not want to make it too soon after his mother-in-law's death. If he did it in mid-December he would be running into the Christmas holiday lull. My own feeling was that it would be best to wait until just after the New Year.

Peter left the hotel on Friday morning, November 22, to catch a plane home to Dallas. There was nothing that demanded his presence at the National Committee regional meeting and he left me to work the remaining sessions. Ione Harrington and Tom Van Sickle were with me. Charlie Barr was also in to help us and Pat Hutar was due to arrive from Chicago shortly after noon.

I had just finished lunch and was about to go up to the afternoon session of the conference when Talbot Peterson, the Wisconsin GOP state chairman, stopped me in the lobby. "Did you hear it?" Peterson asked in a subdued voice. "The President has been shot." Although it wasn't like him, I thought he was manufacturing a bad joke. I said, "Oh, come on, Talbot. Stop kidding." He assured me he wasn't kidding, and the tone of his voice confirmed it.

I tore over to a telephone in the lobby and tried to get hold of Associated Press or UPI to find out how badly Kennedy had been hurt. All the lines were busy. I started to dial the *St. Louis Globe-Democrat* when Ab Hermann came by and told me the story was coming in on television. I took an elevator up to my room and switched on the set. Within a few minutes Ione Harrington, Charlie Barr and Tom Van Sickle joined me. The TV commentator finally verified our worst fears. The President was dead.

The assassin had not been caught, but like many others that day the commentator attributed the crime to "right-wing fanatics."

I will confess that the same thought initially crossed my mind, as it did that of a good many other people in the Goldwater movement. But I preferred to wait until there was more evidence before condemning anyone. Unfortunately, many others refused to wait. Even the Voice of America, in its first broadcast announcing the President's death, went out of its way to describe Dallas as "the center of the extreme right wing." Small wonder then that the Soviet propaganda machine should pick up the same theme. As Arthur Krock of the *New York Times* said, the Voice broadcast provided "grist to Moscow's mill."[1]

Pat Hutar arrived and the five of us stayed glued to the television set for the rest of the afternoon. A number of our friends who were attending the National Committee meeting came in but there was very little

[1] *New York Times,* November 26, 1963.

conversation. We were expecting Senator Tower, who was scheduled to speak at the regional conference that evening. But in the middle of the afternoon we got word that Bill Miller had canceled all the remaining sessions. About three o'clock, Tower's Washington office called. They said there had been a number of telephone threats against Tower and his family and urged us to have him call back as soon as he got in.

Tower, who had been on the plane when he learned of the assassination, arrived soon after this and I apprised him of the threats. He wanted to turn right around and fly back to Washington to be with his family. But I advised him to have his wife and children moved out of their Washington home and into a hotel before he returned. By the time he got back to the capital it might be too late. And there was the chance that some fanatic might be waiting for him at the airport or at his home. In the confused atmosphere that prevailed that afternoon anything seemed possible.

"Why would anyone want to shoot me?" Tower protested. "I'm sure they wouldn't shoot me."

"John," I said, "this is no time to find out. If they shot the President, they'll shoot anybody. Besides, there'll be a terrible backlash against all Texans now." Again I urged him to call his office and have his family moved. Finally, he got on the phone and had it done, after first checking with his wife to make certain she and the children were all right.

When he was off the phone I called our Draft Goldwater headquarters in Washington. Jim Day informed me that they had received a phone call from an obviously distraught man who had vowed that he would bomb our Connecticut Avenue offices. I told him to lock up the office immediately and make sure all the girls got home safely. I also dictated a short telegram offering our deepest sympathy to Mrs. Kennedy and the family and asked Jim to send it just as soon as possible.

Next, I phoned Peter O'Donnell in Dallas. I asked him what was happening down there, whether he had heard anything further on the "right-wing plot" the news commentators were hinting at. But Peter said he couldn't tell me a thing I wasn't getting on radio and television. Dallas was in absolute turmoil, he said. Everything was at a standstill. You couldn't get anywhere. There were no taxis moving. The whole city was in a state of shock.

Later, the news came through that a man named Lee Harvey Oswald had been captured in Dallas. He had been dragged kicking and screaming from a movie theater shortly after he had shot and killed a police officer named J. D. Tippit who had apparently tried to question him about the assassination. Oswald was believed to be the President's murderer. He was, the commentator said, a known activist for the pro-Castro Fair Play for Cuba Committee. Still later it was found that Oswald had once defected to Russia after serving a hitch in the Marine Corps. He had spent three years in the Soviet Union, where he had married a Russian girl who had borne him a child there. He had brought them both to the United States the year before.

This development came only after many hitherto responsible citizens had already convicted the conservative cause, indeed the American people, for the murder of John F. Kennedy. In those ugly hours that followed the assassination a great nation was placed on trial for a crime committed by an avowed Marxist. When the murderer was arrested and his true allegiance revealed, I thought the ridiculous attempt to place the burden of guilt on our whole society would end.

But I was wrong. A good many influential persons continued by dark implication to blame America, and particularly those many millions of Americans who had been opposed to the policies of the late President. In their attempt to instill a sense of shared guilt in all our citizens, these Liberals actually confessed their belief in their own omnipotence and their woeful failure to understand that people in our free society still have the right to dissent. It is only when dissent crosses the line into treason, as it did in the case of Lee Harvey Oswald long before he fired those fateful shots in Dallas, that it deserves to be condemned.

After the identity of the assassin was made known, it was only natural that the people in my hotel room that afternoon should turn their thoughts to the future. Our grief at the death of Jack Kennedy did not lessen. But all of us in that room were deeply involved in a campaign to elect a President of the United States and we had no alternative but to consider the relative strength of Barry Goldwater's new opponent, Lyndon Baines Johnson.

Someone volunteered the opinion that Johnson would be easier for Goldwater to beat than Kennedy. I remember John Tower replying, "You may think that now. But I ran for his Senate seat in Texas and I feel that I know a little something of Lyndon Johnson. If you think Jack Kennedy was a tough politician, you haven't seen anything yet."

At the time I didn't completely agree with Senator Tower that Johnson would be harder to beat. But before many months had gone by I was to see the wisdom of his appraisal.

Early that evening I decided to leave. But a storm had swept in over the Midwest and airline flights out of St. Louis became exceedingly uncertain. Charlie Barr and I had a meeting scheduled in Michigan the following morning and we decided to drive in his car as far as Chicago. Ione Harrington had left her own car at O'Hare Airport and Pat Hutar wanted to get back to Chicago too. So the four of us drove north out of St. Louis, kept together more by our mutual shock than by the exigencies of travel.

It was one of the most miserable rides any of us ever had. We drove for hours through the fierce storm, with the wind buffeting the car and the rain cutting the visibility along the road to almost zero. An almost palpable pall of gloom descended over our little group in the car, as it did over the whole nation that night. There wasn't much talk on that dreary drive and we were all bone tired by the time we reached Chicago at two o'clock in the morning.

The meeting in Michigan was canceled the next morning and I flew home to New York. Over that interminable weekend, as I joined with all other Americans in mourning the death of President Kennedy, I forced myself to reassess the political situation that had been so tragically altered by his assassination. Once again I wondered whether Senator Goldwater, so close just a few days ago to announcing his candidacy, might possibly change his mind.

Although in my recent meetings with the Senator there had been no apparent doubt that he would run, every once in a while there was evidence that his old reluctance had not completely vanished. Only a week before he had told a reporter: "God knows I haven't sought this position. I'm still wishing something would happen to get me out of all this. It's all a little frightening. . . ."[2]

Nonetheless, I had reason to believe that Goldwater had been looking forward with some relish to what had seemed his certain campaign against President Kennedy. Like Kennedy, he anticipated a hard, close battle. But he believed, perhaps a bit ingenuously, that it would be fought out on the issues.

Jack Kennedy and Barry Goldwater had never been close friends in a social sense. But they had entered the Senate together after the 1952 elections and had remained friendly colleagues for eight years despite the fact that they were, in fact and not merely by virtue of party label, on opposite sides of the Senate aisle. This friendly relationship continued even after Kennedy became President.

Not long after Kennedy's inauguration in 1961, Goldwater had shown that he was willing to give the new President a fair chance. He said he wasn't worried about any future errors in judgment that Kennedy might make on his own, but he was concerned about the advisers the President had drawn around him and where they might lead him. A short time later, in April 1961, this concern was justified when the Presidential advisers talked Kennedy into adopting a policy that doomed the Bay of Pigs invasion.

At the outset of the invasion crisis, Kennedy summoned Goldwater to the White House. When the Senator arrived the President had left his office for a few minutes and a secretary showed him into the empty room. Goldwater, who had a back ailment similar to JFK's, sat down in the famous padded rocking chair that Dr. Janet Travell, who was treating both of them, had prescribed for the President.

When Kennedy returned and found the Senator comfortably rocking away in his chair, he smiled and said, "You look fine there. How'd you like to have this damned job of mine?"

"No thanks," Goldwater shook his head. "You can have it." Then, in a more serious vein, he added, "Jack, I don't blame you at all for what happened in Cuba. This is just the result of a great many years of mistaken foreign policy. I hope you can correct this because we're going to be in deep trouble if you don't." Then he urged the President to give the Cuban exile force adequate U.S. air support.

At the moment, of course, Goldwater did not know that the air cover for the Cuban invasion had been called off, and it wasn't until some time later that this critical decision was disclosed. In the meantime, while the crisis was at its height, the Senator made a number of speeches urging all Americans to stand behind the President.

Afterwards, as it became more and more obvious that Kennedy's advisers were leading him to the point of compounding all the old mistakes the U.S. had made in dealing with the Soviet threat, Goldwater became the leading critic of the Administration's foreign and defense policies. It was chiefly in opposition to these policies that Goldwater intended to wage his coming campaign. But he had no intention of permitting that campaign to degenerate into a mud-slinging contest with Jack Kennedy.

"It's impossible to hurl a fistful of mud and still remain spotless yourself," he once told Jack Bell, the veteran Associated Press correspondent and the Senator's Washington neighbor. "President Kennedy and I are poles apart on many issues, and while we are fully aware of the gulf between us, neither has permitted these differences to develop into personal antagonisms."[3]

I was not surprised when I learned over the weekend that Goldwater was taking Kennedy's death hard. The Senator had been notified of the assassination at the airport in Chicago on Friday as he was helping transfer his mother-in-law's coffin from the commercial airliner which had carried it from Phoenix to a private plane which was to fly it to Indiana for the burial. That same day, Goldwater issued the following statement:

The tragedy that struck down our President has struck also at the heart of our nation. It was a vile act. It embodied everything that America is against and against which all Americans should be united. . . .

[3] *Mr. Conservative: Barry Goldwater,* by Jack Bell; MacFadden-Bartell Corporation, New York, 1964. Page 147. (Previously published by Doubleday & Company in 1962.)

Let no man watching us now take twisted comfort from our plight and our pain. Let all men know that America and America's spirit will expiate this crime, will rise from prayerful knees and will face again, in new resolve and resolute knowledge, the future. . . .

The President is dead. That terrible epitaph is before our eyes. Before some of our eyes there is the epitaph of a man with whom we long worked and knew well. No disagreement shadows our memory of those times, for no disagreement or agreement makes us more or less brothers in loss at such a time.

It was several days before I learned that Kennedy's assassination had radically changed Goldwater's decision to seek the Presidency. But I had sensed that it would affect his thinking, and I was more determined than ever to continue the work of our Draft Goldwater Committee. Lyndon Johnson's ascendance to the White House would not basically change the governmental policies which had forced the resurgence of the conservative movement, whatever effect his actions might have on the movement itself. Somehow, the Senator would have to be made to see this.

When I returned to Washington after President Kennedy's funeral, I learned that Goldwater was joining a group of other Republican senators in calling for a moratorium on politics during the month-long period of mourning President Johnson had declared. As soon as the moratorium was officially announced, our National Draft Committee sent a telegram to all state chairmen. It read in part:

Our sympathy and most profound condolences go to Mrs. Kennedy and the other members of the Kennedy family in their hour of grief—and our admiration as well. Who will ever forget the splendid example which Mrs. Kennedy offered throughout a most trying 72 hours?

Therefore, in deference to the memory of the late President . . . we will observe a moratorium on public activity for a period of 30 days and we ask all state committees to cooperate.

However, the National Draft Goldwater Committee will continue to work toward its goal. . . . Our Committee is in the American tradition of the two-party system—a tradition which the late President Kennedy understood and supported.

CHAPTER 24

LIMBO

TWO THINGS chiefly concerned me during that gray, uncertain period following President Kennedy's assassination. The first was the possibility that Senator Goldwater might now withdraw from the race, a possibility that very nearly became a fact. The second was the effect of the assassination and Lyndon Johnson's ascendancy upon the momentum of the Goldwater movement.

In the beginning, I did not believe that the events of November 22 would necessarily alter Goldwater's chances of winning the Republican nomination. They would make it more difficult, principally because the assassination was certain to give the other Republican hopefuls false confidence that they could now beat the Senator. But our Draft Committee had built strong organizations all across the country and in the final analysis it is organization that wins a nomination.

The prospects for Goldwater's election were quite another matter. For one thing, the whole strategy upon which our campaign to elect Goldwater had been based would now have to be changed. With Lyndon Johnson as President, we could no longer count on capturing the entire South, and particularly the key state of Texas. However, there was still the chance that Goldwater might counteract the handicap of running against a Southerner in the South if he could maintain and build the surprising strength he had begun to show in the North before disaster struck in Dallas.

What worried me most in looking beyond the national convention to the 1964 election campaign was the loss of momentum we were presently suffering. The Goldwater bandwagon was like a train that had been speeding down the track at 100 miles an hour when it was suddenly flagged down at a siding where it would have to stand still for thirty days. The engine was still intact. All the cars were in working order, as a check of our state organizations soon proved. But the terrific thrust that had been propelling the Goldwater express onward toward the White House had been temporarily cut off.

It would take some time to build up a full head of steam again and get the bandwagon rolling at the same fast clip. But I felt it could be done—provided the Senator emerged victorious in several selected primaries, scored a smashing victory at the San Francisco convention, and went on to wage an intelligent, fighting campaign in the final battle for the Presidency.

The first item that had to be settled, of course, was Goldwater's willingness to climb back into the driver's seat and pull the throttle wide open just as soon as the moratorium ended. The fact that he had not formally announced his candidacy made it immensely easier for him to pull out. Officially, he was not committed. If he issued a simple statement that he did not want to run we could, of course, continue our Draft operation, though under a severe handicap. But if he decided to follow General Sherman's route, and categorically declared that he would refuse to accept the nomination even if it were profferred by the national convention, we would have to quietly fold up our Draft Committee tent and steal away.

In the meantime, there was no choice but to proceed on the assumption that Goldwater would still decide to go for it. During the first week in December I sent a memorandum to our original group on the occasion of the second anniversary of the Chicago meeting in which we had made a firm and final decision to dedicate ourselves to the objective of making the Republican Party the conservative vehicle in American politics. In the memo I gave no hint that Senator Goldwater was again wavering. Instead, I closed with the admonition, "Now we must redouble our efforts for the final year and victory in '64."

I did not see the Senator for several weeks after the assassination but through Mr. X and others I learned that he was in a state approaching deep depression. After the 1964 election Goldwater himself said, "When Kennedy died, I told my wife within a few days that I would definitely not seek the nomination. I didn't feel that Johnson could be beaten, because Johnson was a Southerner and he would or should carry the South. . . . Johnson understood power more than Kennedy did—even though Bobby Kennedy understands it very well. Johnson would be more ruthless, which he is."[1]

---

[1] *U.S. News & World Report*, December 21, 1964.

A situation like this might have served to stiffen the resolve of another man. But for some reason it did not have this effect on Barry Goldwater. He waited two weeks after he made his decision not to run and then held a meeting in his Washington apartment. Present were Senators Cotton and Tower, former Senator Knowland of California, Peter O'Donnell, Denison Kitchel, Bill Baroody and John Grenier, the Alabama state Republican chairman who had recently become our Draft organization's Southern field director.

Goldwater started by reassessing the political situation that had been so drastically changed by Jack Kennedy's death and ended by informing the group that he had made up his mind not to seek the Presidency. Although they had all expected something like this, everyone there was stunned. Each one of these men, with the exception of Baroody, who was not ostensibly in politics, had publicly committed himself to Goldwater's candidacy. Several of them, particularly John Tower and Peter O'Donnell, had labored long and hard in his cause at considerable personal sacrifice. And at least one, Norris Cotton, had displayed great courage in defying powerful political elements in his state to support Goldwater.

It was Cotton who now took the initiative in arguing against Goldwater's decision. In his gruff Yankee manner he pointed out that the basic political complexion of the ruling Democratic Party had not been changed one whit. Expediency, in both foreign and domestic affairs, would be even more the order of the day under Lyndon Johnson. The issues were still the same. No matter what his personal feelings might be, Johnson could not afford to alienate the powerful alliance of Leftist intellectuals and big union bosses by drastically changing the foreign policy that had spawned so many tragic defeats. For exactly the same reason, America's headlong plunge toward socialism would not be halted and indeed might very well be accelerated. Cotton said flatly that Goldwater had a duty to the American people to run for President.

The others agreed, and in varying degrees of intensity supported Cotton. Several said that if Goldwater refused to run it would appear to many of the millions of people who were supporting him that he was betraying the conservative cause.

Under this barrage, Goldwater wilted. However, he still refused to commit himself. He asked for a week or ten days to think things over, but two days later Senator Cotton and Senator Carl Curtis of Nebraska visited him at his office. Kitchel and Burch were also there, observing mostly in silence while Cotton and Curtis turned the heat on Goldwater again. They left without getting his promise to run, but he was visibly softening. He had ordered a private poll to determine just how much the assassination had affected his chances. When it showed that he was still in the running his decision was virtually assured.

Goldwater doesn't recall the exact date when he made his final decision. It was, I think, two or three days after the meeting with Norris Cotton and Carl Curtis, which would make it about December 11. Barry remembers that he was sitting in his den at his Washington apartment. At last he realized there was no way out of his dilemma. He sought out his wife and asked her what she thought about his running. "Well," Peggy replied uncertainly, "if that's what you want to do, go ahead and do it. I don't particularly want you to run, but I'm not going to stand in your way."

With that the die was cast, as much by Peggy Goldwater as by her husband. They knew their lives would never be quite the same again. But there was really nothing else for them to do. The Senator finally saw, as I had told him almost a year earlier, that he had long since painted himself into a corner from which there was no escape except to leap out and actively seek the Presidency. He had vacillated many times in the intervening months. But now there would be no going back. Whether he liked it or not, Goldwater was committing himself for the duration of the 1964 campaign.

Unintentionally, however, Goldwater weakened his candidacy by forcing his supporters into the role of supplicants. We were left without any bargaining power. The price all but a few would have to pay for his reluctant consent was nothing less than delivering total and complete control over his campaign into the hands of whomever he delegated as his managers. We had already had some indication of this with the arrival of Denison Kitchel in Washington some months before. A day or two after the meeting in his apartment we had further evidence that Goldwater did not intend to seek the counsel of experienced advisers like Senators Cotton, Curtis and Tower or Bill Knowland in making key appointments.

Ione Harrington, who had not talked with Goldwater since she became co-chairman of our Draft Committee, went to see him at his office. She submitted her proposal for converting the regional organization of her women's division from the Draft setup to the new campaign committee that would be formed after Goldwater announced.

The Senator thanked her and then he informed Ione that Ann Eve Johnson, the former National Committeewoman from Arizona, would be named to head the women's division in the new committee. This was a rather rude slap in the face for Ione, who was herself a member of the National Committee. Moreover, it was bound to undercut her position with her people back in Indiana. But she took it like a good soldier and told the Senator that Mrs. Johnson was a wise choice.

Ione said she was willing to work wherever she could be most helpful to his campaign. Later, she accepted the position as Mrs. Johnson's
assistant director with good grace. But she was naturally disappointed
that all of her carefully laid plans for converting her regional organizations were never implemented.

On December 11 the Steering Committee of our Draft organization
held a meeting at the Mayflower Hotel in Washington. Peter O'Donnell
presided and, as usual, Rita Bree took down the minutes. Peter reported
on the meeting at Goldwater's apartment and said that plans were going
ahead for the Senator's formal announcement.

O'Donnell gave us an incisive appraisal of the assassination's impact
on Goldwater's candidacy. He outlined the areas and voting blocs from
which Kennedy had drawn his greatest strength and pointed out that
Johnson was, at that time at least, weak in many of these same areas.
He underlined the fact that Johnson had never been widely popular in
Texas, and that a cloud of suspicion still lingered as a result of his first
questionable election to the Senate years ago. Only a few months before
a popularity poll in Austin had shown LBJ running 11 per cent behind
Kennedy.

Peter offered the opinion that Johnson would be particularly vulner-
able in Texas, and in many other states, if he picked Bobby Kennedy
for his running mate. The resentment against brother Bobby ran much
deeper than it ever had against Jack Kennedy among voters in most
sections of the country.

O'Donnell said that the nomination was going to be more difficult
to obtain for Goldwater now, but he maintained it would be worth a
lot more when he got it. A successful nominating drive would help
re-establish the momentum we were currently losing with each passing
day.

Surprisingly, our financial campaign had not faltered since the assassination, despite the fact that we had canceled a half-dozen fundraising
dinners in observance of the moratorium. Frank Kovac reported that
the Finance Committee was greatly encouraged by the large number of
checks that had been written after November 22. And Stets Coleman
commented that the fund drive was doing a lot better in December, a
normally bad month for raising money, than had been anticipated early
in the fall.

There was some discussion about the chances of getting Len Hall
on our Goldwater team. I mentioned that the Rockefeller strategists
had been back trying to line Len up immediately after the assasination,
but that he had held them at arm's length. Stets Coleman said that even
though Kitchel would be campaign manager, he knew nothing whatever
about how delegates to a national convention are selected. Hall could

be of great help to us in that critical area. But the decision was up to Goldwater and the Senator had already said that he didn't feel he needed political pros because every Presidential candidate spawns his own professionals.

O'Donnell strongly suggested that every one of us who could get to Goldwater emphasize now, before it was too late, that he just couldn't run a national compaign on the basis he was operating on at that time. Peter said he had talked to Senator Cotton and had received his permission to go into New Hampshire to confer with the Goldwater people there, including Stewart Lamprey, the Speaker of the State House of Representatives and Cotton's second in command. He added that Goldwater knew he would have to win big in New Hampshire in order to get back into orbit.

Eventually, after the New Hampshire primary in March, Peter said the Republican opposition to Goldwater would center on Bill Scranton. He was already being touted by *Time,* whose president, Jim Linen, is his brother-in-law, and we could expect all the other national magazines and a large number of influential newspapers to play Scranton big from then on. But a smashing Goldwater victory in the nation's first primary would dim Scranton's hopes.

When the meeting ended I felt a sense of pride in this group. Here we were, less than three weeks after Kennedy's assassination, and every Liberal columnist in the nation had all but buried Goldwater's chances for getting the nomination. Yet there had been no talk of defeat in that room all morning. Indeed, the determination of these people seemed to have grown in the face of what many believed would be insurmountable obstacles. I made a little private wish that some of their fighting spirit would rub off on our candidate.

Goldwater and our Draft Committee scrupulously observed the moratorium on public politics until after December 22, confining all our activities to private meetings. But within a few days after Kennedy's burial at Arlington Cemetery it became apparent that we had fallen into a massive trap, partially set by circumstance, but equally the work of a master politician.

Lyndon Johnson had no alternative but to move forcefully onto the center of the stage and lead the nation during those uncertain days that followed the tragedy in Dallas. But we quickly saw that he also intended to use this period, when he knew all opposition in the Congress and elsewhere would be silenced by the moratorium and by public sentiment, to move ahead with a political program in order to establish a record that would plainly bear the LBJ brand. It was a masterful stroke, and as a politician I could not help but feel a certain awe at Johnson's strategy.

The last strains of the bugler's "Taps" sounding over Kennedy's grave were still echoing from the hillside above the Potomac when Johnson started receiving an unending procession of national leaders—union presidents, businessmen and financiers, civil-rights leaders. Everyone came, as if to receive a Presidential blessing. And when they left, they almost invariably pledged their wholehearted support to Lyndon Baines Johnson.

On November 27, just two days after the Kennedy funeral, Johnson addressed a joint session of Congress and urged the "earliest possible passage" of a new civil rights program, a tax-cut bill, and other key legislative proposals that were certain to win him votes from a wide variety of groups, including many who at another time would have been sure to fight such measures tooth and nail.

Civil rights—and peace—were the key themes of his address. It was obvious that Johnson was going to eradicate his old image of a Southerner intent on preserving the status quo in his home region. He was building himself as a Liberal and a man of peace. Yet somehow, when he spoke of maintaining the stability of the dollar and a strong military capability "second to none," Johnson managed to sound like the most solid conservative.

In spite of the conservative mien he presented, which was greatly enhanced by his slow, deliberate drawling speech, Johnson was obviously planning to out-Kennedy the late President. Congress had forbidden Kennedy to continue foreign aid to Communist nations. But Johnson demanded and got Congressional approval for new aid programs for Communist Poland and Yugoslavia. Congress had insisted that Kennedy sell grain to Russia only for gold on the barrelhead. Johnson twisted Congress' unwilling arm until it approved the Soviet grain sale on long-term credit. While stressing his frugality by personally turning off lights in the White House, he sought, and got, an expansion of welfare programs, promising that this was only the beginning of bigger and better spending on anti-poverty measures. And at a White House ceremony he personally bestowed the Fermi Award on J. Robert Oppenheimer, the nuclear scientist who had attempted to block U.S. development of the hydrogen bomb. It was Oppenheimer's denials about his many Communist connections during the Atomic Energy Commission hearings that led to the revocation of his security clearance.[2]

---

[2] Oppenheimer, the director of the Institute for Advanced Studies at Princeton, had been made into a symbol of the persecuted Liberal. The rehabilitation of Oppenheimer had been a major goal of the Far Left for nearly a decade. They knew that if they could restore the reputation of this man they could claim a major victory in their unending drive to break down all internal security standards in our government.

All through the moratorium, the President commanded the headlines. It sometimes seemed as though he was vying with Walter Cronkite to see who could chalk up the most television exposure in a single month.

Nor were the President's Democrat allies in the least inhibited by the period of mourning. For many Democrats it was open season on Barry Goldwater and other Republicans. As just one example, I recall a meeting of top Pennsylvania Democrats held in Philadelphia within a few weeks of the assassination. Senator Joseph Clark, former Governor David Lawrence, and state Democratic chairman Otis Morse attended. Press releases were issued forecasting a great Johnson victory in the state in 1964. Not content with that, they blasted Governor Scranton and made known a list of possible candidates to oppose Hugh Scott for the Senate, threatening to expose Scott for "the phony that he is."

In fairness, however, I must admit that not all the public politicking during this period was done by Democrats. Many Republicans were scurrying around trying to cook up new stop-Goldwater movements. Most of them tried to keep their cooking hidden behind locked doors, which was entirely proper. But sadly, more and more stories on their deliberations kept leaking to the press.

Early in December, former President Eisenhower made a statement which was widely interpreted as meaning that he was supporting Henry Cabot Lodge for the Republican nomination. Ike quickly denied this, claiming that Lodge was merely one of several possible candidates whom he thought deserved consideration. Yet the feeling lingered that he had thrown in with the anti-Goldwater forces despite his disclaimers to the contrary.

On December 12, Governor Scranton declined to tell reporters whether he intended to seek the nomination and, predictably, started the speculation spiraling anew on his candidacy. Three days later Scranton met privately with Eisenhower in Harrisburg. The Governor disclosed the results of this meeting in a lengthy press conference several days before the moratorium ended, after first asking the reporters to keep his comments to themselves until December 23.

Scranton told the press that Ike had urged him to give serious thought to seeking the Presidency. "Because of him," the Governor said, "I probably will give even deeper thought to this matter than I had expected to." He insisted that he was still not a candidate. But he added, with what in retrospect must be viewed as the epitome of political innocence, that he was open to "an honest and sincere draft." By way of assuring any such "draft" a solid foundation, he let it be known that he intended to keep tight rein on Pennsylvania's 64 convention delegates.

In spite of his protestations that he was not yet a candidate, Scranton's statements were widely—and I believe correctly—interpreted as a fairly firm declaration that he intended to toss his hat into the ring. The Associated Press summed it up: "Scranton appears to have opened a door for a build-up similar to that which won the GOP nomination for Wendell L. Willkie in 1940."

The analogy to Willkie was particularly appropriate.

As soon as the moratorium was over, several other Republicans, poised like Olympic track stars at the starting line waiting for the gun to crack, were off and running. The "Friends of Henry Cabot Lodge" made his candidacy official, or at least quasi-official, when his longtime associate Robert R. Mullen announced on December 23 that "Draft Lodge" offices would soon be opened in Boston and Washington. Harold Stassen, the perennial loser, was seen trying to round up support from a phone booth just inside the main entrance to the Capitol. And out in Chicago, supporters of Senator Margaret Chase Smith disclosed that Mrs. Smith had authorized them to enter her name as a Vice-Presidential candidate in the Illinois primary.

Somewhat less obtrusively, Dick Nixon's people were again on the move. His wife's brother had been making inquiries about probable costs for a candidate running in the New Hampshire primary.

Out in Minnesota former Governor Elmer Anderson was aggressively promoting Walter Judd as a favorite-son candidate. In a letter dated December 6, Anderson had written a large number of Minnesota Republicans telling them that "it is not at all impossible that Dr. Judd could emerge from a convention as the Presidential candidate." As Anderson very correctly put it, the submission of Dr. Judd's name to the convention was an honor he "richly deserves."

Meanwhile, the National Draft Goldwater Committee was rapidly nearing the end of its public life span. We were getting ready to mesh gears with the new Goldwater for President Committee that would be unveiled after the New Year under Denison Kitchel's command. For a time during December we had thought that the Draft organization would be kept intact, operating in cooperation with Kitchel's committee as a citizens' group called "Americans for Goldwater." However, Kitchel and the Senator decided this would be too cumbersome and ordered that the Draft operation be turned over to Kitchel in its entirety.

I prepared a status report for Kitchel and Mr. X, who was still under the illusion that he was in the picture. I was able to report that our Draft Committee had established organizations in thirty-four states, with committees formed and ready to go in most of the remaining sixteen. All but a very few of our state chairmen had proved themselves effective and I recommended that they be kept on under the new setup. Most of our groups were already working on the delegate selection process peculiar to each state. Two regional coordinators were out working—

John Grenier for the South and Vern Stevens for the Northwest, and we had a man assigned to New Hampshire.

The assassination of Kennedy had outdated all our Draft Committee literature and I strongly urged that new brochures and other materials be prepared as soon as possible. This was but one of a number of important items that were allowed to slide by the new managers.

"Before November 22," I said in the report, "we could have maintained a successful posture with entries in only three preferential primaries—i.e., the three we could not avoid—New Hampshire, Oregon and California. Now it is probable that we will have to enter additional primaries as a means of establishing the fact that 'Goldwater Can Win.' "

I listed Arkansas, Indiana, Illinois, Nebraska, Florida and South Dakota as the most promising.[3] However, I did not rule out Pennsylvania because even a loss in that state, provided Goldwater made a good showing, would give his candidacy a great psychological boost. I felt that if we could win as many as 25 per cent of the delegates in Pennsylvania we would have stopped Scranton on his home ground and Goldwater would be in a better position to negotiate with him and get the Governor to accept the Vice-Presidential nomination.

And finally, I urged Kitchel to begin immediately the detailed planning necessary for a successful effort at the national convention in San Francisco.

Within a few days after I submitted this report, Barry Goldwater entered a hospital in Washington to have a painful calcium deposit spur removed by surgery from the heel of his right foot. With his foot in a walking cast, he flew home to Phoenix on Christmas Eve. The final decision had already been made. He would formally announce his candidacy on January 3 in Phoenix.

I prepared a list of key people in our Draft organization, including the members of our original group, who I suggested should be on hand when the Senator made his announcement. I thought Goldwater would want to give them a little recognition for the hard work they had done in his behalf, and I rented a ballroom in one of the Phoenix hotels so he could come and spend an hour or two with us. But then I got word that Barry wanted only Arizona people and a few other old friends there when he announced. I had to cancel my plane reservation to Phoenix, along with the plans for the party.

Kitchel, of course, was in Arizona with the Senator. Mr. X and I

---

[3] Primaries are not regularly scheduled in Arkansas and are not held unless a leading Presidential candidate requests it. I told Senator Goldwater that I thought it would be good strategy for him to run in an Arkansas primary because Winthrop Rockefeller, the New York Governor's brother, was the National Committeeman there. However, the deadline for requesting the primary passed without the Senator taking any action.

were handling preparations for the announcement from the Washington end. The earlier plan that he and I would work together as co-directors of organization for the new Goldwater for President Committee had been quietly dropped, partly as a result of his own decision to stay out of the public eye. I would continue to work with him, but I mistakenly assumed that I would now be formally placed in charge of political organization for the new Committee.

THE ARIZONA MAFIA

SHORTLY AFTER TEN O'CLOCK on the night of January 2, 1964 Denison Kitchel telephoned the Washington hotel room where Mr. X and I were working on plans for the impending transfer of the National Draft Goldwater organization to the Goldwater for President Committee. Kitchel told us that everything was all set for the Senator's formal announcement the following day. He quickly went over the arrangements again. Then, almost as an afterthought, he mentioned that his second in command would be Richard G. Kleindienst, a Phoenix lawyer who had served as Arizona Republican state chairman from 1956 until 1962.

This was the first I had heard that Kleindienst would play any role in the national Goldwater campaign. Until then, I was under the impression that he was going to run for Governor of Arizona. At the time there were some broad hints that Goldwater and Kitchel brought Dick Kleindienst into the national campaign to keep him from running for Governor. If this was so, their plan was thwarted. Kleindienst eventually won the Republican gubernatorial nomination, only to be defeated in the general election in November 1964.

Kleindienst himself knew nothing of the plan to bring him into the Goldwater campaign until a few hours before Kitchel called Washington. He was invited to Kitchel's Phoenix law office that day and told about it by Kitchel and Bill Baroody. Dick says he advised them to find a politician with broader national experience but Kitchel and Baroody were adamant. They said Goldwater wanted him for the job and he finally consented to take it.

Goldwater's campaign team was now virtually complete. Kitchel would be general director of the Goldwater for President Committee; Dean Burch drew the title of assistant general director; Kleindienst would be director of field operations, and Mrs. Ann Eve Johnson director of women's activities. Because of his connection with the tax-exempt American Enterprise Institute, Baroody would remain behind the scenes, controlling the speech writers and exerting great influence on the Senator's policies, but it wasn't until many months later that his role was made known to the public.

Except for Baroody, all the key posts were filled by people from Arizona. As a group they soon became known within the Goldwater movement as the "Arizona Mafia," a play on the nickname "Irish Mafia" given the team headed by Bobby Kennedy which had gained a reputation for ruthlessness in running the late President's 1960 campaign and handling the subsequent patronage. There were no members of our National Draft Goldwater Committee represented at this point, despite the fact that Kitchel & Company were inheriting all the state organizations we had built.

The Senator had made it plain that he wanted the national Draft Committee dissolved, though our job still wasn't done. Our first goal—to convince Barry Goldwater that he should run—had been achieved. But we were a long way from our second target of winning him the Republican nomination. And we were further still from the third and most important goal of all—to elect him President. However, we had no alternative—or so it seemed at the time—except to turn our organization over to the people Goldwater had personally chosen to run his campaign.

On January 3, over a television set in our Draft Committee's Washington headquarters, I watched the Senator make his announcement. He hobbled out on crutches in front of his hilltop home near Phoenix and stood in the sun before the microphones and television cameras and assembled reporters from all over the country. Then he read the statement which Kitchel claims to have written for him. He said, in part:

I will seek the Republican Presidential nomination. I have decided to do this because of the principles in which I believe and because I am convinced that millons of Americans share my belief in those principles. . . . I have been spelling out my position now for ten years in the Senate and for years before that here in my own state. I will spell it out even further in the months to come. I was once asked what kind of Republican I was. I replied that I was *not* a "me-too" Republican. That still holds.

I will not change my beliefs to win votes. I will offer a choice, not an echo. This will not be an engagement of personalities. It will be an engagement of principles.

The girls at our Washington headquarters broke out a few bottles of champagne when the Senator finished speaking. I joined in the toast to his successful candidacy and then the reporters backed me into my office for an interview. I told them we were confident that the Senator would win the nomination and go on to victory in the coming election. But when they asked what role Peter O'Donnell and I and the other officers of the Draft Committee would play in Goldwater's campaign, I side-stepped because, frankly, I did not know. The Senator had announced his campaign team in Phoenix but he never mentioned any of us.

Goldwater later informed a friend of mine that he had personally sent O'Donnell back to Texas because, the Senator said he told Peter, "It's my political neck, not yours." However, Peter says no such conversation ever took place. Goldwater merely left O'Donnell's future status in the national campaign up in the air. All the top national campaign posts had been filled by Arizona people. Peter had a job to do in Texas as state chairman of the Republican Party and when our Draft Committee was formally dissolved he of course returned to his home state.

My own status was settled in an equally curious way. After Goldwater announced, his campaign team flew to Washington and on Sunday evening, January 5, Kitchel asked me to attend a meeting in a room at the Mayflower Hotel to brief the leaders of the new committee. Kitchel, Kleindienst, Burch and Mrs. Johnson listened attentively while I spent about an hour explaining the plans for working the winter meeting of the Republican National Committee, which was to open in Washington that week. They asked a lot of questions about the Committee, its members, the rules and procedures, and special situations in a number of states.

I had another meeting scheduled at the Mayflower at nine o'clock that evening with John Tower, Peter O'Donnell and a half-dozen other members of our Draft organization. The Arizonans had asked to come along and about fifteen minutes before we went up to my suite Kitchel moved to the question of what part I was going to play in the campaign.

"As you know, Clif, Barry has asked Dick to be director of field operations. He will report to me. I guess the best thing for you would be to serve as sort of an assistant to Dick."

I shook my head slowly. "Titles aren't all that important to me," I said. "But hundreds of people in this country have been working with me for the last two years on this thing. When they find you've made me somebody's assistant, they will naturally be disappointed and it would be difficult for me to keep their confidence. I'm afraid I can't take that job."

Kitchel got up and stood next to the mantlepiece. "Well," he said, "if that's the case, maybe you could stay with us until Friday—until after the National Committee meeting ends. Then you can decide whether you want this job or whether you want to get out."

"Okay," I said, and started to get up. But Dick Kleindienst rose and stopped me.

"Now, let's wait a minute," Dick said. "I don't think we need to make a decision this way. The way I see this, Clif, is that you and I would be partners. We'd be like partners in my law firm. Ninety-five per cent of the decisions the partners make on their own. There's five per cent where the senior partner has to make the decision, and in those cases I would then have to call the shots. We need you. I don't want a little thing like a job title to force you out after all the Draft movement has done for Goldwater. We can work it out. You've earned a place in this organization."

"I want to work for Barry Goldwater," I admitted. "I've worked for him for a long time."

There was a little more discussion about what title I might take. Finally, Dick and Dean Burch asked how coordinator of field operations sounded. I said I thought that would be all right. Kitchel didn't say anything, but we were all under the impression that he agreed.

It was already after nine o'clock and our Draft Committee people were waiting upstairs in my suite. We all went up and I introduced the Arizona group to those Draft people whom they hadn't met before. Then Kitchel announced that he would be general director of the campaign as the Senator had said in Phoenix and he spelled out the titles Kleindienst, Burch and Mrs. Johnson would have. When he got to me he said I would be Kleindienst's assistant. I think Dick corrected him at this point but my mind was on something else at that moment.

Peter O'Donnell was there, of course, and when Kitchel made no mention of him I realized for the first time that Peter was being left out entirely. I had assumed that either Goldwater or Kitchel had had a talk with O'Donnell just as Kitchel and the others had just had with me. But from the surprised look on Senator Tower's face, and on the faces of some of the others, I could see that all of this was being sprung on them for the first time.

Peter was a good soldier about it. He never batted an eye. And when Kitchel got down to discussing assignments for working the National Committee meeting he accepted his with good grace.

The Arizona group sailed into the National Committee meeting with great gusto and started making deals right and left. Ordinarily, this might have been the way to work it for a candidate who has just announced, though more likely most of the deals would have been made long before. But this situation was different.

We already had our Goldwater organizations active in most of the states. The people who were running them, although in some cases relative newcomers, often had more influence than the National Committeemen from their states. I don't say this to disparage the National Committee people. But in some cases these posts have frequently been little more than honorary, although individual committeemen and women have made them into positions of considerable influence. However, these were usually the people who came to the Committee with a good deal of power to begin with. With the state chairmen who serve on the National Committee it is usually another matter. But even a state chairman's job is only as strong as the man who holds it.

Unfamiliar with the different nuances involved in the party structures of each state, the Arizona group was at a decided disadvantage. Some important wires got crossed during those few days at the National Committee meeting, and it took a little doing later on to untangle them without causing serious short circuits.

Unhappily, this particular National Committee meeting was probably the most important one held in a long, long time. Since everyone believed the assassination of President Kennedy had opened up a brand new ball game for the Republican nomination, practically every potential candidate decided to take a turn at bat in Washington that week.

Nelson Rockefeller and George Romney were both in town for speeches at the National Press Club and they put in appearances at the Mayflower where the National Committee was meeting. Cabot Lodge was still in Vietnam, but his backers were very much in evidence.

Bill Scranton came in on Thursday, January 9, to speak at a dinner in his honor staged by the Pennsylvania GOP Congressional delegation. At a press conference he insisted that he was not a "favorite-son *candidate*," but merely a "favorite son." However, his aides were all over the Mayflower trying to corral support for his candidacy among the party leaders from other states.

Barry Goldwater, who had spent the last three days stumping around New Hampshire, flew into Washington that same night. He looked tired and he was hobbling uncomfortably on the foot cast when he showed up at the Mayflower for a National Committee reception. But he received a warm welcome, though it was apparent that many of the same people who had been carefully courting him prior to November 22 were not going out of their way now to seek him out.

On Sunday morning, January 12, after the National Committee adjourned, we held the final meeting of our National Draft Goldwater organization's Steering Committee. The three people who had started it all back in the summer of 1961—John Ashbrook, Bill Rusher and I— were there. So were several other members of our original group—Bill Middendorf and Jerry Milbank; and three of the women who had served so unstintingly—Ione Harrington, Rita Bree and Judy Fernald. Three of the key Texas people—Senator Tower, Peter O'Donnell, and Art Wesley—were on hand. And Kitchel and Burch attended as guests.

O'Donnell opened the meeting and politely, but very firmly, laid some justifiable criticism on the line. He reviewed the results of the National Committee meeting and noted that while at all the major GOP meetings over the past year we had always been the hard chargers, this time it had appeared that we were on the defensive. He said that members of the National Committee, the various state chairmen and the press all got the impression that the Goldwater forces were in disarray. Peter urged that steps be taken to dispel this impression quickly.

"I have always thought in terms of the Senator's ultimate success," Peter said. "But now I can't help but see some clouds on the horizon. If Barry Goldwater doesn't make a good showing this year, the conservatives in New York, Pennsylvania, Illinois, Indiana and other states may be cut down forever."

Ashbrook was obviously worried that Goldwater had deliberately surrounded himself with loyal "yes men," but he made this point more tactfully than that. John said that he felt the success of our operation over the last two years had been based on the fact that there had always been complete honesty and candor within our group. He added that this is what makes an organization strong, but if you fall into the error of trying to please everyone, you are going to be in deep trouble.

With a little smile, Senator Tower remarked that he didn't think Denny Kitchel would try to please everyone.

Kitchel said he was working on an orderly transition of our Draft apparatus into the new campaign committee. He said he would recommend to Kleindienst and me that the transition be worked out dependent upon the priorities we established, but stressed that the overall responsibility would be his.

Kitchel also gave us his appraisal of the present political situation. He said Lyndon Johnson would be easier to beat than Jack Kennedy. Then he thanked the Draft Committee for delivering our organization to him in such "apple-pie order" and he and Burch left.

When they had gone, Senator Tower emphasized that he was willing to work with anyone who wanted to do a good job for Goldwater. He said that Goldwater's election was vital to the future of the country and if he lost, particularly by a big margin, the nation and the Republican Party would have been dealt a severe blow. He felt that what Goldwater needed most at this moment were political professionals other politicians could respect.

Some of the others observed that Goldwater was taking a serious risk in setting up a campaign team with a purely Arizona flavor. Bill Middendorf said Len Hall had told him during the National Committee meeting that the job simply could not be done on a provincial basis. Although Goldwater had let it be known that he had asked Hall to join his team in December and Hall had turned him down, Len had given Middendorf the impression that he had been pretty much told that his services weren't wanted.

Middendorf also submitted his final financial report. Since its inception in April, our Draft Committee had raised over $700,000. Up until the last month, when the Arizona people started ordering special polls and had rented new office space, we had been operating well under our budget and even had a surplus of nearly $170,000. That had been reduced now to $450, although this took into consideration substantial sums for contingencies. All of our assets would now be transferred to the Goldwater for President Committee.

We voted to disband the Draft Committee as of January 14 and Peter and I both thanked the other members of the Steering Committee for their untiring and unselfish efforts over the past trying year.

That same day, O'Donnell wrote Goldwater a letter, based on the discussion we had had that morning. In it, he said:

We'll probably "catch hell" for saying this, but we want to offer these observations. . . . The survival of the conservative element in our party depends on your success. . . . In each state, conservative Republicans have committed themselves to your candidacy. Should your drive for the nomination fail, they will be buried, politically. It will be a long time before a new generation of conservative leadership asserts itself, particularly in the Northern and Eastern states.

The grassroots of the Republican Party is overwhelmingly in your corner. However, the next six months must be a singleminded quest for delegates, which requires concentration on the leadership elements of our party.

Peter went on to urge that the Senator's top campaign leadership reflect a more national base, and as a step toward this suggested Len Hall as chairman of a delegate advisory committee. Once again, he reminded the Senator that "shooting from the hip" could prove fatal to his candidacy and asked him to take more care in controlling the issues "by only discussing those things which you have considered in advance." Peter closed by pledging Goldwater "our complete support" and expressing our gratitude for his acceptance of "this tremendous responsibility."

Thus ended the first successful bona fide draft of a Presidential candidate in the history of the American two-party system. However, our work was far from finished and the members of the National Draft Goldwater Committee, both on the national and state levels, were all to play major roles in the coming drive for delegates who would vote for Senator Goldwater six months hence in San Francisco. It is a tribute to their political fortitude that they worked right on through to the end, in spite of many personal disappointments caused by the disruptive manner in which the Draft Committee organization was taken from them and handed over to people most of them had never known before.

At the suggestion of Kitchel and Kleindienst, I had moved out of 1025 Connecticut Avenue the week before and into the new Goldwater for President Committee offices on the second floor of the Duryea Building across the street at 1101 Connecticut in the same block as the Mayflower Hotel. We kept the old Draft headquarters for subsidiary activities but Kitchel, Kleindienst, Burch and I worked out of 1101, which now became the national nerve center of the Goldwater campaign.

Jim Day and most of the other members of our Draft Committee staff came over with me to get the new offices in working order. For we were not only handing Kitchel and Company a nationwide organization but a thoroughly tested and extremely competent headquarters staff as well.

Another holdover from our Draft Committee was W. Lee Edwards, ex-press secretary to former Senator John Marshall Butler of Maryland. Lee was later named director of public information for the new Goldwater Committee. The son of Willard Edwards, the able Washington correspondent of the *Chicago Tribune,* Lee had grown up living with deadlines and he did an outstanding job of getting out the countless press releases that issued forth from the new Goldwater command post.

Judy Lewis, the attractive young wife of Fulton Lewis III, remained in charge of keeping the thousands of pieces of mail moving, a job she did exceedingly well. Dorothy West continued to handle the nationwide distribution of supplies and materials, one of the biggest headache jobs in any campaign but one Dottie handled with unfailing cheerfulness and efficiency. The Reverend Charles Hayes was building his own parish in Washington, but became a full-time staffer in the supply department. Always conscientious, Reverend Hayes was a great morale-builder for the rest of the staff and he did much to help us over the trying period of the January transition.

Jim Streeter, who had come down from New Jersey to work on the July Fourth rally and remained to help supervise our many volunteers, also stayed on. Though still in his early twenties, Jim proved himself an astute student of politics as well as a thoroughly dependable eighteen-hour-a-day worker. He handled all kinds of jobs with never-failing good humor, from the news clipping file to general office security.

Donald Saltz was Frank Kovac's chief accountant and he labored assiduously to keep the finance records in order, both during the Draft days and after—no easy job in any political campaign. Barbara Miller had, I think, one of the toughest assignments of all. She was a general secretary and had to serve as backup for all the other secretaries. Like most of the others, Barbara accepted her new tasks under Kitchel's command with graciousness, despite the fact that she was confronted overnight with a whole new set of bosses.

And then there was what my wife called "Clif's harem." These were three young women who shared an apartment in the same building on New Hampshire Avenue where I took up residence in June of 1963. Two of them were Texans—Marsha Brock, who proved a big asset as an attractive and always courteous receptionist, and Judy Harper, a dedicated conservative who was entrusted with many confidential records and maintained them with great efficiency. The third girl was Jean Keikeisen. Originally from Minnesota, Jean did yeoman service as a bookkeeper for both the Draft and Goldwater for President Committees. When I was in town these three delightful girls always waited in the lobby for me each morning so they could walk me to work. I will confess their cheerfulness and youthful optimism did a lot to keep up my morale, especially during this period when I started out more than one morning determined to make it my last in the Goldwater campaign.

During the transition period, the big romance of the campaign very nearly got nipped in the bud. Suzie Galvin of Lima, Ohio, had joined our Draft staff early in the summer and it was only lately that I had noticed a certain warm light in her eye for Tom Van Sickle, the young State Senator from Kansas who continued to serve as my executive assistant. They hadn't much time for dating, but I suspect Tom's presence was an added inducement for Suzie to keep working late at headquarters.

However, a few days after we made the move across the street Dick Kleindienst buzzed Suzie, who was acting as his secretary, and asked her to run downstairs and get him a pack of cigarettes. About twenty minutes went by and when Suzie failed to reappear Dick poked his head out his office door and asked her where the cigarettes were. She explained that she had been busy fielding phone calls, but this failed to placate Kleindienst.

"Suzie," he said, "I'm going to have to fire you."

A sympathetic smile enveloped Suzie's pretty face and her perky little nose almost wrinkled with laughter. "Gee, Mr. Kleindienst," she said. "I'm afraid you can't fire me."

Kleindienst did a doubletake and slammed the door. Then he picked up his phone and asked me to come to his office. "What's that kid mean, I can't fire her?" he asked in obvious puzzlement.

"She's right, Dick," I replied. "You *can't* fire her. We're not paying her salary. She's a full-time volunteer. Her grandfather, who is one of the biggest contributors to the Goldwater campaign, sent her down here."

Dick shook his head, but he accepted the fact that he had a dismissal-proof secretary and Suzie stayed on. Her romance with Tom Van Sickle ripened through all the vicissitudes of the campaign, and the month after the 1964 election I had the pleasure of dancing with Suzie at their wedding in Lima.

We lost one faithful member—in fact the original member—of the Draft staff during the Arizona takeover. Now that Ione Harrington was no longer in charge of women's activities, Rita Bree went back to New York. She returned to Suite 3505 where she continued to work with the Goldwater groups in New York state and the metropolitan areas for the duration of the campaign.

Later in January, Ione accepted the post of assistant director of the women's division under Ann Eve Johnson, fulfilling her pledge to the Senator to work wherever he felt she would be of the most use.

Judy Fernald became coordinator of special activities for this same division and stuck with it until Goldwater was nominated, though by then she was almost six months pregnant. After San Francisco she returned to New Jersey, where she was still co-chairman of the state Goldwater organization and vice chairman of the Upper Montclair Republican committee. Her third child, John Gregg Fernald, was born two days before the November 3 election. But Judy was busy on the phone rounding up election board workers and voters from her hospital room the day after he arrived.

By the end of January, the Goldwater for President Committee was pretty well rounded out. The most important step—and one that Peter O'Donnell had been urging the Senator to take for months—was the appointment of a Finance Committee under Dan Gainey, the former treasurer of the GOP National Committee who had been serving as finance chairman for our Draft organization in Minnesota. Dan always joked, or maybe only half joked, that he was picked for this important post because he spent the winters on his ranch in Arizona and thus was not considered entirely an alien by Kitchel's crew. The assistant chairman, G. R. Herberger, was also a part-time Arizonan who hailed from Minnesota and operates a department store chain in the Midwest.

George Humphrey, Eisenhower's Secretary of the Treasury, accepted the Midwest chairmanship of the Finance Committee, and Lammot du Pont Copeland, Jr. of Delaware headed up the Mid-Atlantic region with J. Fife Symington, Jr. of Maryland.

There were no less than five members of our original group on the national Finance Committee. Ed Lynch and Stets Coleman were named finance chairmen-at-large; Bill Middendorf and Jerry Milbank were co-chairmen for the Northeast; and Roger Milliken helped take charge of fundraising in the South.

Henry Salvatori, the dynamic chairman of the board of the Western Geophysical Company in Los Angeles, was appointed state finance chairman for California and did a whale of a job through the critical California primary and on into the fall campaign. Independent of our national fund drive, he raised nearly $1 million for the primary battle alone.

R. Douglas Stewart, chairman of the board of the Quaker Oats Company, and Art Schupp of Detroit were also on the initial Goldwater for President Finance Committee and other prominent citizens were added later.

The whole committee functioned with an effectiveness rarely if ever known before in political fundraising. In the less than six months remaining before the convention they raised the balance of the $3,500,000 I had estimated it would take to finance the nominating campaign. In fact, our expenditures came within $100,000 of the budgetary target we had set at the secret meeting in Chicago in December 1962.

I don't believe there has been a national campaign in this century financed so efficiently. Unlike so many other campaigns, the money for this one was raised without promises of political patronage. And the money contributed came not from a small group of wealthy contributors seeking a measure of control over the national government, a Cabinet post, or some ambassadorship. It came from thousands of people in all walks of life who saw in Barry Goldwater's candidacy a more lasting promise for their country.

Although the financial problem, which of course can be critical, was now solved with the appointment of Dan Gainey and his committee, there were a hundred and one other knotty problems in those early weeks of 1964. Many of them were brought on by Senator Goldwater's tendency to fire away at almost any target that was held up to him at press conferences. Others were produced by segments of the press that dissected Goldwater's every statement in such a way that the resulting bloodletting would have killed off any Presidential candidate, no matter how carefully he chose his words. But many problems were simply manufactured at 1101 Connecticut Avenue by the Goldwater for President Committee.

Back on December 17 I sent Denison Kitchel a memorandum asking him to establish negotiating deadlines for each of the Presidential primaries Goldwater planned to enter. These, I said, would be the final days we should set to come to an agreement on delegates with Republican leaders in each state. If no agreement could be hammered out, we should then have sufficient lead time to get petitions circulated and a slate of Goldwater delegates lined up before each primary filing deadline. To the memo I attached a list of all the states which held primaries, with a suggested negotiating deadline for each and, of course, the last date on which Goldwater could file.

Several times over the succeeding six weeks I brought up this subject again. But it was repeatedly brushed off. The Arizona people were intent on avoiding primary contests wherever possible. Ohio might have proved one good place to re-establish Goldwater's momentum, but a deal was made with Ray Bliss in which Bliss actually gave us nothing whatever in exchange for keeping the Senator out of the Ohio primary.

In Pennsylvania, no deal was even made. But I was forced to keep our Goldwater people there from entering the Senator in the preferential primary. If he had entered, they were confident that in an all-out fight Goldwater could win at least a third of the state's big 64-vote delegation from Scranton. They knew the Governor had lost a lot of ground with rank-and-file Republicans by boosting the sales tax and handing the taxpayers the biggest budget in the state's history. And they also knew that if Goldwater refused to enter, Scranton would use his state patronage system to club the Goldwater-leaning county chairmen and workers back into line behind his favorite-son front.

Paul Hugus, the Allegheny County GOP chairman, was already being made into an object lesson for all dissidents to see what would befall them if they persisted in opposing Scranton. Even before the moratorium ended on December 22 Scranton had singled out Hugus and eventually drove him from his leadership position in the party.

We had a further indication of the lengths to which Governor Scranton would go to block Goldwater just before the Senator came into Pittsburgh to speak at the $100-a-plate Republican "Go Day" dinner on January 29. This was part of the nationwide extravaganza the National Committee had cooked up to raise funds for the 1964 campaign and at the same time put most of the party's Presidential candidates and other leaders on view. Over closed-circuit television piped into dining rooms in twenty-one cities, the candidates would be competing in their speeches with the most influential Republicans in the nation. Goldwater would be bucking head-on into Scranton, who was speaking from Indianapolis just before him, Romney in Washington, Rockefeller in Los Angeles and Nixon in New York. Senator Thruston Morton was the leadoff man in Houston and Eisenhower and Bill Miller were to wind up the show.

A few days before "Go Day," Kitchel got a distress call from Pittsburgh and he turned it over to me. Less than five hundred $100-a-plate tickets had been sold for the dinner Goldwater was to speak at in the Pittsburgh Hilton ballroom, which can hold over two thousand people. Executives of some of the big corporations in Pittsburgh who ordinarily might have bought a half-dozen or more tables had put up money for only one or two. Our contacts said that the word had gone out from Harrisburg to keep the crowd at the Goldwater dinner to a minimum and most, though not all, of the businessmen were cooperating. The national impact of the Senator addressing a half-empty ballroom while his opponents spoke before jam-packed crowds in other cities was obvious.

Ben Chapple, our Western Pennsylvania chairman, went to work and during the next few days he somehow managed to pack the Pittsburgh Hilton ballroom. Unfortunately, Goldwater turned in a disappointing performance with his five-minute speech before the 25,000 top Republicans who were watching on television. But he followed Scranton, and the instant comparison the viewers made was not unfavorable to the Senator. However, we almost lost our candidate that night.

After the dinner, Ben Chapple's gang threw a party for Goldwater in the Presidential suite at the Hilton. Ben and the Senator were standing with their backs to a glass floor-to-ceiling window when a young drunk who had crashed the crowded party stumbled over and started arguing with Barry. Suddenly, he lunged at the Senator and for a split second Ben Chapple and the other spectators thought he might push Goldwater right through the window. Luckily, someone grabbed the drunk before he threw his punch and hustled him out of the room. If Goldwater had gone through the glass, he would have plunged twenty-four stories to the street. Not long after this a man was killed when he was pushed through an identical window during a scuffle in another room at the same hotel.

After Goldwater's appearance in Pittsburgh I received several complaints from our people there that the palace guard had closed ranks too tightly around the Senator. Even when people did manage to get his ear he invariably told them to give their advice to Kitchel or Dean Burch. I received numerous similar complaints practically everywhere Goldwater went. Some of them may have been groundless, the result of bruised feelings at some imagined slight. But many were justified, principally because the Arizona crowd seldom acted on the suggestions that the people in other states passed onto them.

I have often thought that if the Arizona people had had a chance before the campaign started to work with and get to know the members of the Draft organization, both on the national level and in the states, much of the dissension and confusion could have been avoided. The Arizonans had little confidence in most of the Draft group. Despite the fact that Kitchel and his friends were the people closest to the Senator, most of them lacked confidence in themselves, too, and they guarded jealously what they conceived to be their prerogatives. Too often their defensive actions were tinged with arrogance.

Once, when Ann Eve Johnson was away from Washington, a Goldwater leader in another state wrote our national headquarters and asked for one of Peggy Goldwater's cooking recipes to give to the women's editors on some state newspapers. Ione Harrington sent a recipe back by return mail and thought no more about it since it was a recipe Edna Coerver had been using for years to fill similar requests. But when Ann Eve learned of it she was furious. Rather bluntly, she ordered Ione not to handle any future correspondence without her permission. In the press of a political campaign authority must be delegated, or things just do not get done. And almost every day that winter too many things did not get done at 1101 Connecticut Avenue.

Weeks before the Senator's January 3 announcement I had drawn up a list of our state chairmen with recommendations as to which ones we should keep after the Goldwater for President Committee was formed. But I could never get Kleindienst to sit down and discuss the list with me. The result was that many of the state chairmen were kept on the fence, not knowing whether they were in or out. Finally, after about six weeks, when it became apparent that the morale in many of our state organizations was dangerously deteriorating, I insisted that the appointments be announced. Kleindienst agreed and we sent letters out immediately, but the confidence of some of our people in the states in their national command was seriously eroded by the long delay.

By the second week in February I felt that I had no alternative but to get out. The law firm-type partnership which Kleindienst had suggested had not worked the way he had outlined it. I was forced to clear even the most minor decisions with the high command from Arizona. Because I was the only one at headquarters most of them knew, our state leaders were beginning to blame me for the many decisions that were never made, though I had no authority to make them. Under these conditions it was impossible to work effectively and I could see no alternative but to withdraw completely from the Goldwater campaign.

However, we had an important meeting of the national and state leaders coming up in Chicago that weekend, and since I had been charged with making all the arrangements and preparing the program, I decided to stay on until this meeting was over. I had been given to understand that I would be handling the briefing of the state chairmen in Chicago. But the night before the meeting convened at the O'Hare Inn, Dean Burch informed me that Kitchel would conduct the briefing I had prepared.

There was another meeting at the O'Hare Inn that weekend, one that might well have changed the entire disastrous course of the Goldwater campaign if it had come off as planned.

By this time, many Goldwater leaders in virtually every section of the country knew that something was seriously wrong. They were becoming thoroughly disenchanted with the Senator's campaign, particularly as the signs of his impending defeat in the nation's first primary echoed back to them from the hills of New Hampshire.

The members of my original group were getting beaten over the head for all the mistakes by the people in their own states and regions. They saw that I was in no position to correct these mistakes and so they took matters into their own hands. After conferring among themselves, they decided to nail the Senator in Chicago and read him the riot act.

Frank Whetstone called Goldwater from Montana and arranged a private meeting for the group at the O'Hare Inn on Sunday, February 16. Rather pointedly, Frank told the Senator that they wanted to confer with him alone, and not in the presence of his Arizona people.

On Saturday night Whetstone, Charlie Barr, and about ten of my other old Suite 3505 agents closeted themselves in a remote room at the motel. After reviewing the long list of complaints that had been building up about the campaign, they sorted out the most important ones and arranged an informal agenda for the session with the Senator. Everyone agreed that this was no time to pull any punches.

Frank Whetstone, who had established the closest personal relationship with Goldwater, was chosen as the group's spokesman. It was a wise choice, for I have never known Frank to flinch in the face of any assignment, no matter how tough or distasteful. He agreed to spell out the complaints as bluntly as might be necessary the following day. Then they invited me to attend the showdown session. But since I realized they were bound to raise some questions about my own status in the campaign I begged off.

When Goldwater arrived for the meeting with the group he was very obviously in a highly nervous state. The rigors of the New Hampshire campaign were beginning to show. He had spent a month and a half stumping up and down and across that first primary battleground, most of that time with his foot painfully encased in the plaster cast. And he must have known that he was in for a rough time with this gang that Sunday.

The Senator sat down with the group assembled around him in the motel room and his hands appeared to be trembling. No one there had ever seen him like this before and Charlie Barr decided this was not the time to back Barry Goldwater against the wall. Charlie told Frank

Whetstone the signals were changed. Frank would have to go easy. Seeing the state Goldwater was in, Frank nodded his agreement, discarded the verbal brass knuckles, and donned his best kid-glove manner.

The message was muted. At another time it might have gotten through to Goldwater, but he had closed his mind and he was no longer receptive to polite suggestions. Throughout the half-hour meeting he was on the defensive, but when the group brought up my future role he appeared to promise that I would be given greater responsibility. That placated most of the people there, although I really don't think it should have. There were more important points at stake that day.

Andy Carter and some of the others who attended this meeting now feel that this may well have been the last chance to get Goldwater and his campaign onto the right track. If he had not appeared so distraught, and if the group had laid all their cards on the table, Andy believes Goldwater might have taken their criticism more seriously, and made the drastic changes that were necessary to save himself and the conservative movement from the disaster that descended the following autumn. It was certainly the last opportunity they had as a group to confront the candidate. The Senator never permitted himself to be cornered by them again.

Actually, I'm not at all sure that any of these people would have been willing to use the only real weapon they had, individually or as a group. Ultimately, the only threat they could hold over the Senator was their withdrawal from his campaign. Given Goldwater's mood throughout most of 1964, even that threat might have had no effect. Many an intelligent and effective conservative was forced out by the palace guard and the Senator never, to my knowledge, raised a hand to save them, if indeed he was even aware of the massive throat-slitting that was carried out in his name. Peter O'Donnell, Bill Buckley, Brent Bozell, Mr. X— these were only a few in the long and ever-growing list of casualties mowed down by the Arizona Mafia.

The Barr-Whetstone gang were not the only ones who registered protests about the conduct of the campaign. Dan Gainey and several members of his Finance Committee confronted Denison Kitchel about this time and demanded his resignation. But Kitchel refused to go, though after the New Hampshire defeat he asked a friend of mine if perhaps he shouldn't resign.

Ironically, Tom Van Sickle believes that it was the briefing of the state chairmen at the O'Hare Inn that weekend that saved Kitchel's scalp. Many of these chairmen had also come loaded for bear, but the briefing session went off so well that they felt Kitchel and his crew were developing into real professionals and they decided to hold their fire.

None of them knew, of course, that Kitchel and his friends were merely following a script which I had written for them.

When the Chicago meeting ended I flew back to Washington with Tom Van Sickle. He had been standing guard at the door when Charlie Barr and the group had conferred with Goldwater to make certain no one else crashed the private meeting. Tom was bitterly disappointed that the meeting had failed to accomplish its objective. I was too, of course. But those two days at the O'Hare Inn with the members of our original group and all the state chairmen had made me see that it would be impossible for me to desert these people whatever might happen back on Connecticut Avenue. I had no choice. No matter what kind of a role I was relegated to by Denison Kitchel and his allies I would have to stick it out. From here on until the national convention I never again seriously considered quitting the campaign.

CHAPTER 26

PREVIEW IN
NEW HAMPSHIRE

THE INTRICATE PATTERN of Barry Goldwater's ultimate defeat
on November 3, 1964 was first etched out, indelibly and irrevocably,
in the New Hampshire primary campaign which began ten months
earlier. It was a campaign that I was forced to observe from afar since
I was never permitted to return to New Hampshire after a flying trip
there with Denison Kitchel in October 1963. But I lived on intimate
terms with that initial primary race for more than two months, and with
its effects for weeks afterwards. First-hand reports of the battle daily
crossed my desk in Washington and it is from these that I must draw
in relating the events in this chapter.

By the time Senator Goldwater began his New Hampshire campaign
the full impact of John F. Kennedy's assassination upon the political
scene was clearly apparent. In the polls, Lyndon B. Johnson enjoyed a
commanding lead over every Republican aspirant. A full 70 per cent
of the polled electorate approved of the new President.

However, *vis-à-vis* all the other GOP Presidential hopefuls, Goldwater still maintained a seemingly impregnable position. In the confusion that prevailed in the public mind about his candidacy, much of
it artificially created by the false prophets who counted him out minutes
after Kennedy was slain, he had plunged precipitously in the polls. But
he was still running neck-and-neck with Richard Nixon, who briefly

took over the GOP lead, and he was far ahead of all other Republican contenders.

I knew that Nixon's narrow edge over Goldwater would soon vanish. The former Vice President had no organization to speak of, no political home base to build on, and he was not now, nor was he likely to become, an avowed candidate in 1964. His only chance of securing the nomination lay in a deadlocked convention from which he could conceivably emerge as the compromise candidate.

By contrast, Goldwater had at his disposal the nationwide organization we had spent two years building from Suite 3505 and through our Draft Committee. He had a large, though still undetermined, number of delegates committed informally to his candidacy. And he had a hard core of dedicated volunteers already doing missionary work in precincts throughout the country.

No other Republican could claim anything remotely comparable to Goldwater's organization, volunteer force, and potential delegate strength. Nonetheless, the Senator badly needed a primary victory—or better yet, an unbroken string of primary victories—to prove his vote-getting appeal at the polls. New Hampshire, where the nation's first Presidential primary takes place every four years, seemed a good place to start his winning streak.

At the outset, Goldwater appeared to hold all the cards he could possibly need for a resounding victory in New Hampshire. Our private polls in October had shown that he was preferred by no less than 65 per cent of the Republican and independent voters eligible to cast their ballots in the primary. We knew that this might have dropped somewhat after the assassination. But the Senator had lost no key supporters and he even picked up several prominent backers during the first few days of January. Indeed, all but a very few of the state's leading Republicans were solidly behind him.

Goldwater's state campaign chairman was Senator Cotton, easily the most popular political figure in the state. His field commander was Stewart Lamprey, Speaker of the State House of Representatives and soon to become president of the State Senate. Lamprey was widely regarded as the GOP's best bet to regain the governorship lost to the Democrats two years before. Together, Cotton and Lamprey had done a masterful job of lining up a powerful slate of delegates to run under the Goldwater banner. The slate represented not merely traditional conservatives, but a broad-based cross section of New Hampshire's many warring Republican factions.

Senator Cotton, himself a moderate, headed the list of 14 Goldwater delegates. Mrs. Doloris Bridges, widow of the revered Senator Styles Bridges, brought a large and intensely loyal personal following to her delegate candidacy. Philip Dunlap, the young president of the State Senate, was one of the rising stars in New Hampshire politics. In Manchester, the state's largest city, Goldwater had three of the most popular Republicans going for him—Mrs. Greta Ainley, Chester Jenks and former U. S. Attorney Maurice Bois. In Portsmouth, an upcoming young attorney named Jeremy Waldron, whose vivacious wife was the daughter of one of the state's outstanding judges, announced that he would run as a Goldwater delegate. In nearby Rye, Herbert Philbrick, who had won national fame as an undercover agent for the FBI, added his name to the slate.

On the eve of Senator Goldwater's first campaign sweep through New Hampshire the slate was completed with the addition of Lane Dwinell, twice Governor and a former U. S. Assistant Secretary of State under President Eisenhower. Dwinell had been one of Dwight D. Eisenhower's earliest and most influential supporters in New Hampshire. He had run as an Eisenhower delegate during the crucial 1952 primary while serving as Speaker of the State House of Representatives. As Governor in 1956 he had headed the Eisenhower-pledged New Hampshire delegation to the national convention. Now, the strong statement Dwinell issued in which he announced his intention to run as a Goldwater delegate underlined the solid foundation of responsible support the Senator enjoyed in New Hampshire that first week in January.

Moreover, Goldwater had important backing from the *Manchester Union-Leader,* New Hampshire's largest newspaper and the only one with statewide circulation. Its publisher, William Loeb, a close ally of the late Senator Bridges, fired off front-page editorials almost daily, boosting Goldwater and roundly lambasting his opponents, particularly Rockefeller.

In addition, the top public relations agency in the state, run by Hamilton Putnam, who had been managing publicity for the Republican state committee for years, signed on to handle Goldwater's press relations. To this key job Putnam assigned one of New Hampshire's leading newspapermen, Robert Drury. And George Dawson, head of the largest advertising agency in Concord, confidently took on the Goldwater account, turning down more lucrative offers from other GOP Presidential candidates.

To build a grassroots campaign organization, Cotton and Lamprey marshaled an exceptionally able group of area coordinators. These included Mrs. Judy Levesque, the attractive wife of a Nashua dentist and mother of seven children; Mrs. Marian Haley of Keene, who with her husband, Charles Haley, had organized Cotton's senatorial campaigns in the southwestern part of the state; Mrs. Rita Palmer, of Derry, another Cotton organizer; State Senator Nelson E. Howard and Vic

Cardosi of Rochester, New Hampshire, one of Cotton's most valuable and trusted lieutenants.

Mrs. Norma Currier, the GOP National Committeewoman from New Hampshire, had long been on the Goldwater team, working with the members of my original group as far back as 1962. Now Mrs. Mildred Perkins, president of the state Republican Women's Federation, also came forward to run the Goldwater women's organization in the primary.

Against this formidable team the best Nelson Rockefeller could muster was support from a very few prominent Republicans, and even these demonstrated little real enthusiasm for their candidate. Although they were both avowed conservatives, former Governor Hugh Gregg and his eternal ally, Bert Teague, signed on to manage the Rockefeller campaign.[1]

Rockefeller, in an attempt to offset his failure to attract outstanding allies, dispatched a battalion of New York professionals and public relations experts to Concord. He also shipped in tons of expensive campaign literature and purchased prime radio and television time on stations in Vermont and Massachusetts to beam his message into New Hampshire. The state's statutory limitation of $25,000 on campaign funds expended by any one candidate is a farce to begin with, but Rockefeller elevated it to the level of high comedy.

I will not pretend that the Goldwater forces stayed within this limitation either, though we did observe the letter of the law. Stewart Lamprey, honest Yankee that he is, adamantly refused to let us spend more than the legal limit in the state. He could not control what we spent outside, of course, but even so our costs did not begin to approach the lavish scale of Rockefeller's open-handed spending. Nor did our paid troops from out-of-state ever number a fraction of the force Rockefeller put up at Concord's largest motor inn, the Highway Hotel.

In the beginning, however, money didn't seem all that important to Goldwater's candidacy in New Hampshire. Although Cotton and Lamprey were taking nothing for granted, when the campaign started they had good cause for optimism. Cotton had already convinced Goldwater that he would have to stump the state early and often on the theory that the more hands he could shake the bigger would be his margin of victory.

---

[1] On a radio program, Gregg tried to answer why he, a conservative, should want to lead a Liberal's campaign. "Well," mused Gregg, "if somebody wants you to do them a favor in politics, it makes you feel good, and I've been out of touch for a while, so frankly, I was happy to do it." This frank reply was essentially true. Hugh Gregg *was* a bit "out of touch." He had lost two attempts to win back the governorship and had even failed to win a Congressional primary contest for Bert Teague in 1962 when he acted as Teague's campaign manager. In 1966, Gregg lost again in his effort to regain the governorship.

Thus, it was on a note of high hopefulness that Barry Goldwater began his campaign in New Hampshire.

On the surface, at least, the Senator's first expedition into New Hampshire seemed a smashing success. From the first day he arrived, on Tuesday, January 7, until he departed the state on Thursday afternoon the crowds that flocked to see him exceeded by far all the expectations of his campaign managers. Even at three o'clock in the morning when the chartered DC-3 that had flown him from Battle Creek, Michigan, put down at Concord Airport there was a little crowd out in the snow and cold to welcome him. Some had driven many miles over icy roads and Goldwater himself was surprised to see the hardy little band on the flight line when he emerged from the aging plane. "Don't you New Hampshire people believe in going to bed?" he quipped to Senator Cotton as he came down the stairs one at a time, lifting the heavy cast on his foot gingerly with each step.

At the dinner marking the formal opening of his campaign in Concord's Highway Hotel that evening such a large crowd turned out that it filled two private banquet rooms, overflowed into the big public dining room, and even into several restaurants downtown. When it came time for Goldwater to speak the tables had to be cleared out of the main banquet room and still there wasn't room for everyone to get in.

The Senator's speech, which was mainly a plea for party unity, struck an obviously responsive chord with an audience that had seen a sharp decline in Republican fortunes following a bitter internecine primary battle in 1962. The enthusiastic cheers that punctuated his address must have sent the professionals laboring late in the Rockefeller headquarters downstairs into black despair.

At two coffee hours in Nashua the following morning, the first at the home of Mr. and Mrs. Russell Kennett on Main Street and the next at the suburban ranch home of Mr. and Mrs. Samuel Tamposi, both houses were bursting at the seams. No less than four hundred citizens showed up at the Tamposis, where not more than fifty or seventy-five had been expected. They jammed every room in the house, including the laundry and furnace areas in the basement, and scores of people spilled out onto the snow-covered lawns and into the street.

In Amherst, at the beautiful old Colonial home of George and Phyllis Brown, it was the same story, but with a moving extra touch. The pupils from the Amherst grammar school paraded into George Brown's yard to welcome the man that many of their parents then hoped would be the next President of the United States. Goldwater, always at his best with young people, devoted more time to the youngsters than to the adult voters inside. But the grownups loved it and listened with surreptitious pride at the windows while the Senator and the children solemnly discussed the meaning of democracy.

The highlight of this tour was a speech at St. Anselm's College in Manchester that same night. Knowing how jaded New Hampshire voters have grown over the years with platoons of Presidential aspirants personally pleading for their votes, Goldwater's managers were doubtful that they could fill the 450-seat campus theater for his appearance. But the advance indications of a much larger turnout forced the college authorities to transfer the event into the new 2,000-seat campus gymnasium that afternoon.

Stewart Lamprey learned of this decision in Amherst while Goldwater was talking to the school children in George Brown's yard. With visions of a half-empty college gymnasium staring his candidate in the face, Lamprey sent his area coordinator, Judy Levesque, on ahead to Manchester to see if she could round up at least a few score more people to occupy seats in the cavernous gym. On less than four hours' notice, Judy and her friends, manning a battery of telephones at the Holiday Inn motel, managed to bring out another overflow crowd for Goldwater. The gymnasium was so packed by the time the Senator arrived that scores of students and other spectators had to perch atop the lockers that lined the walls.

The following morning in Portsmouth and Rochester the crowds kept coming. At the American Legion Hall in Rochester, Goldwater was forced to speak standing in the middle of the floor surrounded by people who pressed in so close they were less than an arm's length away from him on all sides. But when he stepped out of the hall, the heavy gray clouds that herald the approach of an ice storm were forming in the sky. As a result, he had to skip his next stop in Exeter, where several hundred people had gathered to meet him at the home of two sisters, Helen Hinman and Henriette Gallant. Instead, he drove straight to Pease Air Force Base near Portsmouth and boarded the DC-3 for the flight back to Washington where he was scheduled to appear at the Republican National Committee meeting that night.

The storm that drove Barry Goldwater out of New Hampshire that January afternoon later loomed as an ominous portent to many of his previously optimistic followers. There was something symbolic about the people left waiting at the house in Exeter. But there were more tangible signs of trouble stirring, signs that showed between the lines of the reports I received in Washington. Beneath the superficial success of the Senator's first New Hampshire tour, disturbing and deeply contradictory crosscurrents were already flowing.

One incident at Pease Air Force Base gave the first hint of what many observers later came to regard as a damaging change in the Senator's friendly, easygoing personality. Though fortunately never noted in the press, this little by-play could have been blown up to equal the famous train incident of Thomas E. Dewey's 1948 campaign. On that occasion, an engineer accidentally backed up the Dewey campaign train, shook up the passengers, and, according to the reporters, sent the candidate into a rage. The incident was used extensively to point up Dewey's alleged irascibility and coldness, and some experts believe it lost him many thousands of critical votes in the close election that followed.

In the little drama at the Air Force base, Barry Goldwater may merely have been an innocent bystander. The storm was closing in fast when his motorcade arrived at the flight line. A reporter who had been in New Hampshire for over a week asked if he could hitch a ride back to Washington on the Goldwater plane if the commercial flights were grounded at Boston's Logan Airport. Tony Smith, the Senator's press aide, said okay and an Air Force major standing nearby volunteered to run back to the control tower to find out if Logan was open to traffic. A few minutes later the major returned. Thinking the reporter was on the plane, he ran up the steps to give him the weather report at Logan. As he reached the top, someone slammed the door in his face.

The major, a command pilot with years of combat and peacetime service behind him, was stunned. He came back down the stairs shaking his head and spotted the reporter standing on the line. "I guess they slammed that door in both our faces," he said. The reporter nodded, and offered the opinion that Senator Goldwater probably knew nothing of what had happened. "Maybe not," the major replied. "But he was standing just inside the door when they slammed it."

A second, and at first less apparent, storm warning had been raised in the Goldwater camp the preceding afternoon in Manchester. After the long day's tour, the Goldwater motorcade wound up at the Holiday Inn motel where the Senator was to rest for a few hours before making his speech at St. Anselm's. During this break, Senator Cotton cornered Stew Lamprey in one of the motel rooms and started reading him a lengthy riot act. The tour thus far had been immensely successful and Cotton was probably only trying to goad Lamprey on to even greater effort. But the heated discussion resulted in an unfortunate misunderstanding between Goldwater's two New Hampshire campaign chieftains that persisted for many weeks.

More serious and lasting in its effect was the visible tightening of control over the Senator by his personal palace guard. On Tuesday a briefing notebook which I had ordered prepared for him—a sort of personal guidebook with information about the political complexion of the towns he would visit, the people he would meet, and the issues which had the greatest vote-getting potential—was turned over to one of his aides. But it was not passed on to Goldwater and it wasn't until the next day that he accidentally discovered that the notebook existed. He never did get his own copy, and was forced to use Senator Cotton's for the balance of the tour.[2]

During the interlude at the Holiday Inn and at St. Anselm's afterwards, Bill Baroody made his first campaign appearance with Goldwater. Oddly, no one in the press, not even the knowledgeable veteran reporters from Washington, was aware of it at the time. But the New Hampshire people were quick to note it, and they wondered at the obviously strong influence Baroody exerted over the Senator. Although some of them laughed, others were puzzled at the jesting manner in which Goldwater addressed Baroody as "the Cardinal," referring to him with mock formality as "Your Eminence." Baroody in turn called Goldwater "Your Holiness," a term of respect reserved for the Pope. However, one of the Hampshiremen, thinking he was calling the Senator "Your Highness," remarked later, "Who the hell do they think they are? Richelieu and King Louis?"

Goldwater and Baroody, who is a Catholic, were only joking, of course. But to many people inside the Goldwater camp, the Hampshireman's quip would not have sounded very far off target. As Denison Kitchel once said of the Goldwater for President Committee, "This is a monarchy, not a democracy." Some people claim that Kitchel fancied himself as the "monarchy's" prime minister, but others believe Baroody was cast in this role. If so, they both missed an all-important point. Cardinal Richelieu's power, as First Minister of France, derived from the unchallenged power of Louis XIII as occupant of his nation's throne. In contrast, Senator Goldwater, though undoubtedly a power in the Republican Party, was still far removed from the real seat of power in modern America, the White House.

All of these disquieting incidents were played out in the wings off stage where they were not subjected to the critical scrutiny of the voting audience. However, another series of incidents took place at stage center on this same campaign swing and were quickly broadcast to the whole nation. Three responses that Senator Goldwater gave at press

[2] The briefing notebook has become a standard manual for Presidential candidates. Meeting hundreds of people along the campaign trail, no candidate can be expected to remember every issue that is important to every city or town he visits, let alone every person he should thank for helping him. On March 5, reporter Mary McGrory wrote in the *Washington Evening Star*, "Senator Goldwater has yet to give a statistic about New Hampshire. He does not even trouble to mention the town in which he finds himself." Although this was certainly an exaggeration, nonetheless I do know that the Senator did not make full use of his briefing notebook on the first three New Hampshire tours. After that, Kitchel and Kleindienst ordered me to remove the man I had working on the notebook from the state.

conferences on this tour were inflated into great national issues that were to haunt his candidacy clear to election day, 1964.

The issues involved were Goldwater's stand on Social Security, the question of control over nuclear weapons, and the reliability of U.S. missiles. In the first two, Goldwater was the victim of gross distortions. In the third, he was placed in an untenable position by a combination of his old tendency to "shoot from the hip" and the failure of the press to dig deep enough beneath the surface to determine the actual facts.

It was at an early morning press conference in Portsmouth on Thursday, January 9, that the Senator remarked, almost offhandedly, "I don't feel safe at all about our missiles. I wish the Defense Department would tell the American people how undependable the missiles in our silos actually are. I can't tell you—it's classified—and I'll probably catch hell for saying this."

The words were hardly out of his mouth and onto the press wires when his facetious prediction came true. Defense Secretary Robert McNamara, in the first of many salvos he fired at the candidate of the party to which he once claimed allegiance, branded Goldwater's statement "completely misleading, politically irresponsible, and damaging to the national security." Significantly, however, McNamara never said flatly that Goldwater's charge was entirely false. And, as a matter of fact, not even McNamara could have proved that it was.

As a major general in the Air Force Reserve, Goldwater was privy to information which he obviously could not divulge. Much of it was "classified," as he said. But there was sufficient data that was even then a matter of public record that would have bolstered his position immensely had he used it during this opening round of the so-called "missile flap."

For one thing, the Senator could have pointed to what General Thomas S. Power, then chief of the Strategic Air Command, has since called "the incredible fact that we have never tested an Intercontinental Ballistic Missile all the way from launch to detonation of the warhead."[3]

---

[3] General Thomas S. Power, *Design for Survival,* Coward-McCann, 1965. General Power served as commander-in-chief of SAC from 1957 until shortly after the 1964 election. Although his brilliant book was not published until his retirement because of a ban imposed by the Secretary of Defense, the portions of his testimony released during the Test Ban Treaty hearings of 1963 said substantially what he writes in the book in describing one of the reasons he opposed the treaty: "Although our current military strategy places increasing emphasis on missiles, the test ban treaty now deprives us of every possibility to ascertain whether our ICBMs will really function as expected. I submit that this is the first time in our history that much or even most of the nation's striking power is to be entrusted to weapons that have never been fully tested operationally."

However, it was also the responsibility of the press to cite this critical fact. Strangely, the same influential segments of our mass media which clobbered Candidate Goldwater on the "missile flap," professed to take seriously Candidate Kennedy's charge in 1960 that an alarming "missile gap" had developed between the U.S. and the Soviet Union. It was not until *after* the 1960 election that the press discovered Kennedy's accusation was essentially fictitious. But Goldwater's charge was instantly labeled as spurious and McNamara's rebuttal widely accepted as gospel.

Even when Goldwater was most thorough and cautious in his replies to the press he could not escape being held up to ridicule or, worse, subjected to outright untruths about his views. This became abundantly apparent at the very first press conference he held in New Hampshire. When the Senator limped into his state campaign headquarters on Concord's Main Street at ten o'clock that Tuesday morning, the reporters immediately began pelting him with questions about stands he had taken as long ago as half a dozen years before. They ran the gamut, from his opposition to the graduated income tax through an ancient suggestion he had made that the U.S. should consider withdrawing from the United Nations if Communist China was admitted. But the two issues which subsequently damaged him most were, as I mentioned before, his stands on Social Security and control of nuclear weapons. In both cases his views were grossly distorted. I have before me as I write this a transcript of the tape recording that was made of this press conference—*a transcript that was distributed to all the reporters present that very same day.*

Asked whether he favored continuing the Social Security program, Goldwater replied that he would suggest only "one change." He felt that participation in the program should be voluntary. "If a person can provide better for himself let him do it," he said. "But if he prefers the government to do it, let him." He pointed out that by 1970 the government would be taking 10 per cent from a person's paycheck for Social Security. For that amount of money, he added, people could "get a better Social Security program" through private insurance.

A few hours later, the *Concord Monitor* ran the banner headline: "GOLDWATER SETS GOALS: END SOCIAL SECURITY, HIT CASTRO." Immediately, the Senator was placed on the defensive regarding what became, with the substantial help of repeated charges by Nelson Rockefeller, a major issue in New Hampshire and in the general election campaign the following fall.

The question on nuclear weapons came up during a discussion of a foreign policy paper which Goldwater had submitted to former President Eisenhower the previous September. He said he did not want to create the impression that Eisenhower had approved his foreign policy "in total." But, he added, "I asked him for criticism; he had none and agreed with what I had said. He was specifically drawn toward NATO and the Western problem." Then came the following exchange:

How about nuclear weapons?

I have said, the commander should have the ability to use nuclear weapons . . . Former commanders have told me that NATO troops should be equipped with nuclear weapons, but the use should remain only with the commander.

It was completely clear that the Senator was referring *only* to the NATO commander. Yet the word was spread far and wide that Barry Goldwater advocated entrusting control over nuclear weapons to field officers. The following autumn *U.S. News & World Report* unearthed the information that what Goldwater suggested in Concord on January 7 had been established U.S. policy under both Presidents Eisenhower and Kennedy. But by then it was too late. Goldwater had been so long depicted as a trigger-happy warmonger who would give even low-ranking officers the power to touch off a nuclear holocaust that the overwhelming majority of voters accepted this totally false picture of him as fact.

Much of the blame for this must fall on the heads of the rival candidates in the Senator's own party. Driven by desperate ambition or uninformed idealism, they seized upon explosive issues and detonated them repeatedly in an attempt to blast Goldwater out of the running. In the process they not only decimated the Republican Party but did their country a grave disservice.

One other warning signal was first spotted during Barry Goldwater's initial swing through New Hampshire. On the night of January 7, while the Senator was speaking at the campaign kickoff dinner in Concord, his supporters in the town of Pittsfield conducted a canvass of Republican and independent voters. Under New Hampshire law, independents can vote in a primary merely by appearing at the polling places and indicating which party they intend to vote with. There were a large number of independents in the state and in Pittsfield they comprised a group half as large as all the registered Republicans.

Of the 480 voters polled that night, 130 said they intended to vote for Goldwater, 50 were opposed to him outright, and 300 said they were undecided.

It was the unusually large undecided vote that jolted Norris Cotton and Stew Lamprey. Subsequent canvasses during the next few weeks showed that this trend was not peculiar to little Pittsfield. It extended throughout the state. Nearly two-thirds of all those eligible to cast their ballots in the primary had not yet made up their minds, although, as I have noted previously, before the assassination 65 per cent claimed they favored Goldwater.

Obviously, there had been a drastic change in New Hampshire. Nor could it be attributed to anything Senator Goldwater had said or done. The Pittsfield canvass, which proved a faithful mirror of statewide voter sentiment, was taken less than twelve hours after his very first press conference of the campaign. The Social Security scare raised by the false headline that afternoon and the nuclear weapons issue could not possibly have had such an instantaneous effect. It was evident that the assassination of President Kennedy had dealt Barry Goldwater's candidacy a far more serious blow than any of us had hitherto suspected, at least in New Hampshire, and probably throughout the whole Northeast. Whether it had had a similar impact in the Midwest, West and South remained to be seen.

Nonetheless, there was still a ray of hope in the New Hampshire situation. The voters had apparently not turned their backs completely on Goldwater. They were *undecided*. But they had not yet swung over to another candidate. I believed, with what I must confess was probably an overdose of faith, that a dramatic and confident campaign could bring them back into the Senator's fold. Unfortunately, this was not the kind of campaign that was waged.

In late January, Dick Kleindienst made a flying foray into New Hampshire. After surveying the scene for less than forty-eight hours he returned to Washington with gloomy news. He was convinced the Senator was going to be beaten badly in the March 10 primary. That being the case, Kleindienst recommended that Goldwater let it be known now that he *expected* to lose so that when the defeat came it would not appear quite so disastrous.

What the Goldwater campaign needed more than anything else at this juncture was a healthy injection of confidence. Elections, particularly Presidential elections, are not won with pessimism. An underdog may come from behind to win, as Harry Truman had in 1948 and Jack Kennedy had in 1960. But the underdog must show a fighting spirit and cloak himself in the sturdy armor of self-confidence if he hopes to spring an upset. His private appraisal of his slim chances should never be displayed in public. Yet two days after Kleindienst made his recommendation, Barry Goldwater announced to the press that he was going to lose badly in New Hampshire and would be happy to get one-third of the total primary vote. The Senator, who had not lost an election in more than fifteen years in politics, not only assumed the unfamiliar role of underdog, but revealed himself as perhaps the least confident underdog ever to enter the Presidential lists.

From there on, Goldwater's stock in New Hampshire sank further with each passing day. He appeared bewildered by his failure to "get through to those people." Doggedly, he kept right on stumping the state, hoping to find the magic formula for victory. I don't think he ever realized that he had thrown away one very important element for such a formula when he had announced that he fully expected the same voters he was striving to win to repudiate him at the polls on March 10.

There were, of course, many other reasons why the transmission of the Goldwater bandwagon got hopelessly locked in reverse in New Hampshire. Not the least of these was overexposure of the candidate. Although it must have been obvious, even to the Senator, that he was being badly overexposed, he kept returning to the state and during the two months of the campaign he spent nearly half his time there. Everyone connected with his campaign cited its similarity to the Taft-Eisenhower battle in the first primary of 1952. Senator Taft, who campaigned quite hard in New Hampshire, was defeated. General Eisenhower, then in France as commander of NATO, won without ever setting foot on New Hampshire soil.

Goldwater's advisers also made the fatal mistake of trying to change his style. Unlike most politicians, Barry is not a gladhanding hail-fellow-well-met. As he put it himself during a coffee hour in Hanover in late February, "I'm not one of these baby-kissing, handshaking, blintz-eating candidates. I don't like to insult the American intelligence by thinking that slapping people on the back is going to win you votes."

Yet this was exactly what his advisers tried to make him into. Instead of limiting his appearances to major rallies, the pace of the coffee hours, factory visits, school speeches and what-have-you was steadily stepped up. Instead of cutting down the press conferences after the disastrous results of the first tour, they were increased to as many as four or five each day. Instead of allowing him adequate time for rest, particularly in the early stages when he had to drag himself around on a foot weighted with a heavy cast, the schedule often called for fourteen, sixteen, and even eighteen hours of steady campaigning with as many as eighteen appearances per day.

Charlie Justice and Dave Banks, the two men who drove the Senator over every painful mile of the New Hampshire campaign, noticed very early in the game that his stamina was being taxed to the limits of endurance. Some reporters sneered at Goldwater in print for riding around in a Cadillac while Rockefeller hopped hither and yon on a chartered press bus. But Dave Banks, who owns the Cadillac-Chevrolet agency in Concord, purposely volunteered to drive the Senator in a Cadillac rather than a smaller car because he was concerned in the beginning about Barry's bad foot and later about his obviously growing fatigue.

Some tangible evidence that he was winning votes instead of losing them might have buoyed Goldwater up through this trying period. But the harder he ran on the exhausting treadmill manufactured for him, the more ground he lost.

By early February it had become obvious to many of our people far removed from New Hampshire that Goldwater was going backward with each passing day. Two of our volunteer organizers in Illinois, Oscar (Chip) Blomgren and Robert Hayes, became so alarmed at what the Senator's lackluster campaign was doing to their own efforts in Illinois that they flew to New Hampshire to try to talk Goldwater into improving his speeches and public statements.

Hayes was a highly successful private human relations consultant to a number of the nation's top corporations. He believed that if Goldwater would only develop his positions in greater depth and present them in clear, straightforward language, the impression that the Senator was a fast-draw artist could be rectified. He and Blomgren met Goldwater at Laconia Airport the night of February 6. Hayes rode with the Senator up through Franconia Notch to Littleton and outlined his plan en route.

The first thing that should be decided, Hayes argued, was what issues would best serve the Goldwater cause in New Hampshire. At most, two or three issues would be enough and other peripheral points could be tied into these. The important thing was to provide the Senator's campaign with a central theme and give it a positive note that would indicate it was taking the offensive. Hayes recommended that Goldwater let his delegate candidates hammer away first at the main issues. They could set the stage by presenting all the negative aspects of each issue. Then Goldwater could take the positive side by presenting solutions to the problems the delegates had brought to the voters' attention.

Goldwater appeared quite enthusiastic about Hayes's idea. He approved it immediately. Wisely, Hayes insisted that if he were to undertake the project he would have to have a direct pipeline to the Senator. Goldwater appeared to approve that too.

That same night Hayes and Blomgren returned to Concord and began rounding up a team of speech writers. Through an intermediary they lined up four of the country's outstanding conservative writers, all of whom would work—like Hayes and Blomgren—on a purely voluntary basis. They then flew back to Chicago to research the issues they believed would be most appealing to New Hampshire voters.

Within a few days Hayes and Blomgren were back in New Hampshire with a brace of speeches prepared for Doloris Bridges, Phil Dunlap and other key Goldwater delegates. The first issue they had picked was foreign aid. Armed with a trunkful of statistics, they proved conclusively that U.S. tax money funneled to foreign countries was undercutting American industry and causing the loss of thousands of manufacturing jobs. They zeroed in on electronics and textiles which, along with the shoe industry, are the mainstays of New Hampshire's economy.

The speeches Mrs. Bridges and others gave across the state that week seemed to open the eyes of a lot of voters. Then, on a Saturday night, Goldwater came in and offered his solutions to the foreign-aid problem in a major policy speech at Nashua that one of Hayes's writers had authored. Stewart Lamprey jubilantly noted that it was the first speech the Senator had given in New Hampshire that had aroused any real enthusiasm among people known to be in the doubtful column. At last the campaign seemed to have struck on a theme that might win votes instead of losing them.

Foreign aid, national defense, foreign policy—these were to have been the central issues of the Goldwater campaign during the remaining month. However, a few days after the Nashua speech the writers learned that Bob Hayes's pipeline to Goldwater had been cut. He was forced to channel the speeches through Denison Kitchel and the old speech writing team. The writers had taken on their assignments, without any thought of a fee, only because they had been assured Kitchel & Company would not interfere and that Goldwater alone would make the changes in the speeches they were writing. When they found that Kitchel, Tony Smith and the others were editing the speeches they withdrew from the project. They knew that it was useless to try to correct the problem if their work was being edited by the very same people who had helped create it in the first place. No central theme was ever developed for the Goldwater Presidential campaign, though these writers had made a successful start, and given time and the candidate's confidence they might well have provided that all-important ingredient.

One of the writers, an author and prominent newspaper editor, did complete the speech that Goldwater was to have given as his windup for the New Hampshire campaign, hopefully in his final television appearance before the voters went to the polls. It was relayed to the Senator personally in one last desperate effort to reopen the pipeline that had probably never existed. On March 4 the peripatetic Ted Humes, our Draft organization's ethnic-group expert and Western Pennsylvania vice chairman, brought the speech to Keene, New Hampshire. There he found the Senator relaxing in his room at the Winding Brook Lodge after a hard day's campaigning. Humes handed Goldwater the speech, together with a letter from the man who had formed the new speech writing team for Bob Hayes. A few sentences from that letter to the Senator are, I think, worth quoting:

You must be aware that there is a need for improving the quality of the speeches written for you, else you would not have given your blessing to the Hayes-Blomgren project. I do not mean this in criticism of these speeches. Some, in fact, are quite good. But they are not lighting any fires among the great mass of uncommitted voters. You are not getting through to them, and if you hope to win you must find a way to reach them. I tell you all this only because I think you must know there is widespread disenchantment among your supporters all over the country, and, unless something is done soon to greatly improve the quality of your speeches and other public utterances, many of us fear that your campaign will crumble, and the conservative cause that all of us have worked so long and so hard to advance will suffer irreparable harm.

As Goldwater was reading this letter Tony Smith and several other members of the palace guard burst into the room. The letter was put aside and, during the little party that followed, the wrap-up speech was apparently lost in the shuffle too. At least it was never delivered by Goldwater. Instead, he made his final television appearance with a group of housewives and others in a homey panel discussion. They asked him questions about Social Security, the United Nations and other issues that were, of necessity, defensive and diffused. Even his most loyal partisans agreed the Senator's New Hampshire finale was a disastrous performance. And his showing at the polls proved beyond doubt just how disastrous this whole campaign had been.

Long before March 10, however, it had become perfectly apparent that Goldwater had yielded too much ground in the early stages of the campaign to make up very much of it with even the most professional slambang finish. We knew that Rockefeller was slowly taking over some of the ground that kept slipping out from under Goldwater. But we were also aware that the largest part of the big undecided vote, much of which had once been solidly for the Senator, was shifting elsewhere. And in 1964 the New Hampshire connoisseurs could pick and choose from a smorgasbord serving of Republican candidates.

Besides the two major candidates—Goldwater and Rockefeller—there were no less than five other entries. There would have been six, but Bill Scranton wisely decided not to leap on the merry-go-round. He had no intention of facing his opponents—or the voters—at the polls and he quickly squashed an incipient attempt to mount a write-in campaign in his behalf.

Dick Nixon also played hard to get. He flatly refused to let his supporters in New Hampshire put his name on the ballot. But unlike Scranton he looked the other way when a write-in campaign was cranked up for him by former Governor Wesley Powell, a nominal Republican who had kicked over all the party traces to help elect a Democrat to the governorship in 1962.

Margaret Chase Smith, who was making a serious bid for the Vice-Presidential nomination, came in from the neighboring state of Maine and waged a fairly vigorous campaign in this first Presidential primary. Harold Stassen also got on the ballot, backed by a mysterious bankroll and sustained by his quixotic ambition. There was another avowed candidate named Norman LePage, a New Hampshire businessman, whose motives for entering were never made clear. And, finally, there was Henry Cabot Lodge.

Like Nixon, Lodge refused to file formally for the primary. He was still in Vietnam, trying to appear aloof from the mundane rough-and-tumble of stateside politics. But he did nothing to discourage the write-in campaign mounted by his son, George Lodge, and a group of hardworking young Turks from Massachusetts who had aided George in his ill-fated run for the U.S. Senate against Ted Kennedy in 1962. David Goldberg and Paul Grindle came up to Concord from Boston in mid-January, found an empty store on Main Street not far from our Goldwater headquarters, and started rounding up Lodge supporters.

Rockefeller did his best to get Cabot Lodge to call off George and his boys. He even telephoned the Ambassador in Saigon and begged him to order them out of New Hampshire. He must have pointed out that before the Kennedy assassination Lodge had been one of the people who had most strongly urged him to run against Goldwater. Now, by permitting a write-in campaign, Lodge was deliberately siphoning votes from Rockefeller and, in the Governor's view, helping the man they had both vowed to stop. But Cabot Lodge made it abundantly clear that he would do nothing to discourage his agents in New Hampshire. Rockefeller, with justification, felt that he had been stabbed in the back.

Actually, however, Lodge was not so much drawing votes from Rockefeller as giving the preponderant undecided vote an alternative they were clearly seeking. Goldberg and Grindle did a fine job of coalescing this vote around Lodge, thus keeping it from drifting into Dick Nixon's column. Stassen was never really a factor and, as Chet Wiggins, Senator Cotton's administrative assistant, had told me in Washington very early in the campaign, the people of New Hampshire were still too tradition-minded to vote for a female Presidential candidate, even one so well liked as Margaret Chase Smith.

The main thing that Goldberg and Grindle did was to mail sample ballots to all Republican and independent voters showing them how they could write in Cabot Lodge's name and vote for the delegates pledged to him, all of whom were political unknowns. This was rudimentary, of course. But for some reason the Goldwater forces failed to send out sample ballots of their own.

Thus, while Goldwater and Rockefeller were exhausting themselves trudging up and down the state, the Lodge team quietly completed their political homework for a candidate thousands of miles away. How well their homework paid off became known to the nation within minutes after the polls closed in New Hampshire on March 10.

Fewer than 95,000 voters cast their ballots in the Republican primary that Tuesday. More might have turned out if a blizzard had not dumped up to fourteen inches of snow on New Hampshire throughout the day. But more likely the light vote can be attributed to the fact that many citizens decided it was just not worth the effort to go to the polls. They had been promised a choice. They had been unable to discern what the choice was amid the confusing echoes that had reverberated from the Canadian border to the Massachusetts line for two interminable months.

Most of the polls closed in New Hampshire at 7 P.M. Watching the CBS computer, Walter Cronkite was able to report a scant eighteen minutes later that Henry Cabot Lodge had won the Presidential preference primary. The final tally confirmed this forecast. Lodge garnered 33,521 of the 94,641 votes cast, a very good showing for a write-in candidate. Goldwater was a poor second with 21,775, barely 23 per cent of the total vote. Rockefeller came in third, with 19,496 or 20.6 per cent. Nixon got 15,752 write-in votes, a fairly respectable performance but not respectable enough to enhance his tacit candidacy appreciably. Margaret Chase Smith, as Chet Wiggins had forecast, proved that New Hampshiremen—and women—were not yet ready to take any woman Presidential candidate seriously. Senator Smith picked up only 2,812 votes. Harold Stassen's initial effort in his 1964 last hurrah came out sounding more like a Bronx cheer. He received a microscopic 1,285 votes. And Bill Scranton brought up the rear with a grand total of 77 write-ins.

At the Madison Hotel in Washington I watched the returns coming in from New Hampshire with Senator Goldwater, Denison Kitchel, Dean Burch and the other members of our national campaign team. The true dimensions of the Senator's defeat were only partly apparent in his dismal 23 per cent showing in the Presidential preference primary. They were revealed more accurately, and more tragically, in the loss of every one of his delegate candidates, including Senator Cotton, former Governor Dwinell, Doloris Bridges, Herb Philbrick and State Senate President Dunlap. Cabot Lodge's slate of unknowns swept the field, a feat no one ever suspected they could bring off. For Goldwater it was more than a defeat. It was a thoroughgoing rout.

In our suite at the Madison, the Senator seemed to accept the results with equanimity. When the returns were all in, he rose from his chair, squared his shoulders, and went down to the ballroom to face the television cameras. He refused to pass the buck for his defeat, saying simply "I goofed." But he promised that he would do his best not to repeat the mistakes of New Hampshire and when he left the ballroom I sensed a new determination in his stride.

Lee Edwards, our press man, came up to the suite and said the press was expecting an appraisal from the Senator's campaign managers.

Neither Kitchel nor Burch felt inclined to take on this chore, so I was appointed. I did my best to put a good face on what was obviously a bad situation. I reminded the reporters, and the millions of television viewers, that New Hampshire was merely the first of a number of primaries and I expressed confidence that Senator Goldwater would come back from this defeat to win the nomination at San Francisco.

I don't think any of the reporters took me very seriously that night. Some of them all but nominated Ambassador Lodge in their stories and columns the next day. Invariably, they harked back to General Eisenhower's defeat of Senator Taft in 1952, though they must have known that much had changed in those fourteen intervening years.

It has long been my belief that the New Hampshire primary has been puffed up out of all proportion to its actual significance. The press tends to forget that this is a very small state (the 1960 census placed its population at 606,921), and that it is ridiculous to expect fewer than 100,000 citizens voting in a primary to have the final word in determining the candidate of either major party in a nation whose population is now nearing 200 million. Yet a victory in New Hampshire had always been considered mandatory for a serious Presidential candidate. It is one of those ancient political myths that everyone just accepts at face value. Politicians are wedded to it as much as the press is.

Political myths die hard, especially in an age of myths. But as I addressed the television audience from Washington that Tuesday night I knew that the myth of the New Hampshire primary was even then being slain in a most efficient manner by the men and women who had been working with me in the forty-nine other states since the days when we set up our modest office in Suite 3505.

BOOK FOUR

COUNTDOWN

CHAPTER 27

COUNTDOWN I

IN THE WAKE of Senator Goldwater's devastating defeat in New Hampshire his candidacy, solemnly pronounced dead on November 22, 1963, was ceremoniously interred by virtually all the great oracles of the nation. His chances of winning the Republican Presidential nomination were buried deep under tons of newsprint and further concealed by a mighty torrent of commentary issuing forth from radio and television studios across the land. The Senator's opponents in both parties vied with one another in placing the seal on the tomb of his political fortunes.

The Goldwater camp itself was in a state of shock. For a week practically nothing was done at the campaign headquarters in Washington. Once again I checked by phone with most of our state chairmen. Some of them were discouraged by the magnitude of the Senator's loss in New Hampshire. But they all showed an iron determination to fight on and not one of them spoke of quitting. I reminded them that the press had largely overlooked the fact that Goldwater already had nearly four times as many delegates irrevocably committed to him as he had lost in New Hampshire. In the last two days of February Denny Garrison's and John Thomas' people had swept the Oklahoma state convention and produced 22 delegates firmly pledged to the Senator. At the North Carolina convention held that same weekend we picked up all but one of the 26 delegates chosen. Four more had been selected at district conventions in Tennessee and two in district contests in Kansas.

Moreover, we were getting good reports on the crowds that were turning out to welcome the Senator in California, where he had flown right after the New Hampshire primary.

At our Goldwater national headquarters, however, nothing had changed. The day following the New Hampshire primary Denison Kitchel issued a press release which said: "It is most gratifying that a candidate from the Far West, Senator Barry Goldwater, could do so well in the New England state of New Hampshire." After that Kitchel retired to his big corner office and we saw very little of him for the next week.

A group of the top members of the Finance Committee did succeed in getting a meeting with Kitchel. They demanded his resignation and it was understood that he was seriously considering whether he should submit it. He asked one of the former leaders of our Draft Committee if he should get out. But although for several days he seemed to waver, it was obvious that he had made up his mind to stay.

The morale at headquarters was at low ebb. Something had to be done to halt the aimless drifting and get some direction into the campaign. On Wednesday, March 18, I sent a two-page memorandum to Senator Goldwater and Kitchel requesting that "clear-cut lines of authority and responsibility be established" in the quest for delegates. Then I added:

Politicians being what they are, will seek every potential avenue to achieve *their own desired ends.* Thus, if it is possible for them to discover any way to seek decisions from more than one person, they will do so. . . . Therefore, I believe that it is essential that one man working immediately with the candidate and the candidate's personal campaign director should be assigned this authority [in the delegate operation].

I also suggested that weekly meetings of key division chiefs be held so that they would all know their assignments and responsibilities for the week ahead. And I further proposed that the political director hold briefing sessions with the press once a week so that the public could be better informed of what was actually going on in the continuing battle for delegates. In conclusion, I went further than I had ever gone in any conversation or communication with the Senator. I wrote that I firmly believed he had the potential for a great victory. But, I emphasized, "you cannot do it alone, and no man can."

"It is regrettable," I added, "that you should have to take time to concern yourself with the details of organization. But I believe that if you would do this now and establish the most effective organization we can visualize, then the rest of the campaign will be made easier for you and will result in victory in July and in November. If this is not done, it is equally possible for that victory to disintegrate."

When I wrote this memorandum I had little hope of getting through.

But a few days later Dick Kleindienst bustled into my office in mid-afternoon and said: "Get your hat. We're off to Barry's apartment." I had never been invited to the Senator's apartment and I was rather surprised to be going now. We rode out in a cab with Kitchel and Dean Burch and when we arrived at the Westchester Apartments we found a big crate of grapefruit almost blocking Goldwater's door.

The Senator, in high spirits after his first successful campaign tour of California, joked for several minutes with his Arizona friends. Then he sat down on the L-shaped couch in his living room and got down to business. He said he had called the meeting to review the campaign and discuss plans for the future. Kitchel, who was sitting a little apart in a straightbacked chair, tossed the ball to me. I had had no fore-warning about this meeting, but fortunately I was able to refer to my memorandum and I repeated the main points I had made in it. Dick Kleindienst, who paced the floor throughout, stopped a few times and interrupted, but for the most part he agreed with my recommendations.

When I finished Dick said: "One thing we ought to get straight right now is this question of who is going to run the convention." He added that he thought I was the one who ought to do it and the Senator said that he agreed. Neither Kitchel nor Burch dissented. We talked a bit about the communications setup for the convention and then the Senator steered the conversation into another channel. He asked how we could tighten up the lines of authority and whether it would be possible to divide up the states between Kleindienst and me.

Actually, Kleindienst had asked me briefly about this before we left headquarters. I had said that I wasn't sure you could divide up the country by drawing lines on a map. There were more than geographic considerations involved and each state had to be dealt with as a separate entity. Now, however, Dick told the Senator that "Clif and I will work that out." He said we would decide which states each of us would take and that we would have equal but independent authority in whichever ones he and I selected. He added that since he had been in Oregon he thought he ought to keep that one. But from here on, he said, he and I would be co-directors of all the field operations.

The Senator agreed to this arrangement and again neither Kitchel nor Burch objected. In fact, neither one of them said much throughout the meeting. We left right after this and at the door the Senator handed me one of the grapefruit from the crate in the hall. I seem to recall that it was an Arizona grapefruit and I wondered if there was supposed to be something symbolic about his giving it to me.

Kleindienst was as good as his word. He lived up to the letter of the agreement and one of the first things he did when we got back to headquarters was to order new calling cards printed for both of us.

Mine bore the inscription "Co-director of Field Operations," the same as his. Then we sat down and discussed the division of the states. Dick took all the remaining fourteen primary election states, except for Illinois, which we agreed to work together, and California, where he would have senior responsibility and I would help out whenever I could. All the rest of the states, in which delegates would be selected at state conventions, would be my personal responsibility. Actually, as we shall see, this arrangement worked out quite well.

Dick Kleindienst was by far the most politically knowledgeable member of the Arizona group which, as I have noted, included several non-Arizonans. In addition, he had the courage of his convictions and was not afraid to speak out against decisions he considered unwise. Unfortunately, not long after the meeting in Goldwater's apartment Dick was frozen out of the inner circle. He openly disagreed with a group decision at a strategy meeting that was also attended by George Humphrey and Arthur Summerfield. Afterwards, Bill Baroody took him to task for displaying disloyalty to the group. In reply, Kleindienst minced no words. He said that his first loyalty in the campaign was to Barry Goldwater. "If disagreeing with *you* is being disloyal," he added, "then I don't understand your definition." Kleindienst was never again invited to a strategy meeting.

The first Republican convention after the New Hampshire primary was held in the Virgin Islands on March 15. As predicted, all three delegates went to Governor Rockefeller, whose family has large real estate and other holdings in the Islands.

Next came South Carolina, which just as predictably went entirely to Goldwater. The Republican State Committee, headed by Drake Edens and Mrs. Julia Dougherty, had previously constituted itself the official Draft Goldwater Committee. The only problem in South Carolina was which of Goldwater's many supporters would be named as delegates. Bob Chapman, who, with Roger Milliken and Greg Shorey, had been a charter member of our old 3505 group, had lost out to another Goldwater man, William Workman, in the 1962 Senate primary. Drake Edens, Workman's campaign manager, then became state chairman so we had in effect two Goldwater groups vying for delegate seats and control of the Republican Party in the state. However, at the state convention on March 21 both groups were given representation in the delegation to the national convention, and Roger Milliken sent me a telegram joyfully proclaiming that "South Carolina will cast its 16 votes for Barry Goldwater forever."

In the Wisconsin primary on April 7 we did a fadeout. I had recommended to Dick Kleindienst and Kitchel months before that the Senator stay out of this state, Wisconsin is one of the few states where crossover voting is still permitted in the primary. Since the Democrats had no contest, they would have voted in droves on the Republican ballot and they would have voted, under orders, against Barry Goldwater. Thus, when Congressman John Byrnes decided to run as a favorite son, Wayne Hood and Sam Hay agreed to back him if he would keep all the other serious candidates out of the primary too. Byrnes and his fellow Congressman, Melvin Laird, prevailed on Rockefeller to stay out. Rockefeller knew that with Goldwater out of the picture he would lose even if he won. A victory over a favorite son would not enhance his candidacy; a loss would probably bury it forever.

Thanks to the splendid organization put together by Wayne Hood and Mary Kay Hanson, our state co-chairman, together with Sam Hay and Jim Mack, during the Draft days we were able to get elected in the primary virtually all of the 20 delegates running in the Congressional districts. They were committed to John Byrnes on the first ballot at the convention but I knew that they would be safely there if we needed them. And we could count on several of the 10 delegates elected at-large as well. The Wisconsin primary brought our delegate total to well over 100—and we still had forty-five states to go.

The pace of our delegate countdown now began to accelerate. The day after the Wisconsin primary we pulled nine firm Goldwater delegates out of the North Dakota state convention, with two more leaning his way, though officially they were all uncommitted. Our state chairman, P. J. Carey of Fargo, and his co-chairman, Mrs. Phyllis Connolly of Dunn Center, were ably assisted by Brooks Keogh, the president of the National Livestock Association, in this successful operation.

On April 11 the Kentucky state convention added at least a dozen more delegates to the Goldwater tally, though again they were pretty well hidden. Ostensibly, the 24 Kentucky delegates were committed to the favorite-son candidacy of Senator Thruston Morton, but Congressman Gene Snyder and our friends there had worked out an arrangement similar to the one we had made in Wisconsin. Ultimately, Senator Morton, who ably acted as chairman of the national convention, decided not to run as a favorite son and released his delegates, giving us 21 from Kentucky on the first ballot.

Then came the big one in Illinois. Neither Nelson Rockefeller nor any of the other Republican Presidential aspirants could muster enough courage to challenge Barry Goldwater in the April 14 primary there. But a brave little lady from Maine, Margaret Chase Smith, who was not really running for President, took him on. Considering the tremendously effective grassroots organization that Charlie Barr, Hayes Robertson, Ed Derwinski, John Milliken and Mrs. Patricia Hutar had built for

Goldwater in Illinois, Senator Smith did very well indeed. She polled more than 209,000 votes in the Presidential preference primary. But Senator Goldwater did even better. He racked up nearly 509,000, or more than 62 per cent of all the votes cast. Cabot Lodge, until then still the choice of many influential but unrealistic pundits, was lucky to get 68,000 write-in votes, and other hopefuls trailed farther behind—Nixon with 30,000, Rockefeller with 2,000, Scranton with 1,800 and Romney with 465. Even a Democrat, Governor George Wallace of Alabama, polled almost as many Republican write-ins as Scranton and Romney combined.

The preference vote told only part of the story, however. Of the forty-eight delegates elected in the Congressional districts that day, nearly forty were solid Goldwater adherents. Most of the rest were either leaning—or being pushed—in his direction. Ten more at-large delegates would be named from Illinois at the state convention in Springfield on May 1. After the Senator's solid showing at the primary polls there was little doubt that the majority of these ten would also be in his corner. Although I did not publicly claim it at the time, I added the figure 50 to our growing total of Goldwater delegates and put a little plus sign after it to leave the door open for any of the eight others Charlie Barr and Company might win over before we got to San Francisco.

Amazingly, many newsmen and commentators perversely interpreted Goldwater's triumph in Illinois as a defeat. It was the first election I have ever been involved in where a candidate won more than 62 per cent of the vote and still came out a loser in the press. Most of the columnists based their conclusions on the results of the gubernatorial primary battle between Charles M. Percy and State Treasurer William J. Scott. Percy beat Scott nearly 2 to 1 but since both were avowed Goldwater supporters it was difficult to determine the premise for those conclusions. To be sure, Percy was known to be somewhat less enthusiastic about Goldwater's candidacy than was Scott. But on the night of the primary Percy issued a statement in effect pledging his own convention vote to Goldwater.

Few of the pundits troubled to point out that Scott had entered the primary campaign very late in the game, after Illinois Secretary of State Charles Carpentier had suffered a heart attack and was forced out of the contest.[1] Cook County chairman Hayes Robertson also withdrew and Scott, in effect, replaced both of them. Moreover, many of the people in the top echelons of Chuck Percy's campaign were solid Goldwater supporters and it is safe to say they would not have backed him if he had repudiated the Senator.

[1] Tragically, a second heart attack not long after this proved fatal to Charles Carpentier.

For whatever reason, it was perfectly obvious to any objective observer that a substantial segment of the press was deluding itself in reporting the results of the Illinois primary. But more important, by indulging in self-delusion it was also deluding the public. Even when Barry Goldwater won, and won big, a numerous and frightened segment of the fourth estate were determined to perpetuate the myth that Goldwater was a loser. Columnist David Lawrence put the case in proper perspective two days later:

> Maybe two and two don't make four, after all, in national politics. Judging by some of the TV and radio broadcasts on Tuesday night and subsequent comments in the press, Senator Goldwater got the highest number of votes in the Republican presidential primary in Illinois but nevertheless suffered a "setback". . . .
> Such commentaries . . . serve only to mislead many people and take away from the victor in the election contest some of the prestige which he deserves when he gets a majority or more.[2]

Senator Goldwater, speaking at the American Society of Newspaper Editors convention in Washington that week, caustically remarked that "the published reports of my being out of the race are a bit premature." Then, with a wry smile, he added, "I'm beginning to know exactly how Harry Truman felt as he read the polls and the papers in 1948."

At Goldwater headquarters, however, we had by this time become virtually immune to the opinions of the majority of mass media's political "experts." We never permitted the constant barrage of propaganda to deflect us from our main purpose, which was to keep adding to Senator Goldwater's delegate total. Four days after the Illinois primary, on April 18, we reaped another sizable harvest of delegates in three states— Arizona, Louisiana and Kansas.

Sixteen of the Louisiana delegates had already been picked in district elections ten days earlier. Now, at the state convention, my old friend Charlton Lyons led the Goldwater forces to a clean sweep of the remaining four at-large delegates to give the Senator all 20 of Louisiana's votes.

The result in Arizona was, of course, a foregone conclusion. Favorite son Goldwater nailed down all sixteen delegates without lifting a hand. The Kansas convention, however, was something else again.

I flew to Topeka to address a Goldwater dinner that was held on the eve of the April 18 state convention. Former Senator William Knowland of California was the principal speaker and he charged up the audience with a fiery speech on foreign policy. My talk was confined to the necessity of getting as many delegates as possible from Kansas behind Barry Goldwater.

[2] David Lawrence, *Washington Star*, April 16, 1964.

Psychologically, Kansas was a key state because Nelson Rockefeller hoped to win a number of delegates there to prove he had support in the Midwest. The Governor of Kansas, John Anderson, was a staunch Rockefeller man but we had already defeated a number of his hand-picked Rockefeller delegates in the district contests. We were going into the convention with ten delegates from the districts, but ten more were to be selected at-large. Five of the latter had already been decided on, and only one was a solid Goldwater supporter. Tradition dictated that the Governor would select the remaining five, all of whom would almost automatically be ratified by the convention. Governor Anderson had arranged that he would be one of these five.

I knew that if we let John Anderson beat us it would stiffen the determination of several other governors who were inclined to back Rockefeller. However, if at all possible, I wanted to avoid embarrassing Anderson, who was then chairman of the Republican Governors' Conference. We sent overtures to him promising our support for his delegate candidacy if he would change his stand and support Goldwater. Unfortunately, Governor Anderson refused this offer. We now had no alternative but to oppose his candidacy on the convention floor.

Immediately after the dinner, I went to a hotel room to confer with our Kansas team: State Senator Tom Van Sickle, Ned Cushing of our original group, Bill Whorton, our state Goldwater for President chairman, and Mrs. Betty Mendenhall, the state co-chairman. At first, there was the feeling that we should oppose all five of the delegates to be elected in the morning, including the Governor, the state chairman, and three other high Republican officials. However, as we went down the long list of state delegates I saw that we might not have quite enough strength to buck all of these prestigious officials head-on. Besides, Van Sickle and Cushing did not want to openly repudiate the state chairman and one or two of the others.

Finally, about one o'clock in the morning, we decided to let the state chairman and three others go in unopposed. Then we would try to beat the Governor, who had made himself the symbol of the Rockefeller cause in Kansas and the rest of the Midwest. The question then arose as to whom we could find to oppose him. It had to be someone both with high standing in the party and with enough courage to lock horns with the Governor of the state. Luckily, we had someone who filled both of these qualifications perfectly—Mrs. Effie Semple, the retiring National Committeewoman from Kansas and a woman who had long been ideologically committed to Senator Goldwater. We called Mrs. Semple, getting her up out of bed about two o'clock, and after we explained the situation to her, she agreed to run against Governor Anderson.

The few remaining hours of that night were spent trying to corral as many delegates as we could find to back Effie Semple. The key man in this pre-dawn delegate hunt was Vernon Williams, the Sedgwick County Republican chairman and leader of one of the biggest delegations to the state convention. We hauled Williams out of bed and got him up to our hotel room. I asked him how many delegates he could produce for Mrs. Semple. He explained that his county delegation was going into the convention under the unit rule, with half of his 123 delegates committed to the Governor and the other half to whoever the Goldwater candidate would be.

"How many would we get for the Goldwater candidate if you were operating without the unit rule?" I inquired.

Williams thought a minute and then replied: "We should have more than a hundred. Maybe a hundred and ten."

I said, "Okay. Release your people from the unit rule and let them go for Effie. Your votes should just about put her over the top."

Before we went to bed we got the word out to as many Goldwater delegates as we could reach that they were to go straight down the line for all of the Governor's candidates. All, that is, except the Governor himself. Then I snatched about forty-five minutes' sleep, got up, showered, shaved and went forth to the fray.

From the balcony of the convention auditorium the whole scene was laid out before me. Anderson's people fully expected us to fight them every inch of the way, but when our Goldwater delegates cast their ballots for the state chairman the confusion began to spread. It spread further as each succeeding Anderson candidate went in unopposed. I could see the Governor's people scurrying about the floor wearing puzzled frowns and trying to find out what was happening.

Finally, former Congressman Cliff Hope rose and placed Governor Anderson's name in nomination. Then our man Odd Williams rose and made an impassioned nominating speech for Effie Semple, emphasizing that her long years of faithful and effective service to the Republican Party deserved to be rewarded. The demonstration for Effie easily outdid the one that had been staged for the Governor. But while it was going on I saw Anderson's men running up and down the aisles and the next thing I knew a woman mounted the rostrum and nominated Miss Lahoma Dennis, the president of the Kansas Republican Women's Federation and a solid Goldwater supporter.

It was one of the oldest political ploys in the book. What they hoped to do was split Effie's vote. And on that basis I was by no means certain that we had enough margin to get her by. Now, however, it was our team's turn to run down the aisles. I saw several of our people descend on the Women's Federation president, and one of them managed to grab a microphone. He handed it to her and she demanded recognition. Then, speaking in a firm, clear voice, she withdrew her name from nomination.

Now it was a clearcut battle between Goldwater supporter Effie Semple and Rockefeller backer John Anderson. The roll call that followed was nip and tuck—until it got to Sedgwick County. Vernon Williams rose and announced, "Sedgwick County, operating under the unit rule, but not enforcing it, casts 13 votes for Governor Anderson and 110 votes for Effie Semple."

The convention exploded. The cheers that shook the auditorium left no doubt as to where the sentiment of the majority of the delegates lay. The Governor, who had stubbornly persisted in going against the wishes of the majority, was obviously whipped. The roll call continued, but when it reached the point where Mrs. Semple had 626 votes to 282 for the Governor I saw John Anderson fighting his way to a microphone in the middle of the floor. Suddenly, his voice came booming over the public address system:

"In the interest of the unity and harmony of the Republican Party in the State of Kansas, I ask that my name be withdrawn. I urge this convention to unanimously elect Mrs. Effie Semple as delegate to the national convention."

It was a sporting gesture, and one that saved the Governor from an even more severe beating than if he had permitted the roll call to spin out to the end. I descended from the balcony and the first person I ran into downstairs was Governor Anderson. We shook hands, and I congratulated him on his sportsmanslike action. But the *Time-Life* reporter, Murray Garst, grabbed my arm as I walked away. "Clif," he said, "you were awfully nasty." I said that I didn't look at it that way and I was sure Governor Anderson didn't either. He would have done exactly the same thing had he been in my place.

That afternoon we finished up our work in Kansas by electing two more Goldwater people, Sam Mellinger and Mrs. Donna Addington, to the National Committee. We ran them as a team. They were picked by the twenty national convention delegates. The vote went through four ballots but on the fifth they were finally elected on an 11 to 9 vote. Thus, the convention that had started in the morning with an apparent rout for the Goldwater forces in Kansas ended up as a smashing victory.

Ned Cushing was beside himself with joy. For him, this day was the culmination of the organizing effort he had begun in Kansas immediately after our second meeting in Chicago in December 1961. We had spent many long hours together since, making plans in hotel rooms and talking on the phone between my office in the Chanin Building and his home in the little town of Downs. Now it was Ned's turn to howl—and howl he did.

Before we went to the party I tossed for the Goldwater state delegates, Ned dragged me off to a cocktail lounge in downtown Topeka. As we entered, he let out a resounding "Whoopee!" The piano player, a Goldwater man who had been corralling delegates for us, stopped in the middle of a tune and started pounding out "When the Saints Come Marching In." Everyone in the place joined in the chorus, though I suspect half of them had no idea what they were celebrating. Ned kept saying, "Boy, it feels *so* good!" Then, just as the piano player finished banging out "Saints," Ned turned to me and said, "Clif, can I do it just once more?" I laughed and said to go ahead. With that, he gave forth with the most piercing "Whoopee!" I ever heard. My eardrums felt shattered, and Ned must have rattled all the bottles behind the bar. I suppose everyone in the place thought he was crazy drunk. Actually, he had not had a drink. He was just deliriously happy—as he had every right to be.

Kansas produced only a dozen hard core Goldwater delegates and six more that Tom Van Sickle and Ned Cushing knew were in our corner. But the display of Goldwater power at the state convention placed all the other Rockefeller-leaning governors on notice. It paved the way for easy wins in several other states where governors were getting ready to oppose our Goldwater people. From there on they knew that if they did not want to risk open defeats when they ran for delegate posts they would have to pay more heed to the wishes of the rank-and-file Republicans. In the end I believe Effie Semple's victory in Kansas helped avoid potentially divisive situations which could have split the party badly in several states. But there were some splits that could not be avoided. Unfortunately, not all the Republican governors displayed the same fine sportsmanlike spirit as John Anderson had in Kansas.

As I flew back to Washington, I added up our current total of Goldwater delegates. The Kansas convention, plus the sweeps in Arizona and Louisiana, put us well over the 200-mark. We were less than a quarter of the way through the crucial delegate countdown, but Goldwater had already left all the other Republican aspirants far, far behind. For the time being, at least, it would be just as well if none of them fully realized what a flying start he had made. I decided to claim only 165 delegates when I got back to Washington. Most of the others were well concealed, and I felt we should hold them in reserve just in case we needed them to counteract some future setback along the way.

CHAPTER 28

COUNTDOWN II—THE BOUNTIFUL FORTNIGHT

IN THE LAST DAYS of April and the first week of May the tempo of the delegate countdown rose like the staccato beating of a military drum calling men to arms. During one brief fifteen-day period Barry Goldwater won more than two hundred delegates in seven primaries and six state conventions.

The first contest after the Kansas convention was the New Jersey primary on Tuesday, April 21. I had returned to Washington from Topeka to help unravel some knotty problems that confronted the Goldwater forces in New Jersey. Our exceptionally able New Jersey state chairman, Mark Anton, had made a firm decision to ride with the regular Republican organization in the primary delegate elections in exchange for certain important concessions. Mark and Judy Fernald, our state co-chairman and former Draft Goldwater national secretary, were both guaranteed delegate seats and so were two other avowed Goldwater supporters. However, some other Goldwater partisans insisted on running for delegate posts against organization candidates.

To these partisans it appeared that Mark and Judy had engineered a deal tantamount to surrender. Nothing could have been further from the truth. Mark Anton, a former state senator and president of the Suburban Propane Gas Company, was one of the most popular figures in New Jersey Republican circles. He had decided to go along with the regular organization in the selection of delegates for two very good reasons. First, he wanted to avoid splitting the party in his state, a party that was already divided between the Liberals, who were polarized around Senator Clifford Case, and a strong conservative grouping of Goldwater supporters. Secondly, Mark was thoroughly convinced that by working through normal party channels he could pull a significant number of Goldwater votes out of his delegation in San Francisco.

When all our efforts at persuasion failed with the zealous partisans, Mark had no choice but to repudiate their candidacies for delegate seats and support the organization people running against them. In the primary that Tuesday, all of the dissidents were soundly trounced. But the two other Goldwater candidates Mark and Judy backed—Robert MacPherson of Fanwood and Richard F. Plechner of Metuchen—handily defeated the Liberals opposing them.

After the dust settled, four more New Jersey delegates publicly committed themselves to Goldwater, giving us an ostensible total of 8. This represented quite a group in a state where Nelson Rockefeller had fully expected 100 per cent of the delegation to be handed him on a silver platter. But the Goldwater coup was much more far-reaching than even Rockefeller suspected at the time. In July, when the roll call at the Cow Palace reached New Jersey, Mark Anton, as good as his word, delivered 20 votes for Barry Goldwater—exactly half of the entire state delegation.

The day of the New Jersey primary I flew to Des Moines to tackle a problem very similar to New Jersey's that was about to burst into the open at the Iowa state convention the following day. My old ally, John Keith Rehmann, and our Goldwater state co-chairman, James W. Wilson and Maurice Van Nostrand, also had a serious revolt on their hands. They had worked out what they believed to be an equitable arrangement concerning delegates with Senator Bourke B. Hickenlooper and the state Republican organization. But once again a dissident group of Goldwater partisans threatened to upset the apple cart.

John Keith Rehmann was an old friend of Senator Hickenlooper's and he had good reason to believe the Senator, who would head the Iowa delegation, was favorable to Goldwater. However, Hickenlooper was also chairman of the Senate Republican Policy Committee. Congress was still in session and he needed the cooperation of all Republican senators on important legislation that was coming up before adjournment. He could not at this stage publicly endorse his colleague from Arizona. Nonetheless, the dissident Goldwater faction insisted on opposing selected members of Hickenlooper's delegate slate.

We could not afford to alienate Senator Hickenlooper and our other more or less clandestine friends in Iowa. Rehmann, Wilson and Van

Nostrand, having exhausted all their powers of diplomacy in conferences with the stubborn dissidents, sent up a flare for help. I came as quickly as I could and the night before the convention I managed to talk several of the rebels into line. But the next morning when we arrived at the National Guard Armory in Des Moines for the convention balloting there was still a group intent on rebellion.

The leader of this group was a man named John Burroughs of Davenport, Iowa. He was one of those sincerely aroused citizens who had helped give the Goldwater movement its tremendous grassroots strength. But on this particular morning we found ourselves locked in a long and at times angry debate.

We met on a ramp outside the Armory and I told John Burroughs that I wanted his group to hold their fire on the convention floor. He was adamant, and so were the four other men with him. They were going to oppose the convention nominating committee's slate come hell or high noon. They felt they knew more about the political picture in Iowa, and that was probably true. I pointed out that someone had to make decisions of this nature on the basis of how they related to the overall national situation. I freely admitted that I was not infallible. But I had been charged with the responsibility of making these decisions and in my judgment they would be doing Senator Goldwater's candidacy serious harm if they persisted in fighting Senator Hickenlooper and his people. "If I'm proved wrong," I concluded, "you can drop me in the bay at San Francisco and let me try to swim to Alcatraz for sanctuary."

Burroughs finally acceded and the balloting went off without a hitch. We claimed only six committed delegates out of Iowa's twenty-four. But when the roll call came at San Francisco Senator Hickenlooper rose and announced that Iowa cast 14 votes for Barry Goldwater. In so doing, he saved me from a dunking in the cold, choppy waters under the Golden Gate.

In Nevada, on April 24 and 25, our state chairman, William B. Wright, Sr., former president of both the Nevada Cattlemen and American National Livestock Associations, corralled all six of his state delegates for Goldwater at the state convention. Helping Bill Wright round up this delegation were Mrs. Amy Gulling of Reno, his co-chairman, and Lieutenant Governor Paul Laxalt.

Three days later, on April 28, two big primaries in the East received national attention, although neither was really significant in terms of the nominating process in the Republican Party in 1964. Both states had prominent favorite sons—Governor Scranton in Pennsylvania and Ambassador Lodge in Massachusetts. Yet Barry Goldwater yanked delegates out from under the noses of each.

In Massachusetts, thanks to the diplomatic organizing efforts of our state chairman, Lloyd Waring, and Roger Allen Moore of my original group, we got five committed delegates—including Moore. And in Pennsylvania, where the full power of the state administration was ruthlessly unleashed against all Goldwater supporters, we picked up two more for the record, though we actually got four on the first ballot at the convention and would have had more if a second roll call had been necessary.

One of the two Pennsylvanians publicly committed to Goldwater was Ted Humes, our state vice chairman in the Draft days. Humes had continued to work with Ben Chapple in the state Citizens for Goldwater and thus his victory was particularly significant. But Paul Hugus lost and his defeat was a bad omen.

Although no Presidential candidates were listed on the ballot in either Massachusetts or Pennsylvania, extensive write-in campaigns were conducted for the favorite sons. Yet Goldwater received more than 32,000 write-in votes in Pennsylvania despite the fact that he had specifically and firmly requested his supporters not to mount a write-in campaign. Governor Scranton, who had permitted his state organization to mail more than a million Scranton stickers with instructions to use them on the ballots, ended up with 58 per cent of the total write-in vote; an unimpressive showing for an incumbent governor in his own home state.

That same week Goldwater received more than 75 per cent of all the votes cast in the first Texas Republican Presidential preference primary in history. Governor Rockefeller, who had tried but failed to have his name removed from the ballot, garnered less than 5 per cent of the Texas vote. Rockefeller charged that the Goldwater forces in Texas, led by state Republican chairman Peter O'Donnell, our former Draft chairman, had staged the primary and put his name on the ballot just to embarrass him by showing how weak he was in that state.

The Texas primary was not binding on the state's big 56-man delegation, which was officially selected at the state convention on June 16. However, Peter's primary, as I was wont to call it, left no doubt as to which candidate the delegates would vote for come July.

Three state conventions—in Georgia, Maine and Tennessee—added over fifty more delegates to my growing list on May 2, the same day as the Texas primary. In Georgia and Tennessee, a number of these had previously been elected at the district level. But at the Tennessee convention, my old friend Representative Sam Claiborne, who was serving as our Goldwater state chairman, and his co-chairman, Mrs. Francis Rice, with the help of Congressman William E. Brock, put the icing on the cake by getting all of the twenty-eight delegates committed to Goldwater, though we only claimed twenty-two and held six in reserve.

Our people in Georgia did almost as well that day. The Goldwater chairman, State Senator Joseph J. Tribble of Savannah, had a fine team working with him, including Howard Callaway, who was elected to Congress that November, and Paul Wolf, who in 1965 became Republican state chairman. For more than a year they had been organizing at the district, county and precinct levels, getting rid of the party hacks who had lived off the crumbs of federal patronage for decades and replacing them with aggressive young people intent on building a bona fide two-party system in Georgia. At the state convention they added significantly to the Goldwater delegates already elected in the districts and emerged with all but two of Georgia's twenty-four delegates firmly committed to the Senator.

Maine, of course, was another matter. Senator Margaret Chase Smith got all fourteen delegates as Maine's favorite daughter. However, one of them was, of course, the Republican state chairman, Dave Nichols, the silent member of my old 3505 group, and he had strong backing from our Goldwater chairman, Cyril M. Joly, Jr. of Waterville and an effective co-chairman, Mrs. Eleanor Higgins of Bangor. Like the loyal State-of-Mainers they all were, our Goldwater group backed Senator Smith's candidacy right on through the national convention roll call, though we knew we could have counted at least four, and possibly a half-dozen, delegates out of Maine if Mrs. Smith had released them after the first ballot, as I fully expected she would.

A fourth state convention was held that same weekend in Illinois where ten at-large delegates were selected. The hearts—and the votes —of all but a few belonged to Barry. We were moving closer and closer to a virtual sweep of Illinois' hefty 58-man delegation.

Tuesday, May 5, marked another banner day for Barry Goldwater. Three primary elections on that date ultimately produced 83 votes for him at San Francisco. They were held in Ohio, Indiana and the District of Columbia. The fate of Ohio's big bloc of 58 delegates was, however, by no means clear at the time.

Dick Kleindienst had taken over our operation in Ohio early in January and he quickly worked out a deal with the state Republican chairman, Ray Bliss. Kleindienst agreed to let the "normal processes" in the selection of delegate candidates run its course. He also agreed to keep Goldwater's name off the ballot and let Governor James Rhodes run unopposed as a favorite son.

After the agreement was sealed it was presented to me as a *fait accompli* and I had no choice except to concur. My assignment then was to keep our Goldwater people from fighting it out with Bliss and Rhodes. I telephoned our Goldwater leader in Ohio, Dr. Norris B. Livingston, from Washington and Dick Kleindienst also took part in the discussion from another line at our headquarters. The doctor, who had been gearing for a fight in Ohio for nearly a year, was quite upset. He said he was certain he could win a large number of Goldwater delegates if we would only let him go. My heart wasn't in it, but I pleaded with him not to take any action that would disrupt our agreement with Bliss.

Finally, Dr. Livingston said, "Is this what *you* want, Clif?" I swallowed hard at the other end of the line and said yes, this was what I wanted. He said, "Okay, we'll accept it." He was still free to drum up support for potential Goldwater delegates within the party organization, but there were to be no contests nor any open attacks on the state GOP committee. Everything had to be done within the "normal processes."

When the delegate slate was finally hammered out in Ohio, Dick Kleindienst and I went over it and came up with more than 20 Goldwater votes. However, whether we would get them on the first, second, third—or one-hundredth—ballot depended entirely on when Governor Rhodes and Ray Bliss decided to release them.

Not long after Dr. Livingston acceded to the Bliss-Kleindienst arrangement, Senator Goldwater flew to Columbus to speak at a Republican fundraising luncheon Bliss had arranged. With Bliss' consent, Livingston had a big crowd at the airport to greet Barry. They came from all over the state, expecting that their candidate would address them at least briefly.

Unhappily, when the Senator alighted from the plane the reporters surrounded him immediately. One of them asked if he planned to confer with Dr. Livingston, who was standing a little way off waiting to meet him. Goldwater replied that he didn't know who the doctor was. Then, after a perfunctory address to the assembled crowd, he was whisked off to the luncheon.

Dr. Livingston phoned me in Washington and reported what had happened. I asked him to hold some of his people at the airport and I would arrange for the Senator to meet them before he took off. I got through to Tony Smith at the luncheon and he said he would set up the meeting. But when Goldwater returned to the airport several hours later he brushed by Dr. Livingston and his group and went directly to the plane. Understandably, Dr. Livingston and his people felt that they had been double-crossed. They had given in to all our demands but the candidate wouldn't even take the time to acknowledge their existence.

All this had transpired months before the May 5 primary. Although Dr. Livingston and his people would have been justified in kicking over the traces and fighting the state organization's candidates they continued to cooperate, and the regular slate, committed to Governor Rhodes, sailed in without opposition. We claimed no delegates in Ohio that day. However, we had enough—including Congressman John Ashbrook, who with Bill Rusher had helped map the original plans for our operation back in 1961—to establish a solid bridgehead in Ohio.

The results of the Indiana primary were more immediately apparent. Ione Harrington, Bob Hughes and Bob Matthews had helped pick an eminently effective Goldwater for President leadership team in Leslie Duvall of Indianapolis and Mrs. Ray Marr, Jr. of Columbus, Indiana. Their combined efforts delivered all 32 of Indiana's delegates to Goldwater and piled up more than 260,000 votes for him in the Presidential preference balloting. Former U.S. Senator William Jenner of Indiana deserves a major share of the credit for this stunning victory.

Rockefeller and the other prominent GOP candidates had wisely side-stepped the Indiana primary. Instead of entering themselves, they quietly threw their weight behind the Don Quixote of the Republican Party, Harold Stassen. However, Stassen—drawing all the anti-Goldwater votes in the state—still could manage to garner only a little more than a quarter of the total vote. The press, of course, made much of this, often to the point of obscuring the fact that Barry Goldwater had carried the entire delegation in Indiana.

The big surprise in Indiana on May 5 was not the Republican, but the Democrat primary. Governor George Wallace of Alabama, openly campaigning as a segregationist in a Northern state, won more than 30 per cent of the Democrat vote against Indiana Governor Matthew Welsh, Lyndon Johnson's stand-in. Amazingly, Wallace got his biggest vote in Lake County, the steel-producing area of northern Indiana right next door to Chicago. The white backlash the Democrats feared suddenly loomed much larger than they had anticipated. Two weeks later Wallace threw another scare into his party's hierarchy by winning nearly 43 per cent of the primary vote in Maryland against another Presidental stand-in, Senator Daniel B. Brewster.

The District of Columbia primary was, of course, overshadowed by Ohio and Indiana. But it dropped four more delegates in Barry Goldwater's already crowded basket. These resulted from a little arrangement I had made months before the assassination with Carl Shipley, the local Republican leader in Washington. He had agreed to give us four of the nine delegates and he faithfully kept his word. Phil Guarino, prominent restaurateur and vice chairman of the D.C. Republican committee, was one of our earliest and most enthusiastic organizers in the District and it was largely through the efforts of Phil and his friends that we were able to demand nearly half the D.C. delegation. Actually, I must be frank and admit that the Senator's vote-getting potential was not exactly phenomenal in the national capital. The overwhelming majority of the federal bureaucrats were frightened to death that a Goldwater victory would cost them their jobs and we were indeed lucky to get as many delegates as we did out of Washington, D.C.

These two weeks, beginning with the New Jersey primary on April 21 and ending with the Indiana, Ohio and District of Columbia primaries on May 5, put Goldwater so far out front in the crucial quest for delegates that he was now guaranteed a position of commanding strength at the national convention. He was, however, still a far piece from a first-ballot victory.

Publicly I claimed only 112 of the delegates selected during this period. But my private tally showed a bedrock 148 which swelled to 204 with the addition of the 56 Texas delegates not yet officially chosen but virtually committed to Goldwater as a result of his tremendous showing in the preferential primary. Nor did this include any votes at all from the Ohio delegation, all of which I placed in Governor Rhodes's column for the time being.

With the more than 200 delegates I had counted when I left Kansas on April 18 we were now easily over the 400-mark, or about four-fifths of *all* the delegates named to date. But for the record I claimed less than 250. My reason for doing this was quite simple. Frequently, Presidential candidates claim more delegates than they actually have in an attempt to create a bandwagon psychology. In the past, this tactic has often worked. But very early I decided to play this game in reverse, announcing only those delegates who were publicly committed and whom I could not very well hide. All the others—the Goldwater votes that did not show on the surface—I held in reserve.

My strategy was to pace the Senator's candidacy as slowly as possible during the spring and at the same time gradually heat up the momentum, building to a climax just before the national convention opened. I was also aware that we might need my hidden reserves if the candidate suffered a real setback along the way, particularly in the California primary on June 2. If he lost all of California's 86 delegates I wanted to unveil two or three times that many the following day to send him back into the ring swinging haymakers after the press counted him out.

Fortunately, most members of the mass media, intent on playing down Goldwater's candidacy any way they could, were only too anxious to help me play my little game. However, after the first week in May some of the more astute reporters and commentators, whatever their personal political prejudices, refused to blind themselves to reality and began to catch on. *Time*, which for the most part did an objective job of reporting throughout the pre-convention campaigning, was among the first to discern the trend. In its May 8 issue *Time* reported:

Suddenly, like a brush fire racing out of control, the word crackled among informed Republicans: GOLDWATER'S ALMOST GOT IT! It seemed hardly possible. Here was Arizona's Barry Goldwater, who only a few weeks ago appeared to be flat on his back in his quest for the GOP Presidential nomination. . . . Yet, as of last week, Goldwater was clearly the man to beat in San Francisco. . . .

Time noted that there were several reasons for the delay in assessing Goldwater's true strength. First of all, the magazine perceptively observed, "There was the national preoccupation with primaries, which usually make more headlines than delegates." Secondly, it said, "There was obsession with the polls. But no pollster has ever nominated a Presidential candidate. . . . Thus, slowly but steadily, Goldwater kept collecting delegates while the unavoweds and disavoweds collected press clippings." *Time* projected the Senator's first-ballot vote at 550. Then, with an insight very few other publications displayed, it revealed that the Senator "also has impressive reserve strength in some of the states presently planning to support favorite sons on the first ballot."

Actually, *Time* was a bit premature in reporting the assessment of "informed Republicans" that "Goldwater's almost got it!" He was still a long, long way from home plate, and at our Washington headquarters we were taking nothing for granted.

The Senator had enjoyed a bountiful fortnight in the quest for delegates. But ahead lay the Oregon and California primaries, both potential stumbling blocks in his path. In was my job to see that he would have enough delegates cemented to his candidacy so that he could hurdle defeats in each of these states and still stay in the nominating race. Getting him past Oregon would be easy. In fact, we had already decided to walk Goldwater around Oregon. But California was the big one and if his campaign was going to go up in smoke there, we had less than four weeks to finish building a fire escape for him out of degelate votes in nine primaries and conventions before the voters in the Golden State went to the polls.

CHAPTER 29

COUNTDOWN III—THE FIRE ESCAPE

ONE ASPECT of the mad scramble for the 1964 Republican Presidential nomination that was ignored almost entirely by both the politicians and the press was the true status of George Romney. As late as June 7, at the Governors' Conference in Cleveland, people kept trying to revive the Romney for President boomlet that had died a-glimmering more than a year before. But the Governor of Michigan was never a candidate. In fact, he had signed a pledge swearing that he had no intention of becoming a nominee for President in 1964. He took this oath before March 9 in order to remove his name from the ballot in the Oregon primary. Since I knew that George Romney was not a man who would easily break his word I did not consider him in the same light as the other "unavowed" favorite-son candidates. Romney was in my view a bona fide favorite son and entitled to be treated as such.

Thus, when I flew to the Michigan state convention the weekend following the primaries in Indiana, Ohio and the District of Columbia, I had no intention of getting into a bloody battle with Romney over delegates. I had been assured that the Governor would maintain a position of neutrality in the continuing struggle for the Presidential nomination. Senator Goldwater was guaranteed at least half a dozen Michigan delegates as a result of the selection processes in the districts.

If we could pick up a few more, fine, I would gladly take them. But if we could not, there would be no fight on the convention floor.

There were more than enough problems in Michigan without our getting into a slugging match with the Governor. The biggest one was the bitter feud between Romney and Richard Durant, the ex-Birch Society member who was chairman of the Republican 14th Congressional District organization. Durant, a Goldwater supporter, had recently sued Romney for libel. This caused great consternation among our official Goldwater leadership in Michigan, headed by Creighton Holden, Mrs. Betty Jones, and a member of my old 3505 group, Ty Gillespie. All of them were friends of Romney and had worked hard for him in his first gubernatorial campaign in 1962.

The impression had been created in Michigan that Dick Durant was the spokesman for the Goldwater state organization and my team there asked me to set the public straight. On Thursday, May 7, I issued a statement from Washington pointing out that Durant had "no official relationship with our organization." I emphasized that Creighton Holden was our Michigan chairman and that "no other person is or has been authorized to represent our committee." In conclusion, I expressed "our great admiration and respect for Michigan's distinguished Governor, George Romney." And I added that we would continue to work for a strong, unified Republican Party in Michigan to aid in the election of Barry Goldwater as President and the re-election of Romney as Governor.

The next day I hopped a plane for Lansing to lend our Michigan committee a hand at the convention which was to open there on Saturday morning. Ty Gillespie met me at the airport and we drove to the hotel, where we met with Holden, Mrs. Jones and some other members of our Michigan group. Once again, they impressed upon me the importance of staying out of a pitched battle with Romney.

It was imperative, they felt, that we should do all we could to preserve party harmony in a state which had been controlled for so many years by a Democrat machine owned lock, stock and barrel by Walter Reuther's United Auto Workers and the AFL-CIO. They wanted to avoid any disputes that might endanger Romney's chances for re-election in November. Creighton Holden and his team were doing a delicate balancing act on a high wire that was being roughly shaken at one end by some rather obstreperous Goldwater supporters and at the other by a much larger gang of rule-or-ruin Liberals.

As soon as we had all agreed on our convention strategy, I phoned the Michigan Republican chairman, Arthur Elliott, who had asked Ty Gillespie to have me call him when I got in. Art said the Governor wanted to see me and we set up an appointment for right after dinner.

That evening a series of tragic tornadoes ripped through Flint and several other Michigan cities. Governor Romney left immediately for the disaster areas and our appointment, of course, had to be postponed. I stayed up waiting for him to return to Lansing and finally went to bed about 3 A.M. At 6:30 the phone in my hotel room rang. It was Art Elliott and he told me the Governor had just returned and would like to talk with me now if I could come down to his suite. I said that I would be there just as soon as I could get shaved and dressed.

Despite the early hour, there was a lot of activity around the Governor's suite when I arrived about fifteen minutes later. Romney looked as fresh and chipper as if he had just returned from a long and restful vacation, though he hadn't even been to bed. He had come in from the tornado-stricken area after a night of climbing over rubble inspecting the damage, and had showered, shaved and changed his clothes. Now he was ready to begin a tough day of politicking and he wanted to get things settled before he went out on the convention floor.

Our discussion centered around the distribution of the twelve at-large delegates who were to be chosen that day. I felt we should have a minimum of two from this group to add to the half-dozen we had already won in the districts. Romney pointed out that he wanted to be a delegate and that the state chairman, the two National Committee people, the other state and party officials who were traditionally named as at-large delegates also deserved recognition. I could understand his problem. There were just so many seats to go around, and he had more than enough people to fill them.

However, I insisted that if he had a Rockefeller man on his list—as I knew he had—that we should have at least two, considering the extent of Goldwater support in Michigan as compared with Rockefeller's. I wanted Creighton Holden on the slate and the then majority leader of the state House of Representatives.

The Governor promised to give my requests serious consideration but he did not make a firm commitment. As I emerged from his suite I bumped into my old friend Larry Lindemer who was waiting outside the door for his turn to confer with Romney. Larry, a former Republican state chairman in Michigan, was Nelson Rockefeller's Midwest coordinator, and I felt that Governor Romney had at least established the proper order of priority that morning by seeing Senator Goldwater's representative first. However, I left knowing that we had received very little else.

There was nothing we could do to force Romney to give us more delegates short of waging an all-out fight against some members of his slate on the convention floor. Our Michigan people had already decided to sidestep such a fight. And, although our state organization was strong and aggressive, there was a serious question in my mind whether we could have beaten Romney's candidates with only a few hours to marshal our forces.

The situation was not analagous to Kansas, where Governor Anderson was the leader of the Rockefeller forces not only in his state but in the entire Midwest. Romney was a favorite son intent only on holding his delegation in line through the first ballot and I had no reason to believe that he would throw his vote to another candidate.

In the end we received one at-large delegate and one alternate at the Michigan convention, giving us a total of 8 overall. Romney kept the other 40 delegates tightly in line and neither Rockefeller nor Scranton got a single vote out of Michigan at the Cow Palace.

On that same day there was another Republican state convention, in Wyoming. Luckily, Wyoming was no problem. Senator Milward L. Simpson, a thoroughly dedicated citizen, was the Goldwater chairman in that state and we also had important support from Governor Clifford P. Hansen, the two members of the National Committee, Joseph L. Budd and Mrs. Edith M. Daley, and both the outgoing and in-coming state Republican chairmen, John S. Wold and Stanley K. Hathaway. Our Goldwater co-chairman, David Kidd of Casper, had made certain that no potential backsliders got on the delegate slate and we romped home at the state convention on May 8 and 9 with all 12 delegates from Wyoming committed to vote for Barry Goldwater until hell underwent a severe and dramatic change in climate.

The combined total of Goldwater delegates from Michigan and Wyoming was 20, giving us 56 for the week with those we had won on Tuesday in Indiana and the District of Columbia. The following week the pace of our advance slowed somewhat although four states picked delegates. There were two primaries on Tuesday, May 12, one in Nebraska and the other in West Virginia, a third in Oregon on Friday, and a state convention in Vermont on Saturday.

Only six delegate seats were at stake in Nebraska, all in district elections. The remaining ten at-large delegates would not be selected until the June 1 Republican state convention. On the preferential ballot, Senator Goldwater was running without formal opposition. However, both the Lodge and Nixon forces had mounted concerted write-in campaigns.

Nebraska was the first state in which Dick Nixon made any serious move. Five days before the balloting he appeared in Omaha to deliver a speech before the National Conference of Christians and Jews. The following day, former Secretary of the Interior Fred Seaton, who was masterminding the Nixon campaign from his newspaper in Hastings, blanketed the state with mailing pieces showing voters how they could cast write-in votes for the ex-Vice President. It was a good try, and Nixon demonstrated that he was still popular with the voters by winning nearly 43,000 write-ins, about 32 per cent of the vote. Lodge limped in with a feeble 22,000 votes, or 16 per cent. Amazingly, more was made of this by some segments of the media than Dick Nixon's really impressive showing.

But the combined vote of both these prominent Republicans failed to equal Barry Goldwater's Nebraska primary total. He came in with 67,369 votes, nearly half of all those cast, despite the fact that he had hardly campaigned in that state. Moreover, he swept in all his delegates in the district elections with him. His Senate colleague, Carl Curtis, assisted by our Midwest regional director Dick Herman, who was doubling as the Nebraska Goldwater chairman, and co-chairman Mrs. Doris Wood of Omaha, were confident that this display of strength in the primary would guarantee Goldwater all the 10 at-large delegates at the Nebraska convention.

West Virginia was a horse of a very different color—mostly green. As everyone knows, West Virginia primaries are often for sale. From the beginning, I was opposed to any attempt to bid for votes that could be bought. Senator Goldwater never had any intention of trying to buy votes either, and in that he was in complete agreement with the policy laid down long before by our original group. Thus, Rockefeller went on the West Virginia ballot unopposed and since no write-ins were permitted he got all the votes. Unfortunately for him, his investment did not pay off in delegates. The primary was non-binding on the delegates and five of them, including former U.S. Senator Chapman Revercombe, were avowed Goldwater supporters while four more were leaning heavily in our direction. Ultimately, Goldwater received 10 of the 14 West Virginia votes, with Rockefeller and Scranton dividing the other 4 evenly between them.

Nonetheless, this proved to be Rockefeller's best week—the highwater mark of his pathetic comeback campaign. On Friday, he managed to win the Oregon primary with 33 per cent of the total vote. In Oregon the primary was binding, and Rockefeller got all eighteen delegates.

In Oregon, all five of the serious Republican Presidential candidates were on the ballot, plus Margaret Chase Smith, whose aspirations never exceeded the Vice-Presidential nomination. Both of the announced candidates, Goldwater and Rockefeller, were on it, and so were the names of the two leading "unavowed" candidates, Nixon and Lodge. Even Pennsylvania's Scranton, who avoided confrontations with the voters as if fearing they might contaminate him with a fatal disease, was entered.

There is no honorable way of getting out of the Oregon primary if you have any plans at all for seeking the nomination. Under Oregon's curious law, its Secretary of State must list *all* persons on the ballot who have been prominently mentioned as possibilities for their party's nomination. After that the only way you can erase your name is to sign an affidavit swearing you do not intend to become a candidate that year. In 1964, only George Romney signed this pledge. All the other "unavoweds"—Nixon, Lodge and Scranton—refused to sign and their real intentions were thus smoked out when the deadline for filing the affidavits passed on March 9. The Oregon Secretary of State, Howell Appling, then had no choice except to put them on the ballot with Goldwater, Rockefeller and Mrs. Smith.

If the three "non-candidates" had taken the pledge, the Oregon primary could have been an important and interesting race. But as it was, the field was so big that it could only develop into a contest of confusion.

From the outset, our Goldwater effort in Oregon was subject to conflicting crosscurrents. In the Draft days there was a quite zealous faction clamoring for recognition and I refused to give it to them. When the Arizona group took over the national campaign Dick Kleindienst tried to get Sig Unander, who had run very strongly against Wayne Morse in the 1962 Senate race, for our state chairman. But Sig turned him down. For some reason, Wes Phillips, who had done a bangup job as Unander's campaign manager in 1962, was not consulted and for a while this caused more hard feelings.

Finally, late in January, Kleindienst appointed Dr. Edwin Durno, a retired physician from Medford and a former Congressman who had lost to Sig Unander in the 1962 Senate primary. Mrs. Esther Pallady, who had once headed the state Republican Women's Federation, was named co-chairman.

To give Dr. Durno and Mrs. Pallady as much professional support as possible, Kleindienst next pulled in Steve Shadegg, the former Arizona state GOP chairman who had managed Barry Goldwater's two successful campaigns for the United States Senate. It was a smart move and I for one was glad to have Steve back on board. As our Western States' director, he played a key role in the last big push of the California primary and in our delegate countdown in half a dozen other states.

Under Shadegg's expert guidance our Oregon forces went to work early in February and started tooling up for the coming campaign. Goldwater made one brief foray into the state on February 12 to address a Lincoln Day dinner in Portland. He returned again on April 5 to begin a three-day campaign tour and everywhere he went he was greeted by enthusiastic crowds. But there was something ominously reminiscent about this performance. It later occurred to the Senator and his aides that Oregon looked like New Hampshire all over again. This time, moreover, Dick Nixon was on the ballot and his supporters were conducting an aggressive campaign. Nixon undoubtedly would siphon off a good many conservative votes that would normally have gone to Goldwater. Then too, Goldwater would have to wage a campaign in California at the same time, to say nothing of tending his duties in the Senate where the critical debate on the Civil Rights Bill was already raging. Given a choice between battling for California's 86 delegates in a stand-up fight with one opponent, Nelson Rockefeller, and the free-for-all in Oregon with five other candidates and only 18 convention votes at stake, the Senator was well advised to walk away from Oregon. And this is exactly what he did.

Goldwater's decision to pull out of Oregon and cancel the remainder of his scheduled appearances there was made about the middle of April. I fully concurred with Kitchel and Kleindienst, who originally advised this move. Looking back, I think it was one of the wisest steps the Senator took during the pre-convention campaign.

Predictably, the already antagonistic segments of the press had a field day. Goldwater was accused of surrender, and there were broad hints that he was guilty of something close to cowardice. Some columnists went so far as to claim that he was preparing to quit his campaign for the nomination entirely. But in reality all he did by refusing to campaign was to deflate the exaggerated importance of the Oregon primary.

With Goldwater gone, Rockfeller now had the field all to himself. He immediately saw his chance and seized it. He stepped up his campaigning in Oregon appreciably, using a clever slogan that placed Goldwater and all the "unavowed" candidates in an unfavorable light with the Oregon voters. "I cared enough to come," became Rockefeller's battle cry. He shouted it at the conclusion of almost every speech he made during the final three weeks of the Oregon campaign. And he worked Barry Goldwater over unmercifully, ripping him with wild charges that surpassed in fury the dum-dum bullets he had repeatedly fired at the Senator in New Hampshire.

Despite Rockefeller's hard charging up and down the state of Oregon, the pollsters all favored Henry Cabot Lodge, who was still trying to hatch his Presidential nest egg from far-off Saigon. Right up until a few days before the balloting the highly regarded Harris Poll gave Lodge 35 per cent of the vote with Rockefeller trailing a lengthy 11 percentage points behind. Harris placed Nixon in third place and predicted Goldwater would run a very poor fourth.

But when the votes were all in Rockefeller won handily with 94,000 and Lodge came in second with 78,000. Goldwater chalked up 50,000 and Nixon was fourth with 48,000. (I could not help but speculate that if Nixon had thrown his considerable weight behind Goldwater, their combined total of 98,000 votes might well have given the Senator the victory in Oregon despite his "non-campaign.") Mrs. Smith placed fifth with 7,000 votes and Scranton scraped about 4,000 off the bottom 2 per cent of the barrel.

The main result of the Oregon primary was that it elminated both Lodge and Nixon from further serious consideration for the Republican nomination. Though neither of them campaigned personally, they both engineered vigorous campaigns through their influential supporters in Oregon and sent in professionals to back them up. Nixon had even dispatched his old aide, Bob Finch, from Los Angeles to the scene of the battle. It was a valiant effort. But its failure irrevocably dashed Nixon's chances for 1964.

The Oregon primary also showed—or should have shown—the utter futility of Bill Scranton's supposedly reluctant candidacy. It was the first and only time he permitted his name to be placed on a primary ballot that spring and the almost invisible vote he received revealed how weak he was among the voters outside Pennsylvania. But Scranton and his aides still maintained a quixotic faith in the powers of publicity and I knew that we had not heard the last of the Pennsylvania Governor despite his miserable Oregon showing.

The third effect of the Oregon vote was by far the most serious from my point of view. There was no doubt that in Oregon Rockefeller had at long last resurrected his candidacy. I knew that it was only a temporary resurrection and that he could never hope to pile up enough delegates in the two remaining months of the countdown to even come close at San Francisco. But his unexpected Oregon victory, coming as it did on the heels of a meaningless win in West Virgina, gave great impetus to his lagging campaign in California. Overnight, Rockefeller shot ahead of Goldwater in the California polls and with only seventeen days left before the California primary it appeared as though he were about to spring another upset.

There was not much I could do about California. This was Kleindienst's territory and I had moved in and out of it only at his request to handle special assignments. But I was determined to rack up as many delegates for Goldwater as I possibly could before the California voters went to the polls on June 2.

The day after the Oregon primary I flew to New England where we had another weekend Republican state convention going in Vermont. Our Goldwater chairman there was the former Secretary of the Navy, William B. Franke, who had retired to his home in Rutland. Like most of the Goldwater for President chairmen, he had first been appointed by our Draft organization. Secretary Franke was ably assisted by Dr. William Mann, an early contact of mine in Vermont, and between the two of them they managed to squeeze three Goldwater delegates out of the state convention.

This was better than I had hoped for in a small state sandwiched in between Rockefeller's New York, Lodge's Massachusetts and hostile New Hampshire. Dr. Mann flew down to Boston right after the convention adjourned to report the results at a regional meeting of our New England leaders. Although he had been elected a delegate himself, the good doctor was somewhat shaken by the unfamiliar display of rough-and-tumble politicking he had just come through. He was still simmering over all the things that the Rockefeller crowd had done to him and Bill Franke, but I tried to buoy up his spirits and I praised him before the regional meeting for what was really a splendid job.

The week after this we experienced the slimmest pickings of our entire four-month countdown. There were no primaries that week, and only one state convention—in Alaska. I sent Frank Whetstone from Cut Bank, Montana, up to Anchorage to handle this one, but by the time Frank arrived the Rockefeller forces had the convention boxed in. This was only eight weeks after Alaska had been shattered by one of the worst earthquakes in modern history. Communications and transportation were still badly disrupted and many delegates were unable to reach Anchorage over roads that had buckled in the quake.

Frank and our Alaskan leaders, Dr. Lee McKinley and Mrs. Tillie Reeve, decided to make a fight of it on the convention floor. But they went down to defeat by a small margin and, despite their courageous efforts, were completely shut out of the 12-man Alaska delegation. Alaska was the only convention state where we failed to score, and was one of the three—with New Hampshire and Oregon—where I failed to make good my promise to obtain Goldwater delegates in every state.

However, we bounced back strong the following week. In the Florida primary on Tuesday, May 26, Goldwater won all but two of the 34 delegates, and he went on to sweep the entire 13-man Mississippi delegation at the state convention four days later.

Mississippi, of course, was no problem. The Republican state chairman, Wirt Yerger, was doubling as our Goldwater chairman and he had substantial backing from the National Committee members, Fred La Rue and Mrs. James F. Hooper, plus our old 3505 ally, Charlie Klumb, and Yerger's co-chairman, Mrs. Esther Scott Barrett. There was only one way the party in Mississippi could go, and it did.

Florida, on the other hand, was chock-full of problems. It has been widely and erroneously reported that we lost the Florida primary because the "official" Goldwater slate of delegates was trounced by a rival slate fielded by the state Republican chairman, Tom Fairfield Brown. Actually, both slates were pro-Goldwater, though there were two dissidents in the Brown slate and there could have been more. Ironically, Tom Brown was our original Goldwater leader in Florida. But we got caught between two factions fighting for control of the Republican Party in Florida and the bloodletting that followed eventually led to Goldwater's loss of the state in November by some 42,000 votes out of a total of 1,854,000 cast.

Our difficulties in Florida dated back to the Republican National Committee meeting in January 1964. The Arizona group had just taken over and William Cramer, the senior Republican Congressman from Florida, nailed Dick Kleindienst at the Mayflower. Dick, of course, had not had time to familiarize himself with the political crosscurrents in Florida or any other state outside Arizona. When Cramer asked him whom he was going to deal with in Florida, Dick said, why, of course, we were going to deal with him.

Now, both Bill Cramer and Tom Brown are good friends of mine. In 1952 I had nominated Bill for a Young Republican post to build him for his first race for Congress that year. He lost by a narrow margin but later won an appointment as a county attorney. Once he was elected to Congress in 1954, Bill got into a long-running feud with the entrenched state Republican organization headed by Harold Alexander and Tom Brown. This was one feud I refused to get involved in and thus I had always been able to maintain friendly relations with both sides. Dick Kleindienst, of course, had no way of knowing about this struggle and he was delighted to get the senior GOP Congressman in Florida as our man in the state.

However, Tom Brown was under the impression that he had a prior commitment from Denison Kitchel naming *him* as the Goldwater chieftain in Florida. After Kleindienst made his commitment to Cramer, Tom came banging on my door at the Mayflower about two o'clock in the morning. He was furious, as he had every right to be. But since I had been downgraded to Kleindienst's coordinator of field operations barely twenty-four hours earlier, there wasn't much I could do for Tom now except to suggest he talk with Kitchel.

The following morning when I arrived at our new headquarters at 1101 Connecticut Avenue there was Tom Brown waiting to see Kitchel. He was kept cooling his heels until almost eleven o'clock before he was finally granted an audience. At first Kitchel denied that he had given Brown a commitment. But later he called Kleindienst and me into the meeting and told Brown that at least he had not given him any commitment that would exclude Cramer.

Still angry at what he regarded as a cheap double-cross, Brown left and later put in a call to Goldwater. But Cramer got to him first and the Senator had already supported the Congressman's claim to the Florida leadership, although Barry later said that he did not realize Cramer would be opposing Brown's man for the National Committee seat.

Cramer and Brown then started putting together rival delegate slates for the Florida primary. Repeated attempts were made to get them to compromise. One of the first was made by Goldwater himself. He was scheduled to speak at a private fundraising dinner in Palm Beach which Stets Coleman and some of our other people had arranged. But when the Senator arrived with Dick Kleindienst, Stets told him bluntly that neither he nor any of his friends would be at the dinner if Kleindienst was there. Dick, of course, did not attend.

After the dinner, the Senator went out on a yacht with Cramer, Congressman Edward J. Gurney and some of the other Florida people to see if he could get them to cooperate with Brown and Alexander. But the meeting ended in a shouting match between several members of the Florida group and this effort at conciliation failed.

The deadline for filing delegate slates was nearing and, as expected, both Cramer and Brown entered rival slates. But to be designated on the ballot as the official Goldwater slate, one or the other had to get authorization from the Senator. At this point John Grenier, the state chairman of Alabama who was our Southern regional director, produced a telegram authorizing the Cramer slate. Grenier had not consulted anyone at our Washington headquarters and when Kitchel learned of it he wanted to fire him. However, Kleindienst took the position that we could not afford to repudiate our regional director, who was also a GOP state chairman. Kitchel then sent another authorization telegram to the Florida Secretary of State, which only served to infuriate Tom Brown even more.

Finally Tom telephoned me and asked if I would come down and help him work out a compromise with Cramer. By this time the New Hampshire primary was over and done with and I had been rehabilitated as co-director of field operations. I informed Kleindienst that I was going to Florida and he decided to come too. Dick felt we also had to take Grenier along, although Brown had specifically asked me to keep Grenier out of the state.

We wound up in a motel near the St. Petersburg airport with Cramer and his aide in one room on the second floor and Tom Brown and Harold Alexander in another downstairs. I was trying to get them to agree to a slate that would give representation to both sides and after much running up and down the stairs we finally got it down to only one delegate seat that was still in dispute.

I left Brown and Alexander to go up and work out this one final bone of contention with Cramer. Kleindienst, who had been working on Cramer, went downstairs to join Brown and Alexander. By this time, both sides were almost ready to bury the hatchet and I got Cramer to agree to sit down in the same room with the others and compromise this last remaining problem of the one disputed delegate seat.

After all the months of everyone agonizing over Florida, I felt pretty good about the prospect of finally ironing out this sticky problem. But when I got downstairs to the other room Brown and Alexander were stalking out. I never did find out exactly what happened, but they had gotten into a verbal brawl with Kleindienst and the whole thing blew up. All our work was wasted. The rival slates that Brown and Cramer had previously marshaled went on the ballot. Brown, with the resources of the state organization at his command, had little difficulty in winning, although Congressman Cramer was elected to the National Committee.

Brown and his people were so angry at the handling of this whole matter that we could not be absolutely certain they would deliver their votes to Goldwater at the convention. However, I had a good talk with Tom Brown after the primary and there was never any doubt in my mind that he was for us. I put him down for 32 votes at San Francisco and Tom came through with 32 votes.

For the record, I claimed only the six Florida delegates who were publicly committed to Goldwater. But on my private tally I entered the number I knew Tom Brown would deliver. With those delegates we had won in Michigan, Nebraska, Vermont and Wyoming since May 9—plus more than 50 others we had taken in district contests in Delaware, Minnesota, Missouri, Rhode Island and Virginia—I was able to tote up 155 more Goldwater votes to add to the 400-plus I'd counted before my trip to Lansing.

Barry Goldwater's fire escape was now complete. If all his bridges went up in flames in California on Tuesday, I knew that we would have at least 550 fireproof votes surrounding and protecting him on Wednesday morning. No amount of pressure or heat would melt them away, and I would have many more like them coming in after California. In fact, I could see 70 more dedicated delegates right now marching into camp from Alabama, Montana, New Mexico and the State of Washington, all clad in asbestos-like suits, all prepared to fight it out in San Francisco if the convention went through one or one hundred ballots. There had never been an army like this in the whole history of American political warfare, and I knew that no matter what the outcome of the convention, and of the election that would follow, this army had now been solidified into a cohesive and effective force. It might suffer defeat, but it would never surrender, and it would live to fight again another day.

CHAPTER 30

COUNTDOWN IV—
CALIFORNIA

EVERYTHING ABOUT CALIFORNIA seems to have been drawn to fit the descriptive old Hollywood press-agent word "supercolossal," and the Republican Presidential primary that was waged there in 1964 was no exception. There were 86 national convention votes at stake, a delegation second in size only to New York's, although California was in the process of overtaking and passing the Empire State in total population that same spring. By June 2, when the primary election took place, more than eighteen million people were residing in this golden land that stretches for 1,200 fantastic miles along the Pacific coast from Oregon to the Mexican border.

A sizable proportion of these people—more than seven and a half million, to be precise—are clustered in and around the sprawling City of the Angels, Los Angeles. And it was there, in this greatest of all the metropolitan complexes west of the Hudson, that Barry Goldwater enjoyed his strongest following anywhere on the continent.

By all the tired rules that guide modern politicians, Goldwater's strength in the Los Angeles area should have resembled nothing more than a scrawny shadow. Here was a great and growing megalopolis, peopled with a polyglot population that included large minority groups and thousands of union members. Moreover, the economy of the region was and is heavily dependent upon federal contracts in the huge aircraft-missile-electronics industry. On top of that, the State of California has had a long tradition of paternalistic government of the type that Senator Goldwater consistently deplored. And yet it was here he had attracted the biggest and most enthusiastic army of volunteer workers that any political candidate had ever marshaled, not only in California but in the United States.

Part of this was undoubtedly due to the strong strain of pioneering spirit that dwells within so many of the people who have made America's last great westward trek. By and large they are rugged individualists of the old stamp. Many came from the ancient Republican heartland in the Midwest, and they brought with them the same ideals and traditions which spurred their ancestors to plough and build a mighty and prosperous empire out of empty wastes of swamp and prairie. Their livelihood might be dependent upon jobs directly or indirectly created by government money. But they no more want that government to tell them how to live their lives than their homesteading forebears had when they settled the land grants doled out by the bureaucrats of the last century.

It is difficult, if not impossible, to clamp the yoke of a political machine around the necks of people like this. Democrats may outnumber Republicans in registration by nearly three-to-two in California, but the people vote as they please.

No one has ever been able to quite fathom the depths of all the intricate whirlpools that spin and churn across California's constantly changing political landscape. I doubt if anyone ever will. For want of better guidelines, the experts invariably fall back on personalities when dealing with California. And, no doubt, there is some validity to this approach.

Hiram Johnson, a bristling little rooster of a man, held sway in state and Republican politics for more than thirty years and left his mark on California, though perhaps not as permanently as many believe. Earl Warren more or less inherited Johnson's progressive Republican mantle, weaving into it a more "modern" Liberal hue during his terms as Governor. But Warren ran on tickets with GOP candidates who were then considered arch-conservatives, most notably Dick Nixon and Bill Knowland. When Warren took California's big delegation to the 1952 convention and swapped it for a lifetime position as Chief Justice of the United States Supreme Court, he left his gubernatorial chair at Sacramento to a Liberal heir, Goodwin Knight. Yet "Goodie" Knight had to share his power with conservative Senator Knowland and with Vice President Nixon, who in far-off Washington seemed to be shifting from the traditional conservatism that had earned him the wrath of the press to a more "moderate" position which, no matter how hard he tried, seemed to win him only an even more vicious brand of suspicion.

The Republican Party probably would have continued to reign in California in the early 1960s if Senator Knowland and Governor Knight had not attempted to switch jobs in 1958. Both were defeated that year, Goodie Knight by the late Senator Clair Engle and Bill Knowland by Pat Brown. And although Dick Nixon carried the state in the 1960 Presidential election, he lost out to Brown in the gubernatorial contest two years later.

Now, in 1964, the deep division in the California Republican Party, which I had observed firsthand during the '62 gubernatorial primary, loomed wider and more unbridgeable than ever. The conservative wing was on the upsurge but the still powerful remnants of the Liberal faction, led by Senator Thomas Kuchel, wanted to keep the party all to themselves. Neither side was in any mood for compromise and the Presidential primary gave each a chance to test its mettle.

The first open skirmish between conservative and Liberal Republicans was a fight for control of the California Republican Assembly, which Earl Warren had set up years ago to give his Liberal phalanx a power base outside the regular GOP state organization. Surprisingly, the conservatives won, and forced through a resolution endorsing Senator Goldwater for President. The United Republicans of California (UROC), organized by a brilliant young politician named Rus Walton, and the state Young Republican organization had already taken similar action. But the Liberals had no intention of accepting these setbacks lying down.

Under California law, the Presidential primary is not a winner-take-all contest as was widely reported in 1964. The primary election does not bind delegates irrevocably to the victorious candidate. However, it became an all-or-nothing battle when our state chairman, Bill Knowland, drew up a slate of Goldwater delegates and wisely made each one sign a written pledge to support the Senator at San Francisco until such time as he might release them.

The Rockefeller forces attempted to make equally certain that their slate was similarly comprised of loyal partisans, but I am not certain that they entirely succeeded. Many Rockefeller delegates were actually Lodge devotees, and there were even some Nixon people among them.

With the delegate slates complete, the stage was now fully set for the costliest, most bitter primary election fight in the history of this country. At stage center, squaring off in a prize ring whose ropes had been stripped of protecting velvet, stood the two candidates, Goldwater and Rockefeller. In their corners, but still well within the glare of the publicity floodlights, were grouped all the prominent politicians in their supporting casts.

It was a tense and climactic scene, a scene worthy of Hollywood at its best, a Cecil B. DeMille extravaganza acted out in mid-twentieth century costumes, speech and manners. And yet the central drama was unfolding beyond the range of the cameras. For while the candidates and their prestigious backers monopolized the attention of the press and public, the real struggle in California was taking place outside this carefully constructed set. It was a struggle not merely for votes but for the minds of men and women, and it was being waged in thousands of neighborhoods and communities strung out along the freeways and clustered in the majestic hills, fertile valleys and air-conditioned desert oases of this great nation-state.

The stars of this drama were indisputably the Senator from Arizona and the Governor of New York. But the principal protagonists were, as some newsmen belatedly discovered, the Goldwater volunteers and the Rockefeller professionals.

Early evidence of this momentous behind-the-scenes clash was revealed on March 4 when an unprecedented army of volunteers unleashed Operation Q. Within the space of a few hours before noon they obtained more than 50,000 signatures for Senator Goldwater on the primary filing petitions, nearly four times as many as were needed. By contrast, Governor Rockefeller's paid professionals took a whole month to secure the minimum number of signatures required to get his name on the ballot by the April 3 filing deadline.[1]

Our Goldwater volunteers in California, numbering more than 40,000, were virtually all so-called "ordinary" citizens. Most were taking their first fling at politics, but they were not motivated by a quest for political power per se. They were people who were deeply and profoundly disturbed by the direction in which America was drifting and they willingly gave of their time, money and effort to do whatever they could to alter that course.

Volunteer groups marching under the Goldwater banner proliferated everywhere in California, and particularly in the Los Angeles area. Some were organized under the direction of Rus Walton's United Republicans of California. Others took their cue from the Young Republicans. But a good many simply sprang up on their own, spontaneously formed by citizens anxious to do their bit for the conservative cause.

In an earlier chapter I mentioned encountering one such group in San Francisco which was organized by Mrs. Bobbie Vargis and her friends as early as the spring of 1963. There were countless others which, like Mrs. Vargis', set up shop on their own hook, paying the headquarters rent, the cost of campaign materials and all expenses out of their own pockets. Hundreds of individuals, with no ties at all to any group, were out ringing doorbells. Mrs. Hannah Nixon, the former Vice President's mother, was one of these—until she was whisked off to New York for a lengthy visit with her famous son.

This is not to say that our California volunteers operated without

---

[1] Rockefeller's petition circulators were paid for each signature they obtained. There is nothing illegal or unethical about this. Under California law, the practice is permitted and used by many candidates.

professional direction. After former Senator Knowland took over as the state Goldwater chairman he forged an effective organization with Pete Pitchess, the Sheriff of Los Angeles County, as his commander in Southern California and Bernard Brennan, who had run Dick Nixon's 1960 Presidential campaign in the state, as our Los Angeles campaign manager. In addition, Henry Salvatori did an amazing job as the Goldwater finance chairman in California with the help of a group of prominent businessmen which included the dynamic young chairman of the Schick Safety Razor Company and Technicolor, Inc., Patrick J. Frawley; Cy Rubel of the Union Oil Company; Leland Kaiser; and many others. On top of that a star-studded galaxy of movie and television actors, many of whom were personal friends of Senator Goldwater, put their shoulders to his campaign wheel. Among them were John Wayne, Ronald Reagan, Raymond Massey, Walter Brennan, Efrem Zimbalist, Jr., Clint (Cheyenne) Walker and Hedda Hopper.

However, faced off against Senator Knowland's impressive team was a formidable band of prominent GOP professionals and industrialists that read like a *Who's Who* in California Republican politics, 1964. Rockefeller's state campaign chairman was Senator Kuchel, one of Earl Warren's more successful protégés. Serving under him were former Governor Goodie Knight; John Krehbiel, the immediate past state Republican chairman; Joseph Martin, Jr., who stepped out of his National Committee post in March to back Rockefeller; Edward Shattuck, another former National Committeeman; Jack McCarthy, the minority leader of the State Senate; George Christopher, former Mayor of San Francisco; and James P. Mitchell, former U.S. Secretary of Labor.

A substantial number of the really big guns in California's business and financial community were also lined up against Goldwater. Most prominent among them were Leonard Firestone of the rubber company family; Theodore S. Petersen, former head of Standard Oil of California; Justin Dart, the chairman of Rexall Drugs; and motion picture mogul Jack Warner.

It has been estimated that Nelson Rockefeller spent between $3,500,-000 and $5,000,000 on his primary campaign in California. A sizable portion of this huge sum was channeled through Spencer-Roberts & Associates, a political advisory firm based in Los Angeles. No one will deny that they spent the money effectively. Among other things, they helped Rockefeller hire a whole platoon of public relations agencies, each assigned to whip up support for the Governor among a different minority or special-interest group. And they bore down hard on getting members of certain of these groups, especially those in the Negro and Mexican communities, to switch their registration from Democratic to Republican so they could cast their ballots for Rockefeller in the June 2 primary.

Nonetheless, all of Rockefeller's money and Spencer-Roberts' polished professional know-how could not withstand the steady day-to-day, house-to-house, person-to-person campaigning of the vast army of Goldwater volunteers. No matter how dismal things looked for their candidate, the volunteers never let up. Two weeks before primary day, for instance, our volunteers in Los Angeles County, where almost 40 per cent of all California Republicans reside, conducted a massive canvass of more than 300,000 voters. Most of them did much more than ask people whom they favored in the election. They sold Goldwater at every door. They also determined who and where the waverers were and went back again and again to win them over.

With Rockefeller unable to attract votes on his own, his managers conceived the clever idea of presenting him to the electorate as a "proxy candidate" for all the Liberal and "moderate" Republican aspirants—Nixon, Lodge, Romney, Scranton and even Stassen. This later backfired, as we shall see, but the Governor got one break fairly early in the game when the California courts invalidated a number of Harold Stassen's petition signatures and thus wiped him off the primary ballot. Up to this point, in early April, Stassen had been drawing 10 per cent of the poll votes, votes which presumably would go to Rockefeller. Now, with no write-ins permitted, the Governor and Goldwater were at last face to face in a two-man battle.

Some members of Senator Goldwater's campaign team recommended that we challenge the signatures on Rockefeller's petitions to force him off the ballot too. They felt certain that this could be done because, as I have already noted, the Governor's paid petition circulators had barely scraped up the necessary number of signatures. There is always bound to be some duplication of signatures, and in a case like this where the minimum was barely obtained it would have been no great trick to have enough invalidated to erase Rockefeller's name from the ballot.

But I was opposed to this move for several reasons. First, I felt that our volunteers would come through strong enough to give the Senator a victory over Rockefeller in their first clearcut contest. And second, if we had him removed from the ballot the Governor could, with apparent justification, accuse Goldwater of being afraid to face him in a head-on clash at the polls. Fortunately, this was one argument I was able, with Senator Goldwater's support, to win. Rockefeller stayed on the ballot.

At the point when this decision was made the Senator was regaining some of the confidence that had been knocked out of him in New Hampshire the month before. Moreover, he had taken firm control of his own campaign schedule, something he had never done in New Hampshire, where he had permitted himself to be horribly overexposed.

On April 4, the day after the primary filing deadline in California,

Goldwater met with Bill Knowland, Henry Salvatori and his other state campaign leaders at a motel near the San Francisco Airport. Knowland had previously arranged a crowded schedule for the Senator for the balance of the California campaign. Like Senator Cotton in New Hampshire, Knowland believed that the more people a candidate could get to meet or speak to, the more votes he would reap at the polls. In March, for instance, he had set up no less than two dozen separate appearances for Goldwater in a single day.

There is a lot to be said for the saturation campaign. Certainly Jack Kennedy benefited from it in both the primaries and general election drive in 1960. But it was perfectly apparent to Barry Goldwater, particularly after his experience in New Hampshire, that this kind of campaign just did not fit his personal style.

At the April 4 meeting Goldwater ruled out any more multi-stop schedules. From now on, he said, his campaign would be limited to large rallies, preferably televised live or videotaped for telecast later. He insisted on cutting down drastically on press conferences (he had held four in one day in San Diego in March with dismal results), and these too would be televised wherever possible so the people would not have to rely entirely on the interpretive accounts of reporters to determine his position on important issues.

Bill Knowland, faced with scrapping a substantial part of the schedule he had painstakingly arranged with his lieutenants for Goldwater's coming campaign tours, argued strongly against the new format laid out by the candidate. But Goldwater stood firm. He was simply not going to let himself in for a repetition of the New Hampshire fiasco.

As a result, Goldwater's California schedule was slashed by more than 75 per cent. Instead of fifteen or twenty appearances a day, he made four or five at the most—and he cut the total number of campaign days in the state nearly in half. He also changed his speech style considerably, replacing the fire and brimstone with a softer sell designed to appeal to people less deeply concerned than those who had done their homework on what had been going on in Washington and in the world.

The new strategy paid off. With the help of his tireless volunteers, the Senator maintained a comfortable lead over Rockefeller in all the California polls during the balance of April and midway through May. He was able to spend more time tending his duties in the Senate, a task he always enjoyed much more than the sweat and thunder of the campaign trail. And he even contrived to make one campaign appearance beamed at California by merely traveling the relatively short distance from Washington to New York.

On the night of May 12 a mammoth National Goldwater Rally was staged in Manhattan's Madison Square Garden, mainly to impress the people of California that the Senator had substantial support in the East and that they need not consider themselves provincial Western kooks if they voted for him. The rally was also designed to show that Governor Rockefeller did not enjoy anything approaching unanimous enthusiasm in his own home state, which was holding a supposedly one-man primary on the same day as California's. Rita Bree, Mrs. Russell Colt and the dedicated volunteers in the metropolitan New York area had been planning the rally for six months, first from Suite 3505 and later from another midtown office. They managed to tie it indirectly into the California primary campaign by getting Bill Knowland to serve as the rally chairman.

With the help of Marvin Liebman, the enterprising entrepreneur of numerous conservative and anti-Communist causes, the rally was a huge success. Marvin even rented an elephant from the Ringling Brothers—Barnum and Bailey Circus, which was also playing the Garden early in May, to promote the event.

A sellout crowd of more than 18,000 packed the venerable Garden for the rally. Once again we successfully defied the old tradition of free tickets for political events by selling seats to offset costs. They went for $2, $5 and $10 per person, with a number of sponsors' seats at $100. The profits were used to finance the videotaping of Goldwater's speech for re-broadcast in California.

Despite this effort, three days later the Oregon primary catapulted Rockefeller into the lead in all the polls in California. The first Harris Poll after Oregon gave the Governor 47 per cent of the vote to 36 per cent for Goldwater. The remaining 17 per cent were listed as undecided. Even granting the erratic performance of the pollsters in Oregon and elsewhere that spring, it was obvious that the Senator was now in deep trouble. And he had only two weeks left to regain his lost ground.

Unlike the general election campaign the following fall when Goldwater and his palace guard seemed to throw up their hands and surrender more than a month before election day, everyone went all out in the homestretch in California. Dick Kleindienst, Dean Burch, Lee Edwards, Ed Nellor and Vern Stevens were all detached from our national headquarters in Washington and thrown into the gap. Steve Shadegg, still weary from the Oregon debacle, was pulled in from Phoenix.

They set up an emergency campaign headquarters in an aging apartment on Los Angeles' Wilshire Boulevard that was once the residence of Greta Garbo. During the next eighteen days, with the help of Rus Walton, Bernie Brennan and some of our other California people, they ground out an unbelievable number of newspaper ads, radio spots and television commercials while expertly meeting a whole herd of crises that came stampeding down and across the state in never-ending waves.

The first big flap after Rockefeller's Oregon victory was caused by a mailing piece sent to hundreds of thousands of California voters by the Governor's strategists. This pamphlet sought to create the very definite impression that Rockefeller had won the unqualified endorsement of all the other major Republican Presidential aspirants. His picture appeared with smaller photographs of Nixon, Lodge, Romney and Scranton under the heading, "These Men Stand Together on the Party's Principles." On the facing page was a solitary photo of Senator Goldwater and the head, "This Man Stands Outside—by Himself." The text unmistakably linked Lodge, Nixon, Romney, Scranton—and even Stassen—to Rockefeller's candidacy and made them appear as members of a united front against Goldwater. "Which Do You Want," the lead headline asked, "a Leader? Or a Loner?"

Like so many of Rockefeller's desperation tactics throughout 1963-64, this one backfired badly. He might safely claim the support of Cabot Lodge, who indeed had permitted his Grindle-Goldberg team to rush to Rockefeller's aid after Oregon. But he had failed to reckon with the personal ambitions of Scranton, the neutrality of Nixon and the independent nature of George Romney.

Romney was the first to repudiate Rockefeller's spurious claim to his allegiance. He sent a telegram to Bill Knowland in California forthrightly stating, "I am neither supporting nor opposing any candidate." Almost simultaneously, Nixon issued a statement to the press disclaiming any connection with Rockefeller's campaign.

On the urging of our embattled band on Wilshire Boulevard, Senator Goldwater sent one of the pamphlets to Bill Scranton in Harrisburg and asked him if Rockefeller "does in fact represent you in California." Scranton replied forthwith. In a special-delivery letter dated May 26 he sounded quite unlike the same Bill Scranton who a little more than two weeks later threw himself into the last desperate assault on Senator Goldwater's candidacy:

Dear Barry:
   I have not been asked by anyone for permission to include my name or picture in this literature. Since I am not a candidate, no one "represents" me in California or anywhere else. . . .
   My one overriding interest is for unity within the Republican Party. Consequently, I have refused to join "Stop Goldwater, Stop Rockefeller, or Stop Anybody" movements.
   I believe that a unified Republican Party can score a resounding victory this Fall. . . . We cannot do this, however, unless we are unified and strong.
   With warm personal regards,

Most sincerely,
Bill /s/
William W. Scranton

Rockefeller's attempt to claim the endorsement of prominent Republicans without even bothering to consult them had completely collapsed. But let no one say that the Governor of New York gives up easily. Ignoring the repudiation of Nixon, Romney and Scranton, his fellow Liberals next contrived to make it appear that no less a personage than Dwight D. Eisenhower was, if not openly endorsing Rockefeller, at least thoroughly opposed to his adversary in the California primary, Barry Goldwater. This little piece of legerdemain was pulled off in a most curious manner and, to be perfectly fair, I don't believe Governor Rockefeller had as much to do with instigating it as many people think.

Actually, the magician who pulled this rabbit out of the hat was a much more devious Houdini. Some say it was Walter Thayer, president of the *New York Herald-Tribune.* Although Thayer was not exactly a Rockefeller partisan, having lately switched his allegiance from Nixon to Scranton, he was determined to halt Goldwater in California. Somehow, Thayer managed to get General Eisenhower to sign an article giving a detailed description of the type of man he believed the Republicans should nominate for the Presidency. The article, carried under a banner headline on the front page of the *Herald-Tribune* on May 25, seemed to support all the things Nelson Rockefeller stood for. By inference, at least, it appeared to rebuff Barry Goldwater.

To make certain that Rockefeller got maximum mileage from the Eisenhower article, the *Herald-Tribune* waived its copyright and released it simultaneously to the wire services and even to its chief competitor, the *New York Times,* which was delighted to carry it on its own front page. Just so no one would miss the point, the *Herald-Tribune* also ran an interpretive sidebar by its syndicated columnist, Roscoe Drummond, emphasizing that the former President's hypothetical description of the ideal Republican candidate was an outright repudiation of Senator Goldwater.

Goldwater, campaigning in California, tried to put the best face he could on this sad bit of business by forthrightly endorsing the views General Eisenhower had expressed in the article. But later in the day his sense of humor, which sometimes flashed in unpredictable ways, got the best of him. Rising to speak at a rally at Shasta College, he turned his profile to the crowd and displayed a long arrow sticking out of his back. The audience roared and newspapers from coast to coast ran a photograph of the scene which set the whole country laughing.

Rockefeller, however, soon found the whole incident terribly unfunny. Once again, our GOP "moderates" had overplayed their hand. When Ike read Drummond's column and the flood of other interpretive stories and editorials labeling his article anti-Goldwater, he hit the ceiling. George Humphrey, his former Secretary of the Treasury and one of his closest friends, telephoned him from Cleveland and in effect told Ike that if he wished to maintain his neutral stance in the party's nominating process he had better disavow the widely held interpretations of his article. On the following Monday, the day before the California primary, General Eisenhower held a press conference in New York. Angrily, he told the assembled reporters, "You people tried to read Goldwater out of the party, I didn't."

The timing couldn't have been better. Instead of trooping to the polls under the illusion that the former President of the United States was supporting Nelson Rockefeller, the California voters were impressed at the most fortuitous possible moment that Eisenhower was doing no such thing. I am sure that many thousands of them now saw that the whole incident was a trick designed to fool them, which it certainly was. And they rightly resented it when they reached the voting booths.

Another major crisis in the waning days of the California campaign was unfortunately not as easy to handle. Senator Goldwater's experience with the press distortions of his statement on NATO commanders controlling nuclear weapons had forced him to shy away from any mention of atomic weapons. But on a program telecast on Sunday, May 24, an innocuous mention of this subject was again exploded into a major issue. Goldwater appeared on ABC's "Issues and Answers" with commentator Howard K. Smith. During a discussion of the Vietnamese war, Smith asked the Senator how Communist supply lines from the north over the jungle trails along the Laotian border could be cut. The following was Goldwater's reply:

Well, it is not as easy as it sounds, because these are not trails that are out in the open. I have been in the rain forests of Burma and South China. You are perfectly safe wandering through them as far as an enemy hurting you. There have been several suggestions made. I don't think we would use any of them. But defoliation of the forests by low yield atomic weapons could well be done. When you remove the foliage, you remove the cover.

Unbelievably, both major wire services, which together serve virtually every newspaper, news magazine, radio and television station in the country, ran stories claiming or broadly hinting that Senator Goldwater had called for the use of nuclear weapons in the Vietnamese War. UPI later retracted its story; but, of course, the retraction was hardly noticed.

Once more, Goldwater had fallen into the fatal trap of assuming that people would understand as much as he did about highly complicated defense technology. It seemed evident to him that "low yield atomic weapons" meant weapons that yield very little fatal fallout. And, in the context of the discussion, it was equally evident that he was not suggesting the use of such weapons to kill human beings, but merely to strip leaves from trees so our fighting men could find the enemy and interdict his supply routes. As a matter of fact he had said on the program that he believed that this job could be accomplished "in a way that would not endanger life." Moreover, he had of course clearly stated that he did not think we would use the method he went on to describe.

However, the Senator once again failed to reckon with the general lack of understanding about a subject that has been forged into the most emotionally charged issue of our age by nearly two decades of irresponsible—and often carefully designed—propaganda. This second "nuclear flap" branded him indelibly as an advocate of atomic warfare. Tragically, it was his Republican opponents for the nomination who kept applying the brand long after the news media issued the retractions. By the time he had won the nomination, the terrible burns they had applied so often in searing him with groundless charges of nuclear irresponsibility ultimately proved fatal to his candidacy for the nation's highest office.

The day the pre-taped ABC show was telecast I was suffering the full effects of its fallout at the last Republican National Committee meeting to be held before the San Francisco convention. The meeting informally opened that Sunday afternoon at the Marriott Twin Bridges Motel just across the Potomac from Washington. Almost everyone else was in California and Denison Kitchel was holed up in his Washington apartment. I was left to work the meeting with Ione Harrington, Tom Van Sickle and Jim Mack, the former executive secretary of the Milwaukee County Republican Committee who had recently joined our team.

From the standpoint of Presidential nominations, this final session prior to the convention is always the most important meeting the National Committee holds. It is the one in which all arrangements for the convention are completed, and all the assignments made to the key jobs from convention chairman on down to chief page. In a tight convention these posts can be critical. If they are held by people hostile to your candidate, they can conceivably make the difference between victory and defeat.

As a result of what now loomed as a Goldwater defeat in California, I did not find myself quite so magnetic as I had been at previous National Committee meetings over the last two years.[2] I was amused to see some of those who had been devotedly courting me in the past now casting covetous glances at the representatives of other candidates. Scranton's team was getting quite a play and even Rockefeller's men were the objects of little political flirtations.

[2] Some of the polls had Rockefeller winning California by as much as 57 per cent of the total vote. The Harris Poll pared it down to 55 per cent the day before the primary.

Rockefeller had some of his key men working the meeting, including George Hinman, Jack Wells and his regional directors, Larry Lindemer, Jean Tool and Tom Stevens. I must say they did a great job for their candidate. Aided by their aura of confidence in what seemed to be Rockefeller's impending California victory, they managed to pick off several of the key convention assignments. The chief doorkeeper's post, which controls the flow of spectators to the galleries, went to Art Richardson, a Young Republican leader in New York. Bob Carter, a neutral, was unopposed for sergeant-at-arms, the man who maintains order on the convention floor, but his chief assistant turned out to be Sandy Lanker, a member of Nelson Rockefeller's personal campaign staff.

I wasn't too unhappy about some of the assignments. I knew that we would have enough delegate votes, no matter what happened in California, to demonstrate where the real power lay. Some of the people in these jobs would come around. I remember that our National Committee allies opposed the appointment of Mike Gill, Mamie Eisenhower's nephew, as chief page. But Mike eventually proved most cooperative and did a bangup job for us in San Francisco.

However, the Rockefeller forces scored a real coup when they slipped in Mark Hatfield, the engaging young Governor of Oregon, as the keynote speaker and temporary chairman of the national convention. Not long before, Senator Goldwater, Kitchel and I had had lunch with the National Chairman, Bill Miller, and he had agreed to reserve these assignments for himself.

I had just arrived at the Marriott and was setting things up in our Goldwater hospitality suite when someone came in and told me that Miller wasn't going to be the keynoter. I went straight up to the National Chairman's reception and cornered Miller. "Bill," I said, "are the signals still on?"

He raised his eyebrows. "Haven't you gotten the word?"

"If there's been a change," I said, "I haven't heard of it."

Miller took me by the arm and we went off by ourselves. "I called Barry," he said. "I told him I just can't do this keynote speech. I don't have time to write it with all the other things I have to do before the convention. Barry agreed with me."

"Who *is* it going to be?" I asked.

Miller hesitated a moment. "Well," he replied, "Mark Hatfield, he will be temporary chairman and keynoter, and Thrus Morton will be permanent chairman."

Since we had previously agreed to Senator Morton, that part of it wasn't news. But Hatfield's appointment was something else again. I had great respect for the distinguished Governor of Oregon, but he had never made any bones about his allegiance to Nelson Rockefeller. A keynote speaker can exert great influence on a convention, particularly a tight one, which the San Francisco conclave might have become if Goldwater lost California. I have never determined exactly why Bill Miller deserted us at this point, unless he smelled a defeat for the Senator and figured he had better have some irons in a few other fires.

When I left Miller I called Kitchel at his apartment and asked him why the signals had been switched on the keynoter. He said he knew nothing about it. Since Goldwater was on a plane en route to the Coast I couldn't reach him to impress the importance of his designating someone to oppose Hatfield.

Without a candidate for keynoter we were left adrift and by the next morning, when the Senator called me, it was too late to act. The first thing he asked me was how things were going at the National Committee meeting. I replied, "We're getting the hell beat out of us. I guess you know by now that Hatfield has the keynoter's job sewed up."

"Oh, don't worry about it," the Senator drawled. "It isn't worth it."

It was too late to debate him, so I completed my report and we rang off. That night, after most of the convention assignments had been decided on, I ran into George Hinman and Jack Wells. We had a drink together and Jack said, "Clif, give us a call on June 3rd. We want you to work with us." I laughed and said I thought it would be more appropriate if they called me. Then I went downtown to our Connecticut Avenue headquarters to finish supervising an operation I had started a week before.

I had already sent out an alarm to our state chairmen urging them to get people in their states to write letters to friends and relatives in California asking them to vote for Senator Goldwater. I suggested that they instruct the people to go back over their Christmas card lists and address books to refresh their memories. And I emphasized that the people should draft their own letters, stating their personal reasons for backing Goldwater and adding whatever touches they thought might be helpful in swinging votes.

It was obvious that thousands of people in every other state had connections in California, which since 1940 had drawn nearly ten million new residents from the Northeast, the South and the Midwest in the greatest of all American migrations. It would certainly do no harm for these transplanted citizens to know that there were many, many friends and kinsfolk back home supporting Barry Goldwater.

In many communities Goldwater volunteers organized letter-writing bees. People assembled in homes, church basements, firehouses—anywhere they could set up tables and chairs. One little group in Kansas penned more than 250 letters in a single evening. I remember they phoned me after midnight when they were finished to tell me that they had also raised $200 among themselves for the Senator's California campaign and would I please tell them where I wanted the money sent. One friend of mine in upstate New York, Albert Winslow, who was our Goldwater chairman in Orange County, personally wrote 76 letters to friends and business acquaintances in California. I felt that the letters from Republicans in New York State were the best of all because they showed Californians that Governor Rockefeller was by no means the Presidential choice of all his own constituents.

The efforts of all these thousands of people around the country and of our hardworking California volunteers notwithstanding, Senator Goldwater was undeniably up to his neck in trouble going into the final week of the primary campaign. After the nuclear flap and Dwight Eisenhower's article I sensed that he had already resigned himself to defeat. On top of everything else, the Rockefeller headquarters in Los Angeles claimed that it was receiving phone calls threatening the Governor's life, and the tired old slogan of "right-wing fanatics" was again revived. None of these calls was ever substantiated but they got a big play in the press. Unaccountably, an apparently genuine assassination threat against Goldwater was buried on the back pages or ignored entirely. But the FBI took it seriously enough to urge the Senator to cancel his final rally at Knott's Berry Farm, where the threatened attack was to have taken place on Sunday, May 31. The rally was held up for half an hour, but in the end the Senator insisted on speaking, and, with police and FBI men fanned out through the crowd, the threat was not carried out.

On this same weekend a crisis of a very different kind descended upon the Rockefeller camp. Shortly after four o'clock in the afternoon of Saturday, May 30—less than seventy hours before the primary polls opened in California—Happy Rockefeller gave birth to a baby boy in New York Hospital. She named it Nelson Rockefeller, Jr. Suddenly the old issue of the Governor's divorce and re-marriage, almost forgotten in the turmoil of recent months, was again impressed upon the public conscience.

Many political observers claim that the birth of the Rockefeller child reversed a tide of victory that was running for the Governor in California. Actually, I don't believe its impact was nearly so great as that. In fact, the day before the baby's birth, which I had no way of knowing was imminent, I held one of my regular background sessions for the press in Washington and confided to the reporters that Goldwater would beat Rockefeller in the primary by about 50,000 votes. For the record, of course, I claimed a victory of much greater magnitude, because I never believe in discounting the psychological importance of behaving like a winner no matter how close or hopeless an election may appear.

The reporters were packed into my office for this session, and if they were skeptical of my confidential prediction of a 50,000-vote win for Goldwater, they downright scoffed when I told them that the Senator would be nominated even if he lost California. Not even Goldwater believed this. He and Kitchel always said that if he went down in California that would be the end of it. But I knew our delegates better than Barry. They would never surrender. There were already enough of them to at least deadlock the convention indefinitely. And there would be more of them before we got to San Francisco.

I was happy, of course, that my thesis did not have to be tested. On Tuesday, June 2, our California volunteers were out en masse. Armed with detailed maps and information kits containing the names and addresses of known Goldwater supporters circled in red, they made certain that these people got to the polls. If they found no one at home, they went back—two, three, four or more times—until they had rounded up virtually every citizen who could cast a ballot for Barry Goldwater.

I took the returns at our Washington headquarters. The polls closed an hour earlier in Los Angeles than in the San Francisco area and within twenty minutes after they shut down in the City of the Angels the CBS computers forecast a Goldwater victory. The final vote was 1,089,-133 for the Senator to 1,030,180 for Governor Rockefeller. Goldwater had taken the big prize—all 86 of California's delegates—with 51.3 per cent of the vote cast. His winning margin of 58,953 was in the range that I had predicted the previous Friday.

The volunteers had come through, as I knew they would. They had assured Barry Goldwater the Republican Presidential nomination on the first ballot. Their work was done, at least until the fall campaign began. But I had to get up the next morning and finish preparations for the state conventions that still lay ahead. I didn't want any letup in our delegate quest. I could not content myself now with just a victory at the convention. I wanted our candidate to win big—bigger than anyone had ever won in a contested convention before.

CHAPTER 31

COUNTDOWN V—THE LAST LAP

SCARCELY NOTICED in all the sound and fury emanating from California the first two days of June was the fact that Barry Goldwater picked up 29 delegates in three other states—Nebraska, New York and South Dakota—that same Monday and Tuesday. With those 29 he went over the top. Although we publicly claimed only 500 delegates on Wednesday morning, my private list now numbered 665—ten more than the Senator needed to win the nomination.

California assured Goldwater a first ballot victory at San Francisco. But he would have won on that initial ballot—or, at the very most, on the second or third ballot—even without California's big bloc of delegates.

Many newsmen and politicians have debated me on this, but it is really a matter of simple arithmetic. Subtract California's 86 votes from the 665 in my private book on June 3 and you get 579. Then add to those 579 the bare minimum of 100 delegates we would have pulled out of the remaining state conventions and you have 679—two dozen more than the 655 votes necessary to nominate.

The experts all say that if Goldwater had lost California our already declared delegates would have melted away and we would never have won enough in the remaining states to offset the desertions. But they are thinking in terms of old-fashioned delegates—delegates who were often easily swayed by the promise of a job or a fat business contract.

Our delegates were a brand-new breed. Nothing could shake them. I cannot conceive of any large-scale desertions we could have suffered.

For one thing, many of these delegates were publicly pledged to Senator Goldwater by June 3. In many cases it would have been impossible for them to change their votes even if they were of a mind to do so—and almost none of them were. Moreover, the overwhelming majority of those I counted in my private book who were not pledged were just as solid as those who were legally bound.

As for the states that still had to elect delegates, they included such Goldwater bastions as Alabama, Colorado, Montana, New Mexico, Utah and Washington. I could count a hard core 90 delegates out of these alone, and I was certain of adding at least 20 more from Connecticut, Idaho, Maryland, Minnesota, Missouri and Virginia. Actually, we got twice as many new delegates after June 2 from these last named states, but I was allowing here for the maximum attrition that would have followed a defeat in California.

At the very worst, we would have gone into the convention with 600 hard core Goldwater delegates. With that kind of a start it would have been no great feat to add 55 more on the second ballot—and believe me, I knew where we could lay our hands on at least that many more.

My biggest problem, I believe, would have been the candidate. He had all but conditioned himself to toss in the sponge if he faltered in California. It is possible that one of the other candidates might have gotten to him—most likely Dick Nixon—and convinced him that he had better hand over his delegates in the interest of party unity. But if Goldwater had decided to deliver his bloc to anyone other than Nixon he would have had a major revolt on his hands. He might even have had great difficulty turning them over to Nixon.

However, all this became purely hypothetical after the great victory in California. We were now at the end of the primary election trail. Only fourteen state conventions lay ahead. And despite the constant sniping of the press and pundits at Goldwater's supposed lack of popular appeal at the polls, the Senator had won all but two of the primaries he had entered. Significantly, he had amassed nearly 2,150,000 votes— 372,000 more than John F. Kennedy had received in the same number of primaries in 1960. He had done this as a member of a minority party whose total registration was many millions less than Mr. Kennedy's Democrats. And he had done it in the face of bitter, often vicious opposition from his Republican opponents.

The last three primaries were held on June 2. Besides California, there was one in New York and one in South Dakota. The day before we had formally added ten more delegates at the state convention in Nebraska.

In South Dakota we picked up 14 and in New York I privately counted a minimum of five, with a strong possibility of getting six or seven.

Practically all of the state Republican leadership was pulling for Goldwater in South Dakota, including Senator Karl Mundt, the state's most popular political figure. Our chairman, Roy Houck of Pierre, and his two co-chairmen, Jack Gibson and Mrs. Vi Byg, both of Sioux Falls, had the state well organized. In the primary there were actually two slates, one officially committed to Goldwater and the other uncommitted but almost as solidly behind him.

Although the primary was not binding, we had six delegates firmly pledged and Senator Mundt was so thoroughly committed to Goldwater that there was no doubt we would have gotten the remaining eight even if California had gone down the drain.

The handful of delegates we won in New York were much harder come by, but they represented a great psychological victory. Governor Rockefeller had set the date for the primary in his home state to coincide with California's in the hope of sweeping 178 delegates in a single day— 86 in California and 92 in New York. But he reckoned without the ability of our strong Goldwater for President Committee, headquartered in my old Suite 3505 on 42nd Street, to crack his supposedly solid front.

We had a great team in New York. Vincent L. Leibell, Jr., a highly respected attorney, was our chairman in the metropolitan area and Elmer R. Weil of Buffalo, an old associate of mine, was the upstate chairman. Mason B. Starring III, our state finance chairman, and W. Russell Pickering, the Goldwater Committee treasurer, did a fine job of raising funds under the most difficult possible circumstances and Rita Bree served, in her unfailingly efficient manner, as campaign coordinator. We also had a strong assist from Dr. Anthony T. Bouscaren, a political science professor at Le Moyne College in Syracuse.

Vince Leibell won a delegate seat himself on June 2 in a tough contest in Queens. He later said that he went to San Francisco with the best credentials of any delegate there. It took a court order to verify his primary victory, which the Rockefeller forces attempted to snatch away from him.

We had two other publicly committed Goldwater delegates out of New York—Vincent Walsh from Nassau County on Long Island and Perry R. Trimmer from Buffalo. Perry's running mate in their district, Willard C. Allis, lost by the unlikely margin of 38 votes. In addition, two Congressmen who were widely known as Goldwater supporters—Steven B. Derounian and Frank J. Becker of Nassau—won delegate seats. Thus, we could count five New York votes on the first ballot. If it had gone to a second, I had one more firmly lined up and was assured of several more.

On June 6, the Saturday following these last primaries, we brought in

49 more Goldwater delegates at the state conventions in Alabama,
Colorado and New Mexico. Alabama was perhaps the easiest of all the
states in our long pre-convention countdown. John Grenier, the Republican state chairman, was our Goldwater for President coordinator in the
Southern states. His Alabama co-chairman was Mrs. Virginia Garrett of
Montgomery. Thanks to them, and to a hard-working team of vigorous
young politicians that included my friend Jim Martin, the 1962
senatorial candidate, there was never any question about who would
win Alabama's 20 delegates.

Colorado presented some difficulties, largely due to Governor Love's
inclination to support Nelson Rockefeller. But our state chairman,
Herbert F. Koether, and his co-chairman, Mrs. Jo Anne Gray, both of
Denver, ultimately managed to bring 15 of Colorado's 18 delegates into
the Goldwater fold.

New Mexico's 14 votes were delivered to Goldwater as the result
of one of the most brilliant organizing operations we mounted in any
state. The man chiefly responsible was my old Suite 3505 ally, Anderson
Carter. A big, soft-spoken young rancher, Andy had served in the
State Legislature as a Democrat. He had been regarded as one of his
former party's most promising political personalities in New Mexico.
But in the early part of the Kennedy Administration he finally realized,
as many another Democrat did during that period, that there was no
sense trying to work with a party that had long ago repudiated its most
cherished beliefs.

Many Democrats hang on in the belief that the only way the tide can
be turned is from within their party. But as events have abundantly
proved, this belief is probably the greatest delusion of this century—
a forlorn wisp doomed since the Roosevelt years and eventually bound to
destroy the philosophical integrity of all who persist in holding it. Instead of turning the tide, the Democrats of good will who have clung to
their party's sullied banner have merely aided and abetted the advances
of the Leftist manipulators by lending their names and reputations to a
cause which is slowly destroying the America they love.

Fortunately, Andy Carter, whose family had been registered Democrats for generations, saw this clearly and the Republican Party in New
Mexico won an important convert. As our Goldwater state chairman,
Andy and his associates, including Mrs. Wynema Kroggel of Socorra,
the co-chairman, had been laying the groundwork for a Goldwater victory
at the June 6 state convention for nearly two years. They had considerable opposition from the Rockefeller forces, which spent large sums in
New Mexico in a vain attempt to crack Barry Goldwater's solid front
in the Southwest. And in Los Alamos, the site of the vast federal atomic
research facilities, Andy and his team successfully stopped a surge to

Cabot Lodge mounted by a group of scientists who, alas, were mostly Democrats and therefore not eligible to vote in the precinct and district Republican caucuses which named the delegates to the state convention.

In many ways, our New Mexican operation was a model of what transpired in several dozen states. Andy Carter refused to let his people be trapped into negative attacks on rival Republican Presidential candidates. They were pro-Goldwater, not anti-anyone. The Rockefeller and Lodge groups, on the other hand, concentrated on loosing bitter assaults on Barry Goldwater.

After that Saturday there was no longer even the faintest shadow of doubt about Senator Goldwater's ability to sweep the national convention. But my troops kept right on working and over the following weekend we corralled another 68 new delegates to bring my private tally up to almost 800 convention votes. There were no less than eight state conventions that week and all but one of them came off exactly as we had planned.

The Indiana convention, held on Tuesday, June 9, merely made the results of the primary official. Goldwater got all 32 delegates. If we had lost California we might have dropped half a dozen of these, but no more. Weeks before, Ione Harrington and Bob Matthews had assured me that we had an unshakable hard core of 26 in Indiana and I had made a note of it in my book.

In Idaho, Governor Bob Smylie, who had been casting about for a way to support Nelson Rockefeller, got the message after we beat Governor Anderson at the Kansas state convention. Thus, we sailed home at the Idaho convention on June 12 and 13 with all 14 delegates pledged to Senator Goldwater. James D. McClary, a Boise construction company executive and our state chairman, managed the whole show without causing any serious splits in the Republican Party and he was ably aided by Mrs. Blanche Evans, the popular Boise housewife who served as his co-chairman.

Another Idaho housewife, Mrs. Gwyn Barnett, deserves special commendation for her work on behalf of Senator Goldwater. Gwyn was the Republican National Committeewoman from her state and she remained steadfast to her principles despite persuasive pressures applied by the Governor and certain members of the regular Republican state organization. In fact, these pressures only made Gwyn all the more determined to win Idaho for Goldwater and she traveled tirelessly up and down that vast state winning converts in cities and hamlets and inaccessible ranches.

In Missouri, our people had to show them, and that they did. Jerry Harkins of Kansas City was our Goldwater chairman, and with the expert assistance of Mrs. Nell Reed, widow of U.S. Senator James A.

Reed, he steered his operation around a number of dangerous shoals and emerged with all but one of Missouri's 24 delegates. Most of these had been previously elected at the district level so at the state convention on June 13 it was simply a matter of certifying them and picking four at-large delegates.

The same largely held true in Virginia, where we had already won most of the 20 district delegates. The convention selected ten more who, in all but one case, were favorable to Goldwater. Jack Middleton, our state chairman, had done a masterful job, particularly in the counties close to Washington where there was substantial opposition to the Senator from resident federal employees. We ended up with 29 of the 30 Virginia votes, which was just exactly the way Jack told me I could count them.

In the state of Washington, Luke Williams and his fellow "amateurs" came through beautifully. Having swamped their Liberal opponents in the precincts for more than a year, they had little difficulty wrapping up 22 of Washington's 24 delegates in the convention that weekend. Luke had promised me a bedrock 18 even if we lost California. He was able to deliver an additional four as a result of that victory.

Across the continent in Connecticut, Newman Marsilius, the Bridgeport businessman who was serving as Goldwater state chairman, and Mrs. Louise Olson of Old Saybrook managed to snatch four delegates from the state convention at Hartford. They had substantial help from another 3505 ally, John Lupton, a former advertising man who got himself elected to the State Senate and was rapidly becoming a power in Connecticut politics. Winning four solid Goldwater delegates was a considerable feat in a state which is wedged between Nelson Rockefeller's New York and Cabot Lodge's Massachusetts, to say nothing of the fact that it was also the birthplace of one William Scranton, who ultimately received Connecticut's other dozen votes.

Minnesota was the one state where we anticipated trouble over that June weekend. I flew to Minneapolis to lend a hand to Bill McFadzean, a charter member of my original group. Bill and his state co-chairman, Mrs. Marg Viehman, were faced with the problem of winning Goldwater delegates without ripping apart the regular Republican organization, which had rallied around the favorite-son candidacy of Dr. Walter Judd, the former Congressman and hero of many conservatives across the country. We had already taken six delegates in district races and after an agonizing two days at the state convention we added two more at-large.

It was on this same weekend that Bill Scranton at long last revealed himself as an avowed candidate for the Republican nomination. Flying from Harrisburg on Friday morning, June 12, with his family and a small contingent of aides, Scranton made his announcement at the Maryland state convention in Baltimore that day.[1]

In a speech delivered in the packed ballroom of the Lord Baltimore Hotel, Scranton gave a fine sample of the vituperative attacks which he continued to hurl at his old "friend" Barry Goldwater for the next five weeks. Without mentioning the Senator by name, but leaving no doubt as to whom he meant, Scranton charged that Goldwater's nomination would destroy "all hope of a Republican victory in the fall."

Invoking the hallowed memory of Abraham Lincoln, Theodore Roosevelt and Dwight D. Eisenhower, Scranton claimed that the Republican Party would "send down to defeat good men and good women who stand ready to carry our banner in the several states . . . if we let an exclusion-minded minority dominate our platform and choose our candidates."

It apparently never occurred to Bill Scranton that he now represented a minority in the Republican Party, a minority that was a thousand times more "exclusion-minded" than all but a few of the people who backed Barry Goldwater. Nor did it occur to him that he was now placing himself in opposition to the real majority within the GOP. Actually, these people—the conservatives of our party—had always been in the majority among the rank-and-file. But their views had long been ignored by the apostles of expediency. In Senator Goldwater they had found a voice, and the thousands of individuals who had taken part in the organizing effort begun by my original group back in 1961 had assured them that this voice would not be denied.

Governor Scranton's entry into the 1964 nominating race was more than an exercise in futility. It was the last desperate stand of a group which had dominated the Republican Party for nearly three decades. Scranton's eleventh-hour bid, and the tactics he employed along his frenetic trail to San Francisco, proved once and for all that the central motivating drive of this group was rule-or-ruin.

Many professed surprise at Bill Scranton's announcement of his candidacy. But the only surprise it held for me was the lateness of the hour he chose. I had been expecting him to move out into the open ever since he placed a telephone call to Pittsburgh a few hours after the assassination of President Kennedy on November 22, 1963.

[1] Goldwater got six delegates out of Maryland, Scranton 13 and Rockefeller one.

CHAPTER 32

THE "RELUCTANT" CANDIDATE

THE BIG PUSH to obtain the Republican nomination for William Warren Scranton actually began not on June 12, 1964 at the Maryland convention, but on the day John F. Kennedy was shot to death in Dallas. Scranton had, of course, become a favorite-son "non-candidate" some weeks before. However, until November 22 he continued to tiptoe softly behind the scenes, "permitting himself," as the press put it, to be wooed by his fellow leaders of the Eastern Establishment. Occasionally, as at the GOP rally in Hershey, Pennsylvania on October 10, 1963, he indulged in a little discreet sniping at Goldwater's flanks. But in the main he showed little disposition to stand up against the rising Goldwater tide.

With the assassination came an abrupt change in the Scranton strategy. During December, some elements of the press, encouraged by Scranton's aides in Harrisburg, began a massive campaign to promote his candidacy. By January, Scranton's face was frowning thoughtfully from the covers of almost every mass-circulation magazine. The *Saturday Evening Post,* perhaps the most virulently anti-Goldwater publication of them all, devoted five pages of homey pictures and flattering text to the little-known Governor of Pennsylvania in its January 18 issue. Accompanying the story was a full-page column by Stewart Alsop headed "The Logical Candidate." In it, Alsop set the tone for all the countless articles and editorials that were ground out on Scranton during the next five months.

Although most of the pundits were calling Scranton a "Republican Kennedy," Alsop said that he "is more nearly a Republican Stevenson —a reflective man, oddly reserved, highly intelligent, *but seemingly without ambition or deep political passion.*" (Italics added.)

It was a source of never-ending wonderment to me that the press invariably pictured Bill Scranton as a reluctant candidate, devoid of any political ambition. There are many knowledgeable people in Pennsylvania who will swear that Scranton started running for the Presidency the day he was elected Governor in 1962. There are some, in fact, who insist that his Presidential aspirations date back to his boyhood when his mother, a wealthy dowager and Republican women's leader, allegedly started pointing him towards the White House.

But Pennsylvanians first detected a new earnestness about Bill Scranton's approach to high political office during his gubernatorial campaign. One incident stands out as an illustration.

As the 1962 election neared, Scranton, a one-term Congressman with brief experience in a minor State Department post, seemed virtually assured of victory over his Democrat opponent, the rambunctious outgoing Mayor of Philadelphia, Richardson Dilworth. However, Scranton's running mate, veteran Congressman James Van Zandt, was having a much tougher time of it in his bid for the U.S. Senate seat held by Joe Clark.

On October 25, 1962, Scranton and Van Zandt came into Pittsburgh for the windup rally of the campaign. Allegheny County was a pivotal area in the election. Its new Republican chairman, Paul Hugus, and the rally organizer, Ben Chapple, who later served as our Goldwater chieftain in western Pennsylvania, pulled out all the stops to make the rally a success. They rounded up movie star James Stewart, a native of the region, to act as master of ceremonies, and former President Eisenhower agreed to make the final speech of the evening.

The rally was held under the massive steel dome of Pittsburgh's new civic arena, which had never been filled before. Yet despite a violent rainstorm and icy winds, it was jammed that night with nearly 14,000 wildly cheering Republicans scenting the first big GOP victory in the state in 12 years.

Scranton and Van Zandt were to have equal time on the televised portion of the rally and both had been asked to time their speeches down to the minute. But something went wrong. Scranton, the first speaker, ignored the frantic wavings of the television crew and spoke a full seven minutes over his allotted time. Following him, Van Zandt was forced to slice his speech in half so as not to cut into General Eisenhower's television appearance. Needless to say, Van Zandt's performance was woefully disappointing and it undoubtedly contributed in part to his defeat at the polls just 12 days later. He trailed the ticket badly in the western counties and could not pick up enough votes elsewhere to overcome the big Democratic majority the Bill Green machine turned out in Philadelphia.

The incident revived rumors of a deal between the Bill Scranton-Hugh Scott wing of the GOP and Democrat bosses Green and David Lawrence, the outgoing Governor and former Mayor of Pittsburgh. It was no secret that Green and Lawrence were anxious to rid themselves of the troublesome Dilworth, but whether they actually threw the election to Scranton in exchange for keeping Clark's Senate seat for the Democrats was never proved.

Not many people were privy to the little by-play which upset Van Zandt's television appearance in Pittsburgh because hardly anyone in the audience knew that both candidates were supposed to get equal time. But those who did know later cited the incident as evidence that Bill Scranton had already begun his covert campaign for the 1964 Republican Presidential nomination.

Beginning in the fall of 1963 Scranton was the honored guest at a series of private luncheons in Philadelphia arranged by Thomas McCabe, chairman of the board of Scott Paper Company. These luncheons were attended by many of the men the press still conceived to be the real leaders of the Republican Party, and it was obvious that the fledgling Governor of Pennsylvania was drawing closer to the so-called "kingmakers."

It is difficult for me to believe that Governor Scranton could have taken his chances very seriously until John F. Kennedy's murder seemed to halt Barry Goldwater's headlong drive towards the nomination. But from that point on he took them very seriously indeed.

Within hours after the President's assassination, Scranton telephoned Paul Hugus in Pittsburgh. Nine days earlier Hugus had been one of the large group of prominent Pennsylvania Republicans who had announced the organization of our Draft Goldwater affiliate in the western half of the state. As GOP chairman in Pennsylvania's second most populous county, Hugus was rightly regarded as the statewide symbol of Goldwater leadership.

It was widely reported in the press that Hugus phoned Scranton first to sue for peace after the tragedy in Dallas. But Paul insists he had not even thought of talking politics with the Governor in the midst of a national emergency. Nonetheless, when the phone rang in his office and the Governor invited him to Harrisburg for "a little talk," Paul strongly suspected what was on Scranton's mind. When they met a few days later, his suspicions were verified.

Scranton demanded that Hugus line up in support of his favorite-son candidacy. Since this would have meant that he would have to repudiate Senator Goldwater, Hugus refused. Instead, he proposed that the Governor get together with him and other leading Republicans and draw up a "harmony slate" of delegates which would give all the various groups fair representation on Pennsylvania's big 64-vote delegation. But Scranton would have no part of that. It wasn't harmony he wanted. It was control—total and complete control.

The Governor had done a complete about-face from his position of a year before, when he had piously insisted that he was in favor of letting delegates to the convention "decide for themselves" which candidate they would back. The following is an exchange that took place between Governor Scranton and Jack Bell of the Associated Press on a "Meet the Press" television show in December, 1962:

SCRANTON: I have no intention of being a favorite-son candidate. I would like to have it be as free, wide and open as it possibly could be, sir.

BELL: If you are not a favorite-son candidate, then, in which direction would you point the Pennsylvania delegation?

SCRANTON: I have perhaps an unusual theory about this. I feel very strongly that one of the mistakes that we have made in the past is to try and tell everyone how they should vote with regard to a national convention. My own personal opinion, at least at this time, subject to qualification and better thinking, is that we should give an opportunity to the people who are elected delegates to decide for themselves whom they prefer and then vote it that way. This would mean that we would have a split delegation, sir.

BELL: Do you mean you are going to introduce democracy into the proceedings of the Pennsylvania Republican organization?

SCRANTON: You sound as if you thought that was one of the queerest things you ever had happen, but I think it can be done, sir.

Within hours after his meeting with Paul Hugus, in December, 1963, Scranton publicly began tightening the patronage tourniquet around Paul's political arteries. All state jobs for Allegheny County, which had been battling a severe unemployment problem for years, were summarily cut off. Hugus, who had been having patronage troubles with the Scranton administration for some time, laughed this off with a quip, "Nothing from nothing still leaves nothing." However, when several of his personal friends, who were also his closest political associates, were fired from their state jobs, Paul began to feel the pinch.

In late January Hugus became even more uneasy when James F. Malone, president of the Pennsylvania Manufacturers Association and a former Allegheny County District Attorney, dropped by Scranton's office for a friendly chat. Although not one of our original Draft Goldwater people in Pennsylvania, Malone had joined the organization's advisory board when it was unveiled after the November election. Now he emerged from a meeting in the Governor's office to announce that Scranton was "in a pretty good position to get the nomination." When Hugus heard this he knew that Malone, who had been one of his chief supporters, had deserted ship.

Prior to the Kennedy assassination a poll of the sixty-seven GOP county chairmen in Pennsylvania had revealed that most of them were for Goldwater. But by the end of January Paul Hugus stood all alone. However, he still had hopes of winning a fair share of delegates for the Senator. His hopes hinged on his own candidacy for delegate from his home district.

Before the February 18 filing deadline for the Pennsylvania primary, Hugus received an overwhelming vote of confidence from his Republican organization. In caucus he won a resounding two-to-one majority over a Scranton nominee for one of the two delegate seats from the 27th Congressional District. By contrast, the 27th's Congressman, James F. Fulton, a thorough-going Liberal and staunch Scranton supporter, barely picked up the minimum number of votes he needed to get on the ballot.

The Scranton forces, however, were not quite finished with Paul Hugus. They entered an unknown Pittsburgh attorney in the primary as a Trojan horse write-in candidate against Hugus. Ostensibly, the attorney was an avowed Goldwater man. But when the Senator telephoned and personally asked him to withdraw from the delegate race he refused.

The stage was now fully set for one of the most ruthless displays of party-splitting politics Pennsylvania had witnessed in a generation. While newspapers and magazines nationally trumpeted Governor Scranton's "deep reluctance" to seek the Presidency, his administration employed every known tactic of bureaucratic pressure to defeat Paul Hugus and obliterate Goldwater support within the Keystone State's GOP.

Under the headline SCRANTON UNDERMINING HUGUS AS DELEGATE, the *Pittsburgh Post-Gazette* reported on April 22, six days before the primary, that Hugus had come under "direct fire" from the Governor's "top aides." Pat O'Neill, the *Post-Gazette's* veteran political writer, gave a straightforward account of how state Republican chairman Craig Truax and William G. Murphy, Scranton's executive secretary, had journeyed to Pittsburgh to personally apply the screws to state employees. "It is a question of loyalty to the Governor," Murphy deserves a loyal delegation to the San Francisco convention in July." blandly told O'Neill. "The Governor is a national figure at this time and

Under the threat of losing their livelihood, the state payrollers turned on Paul Hugus. Predictably, Hugus went down to defeat in the April

28 primary. Six weeks later he was forced out of his post as county chairman and returned to his insurance business. Accepting a promotion from his company, he left Pennsylvania, where he had lived for many years, and went back to the company's home office in Ohio. With his departure, the Republican Party lost the most dynamic and effective organizer it had had in Allegheny County in over twenty years.[1]

A straight down-the-line organization politician, Hugus had been willing to meet Scranton half way on a slate of delegates that would have preserved Republican unity in western Pennsylvania. But the Governor saw Hugus as a stumbling block to his carefully concealed Presidential ambitions. The fact that Paul had helped elect him and had revitalized the Republican Party in the Pittsburgh area, where it had been all but dead since the early 1930s, was conveniently forgotten. The treatment of Paul Hugus was the tipoff as to what Barry Goldwater could expect when Bill Scranton came out swinging for the Republican nomination.

All the while Scranton was taking care of Hugus, he was also maneuvering himself into position with the people everyone still believed made the real decisions about selecting Republican Presidential nominees. On January 17 he attended another of Tom McCabe's intimate luncheons in the board of directors' suite at the Scott Paper Company offices in Philadelphia. Several former top officials of the Eisenhower Administration were on hand, including Ike's old press aide Jim Hagerty, now an ABC network executive; former Secretary of Defense Neil McElroy, the head of Procter & Gamble's soap empire; and onetime White House Counsel David Kendall, now of the Chrysler Corporation.

There were quite a few there from the top echelons of Wall Street, among them Keith Funston, the New York Stock Exchange president; George Leness, head of the nation's largest brokerage firm, Merrill Lynch, Pierce, Fenner and Smith; and Thomas Gates, another of Eisenhower's former Defense Secretaries and now president of the Morgan Guaranty Trust Company. But what interested me most about this luncheon was the presence of Bill Miller, the Republican National

---

[1] In two short years as Republican chairman in Allegheny County, Paul Hugus had chalked up a remarkable record. In the 1962 gubernatorial election he had engineered a 53,000-vote plurality for Scranton against an almost two-to-one Democrat registration majority in his county. A year later he had helped give Allegheny its first Republican district attorney in almost a decade, had come within 6,000 votes of handing the GOP control of the county commission in its best showing in thirty years, and had helped capture several important judgeships and numerous municipal offices that had been owned by the Democrats for two generations. In 1966, by contrast, the GOP lost Allegheny County by 60,000 votes.

Chairman, and two of my old friends who had also held the GOP chairmanship, Meade Alcorn and Len Hall.

From that day forth, while the patently synthetic press buildup of Scranton mounted, I waited for the Governor to make his move. But throughout the spring Scranton dallied. It was not that he was having trouble making up his mind to run, as the press claimed. It was simply that he had no intention of getting knocked off in the mad scramble of the primaries. He could not sidestep Oregon, the only primary in which his name appeared on the ballot. But by remaining aloof from the campaign there he was able to avoid having the press interpret his microscopic 2 per cent vote as the dismal defeat that it was.

Scranton felt that the key to his move for the nomination was former President Eisenhower. Since shortly after the Kennedy assassination he had been attempting to maneuver Ike into supporting him. There were several meetings between them and after each Scranton tried to convey the impression that the General had encouraged him to run. But to his dismay Eisenhower always stopped just short of a public endorsement.

On June 4, two days after Barry Goldwater's victory in California, Scranton decided to try Ike again. He telephoned his mentor, Senator Hugh Scott, and asked him to arrange one final meeting for him with the General. Scranton thought this could best be done through Milton Eisenhower, and Scott agreed.

There was a little delay but finally on Saturday morning, June 6, Scranton made another pilgrimage to Gettysburg. This time he emerged from the meeting to disclose that Eisenhower had strongly requested that he make himself "more available" for the nomination. Then, acting as though a momentous event was in the offing, he prepared to fly to Cleveland for the Governors' Conference which was scheduled to get into full swing the next day.

In Cleveland I had already detected the outline of Scranton's plan. I had been temporarily attached to the staff of Governor Fannin of Arizona so that I could work the conference in an official capacity. Dick Kleindienst, Steve Shadegg and some of our other people were there too. As usual I arrived early, and was not surprised to find Scranton's men swarming all over the Sheraton Hotel on Friday night. Bill Keisling, one of the Governor's young aides, was sporting a goldplated Scranton lapel pin that he told reporters he had worn in his boss's Congressional and gubernatorial campaigns. "I only wear this when I got a candidate," Keisling grinned. "Believe me. I've got a candidate now." Then he and Craig Truax revealed to a select group of reporters that Scranton was going to Gettysburg the next morning.

General Eisenhower was scheduled to stay at Humphrey's home

in Cleveland during the conference, and if anyone could talk Ike out of endorsing Scranton it was his old friend, the former Secretary of the Treasury. Humphrey had an equal interest in saving Ike from embarrassment, rescuing the Republican Party from a dangerous rift and seeing that the nomination went to Goldwater. Humphrey placed a call to Gettysburg on Saturday night. He told his old chief that he hoped he would not be a party to deepening the divisions within the GOP.

By this time, Truax, Keisling and Bill Murphy were putting the finishing touches on their plan to unveil Scranton as a "more available" candidate on nationwide television the following afternoon. Late that night I visited them in their suite. Murphy had been one of my field men in the Citizens for Nixon-Lodge in 1960 and we had become good friends at that time. I knew that he and the others were letting themselves in for a tremendous fall, to say nothing of the painful wrench Scranton's candidacy would cause within the party. I argued with them until nearly six o'clock in the morning in an effort to get them to talk sense to Scranton. The Governor had been my choice for the Vice-Presidential nomination but his entry into the Presidential race at this point, when his campaign could sow deep seeds of dissension, was bound to destroy his chances of becoming Barry Goldwater's running mate.

Without divulging where all the delegates on my private list were hiding I tried to make it clear to the Scranton team that we already had the nomination sewed up. There was nothing Scranton or anyone else could do to stop us. Even Eisenhower's endorsement of Scranton would have no effect upon our delegates. But Craig Truax and the others had been as badly bitten by the Presidential bug as their boss. I left the meeting with the regretful realization that my arguments had failed to make the faintest dent in their ambitions.

Before departing I made one final plea. If Scranton insisted on getting into the race, I urged them to make certain that he conducted a good clean campaign. "Don't let him say anything you all will have trouble living with afterwards," I said. "Fight it out on philosophy if you have to, but not on personalities."

What transpired the following day should have finally convinced them of the futility of their effort. When Scranton arrived at the Sheraton that morning there was a message waiting for him that Eisenhower wanted to talk to him on the phone. When the Governor got through to Gettysburg, the General told him, as gently as possible, that the newspaper reports that he was "encouraging" Scranton's candidacy were completely erroneous. According to *Time*, Ike made it plain that he had no intention of getting involved with a "cabal" to halt Goldwater. He said he wondered if he was "getting old" if he had conveyed that impression, for he certainly hadn't meant to in their meeting the day before.

Scranton's normally sallow complexion is said to have turned about six shades paler, and his face seemed deathly gray when he came downstairs a few minutes later to attend a private breakfast for the Republican governors. As he went into the room where the breakfast meeting was already in progress, some of the reporters wondered if he had taken ill. Later, several of the governors told me what took place in that meeting.

For reasons that still escape me, George Romney had suddenly decided to go on the warpath against Goldwater. Needless to say, he had made his decision independent of Bill Scranton and, since he was definitely not a candidate himself, for quite different motives. Perhaps some of his Liberal friends back in Michigan had sold him a bill of goods that Goldwater's nomination would wreck his chances for re-election as Governor. Whatever his motivation, Romney had charged into the breakfast meeting with a demand that the governors summon Senator Goldwater and request that he "clarify" his stand on a list of key issues.

Goldwater's old friend, Paul Fannin of Arizona, asked Romney the obvious question: What gave the Governor of Michigan, a man who had run in 1962 as a virtual independent, the right to put Senator Goldwater under cross-examination? Nor was Fannin alone in his opposition to Romney's proposal. Even Oregon's Mark Hatfield, loyal Rockefeller man that he was, refused to accept it. In rather blunt terms, Hatfield told Romney, "George, you're six months too late. If you can't add, I'll add it for you. Goldwater's got it. I'm not happy about it. I'm going to vote for Nelson at the convention because I'm bound. But these are the facts, and neither you nor anyone else is going to change them."

Rockefeller, who was there, of course, said very little throughout the whole debate. He had just had his wings clipped by Goldwater in California five days before and I think he was in a rather chastened mood at that point. In fact, the only governor who backed Romney's demand was Scranton. But Mark Hatfield quickly shut him up too.

"Nelson has been working his head off day and night for the past six months, while both you and George remained gloriously silent," Hatfield stated. "Any stop-Goldwater movement now by you eleventh-hour warriors hasn't got a chance. My considered advice to both of you is to forget it."

This was the reaction I had expected from Governor Hatfield. Unlike so many politicians, he is completely realistic. He not only knew that Goldwater had the nomination, he also understood perfectly that a move to block the Senator now could only serve to further isolate the Liberal-moderate wing of the party and drive the candidate away from them.

After the breakfast meeting, Scranton and Romney went their separate ways, Romney under the illusion that he could yet blast Barry Goldwater's candidacy into oblivion by simply leveling batteries of righteous criticism at him, and Scranton under the equally unrealistic illusion that he might still win the nomination if only he could get the right people behind him.

Romney let loose his barrage at a prearranged press conference immediately following the breakfast. Making a point of how he was breaking a longstanding personal rule of not indulging in politics on Sunday, Romney challenged Goldwater to make his views known. Then he added, "If his views deviate as indicated from the heritage of our party, I will do everything within my power to keep him from becoming the party's Presidential candidate."

Scranton was a good deal more circumspect. Going from the breakfast to the KYW-TV studios in Cleveland for his network interview on "Face the Nation," he appeared on television as if he had suffered a severe case of shell shock from the undetonated bomb he had planned to drop on Goldwater. For half an hour, as *Time* later put it, "he hemmed, hawed and hedged."[2]

Deprived of Eisenhower's endorsement and forced to stand on his own, Scranton kept his hands folded over the sheet of paper with the unread announcement of his candidacy that Keisling & Company had prepared for him. The interviewers persistently tried to trap him into outright criticism of Goldwater, but the Governor kept side-stepping. One, Allen Otten of the *Wall Street Journal*, asked if he was saying "that Senator Goldwater does not fit the image of Lincoln and Eisenhower." A moment before it had seemed as though Scranton was trying to say exactly that. But now he denied that this was what he intended.

At another point, Scranton said, "I don't plan to go out and try and defeat Goldwater. I have no such intention." But later he found himself going in the opposite direction: "I have said that I am available for the nomination . . . and that if the majority of the delegates at the convention want me, that I would serve." Luckily for him, the interviewers never asked him *how* he was going to get a majority of the delegates *without* defeating Goldwater.

In the end, Scranton went no further than to reiterate Romney's demand that Goldwater make his views better known so he could determine where the Senator stood on vital issues. The irony of the Scranton-Romney position is that here were two first-term governors, neither of whom had filled out more than a year and a half in their respective statehouses, demanding that Goldwater "clarify" his views when, after

2 *Time*, June 19, 1964.

nearly twelve years in the Senate of the United States and two best-selling books, his views were probably better known than those of any other politician in the country, including Lyndon B. Johnson's. Yet I doubt if a dozen people outside the borders of Pennsylvania and Michigan respectively could spell out specifically what Scranton's or Romney's views were on, say, foreign aid or disarmament.

Surprisingly, it was Nelson Rockefeller who summed up the Scranton-Romney dilemma during a deliciously witty press conference at the Sheraton after Scranton finally escaped from the television cameras. Asked if he would support Scranton, Rockefeller replied:

Governor Scranton said that he was waiting to see where Senator Goldwater stood. And after listening to his press conference, I think I've got to wait and see where *he* stands.

Later, a reporter cornered Rockefeller and asked him again what he thought of Scranton. The Governor frowned and sarcastically demanded, "Did *you* see him on television?" Nor was Rockefeller in any mood to spare Romney. During a press conference a reporter wanted to know, "If Governor Romney's rather vigorous position comes too late, what can be done here that isn't too late?" Flashing his famous grin, Rockefeller impishly replied, "More *Romneys*."

By now the Liberal-moderate "cabal" at the Governors' Conference was so badly divided that even Romney started taking pot shots at Scranton. While watching Scranton's dismal performance on "Face the Nation," Romney burst out, "Where are *his* principles?"

I certainly hadn't anticipated the high degree of cooperation I received at the Cleveland conference from Governors Rockefeller, Romney and Scranton, but I was most grateful to them for it. From my point of view, it was a delightful show. At the outset, the press had been endlessly harking back to the 1952 Governors' Conference, at which Tom Dewey had sewed up the nomination for Dwight Eisenhower. Some reporters and commentators were cautiously predicting that the Liberals would spring a similar coup at this one and snatch the nomination from Goldwater as they had from Taft. But at the end of that remarkable Sunday, even the most partisan Liberal members of the press had given up this ephemeral ghost. Strangely enough, some of the governors had not.

On Monday, General Eisenhower arrived and went in to a private reception given in his honor by the GOP governors before the banquet at which he was to be the principal speaker. The reception was supposed to have been a strictly social affair, but Paul Fannin returned to our Goldwater suite and told us that a group of his fellow governors had given Ike a good going-over. Fannin was visibly upset about some of the nasty things they had told the former President about Senator Gold-water. He had done what he could to counter their criticism, but he was worried about the possibility that Ike might waver. In fact, he said, the General was conferring with Scranton again that very moment.

I walked down one flight of stairs to Governor Scranton's suite and pushed open the door. Eisenhower and Scranton were chatting amiably with George Humphrey and several other people. I caught ex-Secretary Humphrey's eye and he came out into the corridor. When we escaped from the little knot of reporters at the door I told him what Governor Fannin had reported.

"Don't worry," George smiled. "Ike's all right."

A little later Senator Goldwater came in to attend the dinner. He made a triumphal entry into the Sheraton and many of the same people who the day before had been fishing for another candidate were there to greet him warmly. One of the reporters nailed him with the question as to whether he was going to submit to a quiz by the Republican gov-ernors, as Romney and Scranton had suggested. Steve Shadegg, Dick Kleindienst and I had warned him about this ploy beforehand and he re-jected the idea, saying that he was sure all Republicans were well aware of his views.

At the banquet, the Senator chatted amiably with Eisenhower, and with all of the Republican governors present, including Scranton and Rockefeller. He left right after the dinner, as did Eisenhower, who re-turned with George Humphrey to the latter's home. Scranton and his wife Mary stayed to dance a polka and for a few hours all seemed well.

Shortly after midnight, however, Dick Nixon suddenly appeared on the scene. He had been traveling through Michigan with George Romney all day at the start of a thinly concealed nationwide campaign tour which he hoped would revive his candidacy. His chance for the nomination, however, still lay in deadlocking the convention, and this could only be done by another candidate who would be willing to face off against Goldwater and try to grab enough delegates to block the Senator for two or three ballots.

Nixon sat up until 3 A.M. with Romney trying to convince him to enter the race. There are those who claim that Romney promised to consider entering, but I don't see how he could have done this in the light of his Oregon pledge not to become a candidate. At any rate, Nixon did attempt to get the Ohio delegation behind Romney. But Ray Bliss flatly rejected the idea and it seems that at this juncture the whole plan collapsed.

At a press conference the next morning Nixon fired the final volley of the Battle of Cleveland—and he aimed it straight at Barry Goldwater. "Looking to the future of the party," the former Vice President said, "it would be a tragedy if Senator Goldwater's views as previously stated were not challenged—and repudiated."

I am at a loss to explain what had gotten into Dick Nixon—as I am in trying to delve into the motives of George Romney, Bill Scranton and Nelson Rockefeller in opposing Barry Goldwater at that late date. If they really disagreed so violently with his philosophy, they could have gotten together months before and settled on a single candidate to support against the Senator. But they had all been pursuing divergent trails, each in the hope that the trail he had taken would lead to the nomination. Now, when the whole world could see that Goldwater already had that nomination, they were still tearing off in different directions—and I don't think any of them quite realized that they were tearing the Republican Party apart in the process.

Damaging as the tragi-comedy in Cleveland was to the GOP, there was worse to come. Sometime between Tuesday morning and Thursday night, Bill Scranton decided that he had lost so much stature in Cleveland that the only way he could regain it was to plunge into the race on his own—without Eisenhower, without his fellow Liberal governors, and without any delegates outside the Commonwealth of Pennsylvania.

There was a confusing spectacle as Scranton dispatched a delegation of Pennsylvania legislators to Gettysburg to storm the Eisenhower citadel once again on Thursday afternoon. But General Robert Schulz, the former President's longtime aide, turned them back at the door of Ike's office.

That evening, Scranton met with his aides and Senator Scott at the Governor's house in Indiantown Gap. He let Scott and the others persuade him for three full hours before he finally told them that he had made up his mind to run. Immediately, phone calls went out to leading Republicans in all parts of the country. Scranton even got Eisenhower on the phone again. But this time, instead of requesting support, he simply told Ike that he was going to run.

The next morning Scranton flew to Baltimore to make his pitch to the Maryland convention. Barry Goldwater graciously welcomed him into the campaign, though he couldn't resist reminding the Governor that back in December he had received a letter from Scranton saying, "I hope you decide to run." With tongue in cheek, Goldwater remarked, "Governor Scranton's persuasiveness is one of the major reasons I announced my own candidacy for the Presidency."

From Baltimore, Scranton took off with his entourage for the Connecticut state convention in Hartford. For the next five weeks he was constantly on the go. And everywhere he lit, he hammered brutally at Barry Goldwater. It was always the same theme: Goldwater couldn't win, Goldwater was "dangerously impulsive" on foreign policy, Goldwater's stand on domestic issues was hopelessly out of date. His attacks exceeded even the vitriolic blasts that Nelson Rockefeller had fired at the Senator, and people who had observed the seemingly mild-mannered Scranton for years were amazed—and repelled—by his free-swinging antics.

To his increasing chagrin, Scranton saw that his bitter attacks on Goldwater were failing to win him delegates. If anything, they were driving delegates away from him by the dozen.

Scranton thought he had a good chance of winning the entire delegation in neighboring New Jersey. But after he addressed a party caucus there the delegates voted to go to San Francisco uncommitted. As my friend Mark Anton could have told him, this meant that he would be lucky to get half of New Jersey's 40 votes.

In Delaware, Senator John Williams, the courageous gentleman who had exploded the Bobby Baker case, listened to Scranton's pleas and then dropped his own favorite-son candidacy to announce for Goldwater, thus releasing his state's delegation.

Even George Romney started to change his tune after watching Scranton in action. When Goldwater and I went into Michigan late in June, Governor Romney welcomed the Senator warmly. Though Romney did not abandon his favorite-son stance, he announced that he still had not picked a candidate and would wait and see what the Republican platform had to offer before he made a decision. Ultimately, Scranton failed to get a single vote out of Michigan.

Meanwhile, my countdown at the remaining state conventions was proceeding as planned. On June 16, Texas verified the 56 votes I had already credited to Goldwater after Peter O'Donnell's primary. Two days later the Montana state convention opened. Frank Whetstone had the situation well in hand and with the aid of Governor Babcock and our state Goldwater chairmen, Jerome Anderson of Billings and Mrs. Helen Chaffin Johnson of Bozeman, all 14 Montana delegates were solidly in the Goldwater column when the convention adjourned.

In Utah that same weekend, chairman Fred L. Finlinson of Salt Lake City rounded up 14 more votes when his convention voted, almost unanimously to commit the entire delegation to the Senator. Arkansas had 12 votes. We got nine of them. Scranton was lucky to get two and of course Winthrop Rockefeller had to cast his ballot for his brother. We had previously been assured a minimum of six votes in exchange for our state organization's support of Winthrop's gubernatorial candidacy against Democrat Orval Faubus. But if Goldwater had lost in California I was prepared to discount all of them.

Even Hawaii came through for Goldwater in June, thanks to a tremendous organizing effort by our state chairman, Robert Hales of Kailua, and Mrs. George Kellerman of Honolulu. Bob, Libby Kellerman and their friends got us four of the eight delegates at the state convention, and they were four who were prepared to stand by the Senator if all the volcanoes in the island suddenly erupted and spewed forth Scranton buttons. The other four went to Hawaii's favorite son, U.S. Senator Hiram Fong, and Scranton never got a one.

The countdown was now complete. With these last state conventions, my private tally shot up to over 800 first-ballot votes for Senator Goldwater. Yet Bill Scranton still kept hustling around the country claiming new delegates. Finally, on June 21, I issued a statement to the press in an attempt to correct the erroneous reports of growing Scranton strength. I noted that the Governor had made forays into eight states during the last week. Then I added:

Governor Scranton has stated publicly several times that he has picked up strength in the states he has visited, but he has declined to give the names of his supporters or the number of delegates who support him.

After a careful survey of the states visited by the Governor, it is clear that the only delegates who have come out for him are those who were previously uncommitted or committed to Governor Rockefeller or Ambassador Lodge. There has been *no* erosion of Goldwater strength.

I then gave the reporters a state-by-state breakdown which proved that Senator Goldwater had actually won 21 *additional* delegates in the states Governor Scranton had been in during that week. Most of these, I will admit, were "sleepers" I had kept hidden in my private book against just such a contingency, but there were a few new ones that I had not previously counted.

It was in that same week that Barry Goldwater cast his vote against the Civil Rights Bill and, in so doing, made a historic speech on the floor of the United States Senate. He had gone along with all but two sections of this bill, having voted *for* most of the others when they came up as amendments. The two sections he opposed were Titles II and VII, dealing with so-called "fair employment" practices and public accommodations. In his stirring speech on June 18, the Senator said in part:[3]

I am unalterably opposed to discrimination of any sort and I believe that though the problem is fundamentally one of the heart, some law can help—but not law that embodies features like these, provisions which fly in the face of the Constitution and which require for their effective execution the creation of a police state.

And so, because I am unalterably opposed to any threats to our great

[3] See Appendix B for full text of this speech.

system of government and the loss of our God-given liberties, I shall vote no on this bill. This vote will be reluctantly cast, because I had hoped to be able to vote "yes" on this measure as I have on the civil rights bills which have preceded it. . . .

If my vote is misconstrued, let it be, and let me suffer its consequences. . . . My concern extends beyond this single legislative moment. My concern extends beyond any single group in our society. My concern is for the entire nation, for the freedom of all who live in it and for all who will be born into it. . . . This is my concern. And this is where I stand.

Goldwater had been under terrific pressure to vote for this bill—from the press, from many Republicans who wanted to go along with his candidacy but feared reprisals in their home districts and states, and even from a few of the people within his own campaign organization. I knew that a nay vote, in the highly charged emotional atmosphere of 1964, would hurt him badly in many areas of the country. But I never sought to advise him on this, nor for that matter on any other measure that came before him in the Senate. I had decided to support Senator Goldwater because I knew him to be a man of conscience, and I never felt it was my place, as one of his political advisors, to ask that he do anything other than vote his conscience. I may have disagreed with some of his votes in the Senate, but one never expects to find a man with whom he can agree entirely on every single legislative issue. The most I can ask of any man in the Congress is that he vote for what he truly believes is best for our country, and this I knew Senator Goldwater would invariably do, as he did on this Civil Rights Bill.

Predictably, Bill Scranton, Nelson Rockefeller and his other opponents for the Republican nomination tried to reap political hay from what they professed to believe was Barry Goldwater's unpopular and "reactionary" vote on civil rights. But there were many others who saw it in a different light. Columnist David Lawrence called it the "courageous act" of "a man who would rather risk the loss of a Presidential nomination, or even an election, than surrender his convictions to political expediency."[4] Arthur Krock, the dean of *New York Times* writers, agreed that "the Senator set an example of political and moral courage that was the more admirable because of the immediate circumstances."[5] In conclusion, Krock wrote:

When Governor Scranton announced his active candidacy for the Republican Presidential nomination at Baltimore last week, he invoked Lincoln in behalf of his argument that the choice of Goldwater would be a "sell-out" of the party's principles. But those who urged Goldwater to vote against his conscience today, and those Republicans who demand

[4] *New York Herald-Tribune*, June 19, 1964.
[5] *New York Times*, June 19, 1964.

his recantation as the price of their support if he is nominated, were pressuring him to do precisely what Scranton said would "make Lincoln cry out in pain"—sell out his principles.

The overwhelming majority of the fourth-estate oracles, however, slashed at Goldwater without mercy for his stand on civil rights, as on virtually every other issue. Nor did they confine their criticism to columns and editorials. In fact, the hue and cry against him reached such a hysterical pitch in the press, during this period of Bill Scranton's quixotic homestretch romp, that several newsmen were repelled by the words and actions of their colleagues. A few even broke the longstanding unwritten law of journalism and struck out at other members of their own profession. One of these was John S. Knight, president and editor of the *Detroit Free Press*. In his "Editor's Notebook" of June 21, Knight made it clear that Goldwater was *not* his candidate and that he had "done nothing to promote his Presidential aspirations." But he could no longer stand silently by and watch what he called the "shabby treatment" Goldwater was getting from "most of the news media":

Their deep concern for the GOP's future would be more persuasive if any considerable number of them had ever voted for a Republican nominee. . . . Of the syndicated columnists, I can think of only a few who are not savagely cutting down Senator Goldwater day after day.
Some of the television commentators discuss Goldwater with evident disdain and contempt. Editorial cartoonists portray him as belonging to the Neanderthal age, or as a relic of the 19th Century. It is the fashion of editorial writers to persuade themselves that Goldwater's followers are either "kooks" or Birchers. This simply is not so. The Goldwater movement represents a mass protest by conservatively minded people against foreign aid, excessive welfare, high taxes, foreign policy and the concentration of power in the federal government.[6]

Knight made it plain that he did not agree with these people because, as he put it, they "yearn for solutions to what are actually insoluble problems." But, he emphasized, "their love of country and patriotism cannot be impugned." Furthermore, he added, although Goldwater's vote on civil rights and his other stands "may give us pause, he has the right to be heard." Then he concluded:

Governor William Scranton's challenge to Goldwater is to be welcomed. . . . But I fail to understand why the hesitant gentleman from Harrisburg is suddenly the hero of the hour in most of the press, and Goldwater the party leper. There was certainly nothing in Governor Scranton's performance at the recent Governors' Conference which

[6] *Detroit Free Press,* June 21, 1964.

would suggest that he is the strong, decisive character now being portrayed in the public prints.

The day after this honest and perceptive piece was published, Governor Scranton flew to Washington to see if he could pick off some Republican leaders in the Congress in the wake of Goldwater's vote on civil rights. His prime target was Senator Everett Dirksen of Illinois, the man who was credited with authoring much of the controversial bill and who, as minority leader of the Senate, helped steer it through to final passage.

Scranton tried to persuade Dirksen to become a favorite-son candidate and thus withhold the Illinois delegation from Goldwater on the first ballot. Ev Dirksen listened politely. But when Scranton left he exploded, "What do they think I am? A rookie or a patsy?"

Not long after this Scranton showed up in Chicago at O'Hare Inn to make an all-out effort to win delegates at the Illinois pre-convention caucus. The lobby was jammed with our people and a jubilant crowd outside happily brandished dozens of Goldwater placards. A covey of Goldwater Girls dressed in sporty straw hats proudly displayed madeup black eyes and big badges proclaiming, "I'd rather fight than switch."

I had flown in with Senator Goldwater that morning and he had gone into a private meeting with Senator Dirksen and Chuck Percy, the Republican gubernatorial candidate in Illinois. Scranton had been trying his darnedest to get Percy's support and apparently he still thought he had a chance with Dirksen. But shortly before one o'clock Goldwater came out of the meeting wearing a "Percy for Governor" button. Senator Dirksen escorted him into the Grecian Room and introduced him to the assembled delegates with a warm show of affection.

I was standing outside chatting with Charlie Barr when I spotted Governor Scranton coming down the corridor. He had slipped in by a back door to avoid the crowd in the lobby. We exchanged polite nods and he continued on to a private room to await his turn to address the delegation. The cheers coming from the Grecian Room must have unsettled him somewhat. I left shortly after that with Senator Goldwater, but Charlie reported to me later on Scranton's performance.

The Governor softpedaled his differences with Goldwater on this occasion and dwelt at some length on his "warm personal friendship with Barry." The delegates had come armed with questions they plucked from a brochure some of our Illinois people had put out showing how Scranton had voted against the Republican leadership—and with the Democrats—on no less than thirty-one key issues during his single term in the Congress. Scranton answered their questions with vague platitudes. After forty-five minutes he seemed happy to escape.

When Scranton was gone, Senator Dirksen rose to speak. "Too long have we ridden the gray ghost of me-tooism," he declared. "When the roll is called, I shall cast my vote for Barry Goldwater!"

The delegation was polled right after that, and all but ten of the 58 votes went to Barry Goldwater. Chuck Percy declared for Goldwater when it was clear the Senator had a majority, thereby honoring the promise he had made after the April primary. Scranton never got a single vote out of Illinois, though Rockefeller received two. Goldwater finally got all the rest.

Scranton had counted heavily on driving a wedge into the Illinois delegation. How he hoped to accomplish this was completely beyond me, but he apparently believed firmly that he could. When he failed, whatever thin hope he still held for getting enough delegates to block Goldwater on the first ballot collapsed entirely. After that, the only wedge that Bill Scranton could hope to drive home was the one he kept pounding into the already divided heart of the Republican Party.

BOOK FIVE

CONVENTION

CHAPTER 33

SAN FRANCISCO I

THE FINAL TEST but one was now upon us. For nearly three years our original group and the thousands of allies we had mobilized throughout the nation had been pointing toward the 1964 Republican national convention and the election campaign that would follow. At last, the first of these two climactic events was at hand. Except in the minds of the most blindly fanatic anti-Goldwater partisans there was no longer the shadow of a doubt that we had enough delegates to win the nomination for the Senator. But as I quietly slipped into San Francisco the last week of June I was determined that there would be no letup in the two weeks remaining before the convention opened on Monday, July 13.

Our principal antagonist, as I conceived it, would be overconfidence. I remembered well what had happened to Senator Taft at a comparable moment in history. When Taft arrived in Chicago on July 1, 1952 he announced that he had 603 delegate votes—just one short of the 604-vote majority then needed for the nomination. Actually, Taft had at least 604. He shaved several votes from his total to withhold his claim to victory and preserve the mood of drama a little longer. Ten days later, on the first ballot, Senator Taft lost to General Eisenhower, who had counted less than 450 votes at the beginning of July.

Essentially the same group that had defeated Taft a dozen years earlier was now arrayed against Barry Goldwater. There were some new leaders, but many of the old faces were still around. Henry Cabot Lodge, who as a Senator from Massachusetts had spearheaded the Eisenhower blitz at Chicago, resigned his ambassadorship in Vietnam to return to the States and help Scranton. Nelson Rockefeller turned over all his staff and facilities to the Pennsylvania Governor. The same elements of the press which Taft noted in a memoir had consistently fought him and "turned themselves into propaganda sheets for my opponent," were even more solidly aligned against Goldwater.

In 1964, however, these people were by no means as powerful as they had been in 1952. They had no Tom Dewey to mastermind the intricate behind-the-scenes dealings and unite Republican governors behind the Eastern wing's candidate. Cabot Lodge's influence had steadily waned, sliding ever since his 1952 senatorial defeat at the hands of John F. Kennedy, dipping lower during his lackluster campaign for Vice President in 1960, and reaching its nadir in Saigon. The Rockefellers could no longer wield the same big stick over delegates that the Eastern Establishment once had. The West and South and Southwest could not now be easily cowed by Wall Street. More important, these regions had developed a new breed of independent conservative who refused to be awed into submission by great wealth of any kind. And finally, the once considerable influence of the press had greatly eroded among thinking Republicans as a result of its undeviating support of Liberal candidates and causes.[1]

But power is seldom surrendered without a struggle. And now, in the twilight of its long reign over the Republican Party, the Eastern Establishment threw every force at its command into the breach. The delegates drifting into San Francisco were subjected to an unbelievable barrage of propaganda to swing them away from Barry Goldwater. Newspaper columnists and television commentators fanned the fires of defeatism in an attempt to bring "grassroots" pressure to bear on them. Letter-writing campaigns were mounted in every state urging them to cast their votes for Governor Scranton. Businessmen delegates had their fiscal arms twisted. The air was filled with unsubtle hints of social ostracism and outright threats of political reprisal.

Through it all, our delegates never wavered. Many were moved to write Senator Goldwater reaffirming their allegiance to his cause. Lester H. Burns, Jr., Commonwealth Attorney for the 41st Judicial District of Kentucky, sent him a letter that set the tone of hundreds the Senator

---

[1] One of our delegates, Mrs. Frances W. Chase, a school-teacher from Easton, Pennsylvania, echoed the sentiments of millions in a letter she wrote Senator Goldwater on June 14, 1964: "I am weary of a foreign policy determined by the *New York Times;* I am surfeited with our party's policy dictated by the *Herald Tribune, et al.* . . . . I must vote my convictions: I must put my country first, my party second, and my state third."

received during this period. Delegate Burns vowed that he would cast his ballot for Goldwater "if my vote alone is the only vote you obtain." Edward S. Swartz, one of the three committed Goldwater delegates in Pennsylvania, wrote from his home in Hummelstown saying that "I am prepared to stand by you as resolutely as did General Thomas for the Union at Chicamauga." Mrs. Lorene Englert of Colorado Springs penned a personal note that stands as a moving tribute to the indomitable spirit of all her fellow Goldwater delegates: "I am writing to tell you that I have been, and will be, subjected to pressures of tremendous force. However, I will be able to stand up to this and come out of the convention with a clear conscience to face our God and our people." And Delegate Harry L. Burns, an attorney from Chinook, Montana, summed up the feelings of virtually everyone in the conservative movement when he wrote that he was not "looking for anything for myself, but only for the good of the party and of the nation."

After receiving two telegrams and a phonograph record message from Governor Scranton within one twenty-four hour period, delegate Charles W. Horn of Los Angeles wired the Governor in reply. Politely, he emphasized his unswerving commitment to Senator Goldwater and then reminded Scranton that those columnists "who immoderately defame Goldwater delegates as 'fanatics' are injuring your and the party's cause."

The Scranton forces refused to heed this and many similar warnings. As the opening of the convention neared they stepped up their attacks and in so doing displayed the apparent hysteria that gripped their camp. I have saved an issue of a tabloid "newspaper," *Convention News,* published by the Scranton for President Committee in San Francisco and dated July 12, 1964. The black banner headline ironically proclaims: VICIOUS DRIVE FOR GOLDWATER OPENED BY RADICAL BACKERS. Another head on page one discloses in retrospect the emptiness of the Liberals' hopes:

GOLDWATER WILL STRIKE OUT AT 623 VOTES;
BILL SCRANTON BOOM PICKS UP AFTER COUNT

Inside, another headline predicts "Black November for GOP If Goldwater Candidate—Barry Would Lose All Fifty States, According to Study." Photographs of a smiling Scranton are plastered on almost every page, but on page four there is a two-column picture of an atomic explosion spewing its black mushroom cloud of death into the skies. Above it, in big bold type stretched in two lines across the page: GOLDWATER'S POST CONVENTION PLANS RAISE QUESTIONS OF NUCLEAR SANITY.

Raymond Moley, the erudite *Newsweek* columnist, commenting from

California on the Republican revolution and the hysterical attacks upon the conservatives, accurately pinpointed the position of the Liberal-moderate phalanx that was relentlessly driving the fatal wedge into the ranks of the GOP:

> Their immoderate language belies their claims to be moderate. They prate about looking forward when they are still scanning the past. The names of the illustrious dead are invoked to drive away Goldwater's demand for a change. They talk about a mainstream, although the main channel has long since left their provinces. These are not the progressives of our times. They are the Bourbons who never learn and never forget.[2]

One need not have been clairvoyant to have anticipated the strategy and tactics of the erstwhile Republican rulers at San Francisco. The fact is that they had never changed their strategy—or their tactics—in the sixteen years that I had been working GOP conventions, and for almost as many years before that. The strategy had worked for Willkie in 1940, for Dewey in 1944 and 1948, for the men behind Eisenhower in 1952, and for Rockefeller when he jammed his platform planks down Dick Nixon's unwilling throat in 1960. The strategy was simplicity itself: to convince the conservatives who make up the majority of Republicans that a conservative candidate can't win and then stampede them by whatever tactics necessary into voting as they are directed. The same methods having worked so wondrously well in the past, they were bound to be used again in 1964.

However, the old strategy seemed to be working in reverse for Bill Scranton. After Senator Dirksen rebuffed him in Illinois, Governor Rhodes of Ohio pounded the final nail into the coffin of his candidacy. Before departing for San Francisco on July 9, Rhodes dramatically revealed that he was releasing his 58 delegates from their commitment to him as a favorite son and announced that he would throw his support to Barry Goldwater. As Robert Novak later wrote, "All that now was left for Scranton was . . . some kind of 'incident' that would miraculously change the mood in San Francisco [and] he was game to try it."[3]

In developing a counterstrategy for Senator Goldwater I was determined that none of our delegates should be goaded into playing Scranton's game for him. We had long foreseen that incidents created by the Liberals would be turned against us. Although we could not prevent them from manufacturing incidents we could reduce their sting by exposing their machinations when possible and by simply turning the other cheek when exposure was impossible.

[2] *Newsweek,* July 13, 1964.
[3] *Op. cit.,* p. 449.

To do this we had to exert a degree of discipline over our delegates never before attempted at a national nominating convention. Very few of our people really needed to be brought under disciplinary control. They knew how to behave themselves without being constantly reminded. But it is inevitable in any large group that there will always be a few who, whether through inexperience or the excitement of a sudden clash, will react heatedly if the opposition starts getting rough. Angry words, cat-calls, booing or even pushing and shoving can reflect upon the whole group or movement, particularly if pains are taken to spotlight these incidents for public consumption.

With a view toward avoiding such incidents, and toward keeping our delegates fully informed of all our decisions, I began preparing for the San Francisco operation as soon as Senator Goldwater placed me in charge of his convention staff early in the spring. The most critical aspect of uniting all our forces under a single command was communications. There would be 1,308 delegates and a like number of alternates scattered in no less than thirty-six hotels and motels throughout San Francisco when the convention opened. We could not depend upon established telephone facilities and normal transportation to keep in touch with our delegates and the hundreds of our other people deployed about the city. For this reason I concentrated on plans for tying all these people together via a private network of telephones and shortwave radios.

Our first meeting with Nicholas J. Volcheff, the electronics genius assigned to us by the Bell System's Pacific Telephone & Telegraph Company, took place on Saturday morning, April 11, at the company's San Francisco offices on New Montgomery Street. Jim Day, Dean Burch and I had already been to the Cow Palace and to the fifteenth floor of the Mark Hopkins Hotel, which was to serve as the Goldwater head-quarters. Now, at this Saturday session, I outlined what we would need to set up foolproof communications between these two central points and the dozens of other strategic locations we would have to cover. Before the meeting ended Nick Volcheff had already started designing the intricate communications system that many reporters—and even net-work television experts—marveled at during the convention.

Jim Day stayed on in San Francisco after we left in April. Through May and June he worked closely with Volcheff, going over every inch of the Cow Palace, inside and out, carefully surveying the locale each state delegation would occupy on the floor, the strategic points in the gallery and the various access routes. Jim also mapped out every room and corridor our Goldwater team would be manning at the Mark Hop-kins and the other hotels, and he made all the arrangements for the housing and transporting of our staff and delegates to the Cow Palace six miles from the central city. In effect, then, we had a working headquarters in the Mark atop Nob Hill a full three months before the convention opened.

By the time I arrived in San Francisco at the end of June, Jim Day and Nick Volcheff had everything laid out. My headquarters, which was to be the nerve center of the Goldwater convention drive, was a fifty-five foot trailer parked at the rear of the Cow Palace just outside its walls. From here I could reach out—over several alternate systems—to every delegation, every hotel, and a fleet of automobiles and buses. We had two direct telephone lines to the Mark Hopkins, one to the Senator's quarters in the Presidential suite on the seventeenth floor and the other to his staff headquarters on the fifteenth. There were thirty other private lines, seventeen linking us to our floor managers in key delegations on the convention floor, the remainder tying us into the main Goldwater switchboard at the Mark and our Goldwater regional posts at other hotels. By pushing a single white button on my console I was instantly in touch with all our people manning the phones at all these locations.

In addition I had a supplemental shortwave radio network which tied the trailer in with dozens of walkie-talkies carried by our people in the state delegations which had no telephones, and placed in key points in the galleries and at all entrances to the Cow Palace. This network also linked us to our fleet of cars and buses, which were all equipped with two-way radios.

Mobile radio equipment had been used in the past at political conventions, but there had often been mysterious jamming, which had rendered them virtually useless at crucial junctures in the proceedings. Nick Volcheff overcame this failing by installing a powerful antenna high up in the steel beams under the roof of the Cow Palace. As a result, we had reception on our system far superior even to the national radio and television networks.

As a further precaution, we purchased commercial advertising time on a local radio station and instructed our staff and delegates to carry pocket transistor radios at all times so they could monitor our announcements when they were away from their hotels.

Charlie Barr was in charge of the Security Detail. Under his command were a group of volunteers equipped with small tape recorders and Polaroid cameras. Most of them operated in automobiles with two-way radios tying them to the trailer. If an incident occurred, they were to get pictures and recordings of what transpired so we would have a factual record of what actually took place. Charlie stationed his people at the entrances to the Cow Palace, on all the approaches, in the parking lot, and there was even one Security Detail car covering our trailer at all times.

Most of these arrangements were never detected by the press. But a good deal has been written about the "buddy system" that I employed in San Francisco. Actually, I implemented this at the end of May. Dick Kleindienst and I instructed our field men and state chairmen to make certain the delegates were all paired off, preferably by teaming a good staunch delegate with one who might be apt to weaken. In most instances it was a tossup as to which member of each team was the stronger. In the end we did not have to use this system for nailing down votes, though it helped avoid incidents by increasing the discipline factor tenfold. During June the two-delegate teams were told to contact each other at least once a week. After they arrived in San Francisco they literally lived with each other, sharing the same room in many cases, eating all their meals in tandem, traveling in pairs wherever they went.

Each delegation had, in effect, two Goldwater chairmen. One, whom we designated as the "inside man," took his state's instructions directly from me and my regional directors. The other was our "outside man." It was his duty to keep tabs around the clock on all the Goldwater delegates from his state. There was at least one room in each hotel equipped with a direct line to my command room at the Mark Hopkins.

As the delegates drifted into San Francisco their state "outside man" called the Mark to confirm their arrival and verify their hotel and room numbers. We kept a running record of these arrivals in our master card file of all delegates. Each card bore the name of a delegate and detailed biographical information about him or her. Contrary to some reports, however, there was not one item of damaging personal information in this entire file. The Goldwater movement was built on conviction, not blackmail, and we had no plans to hold people in line by confronting them with past indiscretions.

Many delegates rode into San Francisco aboard the Freedom Special, a transcontinental train that started from Washington on Friday night, July 10 and picked up delegates at every stop along the way. A group of entertainers were on board to help make the trip more enjoyable. At the San Francisco Airport we maintained a large Goldwater suite with a volunteer welcoming committee to greet the delegates who flew in at every hour of the day or night and to duly report their arrivals.

For a full week before we began work in the trailer outside the Cow Palace, our communications system was operating from shortly after dawn until one or two o'clock every morning. During this period my first-line team made its headquarters in a large suite at one end of the corridor on the Mark Hopkins' fifteenth floor. At the opposite end was our press room and an adjacent radio-TV studio which the Senator and his staff used for interviews and other programs over local and network stations. Off the same corridor in cowboy star Gene Autry's splendid hostelry was a large room housing our private telephone switchboard and other communications gear.

By a curious coincidence our headquarters on the fourteenth and fifteenth floors of the Mark were sandwiched in between Governor Scranton's. His command post was one floor below and his personal quarters were in the Royal Suite on the sixteenth floor, directly under Senator Goldwater's Presidential Suite. This made it mandatory for us to keep tight security on our floors. We blocked off the elevator exits on the fifteenth floor so everyone coming there had to get off at the fourteenth and walk up one flight of stairs. A guard was stationed at the top of the stairs and only authorized staff members wearing lapel pins emblazoned with a Presidential seal were admitted except, of course, during press conferences and visits from prominent Goldwater supporters. Members of my original group wore a similar pin with the numerals "3505" inscribed across the seal.

To keep track of our staff we had locator boards set up. All of us notified the people manning the boards of our whereabouts even if we only went downstairs for five minutes to visit with a friend over a cup of coffee. A closed-circuit television transmitter was trained on the boards and Kitchel, Kleindienst, Burch and I had television sets in our private rooms so we could instantly tell where our people were at any given time.

In crowded San Francisco, with its maze of narrow streets climbing up, down and across high hills, transportation was a major problem during convention week. This was solved by chartering buses and cabs for each delegation so they could travel to and from the Cow Palace in a body. For our regional directors, their assistants and Goldwater's principal staff people we had a fleet of automobiles with shortwave radios. I asked the regional men always to travel separately because in the event of an accident I did not want to lose more than one of them at a time.

The regional directors were the key men in the whole convention operation. They worked with me at all times in the communications trailer when the convention was in session. Each manned a fully equipped position which linked him instantly via telephone or radio to the various states he was responsible for, either separately or as a bloc. The regional directors wore their headsets constantly and above each of their positions was a television set so they could observe what was happening on the convention floor. Behind them sat their assistants, poised to grab the controls whenever the directors were forced to leave the trailer to deal directly with a situation on the floor or in the galleries.

For purposes of working the convention, we divided the nation into six regions, approximately the same as the territories I had mapped out when we had first planned our operation back in 1961. Five of the six directors were men who had worked with Peter O'Donnell and me in the Draft Goldwater Committee. The sixth was Steve Shadegg, Senator Goldwater's former righthand man. Actually we had established liaison with Steve back in the days when we were working out of Suite 3505. But in 1962 he had been busy with his primary campaign for the U.S. Senate in Arizona and it was not until the Oregon Presidential primary that he had joined us once again. Now Steve had the largest geographic region of them all under his wing—Region Six, stretching from Alaska to Idaho and down along the spine of the Rockies and Sierras to the Mexican border below Arizona.

Region One was Lloyd Waring's, a Boston investment banker, onetime Republican state chairman of Massachusetts and chief of both the Draft and Goldwater for President Committees in his home state. Lloyd had all the New England states plus New York, not the most lucrative territory in terms of Goldwater delegates but one which we counted on for important psychological votes.

To handle Region Two—the Middle Atlantic area, the two border states of Maryland and Kentucky, and the District of Columbia—I pulled in Edward Failor of Iowa, a trusted associate of mine since my days in the Young Republicans.

Wayne Hood, our Draft chairman in Wisconsin and one of the most respected political figures in the entire Midwest, commanded Region Three, the old GOP heartland around the Great Lakes: Ohio, Indiana, Illinois, Michigan, Minnesota and Wisconsin. The remainder of the Midwestern states, plus Oklahoma, Missouri, the Dakotas and Colorado, comprised Region Five, which was under the aegis of Dick Herman, one of our original group. Region Four, all the states of the old Confederacy including Texas, was the responsibility of John Grenier, the Alabama state GOP chairman and our Southern regional director since the latter part of the Draft period in the fall of 1963.

Two other people played important roles in our trailer command post. One was State Senator Tom Van Sickle of Kansas, my administrative assistant, who manned the controls of the standby master communications console next to mine. The other was Pamela Reymer, a member of our Washington headquarters staff and now in charge of our delegate charts.

On Saturday morning, July 11, all our trailer communications gear was operable and we went through a dress rehearsal in the trailer just outside the Cow Palace. Everything worked perfectly. If we slipped up somewhere during the next five days, it would not be the fault of Nick Volcheff and the Bell System.

CHAPTER 34

SAN FRANCISCO II

BEFORE THE CONVENTION OPENED on Monday we had already realized the first objective of our old Suite 3505 group. It was the goal which had initially appealed so strongly to Senator Goldwater—a conservative Republican platform.

This is not to say that Goldwater dictated the platform, though he easily could have, just as Nixon had under Rockefeller's prodding in 1960. But the makeup of the Platform Committee was such that the Senator had no need to exert pressure upon it.

The majority of the one hundred delegates on the Committee—one man and one woman from each of the fifty states—were conservatives and they had only to adhere to their convictions to come up with a platform with which Goldwater would feel comfortable. The composition of this Committee was, of course, no accident. The majority were conservatives because the delegations of all but a handful of states were conservative. The Republican state chairmen, who in most cases designate their states' members on the Committee, simply followed the wishes of the majority in making their appointments.

Senator Goldwater's personal representative on the Platform Committee was Congressman John Rhodes of Arizona. With the help of Senator John Tower and others, Rhodes made certain that the document that was finally drafted would be one that our candidate could in conscience run on. However, neither attempted to carve out every plank according to a preconceived pattern. Goldwater merely wanted a "Republican platform," one which practically all members of the party would be happy with and one which would attract Democrats and independents as well.

The Platform Committee had been laboring for days at the St. Francis Hotel on Union Square when the Senator came to address it not long after his triumphal arrival in San Francisco. As *Time* later put it, his appearance "furnished some of the few dramatic moments of the pre-convention week. . . . [He] seemed to electrify his audience, which interrupted him thirty-five times with cheers and hand-clapping."[1] His speech was a stirring plea for party unity:

I will not presume for a moment to tell you what should go into this platform in terms of specific planks or programs. You are Republicans. You know our Republican record. You know where we stand in Congress. You know the programs we have created and fought for. You know the ones we have resisted. You know where we have disagreed on this or that detail. . . . But most important you know the great basic principles on which we agree. . . .

Let those meaningful principles guide your minds and hearts and reject the temptation to make this party's platform a bandstand for any factional cause. You must seek a document that will unite us on principle and not divide us.

We don't come to this time and this place merely to dot i's and cross t's. We have come here to cross the great bridge from weary, futile and fatuous leadership in the national administration to strong, active and hopeful leadership . . . and you must take the first step.

When he was finished and the applause had subsided, the Senator stayed on to answer questions from the Committee. The Liberals, poised for the attack all through his conciliatory speech, sprang at him with scarcely concealed ferocity. They revived the old question of his stand on authorizing NATO commanders to use nuclear weapons and he was forced once again to repeat his position. But they reserved their most withering fire for the civil rights issue. Since he had voted against the new law, one of them asked, wouldn't he attempt to have it repealed if he were elected President? The Senator's reasoned reply extracted the sharpest teeth from this argument:

No. That's not in my opinion the duty of the President. I think the legislative branch has now spoken for the majority . . . of the American people, and while I didn't agree and I represented the minority, I stand with the majority just as Harry Truman did when he vetoed the Taft-Hartley Act. He later used it six times even though he didn't like it.

At this point, George A. Parker of the District of Columbia, the only Negro on the Platform Committee, rose and expressed his doubts that

[1] *Time,* July 17, 1964.

Goldwater would "consistently, conscientiously and in good faith use the powers and prestige" of the Presidency to enforce the law. The Senator bridled a bit at this, but there was no flash of temper in his answer, "When you use that argument, you are questioning my honesty. I should resent it, but I won't."

After this exchange, another delegate bore in with a similar question on civil rights and the Committee groaned its impatience. But Goldwater, the man painted as an "extremist," showed his deeply ingrained sense of fair play. "Now wait," he said. "Let's be fair about this. That was a sensible question and I'm glad it was asked." Patiently, he then explained his position once again. A little later he left, the cheers of all but a few of the assembled Committee members echoing in his ears.

Congressman Melvin Laird of Wisconsin, the Committee chairman, kept ploughing ahead for the rest of the week and on through the weekend with the backbreaking and probably impossible task of constructing a platform that would please all Republicans. Before the job was done, the Committee had listened to the spokesmen of no less than 170-odd organizations. Among them was George Meany, president of the AFL-CIO, who made an impassioned plea for halting trade with Communist countries, a plea that received a far more sympathetic hearing from the GOP than from Mr. Meany's own Democratic Party. Another was Martin Luther King, who made it plain that his civil rights activists would not be satisfied with enforcement of the Civil Rights Act. He demanded that Negroes be "absorbed into our economic system" and sneered at the new law as a "cruel jest," likening it to "giving a pair of shoes to a man who has not learned to walk."

Mel Laird and his Committee heard everyone out. Then they finished drafting the platform. Immediately, unfriendly elements of the press, and even some members of our own party, branded it "reactionary." Actually it was anything but reactionary. It was conservative, yes; however, contrary to popular belief, the two terms are *not* synonymous. It was a platform on which Barry Goldwater could run. But, as *Time* noted, "so, for that matter, could most any other Republican."[2] Nonetheless, it was no sooner approved by the Committee than the Scranton-Rockefeller-Lodge forces laid their plans to tear it to pieces. They sent a delegation of their dissidents on the Platform Committee to General Eisenhower's suite at the St. Francis to enlist his aid. At a televised press conference the next day, however, Ike threw his unqualified support behind the platform as voted out of the Committee and firmly opposed any changes.

Another point of attack we had anticipated was the Credentials Committee. I counted on the Old Guard snatching another leaf from Tom

[2] *Ibid.*

Dewey's 1952 convention book by challenging the right of some of our delegates to be seated, and they did not disappoint me. Fortunately, I had a good insight into this tactic since I had worked under Governor Dewey at that Chicago convention and had observed at close range how he chopped down 42 of Senator Taft's Southern delegates, starting the stampede that ended in the Ohioan's defeat.

Unlike Taft, however, Goldwater held an ace guaranteed to trump any cards the opposition could play, above or under the table. His ace was a brilliant lawyer from Boston and his name was Roger Allen Moore. For months attorney Moore, a member of my original group, had been boning up on state laws and party regulations governing the selection of delegates. He had studied them into the small hours many a night at his home on Beacon Hill, until finally he was unquestionably the country's leading expert on the legal niceties of seating delegates.

When he came to San Francisco, Moore brought all his law books on the subject with him. During a series of meetings with Fred Scribner, the general counsel for the Republican National Committee, he argued our case so persuasively on the delegates contested by the Scranton team that Scribner, who was certainly far from being a Goldwater partisan, wound up pleading our case before the Credentials Committee. I say "our case" advisedly, because actually there was no doubt whatever about the impregnability of our legal position as presented by Roger Moore. And, like the intelligent lawyer that he is, Fred Scribner recognized this. In reality, then, Scribner merely carried the case for the law, and not for us. And on that solid ground was dashed another set of Bill Scranton's ill-conceived plans to create "an incident."[3]

The Scranton forces, however, were preparing to drop a far more powerful bombshell. Until it exploded, none of us in the Goldwater camp saw it coming, though we should have been forewarned by the *Convention News* publication and by a probing attack the Governor conducted in the wake of the famed *Der Spiegel* article.

On June 30 Senator Goldwater suffered one of his now infrequent lapses of shooting from the hip. During an informal interview with a reporter from the West German news magazine, *Der Spiegel,* he was asked if he believed he could beat President Johnson in November. Goldwater replied with his old off-the-cuff candor, "I don't think any Republican can, as of now. . . . I don't think I'd be rash enough to say I could beat Johnson in the South as of now. But come election day, there's going to be another horse race."

Questioned about his vote against the Civil Rights Bill, the Senator

---

[3] The Credentials Committee voted 66 to 19 that there had been no irregularities in selecting delegates in Tennessee, the state the Scranton forces zeroed in on hardest.

defended his stand and added: "If they could have locked the doors to the Senate and turned the lights off, [the bill] wouldn't have gotten 25 votes."

On the worsening situation in Vietnam, Goldwater said he would "make it abundantly clear—and I think President Johnson is tending in that direction—that we aren't going to pull out of Southeast Asia, but that we are going to win, in fact. Now the next decision [must be] based on military decisions. I don't think that's up to a Presidential candidate, or even the President. I would turn to my Joint Chiefs of Staff and say, 'Fellows, we made the decision to win, now it's your problem.' "

When these comments were published, Scranton immediately seized on them to escalate his running attack on Goldwater several more notches. He charged that the Senator had "now decided to defoliate the Republican Party." Then he shouted, "How could the delegates nominate someone who says he can't win?" Scranton hinted darkly that Goldwater was "looking forward" to race riots to "improve his chances in the South."

The Governor reserved his most caustic comments, however, for Goldwater's admittedly facetious-sounding proposal on solving the Vietnam situation. "This is another example," Scranton said, "of his failure to comprehend that being President of the United States is not the same as being a benevolent chairman of the board—letting others decide when nuclear destruction should be unleashed."

Nuclear war was obviously a theme Bill Scranton thought had great possibilities, and we should have seen that he was leading up to a blast of atomic proportions. It came, finally, on Sunday, July 12, less than sixteen hours before the convention was gaveled to order.

At eight o'clock on Sunday morning the phone rang in my room at the Mark Hopkins. It was Senator Goldwater and he suggested that we "get together and run through all the states." Right after breakfast I went up to the Presidential Suite and we spent about an hour going over my projections on each delegation in the roll call. I left right after we finished and spent the rest of the day making last-minute preparations for the convention's opening session and visiting state delegations.

Just before seven o'clock that evening, as I was dressing for the big Republican fundraising dinner, Dean Burch burst into my room at the Mark Hopkins and told me the Senator wanted to see me at once. We stepped across the corridor into another room and Dean shut the door behind us. Senator Goldwater was sitting alone. He looked stunned and a little pale. When I entered he handed me several sheets of paper and murmured, "I just got this from Bill Scranton." He shook his head in apparent disbelief. I took the letter and scanned it quickly. It read in part:[4]

[4] For full text of letter, see Appendix D.

As we move rapidly towards the climax of this convention the Republican Party faces a continuing struggle on two counts. The first involves, of course, selection of a candidate. Here the issue is extremely clear. It is simply this: will the convention choose a candidate favored by the Republican voters, or will it choose you?

Your organization does not even argue the merits of the question. They admit that you are a minority candidate, but they feel they have bought, beaten and compromised enough delegate support to make the result a foregone conclusion.

With open contempt for the dignity, integrity and common sense of the convention, your managers say in effect that the delegates are little more than a flock of chickens whose necks will be wrung at will . . .

Almost laughably—if it hadn't been so tragic—Scranton claimed that he was "providing a rallying point for responsibility in the Republican Party." He then continued with what must stand as the most vituperative indictment ever leveled against an opponent by a serious Presidential candidate—even against a member of another party. The Scranton letter accused Goldwater of "casually prescribing nuclear war as a solution to a troubled world"; of allowing "radical extremists to use you"; of standing for "irresponsibility in the serious question of racial holocaust." Redundantly, the Governor underlined each one of these points, meticulously itemizing them a second time with such phrases as "Goldwaterism has come to stand for nuclear irresponsibility."

"In short," Scranton went on, "Goldwaterism has come to stand for a whole crazy-quilt collection of absurd and dangerous positions that would be soundly repudiated by the American people in November. . . . These are not surface differences between you and the vast majority of Republicans. These are soul-deep differences over what the Republican Party stands for. . . ."

He charged that the convention was "rigged." But piously, and somewhat pompously, he added, "I feel that I have nothing to fear from the convention or from the millions of Americans watching it because my position is a right one." The Governor concluded by challenging Senator Goldwater to a debate before the whole convention "on Wednesday prior to the nominating speeches." However, he expressed doubt that Goldwater would accept the challenge because "you no longer have any regard for the opinions . . . of the American public."

The letter went at least as far as some of the wildest attacks on him by outright extremists of the Far Left. But it did not come from any member of a Marxist cult. It came from the Governor of a great state, from a fellow Republican, from a man whom Goldwater regarded as a friend, a man who had served with him in the Air Force Reserve, a man he had urged to run for high office and who in turn had encouraged him to seek the Presidency. And, the final irony, it came from the Republican whom the Senator had wanted most to be his Vice-Presidential running mate on the ticket the convention was about to choose.

When I finished reading the letter I handed it back to the Senator with the remark, "This ought to make it 1,000 for you on the first ballot." I couldn't fathom Scranton's motives. He seemed determined to destroy himself politically, and I said something aloud to this effect.

"This doesn't sound like Bill," the Senator insisted, shaking his head sadly. "My gosh, we've exchanged dozens of letters and he always signs his 'Bill.' Did you notice that his name is just typed in at the bottom— 'William W. Scranton'?" It was obvious that Goldwater couldn't quite bring himself to believe that Scranton had actually written the letter.

A few minutes later Denison Kitchel came in, followed by Bill Baroody and Ed Nellor. A general and rather confused discussion followed. The suggestion was made to return the letter to Scranton. Since it had been sent as an "open letter" to the Senator, the Scranton forces were obviously planning to release it to the press. It was decided that we should beat them to the punch. Someone suggested that a reply be issued over Senator Goldwater's signature and delivered promptly to every Republican delegate in San Francisco. Kitchel and Baroody went upstairs to draft the reply with their brain trust while Ed Nellor and I left to set up the machinery for its distribution.

Once made, the decision to release the letter was carried out with great dispatch. Harry Jaffa, the political science professor from Claremont College who had joined Karl Hess on Baroody's speechwriting team, suggested that a brief statement by Kitchel accompany it. The letter had reminded Jaffa of an attack launched against another Republican a century earlier. Thus, when Ed Nellor called in the press to distribute the hastily duplicated copies, a brief note was attached stating that the letter had been returned and commending to the Governor's attention a note once sent by Abraham Lincoln to Horace Greeley in response to a blistering editorial published in Greeley's *New York Tribune*. In his note, Lincoln had written, "If there be perceptible in it [the editorial] an impatient and dictatorial tone, I waive it in deference to an old friend, whose heart I have always supposed to be right."[5]

While Nellor was issuing the release to the reporters, my regional directors were deploying their assistants and volunteers throughout San Francisco with copies for every delegate in the city. By morning our Goldwater delegates, far from being split off from us, as everyone

---

[5] The often irrational attacks of Radical Republican Greeley finally wore even Lincoln's prodigious patience thin. In 1864, Gideon Welles wrote in his diary, "Concerning Greeley, to whom the President has clung too long and confidingly, he said today that Greeley is an old shoe—good for nothing now, whatever he has been."

seemed to believe Scranton had intended, were standing more solidly united than ever. The letter even drove a number of delegates we never believed we would get into the Senator's fold.

In a television interview on Tuesday morning Scranton claimed he had not seen the letter before it was sent to Goldwater. He conceded that the wording was "perhaps too strong." But, he said, "I take full responsibility for it . . . I don't apologize." Moreover, he insisted that the basic points made in the letter were "valid" and "most important."

The Scranton headquarters let it be known that the Governor's young assistant, Bill Keisling, had drafted the letter and the late Attorney General of Pennsylvania, Walter Alessandroni, had approved it. But many people in Pennsylvania who are familiar with the way the Governor operates refuse to accept this explanation. They point out that Keisling remained on his staff in Harrisburg and Alessandroni continued to be one of his closest and most trusted political advisors, earning Scranton's endorsement for Lieutenant Governor in 1966 before he was killed in a plane crash that spring. Neither was publicly reprimanded by their boss or downgraded in any way. It does seem incredible that a man of Scranton's stature would permit the most important message of his political career to be sent over his name without at least reading it through once. But apparently this was what happened.

The Scranton letter had far-reaching effects that went way beyond the 1964 Republican convention. People who blame Barry Goldwater for failing to unite the party and for the landslide defeat in November that swept so many Republicans out of office would do well to re-read that letter and ponder its meaning. Author Theodore White, a perceptive reporter but hardly a conservative, struck upon the most immediate effect:

> The letter and the weekend seeking of confrontation ground . . . had made the Republican convention the stage for the destruction of the leading Republican candidate. What Rockefeller had begun in the spring, Scranton finished in June and at the convention: the painting for the American people of a half-crazed leader indifferent to the needs of American society at home and eager to plunge the nation into war abroad.[6]

But Scranton's letter and his other statements in a similar vein did more than seal Goldwater's fate. Symbolically, the Governor seemed to be willing also to seal the fate of the Republican Party and of the two-party system which has contributed so greatly to America's stability for more than a century. What were his motives?

[6] *Op. cit.*, p. 239.

No one can answer that question with certainty. But many experienced observers, including not a few Liberals, believe that Scranton was looking beyond 1964 to the next convention and election four years hence. Just as Rockefeller's dictation of the GOP platform had paved the way for Nixon's narrow 1960 defeat, and for the New York Governor's own candidacy after that defeat, now Scranton's sabotaging of Goldwater would leave the lists open to him in 1968. Or so it might seem. My own opinion is that, if this was in fact Scranton's aim, he missed the target by a very wide mile.

CHAPTER 35

SAN FRANCISCO III

BARRY GOLDWATER'S SMASHING VICTORY at San Francisco actually came the night before the balloting for the Presidential nominee. It came, resoundingly and triumphantly, on a roll-call vote against a civil rights plank to the Republican platform offered by William Scranton. The result of that vote was foreordained. Nonetheless, the tension at the Cow Palace mounted inexorably as the first concrete display of the Senator's total strength within the GOP neared.

Until that roll call there persisted an aura of unreality about the great Goldwater surge. The polls and predictions, the millions of words that had been written about our impending victory, the minor convention tests that preceded it—none of these quite conveyed the full scope of the conservative revolution. Even some of our own delegates and workers had not entirely believed what they were witnessing. For thirty years they had watched conservative candidates and platforms dashed against the seemingly insurmountable wall the Eastern Establishment had constructed around its jealously guarded bastion of power, the Republican Presidential nomination. Three times Bob Taft had stormed that wall, and three times he had been repulsed. Dick Nixon had surmounted it only to find himself a captive, consigned to the dungeon of defeat by men who saw his election as an obstacle to their own ambitions. But now at last the Establishment's mighty fortress was about to come tumbling down.

Outside the Cow Palace the beatniks, civil rights workers and student extremists from Berkeley across the Bay marched and chanted and conducted their sit-down demonstrations on the sidewalk in support of Scranton's candidacy and platform amendments. Shouting "Barry Goldwater must go," they brandished placards that disclosed the true character of their frustrated emotions. "Defoliate Goldwater," read one. "Vote for Goldwater—Courage, Integrity, Bigotry," read another. "Keep NATO Fingers Off the Nuclear Button," proclaimed a third. Strangely, no one asked why these people had come to support a Republican, when few if any of them had ever remotely considered voting for a GOP candidate. Many of them had been taking part in Leftist demonstrations for years. Some had participated in the Communist-inspired riots against the House Committee on Un-American Activities when it had held hearings in San Francisco in 1960. Others had marched with identified Communists in the endless "peace" demonstrations. And a goodly number were involved in the sit-in riots at the University of California campus in Berkeley the following fall. But now all their efforts were directed towards cheering on Republican Scranton and, sad to say, Scranton seemed to welcome their support. He never repudiated them, though ironically he was simultaneously demanding that the Republican Party repudiate the John Birch Society.

The demonstrators were already on the scene when I took up my post in our communications trailer for the opening session of the convention on Monday morning. On the television set above my console I listened to Governor Mark Hatfield's keynote address and waited. The applause had hardly subsided when shortly after noon Newton I. Steers, the Republican state chairman of Maryland and a Scranton supporter, leaped to his feet to present a motion that would bar any state delegation which had refused to accept delegates on the grounds of race. This, of course, was similar to the tactic used in 1952 to unseat Taft delegates. Immediately I pushed the "all-call" button on my controls and flashed the word directly to our people on the floor—"*Vote no.*"

Our floor leader, Senator Carl Curtis of Nebraska, gained the rostrum and made a reasoned speech against Steers' proposal, pointing out that the Credentials Committee would investigate the legality of each delegate's claim to a seat. "Justice will be done," he said. "There is no need for this harassing and diverting substitute." Bill Miller, presiding as temporary chairman of the convention, called for a voice vote on the resolution and a great chorus of "No's" swept up from the floor, drowning out the pitiably weak and scattered voices of our opponents. On this vote the inexperience of the Scranton team showed through their threadbare strategy. They had planned to demand a roll call, but no one bothered to check beforehand with the presiding officer to assure its being held. We had won the opening skirmish without a struggle.

The following night the Scranton-Rockefeller-Lodge forces opened up with three mighty salvos aimed at wrecking the Republican platform. In light of the defeat of the credentials motion on Monday, they obviously knew they were beaten before they started. Their wild barrage on Tuesday can only be viewed as a well-planned, determined and final effort to widen the already gaping division of the Republican Party as much as they possibly could. Politics is often described as the art of the possible. Politicians do not deliberately try to degrade it into an exercise in the impossible unless they have specific plans that stretch off into the future.

The Tuesday session got under way with a fighting speech by the convention's permanent chairman, Senator Thruston Morton of Kentucky. Item by item, scandal by unending scandal—from foreign policy to Bobby Baker, from juggled federal budgets to Billie Sol Estes, Thrus Morton dissected the Democrat administration in Washington. "We're not just fighting for the Republican Party," he concluded. "We're fighting for every American."

Former President Eisenhower came on next with an address that electrified the convention. To the grave disappointment of the Liberals, he sounded much like Barry Goldwater. In fact, he anticipated one of the major themes of the Senator's coming campaign—crime in the streets. "Let us not be guilty," he warned, "of maudlin sympathy for the criminal, who, roaming the streets with the switchblade knife and illegal firearm, seeking a helpless prey, suddenly becomes, upon apprehension, a poor, underprivileged person who counts upon the compassion of our society. . . ."

But Ike drew his greatest ovation when he departed from his prepared text and lashed out at the increasing one-sidedness of the press, which had been roasting Goldwater for months. "Let us particularly scorn the divisive efforts of those outside our family, including sensation-seeking columnists and commentators, who couldn't care less about the good of our party." And he seemed to be addressing himself directly to the Liberal architects of dissension when he pleaded with Republicans to "renew our strength from the fountain of unity, not drown ourselves in a whirlpool of factional strife and divisive ambitions."

Unfortunately, the Liberal wing had long ago turned a deaf ear to such pleas as this, even from the man they professed to honor most highly. Three hours later, after a tedious reading of the platform, their big guns opened up. As Cecil Holland noted in the *Washington Star's* account of the proceedings, now "there was no sign of the party unity former President Eisenhower earnestly advised."[1]

---

[1] *Washington Star*, July 15, 1964.

The Liberal assault on the platform had three prongs—extremism, civil rights and nuclear responsibility. The Scranton strategists had drafted substitute planks on each, all loaded with explosive implied criticism of Goldwater. In the trailer, we had our orders: vote them all down.

Nelson Rockefeller led off, speaking in support of the Scranton amendment which called on the party to denounce extremism, lumping the John Birch Society in with the terrorist Ku Klux Klan and the treasonous Communist Party. In the trailer I issued instructions to the floor and galleries: hear the Governor out, then vote no. But when Rockefeller appeared on the rostrum the booing began before he could even speak. At the sound of the very first jeer, I flashed the signal, *"Cut it."* Still the boos continued, with Rockefeller obviously relishing the role of martyr, smiling his pleasure even as he spoke. "This is still a free country," he shouted. When he stabbed at the Birch Society with the charge of "infiltration and takeover of established political organizations by Communist and Nazi methods" the jeering rose to a deafening crescendo.

The regional directors were pushing all their communications buttons, pleading with our floor and gallery leaders to silence the jeers. When the boos and catcalls continued, I ordered them to check each state delegation and gallery position individually and find out where the noise was coming from. The replies quickly came in from the floor, and were verified by a glance at our television sets. There was no booing there. The delegates were all quiet. But the booing went on.

I quickly dispatched a platoon of workers to the galleries and within minutes the reports came back: "These are not our people." Jim Day, working the galleries with a team of volunteers, concurred. We knew the people we had given tickets to, and we knew where they were seated. The groups that were doing the booing were complete strangers. Some of our troops had briefly joined in chanting "We want Barry." But when they were told to stop, they did. The strangers kept right on, shouting, booing, jeering. In defying our orders, they were obviously carrying out someone else's.

This, then, was the "incident" we had so painstakingly tried to prevent while some of the Liberals were just as carefully plotting it. It had no effect upon the delegates, and indeed at this stage it was not intended to have. This gigantic charade was being played out for the benefit of a larger audience—the millions of voters who would march to the polls in November. Luckily, a good many of them were in bed when Rockefeller began his performance. In the East it was nearly midnight by then, too late for most people there to stay up and watch television. But many viewers saw it in the Midwest, where the clocks had not yet struck eleven, and in the two more westerly time zones practically everyone of voting age was up and watching, particularly in populous California. How many votes Barry Goldwater lost on that one night alone could never be calculated. But I would wager they ran into the hundreds of thousands, perhaps millions, when his opponents were done branding him and his supporters by unmistakable implication as extremists, anti-civil rights fanatics and nuclear warmongers.

After the Scranton extremist amendment was shouted down on a voice vote, George Romney, acting on his own hook, offered an alternate amendment on the same issue, not naming the Birch Society or any group but simply denouncing extremism. It was an amendment we could easily have gone along with. Many of our people, including Peter O'Donnell, the Texas state chairman, and several of our regional directors, wanted us to support Romney's proposal. But after consulting by phone with the Senator's suite at the Mark we decided that our support would only be interpreted as a sign of weakness. Senator Dominick of Colorado was already on the rostrum to speak against the Romney amendment. "The platform is no place for us to set ourselves up as judges of who is and who is not an extremist," Dominick said. On the voice vote the delegates overwhelmingly agreed.

Knowing that we had a roll call coming up on at least one of the upcoming amendments, I picked up the "hot line" to Senator Goldwater's suite at the Mark Hopkins and gave him my projection. "I assume you're watching this on television," I said. He acknowledged that he was. I asked if he wanted me to report to him after the expected roll call. He replied: "You don't report to me. You call if you want me to do something. This is your show."

Congressman John Lindsay of New York argued the case for Scranton's civil rights amendment, which carried a threat to severely cut down the Congressional representation of states denying any of their citizens the right to vote. This was the one on which Scranton's lieutenants had pushed for a roll-call vote in an obvious attempt to show the world that the Goldwater camp was comprised of "lily-white" anti-Negroes. It wasn't, of course, but there was no way we could avoid the vote. I asked my regional directors for a good, hard count on how many votes we would have. Their projected total was slightly higher than we had anticipated. When the roll was called, the Scranton amendment was smothered under a landslide, 897 to 409.

That vote told the story. Goldwater was not only going to go over the top on Wednesday, he was going to win by more votes than any Republican candidate had ever received on the first ballot of a contested convention. The other Scranton amendment, a slap at the Senator's stand on the control of nuclear weapons, bit the dust on a voice vote. We had swept the field clear for the final test.

On Wednesday, the names of no less than eight candidates were presented to the convention—Goldwater, Scranton, Rockefeller, Lodge, Romney, Fong, Judd and Margaret Chase Smith. During the endless nominating and seconding speeches there were problems aplenty on the floor to keep our delegates on their toes. One arose in the Pennsylvania delegation shortly after the session was gaveled to order early in the afternoon.

State Senator Denny Garrison, our Oklahoma chairman, was seated just in front of Craig Truax's switchboard, and he thus had a front row seat from which to observe—and report back to us—every little plan hatched by Truax and the other Scranton aides. The incidents they dreamed up seemed endless—charging that phones to their supporters in other delegations were being tapped, accusing us of keeping their people out of the galleries (when they tried to get in with forged tickets), even claiming that an unknown Goldwater delegate set fire to a Scranton man's coat.

Both Senator Garrison and Ted Humes, our Pennsylvania co-chairman, saw this latter "incident" at close quarters and they tell exactly the same story. Bill Young, the Negro Secretary of Labor and Industry in Pennsylvania and a fine old Republican, had a habit of extinguishing partially smoked cigarettes and dropping them in his coat pocket. (He told Humes he had acquired the habit during the Depression to save money and had never broken it.) One of these cigarette butts smoldered in Bill's pocket and burned a hole in his coat, sending up a small cloud of smoke before he finally noticed it. Apparently forgetting his old habit for the moment, Young told a group of reporters he had been set afire and the television crews scouring the Cow Palace for just such juicy "incidents" descended on him and dutifully transmitted Bill Young's ordeal to the nation.

While George Murphy, now a U.S. Senator from California, was addressing the convention on nominating day, a small group in the Pennsylvania section sent up a mammoth balloon trailing an oversized Scranton banner in violation of the rules against floor demonstrations except during prescribed periods. Lieutenant Governor Ray Shafer, acting as chairman of the delegation, ordered them to pull the balloon down. They refused and Shafer sent for the sergeant-at-arms. A brief dispute ensued but they were finally forced to bring the balloon down. The television reporters converged on the scene and Craig Truax buttonholed Sander Vanocur of NBC, complaining that the Goldwater gang had the convention under such tight control that they couldn't even send up a balloon for Bill Scranton.

Vanocur, without checking further, sent for a camera crew to televise this horrible injustice to the world. Denny Garrison, having watched the whole proceeding, called in on his headset and said he was going to leave his key open so we could record the conversation he was about to have with Vanocur. He was brief and to the point. He informed the NBC man that Truax was lamenting an action that his own Lieutenant Governor had ordered the Scranton group not to take. "If you insist in putting this out on television," Garrison said, "you will be putting out a lie and I will demand equal time to prove that it is a lie." Vanocur, mindful of the open switch on Denny's headset, never said a word. But when he interviewed Truax before the NBC cameras a few minutes later he carefully avoided questioning him about the balloon. We weren't always able to catch these little sideshows in time, however, and many trumped-up "incidents" that put the Goldwater people in a bad light went out over the television networks and into the homes of millions of voters.

It was 3:20 P.M. when Senator Everett McKinley Dirksen of Illinois rose before the convention to nominate Barry Goldwater. He spoke of Goldwater's "blazing courage" in casting votes in the Senate "that won him no applause, gained him nothing politically." "Why is it," Dirksen asked, "that this man, who so certainly has sounded the call to conservatism, should be subjected to the abuse which has been heaped upon him? Is it because he offers a clearcut choice that the Democratic Party, as now constituted, doesn't dare face?"

When he was finished, I punched the all-call button. "Okay," I said, "let them go." There followed the wildest, most joyous demonstration that had ever ignited a Republican national convention. For three days I had been restraining these people, keeping them in tight rein, promising that when the moment came for the official demonstration they could whoop and holler all they wanted. And that they did. Gold glitter sprayed down in showers from the ceiling, sparkling like tinsel against the television spotlights. A huge ticker tape six feet wide dropped through a hole in the roof, unraveling like a visual roll call with Goldwater's name woven in between successively higher numbers until at last it reached the magic 655 necessary for his nomination. Real Indians, actually friends of the Senator from Arizona, came on shrieking war cries. A band from a San Francisco nightclub played all the old marching songs Dixieland style. Hundreds of placards and banners bobbed crazily through the aisles. My favorite was Louisiana's—"*La Louisine dit allons avec L'Eau d'Or!*"

When the allotted twenty minutes were up, Thrus Morton tried to gavel them back into their seats. But they were just getting their second wind. The noise was deafening, and I doubt if very many of them even heard Senator Morton. It took almost fifteen more minutes to clear the floor, and then only after a hundred calls from the trailer to cut it off. It was a beautiful spectacle, one we had all been waiting for years to see. But the convention had to get on with its business.

Clare Boothe Luce, former Congresswoman from Connecticut and ex-Ambassador to Italy, was the first of several illustrious Republicans to second Barry Goldwater's nomination. Senator Tower of Texas and Congressman Charles A. Halleck of Indiana, the House minority leader, followed.

Then Rockefeller was nominated by Senator Keating of New York. The demonstration for the Governor lacked any real spark and his supporters just seemed to be going through the motions. They stopped immediately when their twenty minutes were up, and the signs urging "Responsible Republicanism," "Keep Social Security Secure" and so on disappeared from the floor as if by magic. The Rockefeller delegates knew they were being held, many of them against their will, only to keep as many votes from Goldwater as possible.

Senator Fong of Hawaii, the first American of Chinese descent to be nominated by either major party, dispensed with his demonstration after his name was entered, thus saving considerable time. Senator George Aiken of Vermont gave the nominating speech for Margaret Chase Smith and a fine, lighthearted demonstration followed, with the band happily blaring "Margie" and the "Maine Stein Song." Senator Smith stood in her box, smilingly handing out red roses, and several of her male supporters cavorted on the floor wearing big Goldwater buttons that said, "We're After the Women's Vote." It was a goodnatured interlude, one of the few this acrimonious convention enjoyed.

Milton Eisenhower placed Bill Scranton's name in nomination, underlining all the qualities in which the Governor was alleged to differ from Barry Goldwater ("He is not impulsive, not given to truculence," etc.). The Scranton demonstrators seemed determined to prove that they had as much noisemaking power as our Goldwater people and they put on a good show. But the signs they waved, some borrowed from the Rockefeller forces, zeroed in on candidate Goldwater with such battle cries as "Don't Shoot from the Hip." And when a Negro Scranton demonstrator was hauled away by the police after attempting a one-man liedown in front of the speaker's rostrum, another televised "incident" had been created to underscore the Senator's supposed "prejudice."

George Romney's turn came next. Congressman Gerald Ford of Michigan gave the nominating speech and stuck to extolling his Governor rather than criticizing other Republicans. After the Romney demonstration came another nominating address, delivered by Robert Forsythe, Minnesota Republican state chairman, for his state's favorite son, Dr. Walter Judd.

Thrus Morton, having received a message from Henry Cabot Lodge that the Ambassador was withdrawing in order to support Scranton, announced that Dr. Judd's nomination was the last. But the New Hampshire delegation insisted on nominating Lodge anyway and the crowd groaned its weariness.

It was after 1 A.M. in the East before the roll was called, which deprived us of a large portion of the television audience in the nation's most heavily populated centers as our moment of victory neared. The speechmaking had lasted seven hours, longer than at any previous Republican convention any of us could remember. In the trailer, we had filled the time by taking three preliminary counts to make certain all of our delegates were present and accounted for. On the last one, shortly after midnight, I gave the final battle order to the regional directors. *"Okay,"* I said, *"now I want a hard count, really hard, no nonsense. This will be the one you are stuck with. It's got to be right. I want it to come out exactly the way the roll call does."*

Pam Reymer, keeping the tally on our master chart as we received the reports from the floor, added the total. It came to 884 votes for Goldwater.[2]

At last Mrs. C. Douglas Buck, the secretary of the Republican National Committee, stepped before the microphone to call the great roll of the states.[3] Goldwater was favored by the alphabet as Alabama led off, casting its 20 votes in a bloc for the Senator. Inexorably, the tally mounted, faithfully matching the state totals on our trailer chart. At Georgia, Goldwater passed the 200 mark. At Indiana, the fourteenth state to vote, he shot up to 317.[4] At Massachusetts he went over 400, at New Jersey 500. A small cheer broke the silence in our trailer when New Jersey announced 20 votes for Goldwater. No one beside myself had quite believed Ed Failor, our Middle Atlantic regional director, when he had projected that exact vote on the last hard count.

There were still twenty states to go when we topped 500. Oklahoma's 22 gave us 640 going into Pennsylvania. Scranton had a little more than 100. Ted Humes, knowing that he could easily get the 15 more votes needed to put Goldwater over, tried to get Lieutenant Governor Shafer to poll the delegation one more time. But Shafer was boxed in and he stolidly announced that Pennsylvania cast 60 votes for Governor Scranton, four for Senator Goldwater.[5]

Thus, the honor of nominating Barry Goldwater went to South Caro-

[2] Six votes from Oregon were mistakenly entered on Pam's chart, but I do not include these here in our total. These were votes that were promised to us on the second ballot after Oregon had been released from its obligation to vote en bloc for Rockefeller. It was a purely technical error.

[3] See Appendix C for official roll-call vote.

[4] Scranton had 34 at this same point, Rockefeller 3.

[5] Judge Blair Gunther, Allegheny County commissioner and former chairman of the Polish National Alliance, joined our three committed delegates in voting for Goldwater.

lina. Drake Edens, the state Republican chairman, rose and a great hush fell over the Cow Palace. In our trailer, John Grenier let out a rebel yell and I quickly silenced him. For the next few seconds after that you could have heard a pin drop in our command post. We all listened intently to Drake Edens: *"Mr. Chairman, we are humbly grateful that we can do this for America. South Carolina casts sixteen votes for Barry Goldwater."* A great joyous roar shook the walls of the Cow Palace. I permitted myself a smile. It was certainly fitting that South Carolina should be the state that carried Goldwater over the magic 655 mark. Greg Shorey and Roger Milliken were primarily responsible for starting the whole thing back at the 1960 national convention when they had persuaded the Senator to deliver his famous speech in Chicago.

The light signaling Goldwater's private line to the trailer flashed on my console and I picked up the phone. I switched into the amplifier so the whole team could hear. The Senator's voice came over clearly: "Clif, you did a wonderful job—all of you fellows. I can't thank you enough. See you down here a little later." I thanked him and he hung up.

Some of the regional directors and their assistants had gotten up to congratulate one another and I ordered them back to their posts. "Get your delegates back in their seats," I told them. "This roll call isn't over yet and we don't count this until the gavel raps. You can celebrate after that."

The roll call ended a bare six minutes after it began. Of the 1,308 votes cast, Senator Goldwater received a towering 883, just one less than our final projection. It was the greatest number of votes any candidate in either party had ever achieved on the first ballot of a contested convention that had permitted the roll call to spin out to the end without any interim switchovers.[6] The Senator's total reached more than twice as many votes as were cast for all the other seven candidates combined, and over four times as many as his nearest rival, Scranton.

When the roll call was finished there was only one more scene that still had to be played out that night. A few hours earlier one of our people at the Mark had spotted Governor Scranton leaving for the Cow Palace. His departure was instantly reported to the trailer via walkie-talkie. I had expected the Governor to attempt a performance similar to Goldwater's 1960 appearance at Chicago and I was perfectly agreeable to his speaking. Anything that could help bind up some of the gaping wounds opened before and during this convention was desirable.

[6] Eisenhower ultimately received 845 on the first ballot in 1952 and Taft 280. But several hundred of Ike's votes came after a number of states that had initially cast votes for Taft switched over during the balloting to catch the tail of the bandwagon.

But I had asked Senator Carl Curtis to insist that the roll call be completed first.

However, just before South Carolina cast the deciding vote, one of the men I had stationed outside the Scranton trailer called in on his radio and told me that the Governor had left his trailer, which was next to ours, and was heading for the Cow Palace. On my television set I saw the Governor making his way down the aisle inside the convention hall. The instant the roll call ended he appeared on the rostrum. A short while before I had asked Senator Curtis to call Chairman Morton to remind him that the result of the balloting should be announced before Scranton was permitted to speak. Now, however, the Governor was already in front of the microphones and Senator Morton had to interrupt him in order to give the states a chance to change their votes in an effort to make the nomination of Goldwater unanimous before Scranton addressed the convention.

One by one, nearly all the states, including Pennsylvania, voted their entire delegations for the Senator. There were, however, a few diehard holdouts in Delaware, Kentucky, Maryland, New Jersey, New York, Oregon, West Virginia and the District of Columbia. They probably didn't add up to more than 20 or 30 votes all told, but they were indicative of the bitterness that had been engendered against Goldwater. When the last vote was announced, Scranton moved that Barry Goldwater's nomination be declared unanimous. A great earsplitting roar almost took the lid off the Cow Palace and Thrus Morton ruled that the motion had carried on a voice vote. Scranton now had his chance to speak.

Knowing that many of our delegates and the troops in the galleries were still smarting under the Scranton-Rockefeller-Lodge cabal's destructive attacks, I had passed the word that they should receive the Governor graciously and cheer his requests for party unity. As anticipated, he made an eloquent plea for Republican harmony. He used almost the exact words Goldwater had employed in Chicago when he reminded the convention that "this great Republican Party is our historic home." And he pledged himself to work for the election of the party's candidates. It was a sporting gesture, but one that came a month too late. The harm was already done. Even as Scranton spoke some of his recent allies were stalking out of the hall.

Someone brought a couple of bottles of champagne into the trailer and we toasted the great Goldwater victory. When we got back to the Mark Hopkins the Senator came into my suite, which was across the hall from his own, to thank me once again. I joined the party on the fifteenth floor for about an hour and then went down to the Jack Tar Hotel where Peter O'Donnell and our Southern delegates were celebrating. I went to bed at 6 A.M. and got up at 8:15. When I emerged from my room the committee appointed to officially notify the candidate of his nomination was gathered outside Barry's Presidential Suite. Peter was a member of the committee and we chatted for a few minutes in the corridor. Kitchel came out of the suite and asked me where the notification committee was and I told him. They went in and after they were finished the Senator came out with Kitchel and Dean Burch. The three of them left to meet with the Republican Finance Committee and I returned to my suite.

About ten minutes later Durward G. (Doc) Hall, the Congressman from Missouri, came in to tell me that the GOP state chairmen were in session downstairs. He asked me to go with him and in the elevator we ran into one of the members of the Finance Committee which Goldwater had just addressed. As we got off the elevator, he took me aside and asked, "Is this thing on Dean Burch a secret or can we let it out?" I said I didn't know what he was talking about. "Well," he said, "Burch is the Senator's choice for National Chairman." I thanked him for informing me and continued on with Doc Hall to the state chairmen's meeting.

The meeting was just about to start. Goldwater came over and asked me, "Clif, who is the senior state chairman in here?" I told him that it was Ray Bliss. The Senator was still peeved with Bliss for trying to hold Ohio's delegation for Governor Rhodes' favorite-son candidacy, and he said, "Oh, the hell with that. I'll start the meeting myself."

Kitchel and Burch talked with me for a minute, but neither one of them said a word about Burch's appointment as National Chairman and I didn't ask. They both knew, as the Senator did, that this was the job I wanted to help wage the coming election campaign. I was disappointed that I hadn't gotten it, of course, but I was far more disappointed that the Senator hadn't chosen to discuss it with me before he announced his decision. However, there was still work to be done at the convention. The Vice-Presidential candidate still had to be nominated and Goldwater was to give his acceptance speech that evening. I went right from the Mark to my trailer.

About three o'clock Denny Kitchel called the trailer and asked me to get word to Babette Ransohoff of Connecticut that the Senator wanted her to be co-assistant chairman of the National Committee. He still didn't mention Burch's appointment, but by then the newspapers were carrying the story, which Kitchel had given them right after the Finance Committee meeting, and I guess he assumed I had read it. Half an hour later Ed McCabe phoned from the "brain trust" suite and asked me to call Thrus Morton and arrange to have former President Eisenhower attend the acceptance speech session. I went out onto the convention floor, which I hadn't done before, and visited with some of the delegates I had missed at the parties the night before. I wanted to thank them personally for giving the Senator the nomination. Then I went back to the trailer to work the final session.

Goldwater had chosen Bill Miller to be his running mate without consulting anyone outside his inner circle. Tradition called for discussing this choice with the party leaders and I was dismayed to learn that not even General Eisenhower had been notified beforehand. It wasn't that the Senator intended a deliberate snub. There was just no one around him who could advise him about how such things were done. Miller, of course, was nominated by acclamation.

I have been asked many times why Goldwater chose Bill Miller, a seven-term Congressman from upstate New York who was resigning his seat and would therefore be out of a political job in January. Scranton had been my choice, up until the time his famous letter was sent. Before that I still hoped the Senator might be persuaded to pick Scranton.

It has often been pointed out that Jack Kennedy put personal feelings aside when he selected Lyndon Johnson in 1960 after they had engaged in a running debate at the Los Angeles Democrat convention. He picked Johnson simply because he knew LBJ could hold the South. The question is inevitably posed, why didn't Goldwater swallow *his* pride and select Scranton to strengthen him in the Northeast and among Liberals generally?

But there is no comparison between the Kennedy-Johnson debate and the acrimonious assault Scranton mounted against Goldwater. Johnson had never accused Kennedy of such things as "playing the warmonger's game," nor did he attempt to brand him as a completely irresponsible person. No one who reads the record can blame Goldwater for passing up Scranton. There was no other really prominent Republican political figure in the Northeast he could have named. He reasoned that Miller was a Catholic, a fighting campaigner and fairly well known as a result of his chairmanship of the National Committee. And at least Miller had not been openly associated with the vendetta against him.

After Miller's nomination, Goldwater made his triumphal entry into the Cow Palace amid the shower of colorful balloons. I had not been shown the acceptance speech beforehand and, as I indicated in the first chapter of this book, I was as stunned as anyone that night by the abrasive quality of his words.

The press later said Karl Hess had written the famous line, "Extremism in the defense of liberty is no vice." Actually it was Professor Harry Jaffa, though Jaffa claims he had concocted that phrase in a memo for the Platform Committee and he had not intended it to be used out of context. Nonetheless, both he and Hess had a hand in the final draft of Goldwater's speech, working under the supervision of Bill Baroody. As Steve Shadegg has said, "The manner in which the acceptance speech was written became the pattern for the Goldwater statements during the campaign—ideas and phrases gathered together under Baroody's supervision, edited by McCabe, Kitchel and Hess, until all unity of thought and style was completely destroyed."[7]

My wife went with me to the party for our original group in the Fairmont Hotel when I returned from the Cow Palace. We stayed until nearly three o'clock and then drove together to the home of friends on Belvedere Island, where she had been staying with our children. The next morning I phoned Tom Van Sickle. I asked if the Senator had been looking for me. Tom said no and I told him I'd be at the hotel within an hour to pick up my things. While I was packing in the room at the Mark two of my newspaper friends came by to tell me that the National Committee had officially named Dean Burch National Chairman at the Senator's request. I was writing Dean a note of congratulations when Jerry Milbank dropped in. I smiled and said, "Well, I guess my job is done." Then we shook hands and said goodbye.

I left through the garage to avoid the crowd in the lobby. My wife was waiting in a car at the back of the Mark. As we drove over the Golden Gate Bridge to Belvedere she put her hand on my arm and asked, "Clif, was it all worth anything?"

I shook my head. "I don't know," I said. "All I know is that all of us in the group did what we had to do. And we'll keep right on doing what we have to do."

"Well," my wife said softly, "I guess that's all a wife can ask of a man—or his children either."

I think those words will stay with me as long as I live. They are all the reward I will ever need for those three long years, 1961 to 1964.

---

[7] *Op. cit.*, pp. 165-166.

EPILOGUE

ON NOVEMBER 3, 1964 Lyndon Baines Johnson was elected President of the United States by the largest popular-vote plurality in history. He received 43,126,506 votes—nearly 16,000,000 more than the 27,176,799 cast for his Republican opponent, Barry Goldwater. President Johnson carried 44 states with a total electoral vote of 486. Senator Goldwater won six states with 52 electoral votes, all of them, except for his home state of Arizona, in the South.

Barry Goldwater's defeat was the most thorough-going rout ever suffered by any candidate of a major political party, with the possible exception of Alfred Landon's loss to Franklin Roosevelt in 1936 when the Republicans carried only two states, Maine and Vermont. Moreover, the awesome magnitude of the Goldwater defeat affected Republican candidates at all levels. The GOP lost no fewer than 38 seats in the U.S. House of Representatives and some 530 in state legislatures.

In the wake of this debacle, the Republican Party was pronounced dead by many political experts. Some even ventured that the 1964 election had signaled the end of an effective two-party system in America. Yet just two years later, the Grand Old Party's embattled elephant rose from the shallow grave into which it had been solemnly lowered by the experts. On the night of November 8, 1966 it joyously trumpeted in celebration of its most magnificent off-year resurgence in two decades.

How is it that a party over which so many had chanted requiems in 1964 should come bouncing back with such virility a scant twenty-four months later? The answer to this question has its root in the complex reasons for Barry Goldwater's terrible drubbing. For I submit that it was not Republicanism that was beaten so badly in 1964, nor even the *real* Barry Goldwater. It was radicalism, or rather the illusion of radicalism as represented by a cruel caricature of the candidate.

Senator Goldwater's loss was not an ordinary loss, nor was the campaign waged by his opponents quite like anything we have ever seen before in a Presidential contest. In his book, *The Making of a President —1964,* Theodore White casts the drama of that campaign in iridescent perspective:

Never in any campaign had I seen a candidate so heckled, so provoked by opposition demonstration [*sic*] . . . so cruelly bill-boarded and tagged. . . . For the fact was that Goldwater was running not so much against Johnson as against himself—or the Barry Goldwater the image makers had created. Rockefeller and Scranton had drawn up the indictment. Lyndon Johnson was the prosecutor. Goldwater was cast as defendant. He was like a dog with a can tied to his tail—the faster he ran, the more the can clattered.[1]

In brief, Senator Goldwater was unjustly branded a *radical*—and the overwhelming majority of American voters do not cast their ballots for radicals. This, then, was the basic reason for the disastrous dimensions of the Goldwater defeat. There were, however, other contributing factors, though in the end they all seemed to add, directly or indirectly, to this one central and essentially false label—*radical*.

In this book I have treated all of these factors extensively. To sum up, the principal reasons for Barry Goldwater's rout can be placed under four main headings: the assassination of President Kennedy, the Republican attacks on Goldwater, the ill-concealed prejudice of large segments of the mass media, and, finally, the candidate himself—or more accurately, the candidate created by the first three stated reasons.

Taking them in the order of their importance, the murder of John Fitzgerald Kennedy in Dallas on November 22, 1963 commands precedence above all others. The impact of this tragic event upon both the electorate and the Republican candidate cannot be overestimated.

There is, in the first place, the historic dictum that the assassination of a President molds an emotional climate which has always bequeathed a deep residue of sympathy to his party. The assassinations of Presidents Lincoln, Garfield and McKinley guaranteed the ascendancy of the Republican Party for most of the half-century after the Civil War.

Further, the despondency into which Goldwater sank after Dallas, and the self-defeating mood of fatalism that followed, was apparent to everyone who knew him. His old friend and former adviser, Stephen Shadegg, later said that from November 22 onward "he was never quite the same. The Senator's unfailing good humor vanished. He no longer sought counsel and criticism in the old eager way."[2]

Never having had any real desire for the Presidency, Goldwater agreed to run only to satisfy his friends and the millions of people who had joined the conservative movement. He went through the motions of campaigning for the nomination and election, but his heart was never in it.

---

[1] *Op. cit.*, pp. 328-329.
[2] *Op. cit.*, p. 82.

Goldwater was also deeply hurt by the public reaction to the assassination. Strangely, the tragedy gave rise to a twisted syllogism: President Kennedy was slain in Dallas; Dallas was a conservative stronghold; therefore, conservatives were responsible for the President's death. The fact that the assassin was a Marxist who had defected to the Soviet Union and then returned to America to serve the Communist cause is to this day perversely obfuscated by an avalanche of trivia in endless literary speculations on the crime. "Extremism"—not Marxism—was judged guilty. By some weird involuted logic conservatives had previously been proclaimed "extremists." And in this manner a vast subconscious blame for the assassination rubbed off on Goldwater's supporters, thereby adding another, and perhaps critical, element to the "radical" image.

The second most damaging ingredient in the Goldwater defeat was the vicious, often slanderous, pre-nominating campaign conducted against him by a small but powerful band of his fellow Republicans. "What Rockefeller had begun in the spring, Scranton finished in June and at the convention," Theodore White observed.[3] Actually, Governor Rockefeller began his demolition work on July 14, 1963 when he first linked his friend Goldwater to "extremism." And the public repudiations by Senators Javits, Keating and others continued right down to Election Day. When this relatively tiny group of Republicans were done with Goldwater, all that remained for the Democrats was to swarm in and pick his political bones clean.

The third most damaging factor in Goldwater's candidacy was the vehement prejudice demonstrated by so much of the press and other communications media. Before he became a serious candidate for the Presidency, Barry Goldwater had enjoyed a generally good press. Working newsmen liked him personally. They admired his honesty and candor. But the columnists and commentators, cartoonists and editorial writers increasingly set the tone after the Kennedy assassination. In doing so, they were merely taking their cue from Goldwater's opponents for the nomination.

"Of the syndicated columnists, I can think of only a few who are not savagely cutting down Senator Goldwater day after day," wrote John S. Knight, president and editor of the *Detroit Free Press*. The same held true, he said, of cartoonists, television commentators and editorial writers. Knight was *not* a Goldwater supporter. But his sense of fair play rebelled against what he called the "shabby treatment" of the Senator by "most of the news media."[4]

The hysteria that gripped most of the Fourth Estate swelled to a shrill

[3] *Op. cit.*, p. 198.
[4] *Detroit Free Press,* June 21, 1964.

crescendo as the election neared. It reached its height—or, if you prefer, its most degraded depths—in the autumn issue of a magazine absurdly known as *Fact*. The cover article spoke for itself: *"1,189 Psychiatrists Say Goldwater Is Psychologically Unfit To Be President."*

Not long before, *Fact's* publisher, Ralph Ginzburg, had been convicted by a federal court for peddling pornography through the mails. But this did not deter the *New York Times* from printing full-page advertisements of Ginzburg's *Fact* article. The ads, of course, distilled the distorted story on Senator Goldwater to its most poisonous essence.

Other journalists strove to pin the "fascist" label on Goldwater. From San Francisco, Drew Pearson wrote: "The smell of fascism is strong at this convention." Charles Bartlett, one of Jack Kennedy's favorite reporters, again struck the insidious post-Dallas theme: "The evidence of hate at the convention in San Francisco and the sharpening of the racial issue have raised new fears that it will be physically perilous for President Johnson to campaign extensively. Security experts are keenly aware of the danger to the President from fanatics."

Under the withering barrage trained on Goldwater and his followers, the most staunchly Republican newspapers broke in a mad scramble to dissociate themselves from his candidacy. Even the Hearst chain buckled. In all the land, only a handful of major newspapers stood by Goldwater —the *Chicago Tribune, Los Angeles Times, Cincinnati Enquirer, St. Louis Globe Democrat, San Diego Union,* a few others.

Endorsing the Senator on September 29, 1964, the *Cincinnati Enquirer* said:

Barry Goldwater has become the most slandered man in American political history. . . . He is portrayed as a poisoner of children, as a creature of the night-riders, as a pawn of the militarists and the warmongers. To see the viciousness of the vilification heaped upon him is to begin to understand the desperation with which his enemies are trying to cling to the preverted political order they have been foisting upon America. Their purpose is to do considerably more than defeat him at the polls: they seek literally to crush him lest any other muster the courage to ask them to account for their sordid works.

In fairness to the working press, however, it must be noted that neither the candidate nor his staff went out of their way to endear themselves to reporters. Towards the end, the Senator unbent a bit and on occasion succeeded in re-establishing the old easy camaraderie he had once enjoyed with the press. But many members of his staff remained arrogantly stand-offish towards newsmen till the bitter end. Perhaps they just gave up when they saw that no matter what they or the Senator did he would be violently gored by the media men.

When it was all over, some newsmen recognized the terrible wrong done Goldwater and tried to make amends. On July 28, 1966, Tom Wicker of the *New York Times* Washington bureau wrote:

Barry Goldwater revived today what used to be a substantial love affair between him and the Washington press. . . .

Not enough Americans got a look at this likable Goldwater during the 1964 campaign. . . . It's hard to hold . . . too much against a man who could take the licking he did and then say today that he had "arrived two years late for the Presidency and two weeks early for the wedding." The image never did do credit to the man, and there are not many politicians of whom that can be said.

This brings us to the fourth and final factor that helped loose the deluge which inundated the Republican Party in 1964—the candidate himself. For me, this is the most painful of all. But no one, not even Senator Goldwater, will argue that he waged a spirited campaign that clearly joined the issues. In fact, the Senator has himself said, "Looking back, I see the campaign as less of a debate than two monologues."[5]

The debate that was to give the voters a clear-cut choice never developed for one simple reason: the failure, or reluctance, of both candidates to articulate the issues. President Johnson, of course, had no need to spell out the issues. He had a slogan, and that was sufficient. Curiously, the slogan had been concocted by the Fabian Socialists in England a half-century earlier. It was in 1914 that Graham Wallas, a leading Fabian theorist, published his book, *The Great Society*.[6] The preface is a letter to Walter Lippmann, who Wallas implies inspired the book. Significantly, the last three chapters are titled "The Organisation of Thought," "The Organisation of Will," and, finally, "The Organisation of Happiness." In his campaign, President Johnson wisely bore down on the latter— and then added another, "The Organisation of Fear."

Republicans scorned the Great Society slogan as just another way of promising "something for everybody." What many of them failed to take into account was that in the latter half of the twentieth century practically everybody wanted, indeed, *expected,* something from the government, and large numbers of them were perfectly willing to trade their votes in order to get what they wanted.

Lyndon Johnson, therefore, came through as a conservative defending the established order, while Barry Goldwater, the true conservative, became a "radical" bent on upsetting the applecart of peace and plenty. The labels were turned—and the issues all but forgotten.

[5] *This Week,* October 25, 1965.
[6] *The Great Society,* by Graham Wallas, was published in the United States by The Macmillan Company.

If there was any issue that could be discerned at all in the 1964 campaign it was war, or the threat of war, and peace, or more precisely, the illusion of peace. Johnson played this theme with evangelistic fervor and his fellow Democrats exacerbated the voters' fears of war at every turn. Who can forget the Democrats' television skit which showed a little girl picking petals from a daisy until the film faded to a countdown at a missile launching site and then the grand finale as the whole scene exploded under a mammoth mushroom cloud?

Goldwater never devised a convincing response to the charges and innuendo that made him out a warmonger. Perhaps, as Teddy White has noted, it was because he was "so stunned, so shocked by the attack on him as a killer, that he could not clear his mind to guide a counterattack."

But what of all the other issues—Cuba, the Supreme Court prayer ban, the danger of inflation induced by runaway federal spending? Or the spreading violence in the streets that both Goldwater and former President Eisenhower had underlined so eloquently at the San Francisco convention? The Senator pecked away at some of them in the fall of 1964, but he did so halfheartedly, and he never developed the central theme that so many people had urged him to forge as far back as the New Hampshire primary campaign. The slogan dreamed up by an advertising agency and approved by his managers—"In your heart, you know he's right"—was transparently defensive. And so were all his speeches.

Many times that autumn I had clear evidence that Senator Goldwater had been hurt so badly by Rockefeller, Scranton and other Republicans who had turned on him that all the fight had been taken out of him. "I was pretty fed up at the time," he reflected mildly two years later, noting that he had been "completely taken apart, cut up and spit out by two men I thought were friends."

In the campaign, I served as national director of the Citizens for Goldwater-Miller. Rus Walton, our public relations director, State Senator Tom Van Sickle of Kansas, my administrative assistant, and I originated the concept for a television film called "Choice." Senator Goldwater personally approved the idea when I sent him a memo outlining how the film would dramatize his stand against violence in the streets.

We invested $45,000 in "Choice," which Rus Walton put together largely with television news clips of recent events. Despite the riots which were then erupting in Harlem, Philadelphia, Rochester and other cities, Walton did not underscore the race issue as was later alleged. In fact, there were very few scenes in which Negroes figured at all. We showed "Choice" to a cross-section of the Republican National Committee. They were unanimous in their praise. One of former President Eisenhower's most trusted advisers said it was the greatest political film he had ever seen. "It has got to be shown," he urged.

Predictably, Drew Pearson branded the film as "racist" after viewing the print purchased by the Democratic National Committee. That afternoon, Denison Kitchel called and told me to cancel the press preview I had scheduled for the following day. I asked if Senator Goldwater had seen the film. When he said no, I requested that the Senator be given a chance to see it before a final decision was made. Kitchel finally relented and arrangements were made to show it to Goldwater in Philadelphia the following day.

When Rus Walton and I visited Goldwater in his suite at the Bellevue-Stratford in Philadelphia the next afternoon he had already seen "Choice" and had listened to the objections of his managers. "I'm not going to be made out as a racist," he told me pointedly. "You can't show it."

I reminded him that no Republican who had seen the film had previously raised any question about its being anti-Negro. Only the Democrats and Drew Pearson had done that—for the obvious reason that it was going to lose Lyndon Johnson votes.

"I don't care," he replied.

After that I did not press my case further. It was obvious the Senator had given up, though the election was then a month away. He had already been burned so badly he had no desire to have his hand held to still another fire. He also did not want to go against the wishes of the little group who apparently thought they were insulating him from the flames.

A week later this same group tried desperately to cancel Ronald Reagan's now famous television speech. Luckily, they were overruled. If they hadn't been, I doubt seriously if Reagan would be Governor of California today. For it was that speech which catapulted him into the political limelight in the closing days of the 1964 campaign.

Our Citizens group, working under the aegis of two splendid co-chairmen—Mrs. Clare Boothe Luce and General James A. Doolittle—did what we could to lay the issues before the public. Rus Walton and Travis Cross, the latter a top public relations man loaned to us by Oregon's Mark Hatfield, put out nearly 30 million pieces of campaign literature. And our Citizens Committee spawned a whole galaxy of subsidiary groups—Labor for Goldwater-Miller, Doctors, Dentists and even Pilots for Goldwater-Miller, Mothers for a Moral America, and so on. In the end, our Citizens Group and the Republican National Committee received financial contributions from a record 651,000 voters, most of whom had never made a political contribution before.

However, the really important decisions of the campaign were made neither by the National Committee nor our Citizens organization. They were hammered out in the so-called "Think Tank" on the third floor of an office building at 1625 "I" Street in downtown Washington. There Denison Kitchel, Bill Baroody and their stable of speech writers and research experts held court. It was a court that was notably unreceptive to ideas from outside its own circle. Senator Goldwater's office adjoining the "tank" was open only to a select few.

It would be wrong, however, to point an accusing finger at any individual or group as having been chiefly responsible for Goldwater's landslide loss. The failure of leadership is only one factor, as I have already made clear, though it is the one that probably made the difference between a reasonably respectable loss and a disastrous rout.

I have been asked at least a thousand times whether I really believed Barry Goldwater could have beaten Jack Kennedy had the President lived to run for reelection in 1964. Richard Cardinal Cushing of Boston answers that question with more authority than I possibly could. A close personal friend of the late President and of his family, Cardinal Cushing nonetheless believes Kennedy could not have won a second term.

"The Democratic Party in the North was in a mess," the Cardinal explains. "The South was against him. Cuba would always loom as the Achilles heel of the Administration, and a lot of people who worked for him before, hoping for patronage, were disappointed."

Couple the Cardinal's wise observations with the mounting evidence of rank-and-file labor defections, growing distrust over disarmament programs that failed to guarantee U.S. security, and then add the surging popularity of Barry Goldwater as reflected in the polls in the autumn of 1963 and you have my answer—with one important qualification: if the Senator had waged the same kind of a campaign against Jack Kennedy that he did against Lyndon Johnson, Kennedy's reelection would have been assured. I believe, however, that Goldwater would have fought a far different campaign if Kennedy had been his opponent.

It may well be that Senator Goldwater would have been painted a "radical" even in a race against Jack Kennedy. But certainly not in such vivid hues—nor quite so indelibly. It was the revolt of the Liberal Republicans that made the libelous label stick. And it was the assassination that ignited that revolt by raising the false hopes of the previously avowed "non-candidates" like Bill Scranton and Henry Cabot Lodge.

Nelson Rockefeller had tried to fire an anti-Goldwater insurrection with his slashing Bastille Day manifesto in July. But by November 22 Rockefeller was an isolated and pitifully lonely figure in the Presidential lists. Our Draft Goldwater organization had virtually assured Goldwater the nomination and as this became more apparent to the Governor of New York I am sure he would have exercised more restraint. If it had not been for the assassination, Scranton would never have joined the revolt. In fact, the chances were very good that he would have emerged as the Vice Presidential candidate. With Scranton adding balance to the Goldwater ticket, the "radical" image of the Senator would have faded considerably.

Assuredly, the efforts to portray Goldwater as a warmonger and racist would have been continued by those Democrats who are inspired by the Americans for Democratic Action, by the more extreme diehards in the Liberal faction of the GOP, and, of course, by the Far Left fringe. But deprived of the kaleidoscopic palette prepared for them by Scranton and Rockefeller this slanderous portrait of the Senator would never have adhered to canvas.

Following the 1964 election Opinion Research Corporation of Princeton, New Jersey, took a poll which showed that while 38 per cent of the voters thought Barry Goldwater was "conservative," fully 29 per cent considered him "radical" and another 21 per cent professed they "didn't know."[7] The mere fact that the latter group expressed doubt indicates most of them probably did think he was a radical, or something dangerously close to one. Thus, a potential 50 per cent of the electorate may have bought the "radical" smear of Goldwater.

More significant in terms of the future of the Republican Party was the same poll's findings that, even after a horrendous campaign in which conservatives generally were equated with kooks, *no less than 65 per cent of all Republicans still considered themselves conservatives. Only 14 per cent said they were Liberals, and 21 per cent thought they were "in between."* This should give pause to those GOP leaders who insist upon treating conservatives in our party as a fractious minority.

Moreover, the poll revealed that a healthy 41 per cent of *all* Americans persisted in regarding themselves as conservative, a comfortable 10 per cent *more* than those who clung to the "Liberal" label. The remainder, or 28 per cent, decided they were somewhere "in between." This pattern also held up among the numerous independent voters. Fully 41 per cent of these voters, who are not registered in either major party, felt they were conservatives and only 29 per cent were avowed Liberals. *Even 30 per cent of the Democrats classified themselves conservative, while another 28 per cent refused to be tagged as Liberals, leaving the Liberals as a minority within the party they claim as their traditional preserve.*

Breaking these percentages down into numbers of voters, there were about 29 million conscious conservatives among the 70 million people who trooped to the polls in 1964. Obviously, close to two million of them shunned the conservative candidate. But they still outnumbered the "in betweens"—until recent years the largest of the three groups—by more than 10 million. Normally, about half of the "in betweens"—now number-

---

[7] Amazingly, 5 per cent considered Goldwater a "Liberal." Less surprising, perhaps, 7 per cent tagged him as a "moderate."

ing between 18 and 19 million—will vote Republican regardless of their party affiliation. But in 1964, obviously frightened by the radical tag pinned on Goldwater, they went over *en masse* to Lyndon Johnson.

Opinion Research's exhaustive survey, which delved into many other facets of voter preference, strongly indicated that the conservative cause led by Barry Goldwater in 1964 actually had not suffered as severe a blow as the election returns indicated. It was, and is, a still viable force in American politics. And it is unquestionably the chief source of strength for the Republican Party.

Most political experts noted that while the 1966 off-year elections showed surprising Republican strength, they failed to disclose any clear-cut trend towards conservatives or Liberals. To some extent this is true. However, virtually all of the so-called "peace" candidates who advocated wholesale withdrawal of U. S. forces from Vietnam were soundly beaten and this certainly represented a repudiation of the more extreme Liberal position.[8] In addition, the Republicans' net gain of 47 seats in the lower House of the Congress, though no doubt partly due to the cyclical off-year shift, certainly reflected widespread dissatisfaction with President Johnson's Great Society programs, mounting inflation, and the Administration's failure to bring the Vietnam War to a successful conclusion.

Conservatives generally fared well in Congressional races. John Ashbrook of Ohio, who with William Rusher and myself initiated the Draft Goldwater movement, won easily despite some gerrymandering of his district that was supposed to aid the Democrats. John Rhodes of Arizona, the staunch ally of our Draft organization who later represented Senator Goldwater on the Platform Committee at the National Convention, was returned to Congress with a comfortable plurality. Edward Derwinski, our Illinois Goldwater chairman, won handily. Donald E. ("Buz") Lukens, who won the Young Republican national chairmanship as a Goldwater supporter in 1963, became a freshman Congressman from Ohio. And Gene Snyder, the Goldwater leader in Kentucky, won back the House seat he lost in 1964.

Many other Congressmen prominently identified with the Goldwater movement from the Draft days onward won reelection, including William Brock of Tennessee; James F. Battin of Montana; Durwood G. Hall of Missouri; William Cramer and Edward Gurney of Florida. In addition, Robert A. Taft Jr., son of the late leader of the conservative cause, won back a House seat from Ohio, and conservative Albert Watson of South

---

[8] Many experts classified Mark Hatfield of Oregon as a "peace candidate." However, I do not place former Governor Hatfield in that category. His Senate victory in Oregon was based not on his stand on the Vietnam War, but on his accumulated popularity during his years as Governor.

Carolina, who had switched over from the Democrats, was returned to Congress.

The Goldwater label proved no handicap to Republicans running for the U. S. Senate. John Tower of Texas, our Draft Committee's liaison with Senator Goldwater, scored a smashing victory, capturing nearly 57 per cent of the vote in his race for reelection to Lyndon Johnson's old seat. Carl Curtis of Nebraska, our Goldwater floor manager at the 1964 Convention, romped back to the Senate with nearly 61 per cent of the vote, crushing Governor Frank Morrison, who had been induced to run by President Johnson. Strom Thurmond did exceedingly well in his first campaign as a Republican, and very nearly carried in Marshall Parker, GOP candidate for South Carolina's other Senate seat. In Wyoming, Governor Clifford P. Hansen moved into the Senate without much difficulty, taking over the seat vacated by retiring Senator Milward L. Simpson, also a conservative.

Senator Karl Mundt of South Dakota chalked up the second highest percentage (66) of any GOP Senate candidate. Margaret Chase Smith was tops in that department, with 69 per cent, and I'm sure Senators Mundt, Curtis, Thurmond, Tower *et al.* were delighted to see the lady from Maine first.

A few former Goldwaterites making their first bids for Senate seats did lose—John Grenier in Alabama, Dr. L. L. McKinley in Alaska, Tim Babcock in Montana. But our Draft Goldwater leader in New Mexico, Andy Carter, gave veteran Democrat Senator Clinton Anderson a good run for his money, which came in by the bucketful from the AFL-CIO.

Nonetheless, of the 32 Senate contests, Republicans won 18 overall, for a net gain of three. The party that had been declared dead two years earlier racked up tremendous victories for first-term aspirants in the big population states of Illinois, Michigan and Massachusetts. Charles H. Percy's win over respected Democrat Paul Douglas was truly impressive, as was Robert P. Griffin's triumph over G. Mennen ("Soapy") Williams in Michigan. Both Percy and Griffin walked off with 56 per cent of the total vote in their respective states, and Edward W. Brooke snowed under former Governor Endicott ("Chub") Peabody in Massachusetts to become the first Negro Senator since Reconstruction.

But it was in the 1966 gubernatorial races that Republicans undoubtedly scored their most important gains. They swept 25 of the 34 contests, capturing state houses in eight of the ten most populous states in the Union.[9] As of this writing, the GOP still had a chance to win a 26th governorship if the courts rule in favor of conservative Congressman

[9] In New Jersey, the eighth most populous state, there was no gubernatorial election. Thus, in the top ten, the GOP lost only in Texas.

Howard ("Bo") Callaway, who received more votes than his segregationist Democrat rival, Lester Maddox, but lacked the clear majority called for by the Georgia constitution.

Easily the most impressive gubernatorial victory, on the basis of total votes won, was Ronald Reagan's smashing rout of two-time Governor Edmund G. ("Pat") Brown by a one-million vote plurality in California. Although both George Romney and John A. Volpe registered higher percentages in Michigan and Massachusetts respectively, Governor Reagan's popular vote was nearly two million *more* than Governor Romney's and 2.2 million higher than Governor Volpe's. More significant because their two states are more nearly matched in total population, California's Reagan received some 700,000 more votes than New York's Nelson Rockefeller.

This is not meant to take anything away from the other governors. All the Republican gubernatorial victors deserved highest praise for waging intelligent, well-planned campaigns in 1966 and their combined efforts immeasurably helped to breathe new life into our party. However, the great margin of Governor Reagan's runaway election did not receive as much emphasis in the press as the victories of some others and it needs to be accurately measured.

Further, during the California primary campaign much was made of the fact that Reagan had campaigned so vigorously for Barry Goldwater in 1964. At that time most of the press considered this to be an insurmountable barrier to his election, though they later hedged their bets after his crushing primary victory.

An analysis of other gubernatorial races again clearly proves that a Goldwater or a conservative label was no obstacle for Republican candidates twenty-four short months after the Senator's defeat. Governor James A. Rhodes' great triumph in Ohio warranted far more attention than it received in the post-election stories. Rhodes galloped home with nearly two million votes, no less than 63 per cent of the total. This hardly suggested Governor Rhodes was hurt by his support of Goldwater at the 1964 convention or his loyalty to the Republican ticket during the Presidential campaign.

In Pennsylvania, Raymond P. Shafer also received more than two million votes. A Scranton supporter in 1964 out of loyalty to his Governor, Shafer's free-spending Democrat opponent, Milton Shapp, worked hard to brand Shafer as a Goldwaterite. But it obviously didn't harm Shafer and his quarter-million plurality was excellent in a state where Democrats have a big registration edge.

One of the biggest surprises to the mass media was Claude Kirk's whopping win in Florida. An open Goldwater supporter in 1964, Kirk swept this traditionally Democrat state and in so doing administered a sound drubbing to an avowed Liberal, Mayor Robert King High of Miami. Other conservatives did equally as well in other Democrat strongholds. Paul Laxalt, a 1964 Goldwater leader in Nevada, moved up from lieutenant governor to governor, beating the Democrat incumbent, Grant Sawyer. Don Samuelson, having scored a primary victory over Governor Robert Smylie, whom many voters judged a Liberal, went on to beat a Democrat in the general election.

In Oklahoma, my friend Dewey Bartlett coralled 56 per cent of the vote to succeed Henry Bellmon, proving that Bellmon, the first Republican governor in the state's history, had established an important GOP bridgehead in the Southwest by giving his constituents an honest and responsible administration at Oklahoma City. Also in the Southwest, David F. Cargo lassoed another state house in New Mexico, wresting it away from the Democrats.

Winthrop Rockefeller, who sounds much more conservative than brother Nelson, annexed another new Republican territory in Arkansas. Jack Williams recaptured the Arizona state house for the GOP, and, perhaps most amazing of all, W. J. Hickel beat popular Democrat Governor William J. Egan in Alaska, where Republicans had been in deep freeze since Alaska achieved statehood. Another stunning GOP victory was scored by Harold LeVander in Minnesota. LeVander trounced Governor Karl Rolvaag despite (or maybe because of) the fact that Vice President Hubert Humphrey campaigned strenuously in his home state for the Democrat-Farmer-Labor Party ticket.

A few further notes are needed to cast the 1966 election in true perspective and attempt to determine what it may bode for the future. For one, a very strange thing happened in New York. The Liberal Party, which for a quarter-century has buffaloed both Democrats and Republicans into believing it holds the balance of power in the Empire State, put up Franklin Delano Roosevelt Jr. for governor. Neither Nelson Rockefeller nor Democrat Frank O'Connor were deemed worthy of socialist support. With a Roosevelt topping their ticket, the Liberals reasoned they would show both major parties, once and for all time, where the real fulcrum of power is located in New York's political jungle. But alas, FDR Jr. pulled only a little more than 500,000 votes out of some 7,000,000 cast, proving once again that the American people just don't cotton to dynasties.

While the Liberal Party's star was fading, the fledgling Conservative Party's shot up unbelievably. The Conservative gubernatorial candidate was a man no one in politics had ever heard of before, Paul Adams, Dean of Roberts Wesleyan College in Rochester, a school whose existence was equally obscure. Yet Dean Adams ran neck-and-neck with the famous Franklin Roosevelt Jr. and even beat him by 15,000 votes in

New York City, the capital of American Liberalism. The Conservative Party's sole purpose is to attempt to nudge the Republican Party in New York State back onto its more traditional trail. Although I do not favor third parties, it is possible the Conservative Party may yet fulfill its purpose.

Undoubtedly related to the Conservative Party's strong showing in metropolitan New York was the widespread opposition to a referendum which would have formalized the Police Review Board created by Mayor John Lindsay. Nearly two-thirds of the voters rejected the Review Board, though it had the support of all candidates except Dean Adams. In so doing, New Yorkers showed conclusively that they supported their hard-pressed police in the unending war against crime and violence. Oddly, this is considered a conservative proposition. One would think it might have the support of all Americans. But sadly this is not so. Militant Liberals continue to push relentlessly for measures that would hobble the police more tightly than even the Supreme Court may wish.

There are, indeed, many issues which should not be subjected to ideological patent laws. Basic problems are the property of all citizens in so far as all of us have an equal duty to work towards their solution. I think the 1966 elections showed a dawning awareness of this fact. Perhaps this is why voters generally did not reject candidates on the basis of labels, whether the labels read "Conservative" or "Liberal."

The Republican Party, far from being moribund as its detractors have long contended, has a great future ahead of it—provided it does certain things and refrains from doing others. The most obvious thing that the GOP should *not* do is continue the destructive internecine warfare that has weakened the party for two decades and very nearly consumed it in 1964.

The elections of 1966 would seem to indicate that Republicans have lost their taste for cannibalism. It did rear its ugly head during the California primary campaign. But the GOP state chairman, Gaylord B. Parkinson, gently but firmly put it down. I can think of no better way for Republican candidates to assure future success than to adopt Parkinson's now famous law—"Thou shalt speak no evil of any Republican"— on a national scale.

Beyond this, the party must develop a whole new array of real solutions to the real problems that confront our society. A good start in this direction has already been made by a dynamic young man named Richard C. Cornuelle. In his recent book, *Reclaiming the American Dream,* he poses the thesis that most public problems can best be solved by private, independent action. To prove his idea is more than just another theoretical pipe dream, Cornuelle cites many examples of private groups successfully attacking even the most complex problems that have arisen in our increasingly industrialized urban society.

By now, it must be abundantly plain to even the millions dwelling in our metropolitan centers who have religiously voted the straight Democratic ticket for decades that government cannot provide them with a panacea. There is a place for government in the problem-solving process. There are certain problems which probably are not soluble without enforceable laws. Smog and smoke control is surely one. But after thirty-five years and uncounted billions of dollars in federal, state and municipal expenditures it should be clear that the welfare state simply cannot eliminate all the ills that beset mankind. During this same period, private initiative has done far more in the fields of education, medicine, and, certainly, the reduction of poverty by providing productive jobs, than the New Deal, Fair Deal, New Frontier and Great Society combined.

The stark fact is that the Democratic Party has long been bankrupt of real solutions. It has been adept at putting shining new labels on old worn-out solutions, but these slogans have failed to wash away the problems. In 1932 FDR's New Deal set out to eliminate poverty. In 1964 LBJ's Great Society was still promising to wipe out poverty—although the Democrats had been in control of the national government for all but eight of the intervening years.

Today, the Republican Party, with generally younger and more imaginative leaders than the Democrats, stands on the threshold of an era of unparalleled opportunity. Whether the GOP will seize this opportunity remains to be seen. Intraparty feuds and overconfidence in the wake of the 1966 election victories could halt the Republican resurgence by 1968. However, I would hope that the lessons we learned through such bitter experience in 1964 have become so deeply imbedded in our consciousness that Republicans will not repeat the same mistakes again.

APPENDIX A

Goldwater's Speech on the Test Ban Treaty
September 19, 1963

Mr. President, after reviewing the remarks made in this chamber, and the testimony, regarding the proposed limited nuclear test ban treaty, I am impressed by three arguments—one in its favor, two in opposition.

In favor of it, after all is said and done, is a hope, usually described as a faint glimmer, that this may be the first step toward easing tension in the world. It is difficult, if not impossible, to argue with a hope. It is an emotional thing and arguments appear harsh in its soft and gentle glow. The more fragile an illusion, the more rude must seem the attempts to shatter it.

I have warned and will continue to warn that nuclear weapons are not the cause of tension in this world, that if all were to disappear magically overnight, the tension would remain so long as world Communism remains dedicated to aggression and obsessed by its irrational vision of man as a mere cog in the machine of history.

But hope heeds only itself. How do you remind hope that hitherto on-site inspection has been the qualification of our trust of any arms control scheme? How do you remind hope that the technology of remote detection still has not developed fully to where it can replace such inspection? Or how do you tell hope, sprung from fear, that fallout is less a present threat than smog and fumes of everyday life?

Say these things and hope, revulsed, shrinks from your harsh words. Say these things and you stand alone, a sad and somber, unwelcome guest in a house of celebrants.

We are, apparently, well past arguing with hope. The future will shatter the hope and sober the celebrants. But we must wait.

For my part and the part of those other few who must heed other voices in their consciences, there is only the time now to say why we will vote as we must and oppose this treaty. I perceive two reasons, basically, and I have based my decision upon one.

First there is the reason that this treaty is a political ambush, baited by the necessity of the Soviet to ease the many pressures upon its tyranny. This has been discussed on this floor. The argument impresses me, and I share with those who have made it a bewilderment at why it aids freedom to salve the wounds of tyranny. But that is not the argument which, alone, moves me to vote as I must and will.

I will vote no because of how I read history and perceive the future. I see in our history, in this nuclear age, that what peace we have had has been possible because of our strength. I see in our history the clear course of Soviet aggressions and breaches of the peace. They have poured through gaps in our strength. They have been stopped when those gaps closed or were precluded when our guard remained high.

I see no change in the future until or unless the objectives of Communism, not just their weapons, change. And not even hope has spoken to us so far of a change in those objectives. Rather, all say that the objectives remain unchanged. But hope, it seems, can hear that truth and still proceed, whistling past the graveyard of experience.

Thus, if strength is the shield of peace and weakness the way to war and defeat, it is the impact upon our strength that concerns me most.

What is that impact? Have we not heard assurance after assurance that our strength will be upheld under this treaty? We have, indeed.

But assurances are not facts, promises are not performances, and I do not feel that freedom's strength, in a time of freedom's peril, can be armored by either. Such strength is a matter of here and now, not of "if and when." Real hope must be founded upon real strength.

There is a catalog that has been laid before us of the price in strength we will pay under this treaty. Have we seen a similar catalog of a Soviet price? Hope may see such a catalog, reality does not.

The major heading of this catalog of America's price, in America's strength, is that the treaty, perhaps gently but nonetheless firmly, closes the door of knowledge.

Now you must pardon me for speaking of real weapons in the real world. As I have said, the words sound harsh in the glow of hope. Truth often does.

There has been work under way in our laboratories toward the design, development and test of a device with a yield of 80 to 100 megatons. Now the door will close on that, if this treaty is ratified. Does it close on similar knowledge for the Soviets? We only know that they have tested, tested, mind you, not just conjectured—devices with yields approaching that range, and we have not, and we will not under this treaty.

We have never tested fully the stamina of our hardened missile emplacements. The treaty will close the door against such tests. Will it close such a door for the Soviet? We only know that there is evidence that they have tested—have tested, not theorized—hardened structures.

Through the eyes of hope, of course, we see tests of major weapons and systems as unnecessary. Hope says that what we have is enough, that these high-yield devices are of minimum military efficiency. Lapsing only for a moment into the language of harsh fact, it is asked if several 20 megaton devices are not far better than one 60 or 100 megaton device. Again, the answer must be along the horizons of knowledge and not along the edges of the statistician's ledger sheet.

It is the knowledge of the effect, the environmental effect, of high-yield explosions, the sort we have not tested and will not test under this treaty—it is in such knowledge that we will be weakened by this treaty.

Prompt gamma pulses from high-yield explosions are known devastatingly to distort electronic circuitry.

Interference with electronic triggers is an area of grave concern. So is the effect upon missile guidance systems. So grave is the concern that our military men must ask if the Soviets do not have the capability, with the knowledge gained in their exclusive high-yield tests, of thoroughly disrupting our retaliatory missile systems. They must ask if their systems can survive the meltdown of fissionable materials by neutron impact, the effect of X-rays, the disruption of communications and radar blackout from beta rays, from gamma rays, from fireball effects.

Ask the men who must man the missiles and they say tests are needed. Ask if the Soviets have not already tested in this area and you find that we do not know—but that there is ample evidence upon which to presume that they have.

Ask the man under whose command rests 90 per cent of the strategic striking power of this nation. Ask General Power the impact of this treaty upon the strength about which he knows as much as any man. We have all heard his answer. This treaty is not in the national interest.

Ask the man whose job it has been to work with the most advanced weapons systems, ask General Schriever the impact of this treaty. We all have heard his answer. He felt he could protect this country better without the treaty.

And what of the Joint Chiefs of Staff altogether? Remember now, if you will, only that they finally supported the treaty because of many safeguards, many promises, and political advantages of which others had spoken. But remember every other day of your life, every day that the time bomb of Communist treachery ticks closer to detonation, that they spoke and spoke clearly of military disadvantages under this treaty.

Pray God that we do not have to remember that under attack, weakened and unprepared.

Remember also their warning that a state of euphoria would be the most deadly consequence of the treaty. Remember that as we now officially study increased trade with the Soviets. Remember it when the next steps are taken, the pacts proposed, the agreements signed. It is not too late to remember those things now, but other, more popular tunes seem to dance in the air.

I shall not recite the page-after-page of cataloging of the United States price in strength that this treaty exacts. You know of them; you have heard or read them. You can restudy them. Let me just sum up the price: Under this treaty we close the door on sure knowledge of the survivability of our second-strike capability, the very capability which, until now, has been the shield of peace in this world. We halt the search for the widest span of nuclear know-how at a point where the total test yields of the Soviet are a full third greater than our own.

If I had no knowledge of weapons and of the enemy, then I would wish also to vote for this treaty and share the brief illusion that it brings. But I have lived too long with reality, too long with the men who are dedicated to our defense, too long with the facts of the enemy's dedication, to discard all that I am and all that I know.

I will vote against this treaty because it will erode our military strength. I will vote against this treaty because it preserves the enemy's advances in high-yield weaponry while freeing them to overtake our lead in low-yield research. We pay a price; they do not.

I do not vote against the hope of peace, but only against the illusion of it. I do not vote for war, but for the strength to prevent it.

I have been told as have others, I am sure, that to vote against this treaty is to commit political suicide.

I will vote against this treaty because in my heart, mind, soul and conscience, I feel it detrimental to the strength of my country.

If it means political suicide to vote for my country and against this treaty, then I commit it gladly. It is not my future that concerns me. It is my country—and what my conscience tells me is how best I may serve it.

APPENDIX B

Goldwater's Speech on Civil Rights
June 18, 1964

There have been few, if any, occasions when the searching of my conscience and the re-examination of my views of our constitutional system have played a greater part in the determination of my vote than they have on this occasion.

I am unalterably opposed to discrimination or segregation on the basis of race, color or creed, or on any other basis; not only my words, but more importantly my actions through the years have repeatedly demonstrated the sincerity of my feeling in this regard.

This is fundamentally a matter of the heart. The problems of discrimination can never be cured by laws alone; but I would be the first to agree that laws can help—laws carefully considered and weighed in an atmosphere of dispassion, in the absence of political demagoguery, and in the light of fundamental constitutional principles.

For example, throughout my twelve years as a member of the Senate Labor and Public Welfare Committee, I have repeatedly offered amendments to bills pertaining to labor that would end discrimination in unions, and repeatedly those amendments have been turned down by the very members of both parties who now so vociferously support the present approach to the solution of our problem. Talk is one thing, action is another, and until the members of this body and the people of this country realize this, there will be no real solution to the problem we face.

To be sure, a calm environment for the consideration of any law dealing with human relationships is not easily attained—emotions run high, political pressures become great, and objectivity is at a premium. Nevertheless, deliberation and calmness are indispensable to success.

It was in this context that I maintained high hopes for this current legislation—high hopes that, notwithstanding the glaring defects of the measure as it reached us from the other body and the sledgehammer political tactics which produced it, this legislation, through the actions of what was once considered to be the greatest deliberative body on earth, would emerge in a form both effective for its lofty purposes and acceptable to all freedom-loving people.

It is with great sadness that I realize the nonfulfillment of these high hopes. My hopes were shattered when it became apparent that emotion and political pressure, not persuasion, not common sense, not deliberation, had become the rule of the day and of the processes of this great body.

One has only to review the defeat of common-sense amendments to this bill—amendments that would in no way harm it but would, in fact, improve it—to realize that political pressure, not persuasion or common sense, has come to rule the consideration of this measure.

I realize fully that the federal government has a responsibility in the field of civil rights. I supported the civil rights bills which were enacted in 1957 and 1960, and my public utterances during the debates on those measures and since reveal clearly the areas in which I feel that federal responsibility lies and federal legislation on this subject can be both effective and appropriate. Many of those areas are encompassed in this bill, and, to that extent, I favor it.

I wish to make myself perfectly clear. The two portions of this bill to which I have constantly and consistently voiced objections, and which are of such overriding significance that they are determinative of my vote on the entire measure, are those which would embark the federal government on a regulatory course of action with regard to private enterprise in the area of so-called "public accommodations" and in the area of employment—to be more specific, Titles II and VII of the bill.

I find no constitutional basis for the exercise of federal regulatory authority in either of these areas; and I believe the attempted usurpation of such power to be a grave threat to the very essence of our basic system of government, namely, that of a constitutional republic in which fifty sovereign states have reserved to themselves and to the people those powers not specifically granted to the central or federal government.

If it is the wish of the American people that the federal government should be granted the power to regulate in these two areas and in the manner contemplated by this bill, then I say that the Constitution should be so amended by the people as to authorize such action in accordance with the procedures for amending the Constitution, which the great document itself prescribes.

I say further that for this great legislative body to ignore the Constitution and the fundamental concepts of our governmental system is to act in a manner which could ultimately destroy the freedom of all American citizens, including the freedoms of the very persons whose feelings and whose liberties are the major subject of this legislation.

My basic objection to this measure is, therefore, constitutional. But in addition, I would like to point out to my colleagues in the Senate and to the people of America, regardless of their race, color or creed, the implications involved in the enforcement of regulatory legislation of this sort.

To give genuine effect to the prohibitions of this bill will require the creation of a federal police force of mammoth proportions. It also bids fair to result in the development of an "informer" psychology in great areas of our national life—neighbors spying on neighbors, workers spying on workers, businessmen spying on businessmen, where those who would harass their fellow citizens for selfish and narrow purposes will have ample inducement to do so. These, the federal police force and an "informer" psychology, are the hallmarks of the police state and landmarks in the destruction of a free society.

I repeat again: I am unalterably opposed to discrimination of any sort and I believe that though the problem is fundamentally one of the heart, some law can help—but not law that embodies features like these, provisions which fly in the face of the Constitution and which require for their effective execution the creation of a police state. And so, because I am unalterably opposed to any threats to our great system of government and the loss of our God-given liberties, I shall vote "no" on this bill.

This vote will be reluctantly cast, because I had hoped to be able to vote "yea" on this measure as I have on the civil rights bills which have preceded it; but I cannot, in good conscience to the oath that I took when assuming office, cast my vote in the affirmative. With the exception of Titles II and VII, I could wholeheartedly support this bill; but with their inclusion, not measurably improved by the compromise version we have been working on, my vote must be "no."

If my vote is misconstrued, let it be, and let me suffer its consequences. Just let me be judged in this by the real concern I have voiced here and not by words that others may speak or by what others may say about what I think.

My concern extends beyond this single legislative moment. My concern extends beyond any single group in our society. My concern is for the freedom of all who live in it and for all who will be born into it.

It is the general welfare that must be considered now, not just the special appeals for special welfare. This is the time to attend to the liberties of all.

This is my concern. And this is where I stand.

APPENDIX C

Roll Call Vote
1964 Republican National Convention

STATE	NO. OF VOTES	GOLDWATER	SCRANTON	ROCKEFELLER	ROMNEY	MRS. SMITH	JUDD	FONG	LODGE
Alabama	20	20							
Alaska	12		8			2		1	1
Arizona	16	16							
Arkansas	12	9	2		1				
California	86	86							
Colorado	18	15	3						
Connecticut	16	4	12						
Delaware	12	7	5						
Florida	34	32	2						
Georgia	24	22	2						
Hawaii	8	4						4	
Idaho	14	14							
Illinois	58	56		2					
Indiana	32	32							
Iowa	24	14	10						
Kansas	20	18	1		1				
Kentucky	24	21	3						
Louisiana	20	20							

State									
Maine	14								
Maryland	20	6	13			1			
Massachusetts	34	5	26			1			2
Michigan	48	8			40				
Minnesota	26	8					18		
Mississippi	13	13							
Missouri	24	23	1						
Montana	14	14							
Nebraska	16	16							
Nevada	6	6							
New Hampshire	14		14						
New Jersey	40	20	20						
New Mexico	14	14							
New York	92	5		87					
North Carolina	26	26				3			
North Dakota	14	7				3	1		
Ohio	58	57				1			
Oklahoma	22	22							
Oregon	18			18					
Pennsylvania	64	4	60						
Rhode Island	14	3	11						
South Carolina	16	16							
South Dakota	14	12	2				2		
Tennessee	28	28							
Texas	56	56							
Utah	14	14							
Vermont	12	3				2			
Virginia	30	29			1				
Washington	24	22		2					
West Virginia	14	10		2			2		
Wisconsin	30	30							
Wyoming	12	12							
District of Columbia	9	4	5						
Puerto Rico	5	5							
Virgin Islands	3	3							
TOTALS	1,308	883	214	114	41	27	22	5	2

APPENDIX D

Governor Scranton's letter to Goldwater
July 12, 1964

Dear Senator:

As we move rapidly towards the climax of this convention the Republican Party faces a continuing struggle on two counts.

The first involves, of course, selection of a candidate.

Here the issue is extremely clear. It is simply this; will the convention choose a candidate overwhelmingly favored by the Republican voters, or will it choose you?

Your organization does not even argue the merits of the question. They admit that you are a minority candidate, but they feel they have bought, beaten and compromised enough delegate support to make the result a foregone conclusion.

With open contempt for the dignity, integrity and common sense of the convention, your managers say in effect that the delegates are little more than a flock of chickens whose necks will be wrung at will.

I have doublechecked the arithmetic of my staff, and I am convinced that a true count at this minute puts your first ballot strength at only some 620 votes.

Our count differs from that of your managers because we have calculated an important element which you are incapable of comprehending. That is the element of respect for the men and women who make up the delegations to this convention.

We are not taking them for granted. We are not insulting their intelligence or their integrity.

We're not counting noses, we're counting hearts.

We're not issuing orders, we're providing a rallying point for responsibility in the Republican Party.

You will be stopped on the first ballot because a sufficient number of your nominal supporters have already indicated to us that they will not vote for you.

They are not breaking commitments to you; you have broken commitments to them.

You have too often casually prescribed nuclear war as a solution to a troubled world.

You have too often allowed the radical extremists to use you.

You have too often stood for irresponsibility in the serious question of racial holocaust.

You have too often read Taft and Eisenhower and Lincoln out of the Republican Party.

And that brings me to the second count on which the Republican Party is fighting for its soul.

In the last few days the ill-advised efforts to make us stand for Goldwaterism instead of Republicanism has set off ripples of public opinion across the nation.

All of us in San Francisco are so close to the hour-by-hour story unfolding here that there is a danger we may overlook the overall impression being created in the minds of the American people.

Goldwaterism has come to stand for nuclear irresponsibility.

Goldwaterism has come to stand for keeping the name of Eisenhower out of our platform.

Goldwaterism has come to stand for being afraid to forthrightly condemn right-wing extremists.

Goldwaterism has come to stand for refusing to stand for law and order in maintaining racial peace.

In short, Goldwaterism has come to stand for a whole crazy-quilt collection of absurd and dangerous positions that would be soundly repudiated by the American people in November.

Meanwhile, we have tried as best we can in the rigged situation engineered by your organization to articulate another point of view.

These are not surface differences between you and the vast majority of Republicans. These are soul-deep differences over what the Republican Party stands for.

We cannot lightly ignore the deep convictions of 60 per cent of the Republican Party that Goldwaterism is wrong. Circumstances have given me the responsibility of speaking up for their position. Inclination has given you the task of defending far different opinions.

Neither of us can ignore our responsibilities.

I feel that I have nothing to fear from the convention or from the millions of Americans watching it because my position is a right one.

Certainly you should not fear a convention you claim to control, and

I would hope that we have not reached the point where you fear to face the nation.

Therefore, I am asking that you join me in a request to allow both of us to appear before the convention on Wednesday prior to the nominating speeches.

Each of us should be permitted to speak on the issues.

Then we ought to have the opportunity to question each other.

Frankly, few people expect that you will accept my invitation.

If that is true, the implication will be quite clear: You have taken comfort in the inflated claims of your managers and you no longer have any regard for the opinions of uncommitted delegates or of the American public.

So, it is up to you. You must decide whether the Goldwater philosophy can stand public examination—before the convention and before the nation.

Sincerely yours,
William W. Scranton

Senator Goldwater's Acceptance Speech
at the National Convention

My good friend and great Republican, Dick Nixon and your charming wife, Pat; my running mate—that wonderful Republican who has served us so well for so long—Bill Miller and his wife, Stephanie; to Thruston Morton, who's done such a commendable job in chairmaning this convention; to Mr. Herbert Hoover, who I hope is watching, and to that great American and his wife, General and Mrs. Eisenhower. To my own wife, my family, and to all of my fellow Republicans here assembled, and Americans across this great nation:

From this moment, united and determined, we will go forward together dedicated to the ultimate and undeniable greatness of the whole man.

Together we will win.

I accept your nomination with a deep sense of humility. I accept, too, the responsibility that goes with it, and I seek your continued help and your continued guidance. My fellow Republicans, our cause is too great for any man to feel worthy of it. Our task would be too great for any man did he not have with him the heart and the hands of this great Republican Party.

And I promise you tonight that every fiber of my being is consecrated to our cause, that nothing shall be lacking from the struggle that can be brought to it by enthusiasm, by devotion and plain hard work.

In this world no person, no party can guarantee anything, but what we can do and what we shall do is to deserve victory and victory will be ours. The Good Lord raised this mighty Republic to be a home for the brave and to flourish as the land of the free—not to stagnate in the swampland of collectivism, not to cringe before the bully of Communism.

Now, my fellow Americans, the tide has been running against freedom. Our people have followed false prophets. We must, and we shall, return to proven ways—not because they are old, but because they are true.

We must, and we shall, set the tide running again in the cause of freedom. And this party, with its every action, every word, every breath and every heartbeat, has but a single resolve, and that is freedom.

Freedom made orderly for this nation by our constitutional government. Freedom under a government limited by laws of nature and of nature's God. Freedom balanced so that order lacking liberty will not become the slavery of the prison cell; balanced so that liberty lacking order will not become the license of the mob and of the jungle.

Now, we Americans understand freedom, we have earned it; we have lived for it, and we have died for it. This nation and its people are freedom's models in a searching world. We can be freedom's missionaries in a doubting world.

But, ladies and gentlemen, first we must renew freedom's mission in our own hearts and in our own homes.

During four futile years the Administration which we shall replace has distorted and lost that faith. It has talked and talked and talked and talked the words of freedom but it has failed and failed and failed in the works of freedom.

Now failure cements the wall of shame in Berlin; failures blot the sands of shame at the Bay of Pigs; failures marked the slow death of freedom in Laos; failures infest the jungles of Vietnam, and failures haunt the houses of our once great alliances and undermine the greatest bulwark ever erected by free nations, the NATO community.

Failures proclaim lost leadership, obscure purpose, weakening wills and the risk of inciting our sworn enemies to new aggressions and to new excesses.

And because of this Administration we are tonight a world divided. We are a nation becalmed. We have lost the brisk pace of diversity and the genius of individual creativity. We are plodding along at a pace set by centralized planning, red tape, rules without responsibility and regimentation without recourse.

Rather than useful jobs in our country, people have been offered bureaucratic makework; rather than moral leadership, they have been given bread and circuses; they have been given spectacles, and, yes, they've even been given scandals.

Tonight there is violence in our streets, corruption in our highest offices, aimlessness among our youth, anxiety among our elderly, and there's a virtual despair among the many who look beyond material success toward the inner meaning of their lives. And where examples of morality should be set, the opposite is seen. Small men seeking great wealth or power have too often and too long turned even the highest levels of public service into mere personal opportunity.

Now, certainly simple honesty is not too much to demand of men in government. We find it in most. Republicans demand it from everyone.

They demand it from everyone no matter how exalted or protected his position might be.

The growing menace in our country tonight, to personal safety, to life, to limb and property, in homes, in churches, on the playgrounds and places of business, particularly in our great cities, is the mounting concern, or should be, of every thoughtful citizen in the United States. Security from domestic violence, no less than from foreign aggression, is the most elementary and fundamental purpose of any government, and a government that cannot fulfill this purpose is one that cannot long command the loyalty of its citizens.

History shows us, demonstrates that nothing, nothing prepares the way for tyranny more than the failure of public officials to keep the streets safe from bullies and marauders.

Now we Republicans see all this as more—much more—than the result of mere political differences, or mere political mistakes. We see this as the result of a fundamentally and absolutely wrong view of man, his nature and his destiny.

Those who seek to live your lives for you, to take your liberty in return for relieving you of yours; those who elevate the state and downgrade the citizen, must see ultimately a world in which earthly power can be substituted for Divine Will. And this nation was founded upon the rejection of that notion and upon the acceptance of God as the author of freedom.

Now those who seek absolute power, even though they seek it to do what they regard as good, are simply demanding the right to enforce their own version of heaven on earth, and let me remind you they are the very ones who always create the most hellish tyranny.

Absolute power does corrupt, and those who seek it must be suspect and must be opposed. Their mistaken course stems from false notions, ladies and gentlemen, of equality. Equality, rightly understood as our founding fathers understood it, leads to liberty and to the emancipation of creative differences; wrongly understood, as it has been so tragically in our time, it leads first to conformity and then to despotism.

Fellow Republicans, it is the cause of Republicanism to resist concentrations of power, private or public, which enforce such conformity and inflict such despotism.

It is the cause of Republicanism to insure that power remains in the hands of the people—and, so help us God, that is exactly what a Republican President will do with the help of a Republican Congress.

It is further the cause of Republicanism to restore a clear understanding of the tyranny of man over man in the world at large. It is our cause to dispel the foggy thinking which avoids hard decisions in the delusion that a world of conflict will somehow resolve itself into a world of harmony, if we just don't rock the boat or irritate the forces of aggression —and this is hogwash.

It is, further, the cause of Republicanism to remind ourselves, and the world, that only the strong can remain free; that only the strong can keep the peace.

Now I needn't remind you, or my fellow Americans regardless of party, that Republicans have shouldered this hard responsibility and marched in this cause before. It was Republican leadership under Dwight Eisenhower that kept the peace, and passed along to this Administration the mightiest arsenal for defense the world has ever known.

And I needn't remind you that it was the strength and the believable will of the Eisenhower years that kept the peace by using our strength, by using it in the Formosa Strait, and in Lebanon, and by showing it courageously at all times.

It was during those Republican years that the thrust of Communist imperialism was blunted. It was during those years of Republican leadership that this world moved closer not to war but closer to peace than at any other time in the last three decades.

And I needn't remind you, but I will, that it's been during Democratic years that our strength to deter war has been stilled and even gone into a planned decline. It has been during Democratic years that we have weakly stumbled into conflicts, timidly refusing to draw our own lines against aggression, deceitfully refusing to tell even our own people of our full participation and tragically letting our finest men die on battlefields unmarked by purpose, unmarked by pride or the prospect of victory.

Yesterday it was Korea; tonight it is Vietnam. Make no bones of this. Don't try to sweep this under the rug. We are at war in Vietnam. And yet the President, who is the Commander-in-Chief of our forces, refuses to say, refuses to say, mind you, whether or not the objective over there is victory, and his Secretary of Defense continues to mislead and misinform the American people, and enough of it has gone by.

And I needn't remind you, but I will, it has been during Democratic years that a billion persons were cast into Communist captivity and their fate cynically sealed.

Today—today in our beloved country we have an Administration which seems eager to deal with Communism in every coin known—from gold to wheat; from consulates to confidence, and even human freedom itself.

Now the Republican cause demands that we brand Communism as the principal disturber of peace in the world today. Indeed, we should brand it as the only significant disturber of the peace. And we must make clear that until its goals of conquest are absolutely renounced, and its relations with all nations tempered, Communism and the governments it now controls are enemies of every man on earth who is or wants to be free.

Now, we here in America can keep the peace only if we remain vigilant, and only if we remain strong. Only if we keep our eyes open and keep our guard up can we prevent war.

And I want to make this abundantly clear—I don't intend to let peace or freedom be torn from our grasp because of lack of strength, or lack of will—and that I promise you Americans.

I believe that we must look beyond the defense of freedom today to its extension tomorrow. I believe that the Communism which boasts it will bury us will instead give way to the forces of freedom. And I can see in the distant and yet recognizable future the outlines of a world worthy of our dedication, our every risk, our every effort, our every sacrifice along the way. Yes, a world that will redeem the suffering of those who will be liberated from tyranny.

I can see, and I suggest that all thoughtful men must contemplate, the flowering of an Atlantic civilization, the whole world of Europe reunified and free, trading openly across its borders, communicating openly across the world.

This is a goal far, far more meaningful than a moon shot.

It's a truly inspiring goal for all free men to set for themselves during the latter half of the twentieth century. I can see and all free men must thrill to the events of this Atlantic civilization joined by a straight ocean highway to the United States. What a destiny! What a destiny can be ours to stand as a great central pillar linking Europe, the Americas and the venerable and vital peoples and cultures of the Pacific.

I can see a day when all the Americas—North and South—will be linked in a mighty system—a system in which the errors and misunderstandings of the past will be submerged one by one in a rising tide of prosperity and interdependence.

We know that the misunderstandings of centuries are not to be wiped away in a day or wiped away in an hour. But we pledge, we pledge, that human sympathy—what our neighbors to the South call an attitude of sympatico—no less than enlightened self-interest will be our guide.

And I can see this Atlantic civilization galvanizing and guiding emergent nations everywhere. Now I know this freedom is not the fruit of every soil. I know that our own freedom was achieved through centuries by unremitting efforts by brave and wise men. And I know that the road to freedom is a long and a challenging road, and I know also that some men may walk away from it, that some men resist challenge, accepting the false security of governmental paternalism.

And I pledge that the America I envision in the years ahead will extend its hand in help in teaching and in cultivation so that all new nations will be at least encouraged to go our way; so that they will not wander down the dark alleys of tyranny or to the deadend streets of collectivism.

My fellow Republicans, we do no man a service by hiding freedom's light under a bushel of mistaken humility.

I seek an America proud of its past, proud of its ways, proud of its dreams and determined actively to proclaim them. But our examples to the world must, like charity, begin at home.

In our vision of a good and decent future, free and peaceful, there must be room, room for the liberation of the energy and the talent of the individual, otherwise our vision is blind at the outset.

We must assure a society here which, while never abandoning the needy, or forsaking the helpless, nurtures incentives and opportunity for the creative and the productive.

We must know the whole good is the product of many single contributions. And I cherish the day when our children once again will restore as heroes the sort of men and women who, unafraid and undaunted, pursue the truth, strive to cure disease, subdue and make fruitful our natural environment, and produce the inventive engines of production, science and technology.

This nation, whose creative people have enhanced this entire span of history, should again thrive upon the greatness of all those things which we—we as individual citizens—can and should do.

During Republican years, this again will be a nation of men and women, of families proud of their role, jealous of their responsibilities, unlimited in their aspirations—a nation where all who can will be self-reliant.

We Republicans see in our constitutional form of government the great framework which assures the orderly but dynamic fulfillment of the whole man, and we see the whole man as the great reason for instituting orderly government in the first place.

We see in private property and in economy based upon and fostering private property the one way to make government a durable ally of the whole man rather than his determined enemy.

We see in the sanctity of private property the only durable foundation for constitutional government in a free society.

And beyond that we see and cherish diversity of ways, diversity of thoughts, of motives, and accomplishments. We don't seek to live anyone's life for him. We only seek to secure his rights, guarantee him opportunity, guarantee him opportunity to strive with government performing only those needed and constitutionally sanctioned tasks which cannot otherwise be performed.

We, Republicans, seek a government that attends to its inherent responsibilities of maintaining a stable monetary and fiscal climate, encouraging a free and competitive economy and enforcing law and order.

Thus do we seek inventiveness, diversity and creative difference within a stable order, for we Republicans define government's role where needed at many, many levels, preferably, though, the one closest to the people involved: our towns and our cities, then our counties, then our states, then our regional contacts and only then the national government.

That, let me remind you, is the land of liberty built by decentralized power. On it also we must have balance between the branches of government at every level.

Balance, diversity, creative difference—these are the elements of the Republican equation. Republicans agree, Republicans agree heartily, to disagree on many, many of their applications. But we have never disagreed on the basic fundamental issues of why you and I are Republicans.

This is a party—this Republican Party is a party for free men. Not for blind followers and not for conformists.

Back in 1858 Abraham Lincoln said this of the Republican Party, and I quote him because he probably could have said it during the last week or so: It was composed of strained, discordant and even hostile elements. End of quote, in 1858.

Yet all of these elements agreed on one paramount objective: to arrest the progress of slavery, and place it in the course of ultimate extinction.

Today, as then, but more urgently and more broadly than then, the task of preserving and enlarging freedom at home and of safeguarding it from the forces of tyranny abroad is great enough to challenge all our resources and to require all our strength.

Anyone who joins us in all sincerity we welcome. Those, those who do not care for our cause, we don't expect to enter our ranks in any case. And let our Republicanism so focused and so dedicated not be made fuzzy and futile by unthinking and stupid labels.

I would remind you that extremism in the defense of liberty is no vice!

And let me remind you also that moderation in the pursuit of justice is no virtue!

By the—the beauty of the very system we Republicans are pledged to restore and revitalize, the beauty of this federal system of ours is in its reconciliation of diversity with unity. We must not see malice in honest differences of opinion, and no matter how great, so long as they are not inconsistent with the pledges we have given to each other in and through our Constitution.

Our Republican cause is not to level out the world or make its people conform in computer-regimented sameness. Our Republican cause is to free our people and light the way for liberty throughout the world. Ours is a very human cause for very humane goals. This party, its good people, and its unquestionable devotion to freedom will not fulfill the purposes of this campaign which we launch here now until our cause has won the day, inspired the world, and shown the way to a tomorrow worthy of all our yesteryears.

I repeat, I accept your nomination with humbleness, with pride and you and I are going to fight for the goodness of our land. Thank you.

INDEX